KNIGHTS OF THE FOURTH ESTATE: *The Story of the Miami Herald*

To
John Shively Knight

NIXON SMILEY

KNIGHTS

of the

FOURTH

The Story of the Miami Herald

ESTATE

E. A. SEEMANN PUBLISHING, INC.
Miami, Florida

Contents

Preface

A LTHOUGH *Knights of the Fourth Estate* is the story of the *Miami Herald*, it also is the story of Miami. Both newspaper and city have had their ups and downs together, surviving booms and busts, wars and hurricanes, to make amazing growth within a short time and to share a fame that is nationwide—even worldwide. The story begins in 1910, with the founding of the *Miami Herald,* and ends in 1963 when the newspaper moved into the plant it now occupies on Biscayne Bay between the MacArthur and Venetian causeways.

No small part of the *Miami Herald* story is based on personal recollections of the writer, who began working in the paper's *old* old building, at 200 South Miami Avenue, in 1935. Publisher Frank B. Shutts, the *Herald's* founder, was active then, as was Judge Frank B. Stoneman, a founder of the *Herald's* predecessor, the *Miami Morning News-Record.* In 1937 two brothers from Akron, Ohio, John S. and James L. Knight, purchased the *Herald,* which marked the beginning of a new era for the paper. Personalities came and went. There was H. Bond Bliss, whose column succeeded that of Arthur Brisbane on page one; the colorful Jack Bell, who, having one arm, tapped out his column with one finger; and the unforgettable Arthur Griffith, the erudite editorial writer, who quoted French and Latin scholars while holding court over coffee every morning in the Herald Grille. Moreover, the *Herald's* newsroom in those days was a place to see celebrities—Jack Dempsey, Floyd Gibbons, Phil Wylie, Damon Runyan, Walter Winchell, Eddie Cantor, Johnny Weismuller, Kate Smith. For it was before television, when celebrities leaned heavily on newspapers to run their pictures and keep their names in headlines.

Recollections of veterans long connected with the paper have been tapped freely as sources. Among them are Jack and Jim Knight, John

Pennekamp, Lee Hills, Charlie Ward, Jeanne Bellamy, George Beebe, Ben Maidenburg, Chuck Watters, Don Shoemaker, Kenneth Robson, Jack Kofoed, Cy Berning, Arthur Gucker, Jim Buchanan, Juanita Greene, Leo Adde, John McMullan, and Bill Sandlin, as well as the late Henry Reno, Steve Trumbull, and Arthur Himbert. Most of Chapter 7 is based on Reno's recollections of the 1926 hurricane. Others interviewed include Marjory Stoneman Douglas, Mrs. Frank B. Shutts, former staff members Allen Morris and Kenneth Ballinger, and E. W. Bebinger, a bank clerk who in 1910 accompanied Shutts when he arrived in Miami to take over the receivership of the Fort Dallas National Bank.

Checking the microfilm of the *Herald* back to 1910 as well as the film of its predecessor, the *Miami Morning News-Record,* yielded many details, but neither old papers nor microfilm can match human recollections in producing readable material. While a newspaper may produce a day-by-day history of a community, or even of the world, very little is found about the newspaper itself or about its staff—certainly little of exciting human quality.

The research, writing, and cutting of the manuscript, which had to be reduced by one-half, took six years. It was my intention originally to continue the story through 1963-73, a period when almost as many stirring events seemed to happen as occurred during the previous five decades. But this was abandoned after some 30,000 words had been written. The recent decade is another story—a book for somebody else to do.

I am indebted to Jeanne Bellamy, who helped with the editing and cutting, and I owe much to John Pennekamp for his recollections, particularly of Colonel Shutts. And if John appears to receive more space in the book than anybody else, that's because of his long tenure and the active, sometimes controversial, role he played in the paper's history.

To Lee Hills, who encouraged the writing, must go special credit. He wanted to see the story written while many of the colorful personalities involved were still around, or while those who had passed on were fresh in the writer's memory. As busy as he was—publishing the *Miami Herald* and the *Detroit Free Press,* as well as being involved in the operations of Knight Newspapers, of which he was elected board chairman and chief executive officer in 1973—Lee could find time to talk about the past. He found it relaxing to reminisce, and as a result many recollections of human interest surfaced to give vitality and color to past events.

NIXON SMILEY

Miami, 1974

Gold Mine on Miami Avenue

O N A SUNNY DAY in early March 1937, a massive man whose white hair contrasted with his youngish, florid face, giving him a distinguished bearing, entered the *Akron Beacon Journal* building in Akron, Ohio. He introduced himself to the publisher's secretary as Smith Davis and said he would like to see Mr. John S. Knight. Davis represented a Cleveland newspaper brokerage firm. Knight knew him slightly. In his younger years he had played football with the Western Reserve Redcaps. Although Knight figured Davis had nothing he wanted to buy, he agreed to see him. For Davis was a type the publisher had a fondness for—extroverted and confident, with the bubbling, exuberant personality of a high-class peddler. He was the kind of person you liked immediately, if you were going to like him, and unless you had sales resistance you wound up buying what he had to sell. But this was the kind of challenge Jack Knight liked. As a newspaperman he had known many persuasive types—politicians, promoters, confidence men. At forty-two Knight was a successful publisher and businessman, and he liked to feel that he was a match for the best of the masters of persuasion. So he welcomed Smith Davis with a cordial handshake. Being an avid follower of football, Knight asked Davis about the chances of the new Redcaps team during the coming season.

"The chances of them Redcaps is pretty good," replied Davis.

After the two men had covered a little of the football circuit, the conversation settled down to the purpose of Davis' call.

"I'd like to interest you in some Florida bonds that are to be issued soon by a Boston financial house," said Davis. "These are a different kind of bond from anything that's come out of Florida in the past. They got plenty of solid security behind them."

"Hell, I don't want any Florida bonds," said Knight bluntly. "What are they?"

"Newspaper bonds—the *Miami Herald,*" replied Davis.

"Well, I don't want any newspaper bonds either—but I would buy the newspaper," said Knight, in jest. Knight did know something about the *Herald.* He only recently had returned from a golfing vacation at Miami Beach, and while there he had read the local newspapers. The *Herald* wasn't bad, but Knight did not think of it as being in a league with the *Beacon Journal.*

"You know, there's a good possibility that the *Herald* could be bought," replied Davis. "Would you be willing to risk a week, take a train down to Miami, and talk with the publisher, Colonel Frank B. Shutts?"

Knight thought for a moment. Why not go? Despite the depression that had wracked the country since 1930, he was in good financial condition. Both the *Beacon Journal* and the Massillon (Ohio) *Independent,* which he and his younger brother, James L. Knight, owned, were doing well. They had recently finished paying off the heavy indebtedness left by their father upon his death in 1933. Why not make an offer for the *Miami Herald?*

"I think a trip to Miami could be arranged," replied Knight, glancing out the window at the cloudless sky and bright sunshine. On such a day he had played golf recently at Miami Beach. The recollection evoked pleasant memories and encouraged a desire to own a newspaper in Florida.

"When would you like to go?"

"Well, next week."

"OK. I'll call Colonel Shutts and tell him you're coming. And don't forget to take your golf clubs."

"Hell, I won't do that," replied Knight.

A few days later Knight was on his way to Miami, with his golf clubs among his luggage. After a day of golf and relaxation, Knight took a taxi to the *Miami Herald,* then on South Miami Avenue, for his appointment with Shutts. He immediately liked Shutts, a small town Indiana lawyer who, coming to Miami at forty, had grown with the frontier town and now, at sixty-six, looked upon himself as an important and influential citizen—publisher, lawyer, businessman, civic leader. Shutts had an earthy Midwestern manner that Knight understood. Nor was Knight offended by the older man's emphasis on his own achievements. The walls of Shutts' office were adorned by scores of autographed photographs of important national figures, including presidents and cabinet members. A number of the faces Knight recognized. He and Shutts reminisced about their mutual friends before they sat down in the *Herald* publisher's second floor office.

"So you're interested in buying the *Herald?"* asked Shutts.

"I would consider buying, if I can afford to pay your price," replied Knight.

"As I told Mr. Davis, I'm not interested in selling," said Shutts. "I'm just trying to refinance my debts." Taking a small bottle from his desk drawer, Shutts excused himself, tilted his head back and put a drop of medicine in each eye. He explained that he had glaucoma. His doctor had told him there was no cure, that he faced the possibility of eventually losing his sight. "But I want to keep the *Herald* as long as I can," he added as he returned the bottle to the desk drawer.

"If you were going to sell, Colonel Shutts, what would be your asking price?" asked Knight. He knew that Shutts owed considerable money, inasmuch as he was trying to float a bond issue of more than a million dollars.

"I would have to get at least three million," replied Shutts.

"Would you mind showing me your plant?" asked Knight.

"I would be delighted," replied Shutts, rising briskly. "Afterward we'll go to my home for lunch. My wife is expecting us."

The *Herald,* which Shutts had established in 1910 with the backing of Henry M. Flagler, partner of John D. Rockefeller and builder of the Florida East Coast Railway, had grown until it now occupied three adjoining old buildings facing Miami Avenue, to which a newer four-story mechanical building adjoined in the rear. In its early days the *Herald* had occupied a two-story building on the corner of South Miami Avenue and Southwest Second Street. It later expanded to an adjoining three-story building that had housed the offices of a lumber company on the first and second floors, and a carpenters' hall on the third. At a still later date Shutts had purchased a third adjoining building, of one story, which had been occupied by a garden supply firm. The mechanical building, larger than the three older buildings combined, had been erected in 1925 during the Florida land boom. Knight noted the run-down condition of the business offices, located on the first and second floors of the older buildings, and the shabby appearance of the newsroom, which occupied the onetime carpenters' hall. Although the mechanical building was relatively new and sound, much of the equipment was old. Even at a much lower figure than three million, the *Miami Herald* would be no bargain if you were buying only a plant. But Knight was not so much interested in the plant as he was in the newspaper itself. Despite its conservative format, which he thought was dull, the *Herald* carried a substantial amount of display advertising while its classified section was twice the size of that in the *Miami Daily News,* the afternoon paper. This was significant because the *News* was owned by James M. Cox of Dayton, former governor of Ohio and candidate for president on the 1920 Democratic ticket. Besides being a prestigious figure, Cox was an aggressive and able newspaperman. Although the *Herald* had a morning competitor, the *Miami Tribune,* a sensational tabloid, Knight discounted its an important challenger. Owned by Moses L. Annenberg, the race wire king, the *Tribune* was nearly three years old. But although it boasted a circulation of 100,000, twice that claimed by either the *Herald* or the *News,* Annenberg had been unable to get enough advertising to make his paper profitable. The older papers were too solidly entrenched with readers and with the establishment to be undermined by Annenberg's *Tribune,* despite its muckraking, its crusades, and its sensational presentation of the news.

If Florida had any future, the *Herald* certainly did. And Knight had no doubt about Florida's future. Conversations with friends whose judgment he respected had convinced him that the state would continue to grow. The recent passage of the Social Security Act by the New Deal Congress would guarantee old people a retirement income, and many of them would head for Florida. Although much of the nation in 1937 was still suffering from the effects of a long depression, Miami Beach was in the midst of a resort hotel building boom, and Miami was prospering, too. The *Herald* might well be worth three million, but that was a lot of money in the 1930s, and Knight did not feel he could afford to pay so much for a newspaper. Near the end of the tour the subject of price came up again, and Knight offered Shutts $2.5 million.

After touring the plant the two publishers were driven by a chauffeur to Shutts' home at Point View. Shutts poured Bourbon DeLuxe and again they talked. Although Shutts was a lawyer without background in the newspaper business before he became a publisher, he enjoyed boasting of his success to another successful publisher. Knight encouraged Shutts to talk, and as a result of their conversation, enlivened by several drinks, the Ohio publisher gained new insight into the operations of the *Miami Herald.* He sensed that Shutts was more promoter than publisher. Shutts had more interest in the classified section than in the other operations of his paper. He believed that the size of a paper's classified section reflected confidence by its readers, and that so long as the *Herald* carried twice the amount of classified that its nearest competitor carried, he had nothing to worry about. Although Knight nodded agreement, he privately felt there was considerable room for improvement. If Shutts should sell him the *Herald,* Knight would liven it with a generous use of photographs and increase the paper's readability by adding more columnists and features. But he would make no immediate drastic changes in the format. Experience had taught him that while subscribers welcomed improvements, reading habits caused them to resent major revisions that changed the appearance of their paper. The publishers continued their conversation when called to lunch.

Shutts turned to his wife and said: "Mr. Knight would like to buy the *Herald.* We're half a million dollars apart on the price—but what's half a million dollars to a man like Mr. Knight?"

Whereupon Knight turned to Mrs. Shutts and said: "Yes, it's true that I would like to buy the *Herald,* and we are about half a million dollars apart—but what's half a million dollars to a man like Colonel Shutts?"

On the following day Shutts took Knight to the races at Hialeah Park. Although no enthusiastic sportsman, Shutts kept a box in the new clubhouse. Through the *Herald,* as well as through his personal influence, he had helped to establish thoroughbred racing in Florida and to legalize parimutuel betting. He told Knight he thought horse racing had added "class" to Miami as a winter resort. He was pleased to learn that Knight was a follower of the thoroughbreds. Their conversation continued, more social than businesslike, and after the races Knight returned to his hotel pleased to think that if Shutts were to sell the *Herald* he would offer it to him first. After spending another day at Miami Beach in order to get in one more round of golf, Knight left for Akron keenly aware of his increased interest in owning the *Herald.* He would like to spend more time in Florida each winter. Owning a newspaper would provide him an excuse to do so. For he was a restless person, intensely dedicated to the newspaper profession. He knew he would never be able to spend a winter in Florida without something other than golf and the horse races to occupy his time.

Knight heard no more about the *Miami Herald* for some time, until Smith Davis dropped by to inform him that Shutts had been unable to get his refinancing plan worked out. Florida bonds of any kind were suspect in the 1930s. Many Florida municipalities, railroads, and corporations had defaulted on their bonds, and these bonds were selling at a great discount.

"I hope you're still interested in buying the *Herald,*" said Davis. "I think Colonel Shutts would sell if he could get his price."

"Well, I'm interested in buying," said Knight, "but not necessarily at Colonel Shutts' price. I'm willing to negotiate though."

"Very good," said Davis. "Say the word and I'll get in touch with Colonel Shutts."

Figuring he had carried the negotiations with Shutts as far as he could, Knight asked C. Blake McDowell, the *Beacon Journal's* lawyer, to take over. A few days later McDowell and Davis were on their way east. It was now summer, and Shutts was with his family in their summer home at Lenox, Massachusetts, in the Berkshire Mountains. McDowell took with him a copy of an audit of the *Miami Herald,* which listed the value of the corporation's assets and revealed the extent of Shutts' indebtedness. McDowell had studied the audit carefully. The major creditor was Richard LeBlond, wealthy Cincinnati capitalist who had a winter home in Miami. A longtime friend of Shutts, he had loaned the publisher $750,000 after the collapse of the Florida real estate boom in 1925 to save him from threatened bankruptcy. No payments had been made either on the interest or on the principal. Together with smaller creditors, Shutts' debts, plus interest, amounted to a whopping sum. McDowell figured that at least $1.5 million would be needed to settle those debts. If Shutts hoped to have a substantial amount of money left after selling the *Herald* he would have to receive a magnificent price for it, probably more than Jack Knight was willing to pay. Shutts held sixty-seven percent of the *Herald's* stock. Some of the *Herald's* executives owned shares, but a major part of the remaining thirty-three percent was owned by LeBlond. McDowell was in for some surprises, however, after he and Shutts began negotiations.

"Shutts had only a vague idea of how many creditors he had or how much he owed," said McDowell, later recalling the negotiations. "He not only had borrowed from a Miami bank and from Miami friends, but also from a Boston bank and from Canadian friends—well, from anybody who would lend him money. He liked to live well, and he had spent generously. In better times he had owned a yacht that cost him $30,000 a year to operate. He had not let his debts keep him from living high. What is remarkable is that none of his creditors had put any pressure on him."

McDowell sensed that Shutts was now serious about selling the *Herald,* although he kept repeating that he didn't have to sell. However, he had no son to succeed him, nor had either of his two daughters brought home a husband who had an inclination for the newspaper business. McDowell learned that Shutts had offered the paper to Eugene Meyer, publisher of the *Washington Post.* But after looking over the plant Meyer lost interest. On another occasion Shutts had discussed with the *Herald's* executives the possibility of turning the paper over to them. They would assume the paper's liabilities, and Shutts would hold the stock as security. He must have had second thoughts about this plan, which, considering his heavy indebtedness, was impractical. Moses L. Annenberg, who spent the winters at Miami Beach, had made overtures for the purchase of the *Herald,* but Shutts rated Annenberg with such gangsters as Al Capone and John Dillinger and never seriously considered his offer. Annenberg is believed to have offered as much as $3.5 million. Exasperated, Annenberg began the *Miami Tribune* in 1934 with the avowed intention of forcing Shutts to sell.

Shutts received $10,000 a year as publisher of the *Herald,* as well as substantial dividends from his stock. But the combined income from his newspaper and from his law practice was not sufficient to retire his debts during his lifetime. Shutts held out for the original $3 million price he had asked Jack Knight for the *Herald,* but his main concern was to have something left after his debts were settled.

"He agreed to trim the asking if we could trim his debts through negotiations with creditors," said McDowell. "The negotiations then took a new turn."

Returning to Ohio, McDowell went to Cincinnati and called upon LeBlond.

"LeBlond liked Shutts," said McDowell. "They had been partners in real estate transactions during the Florida land boom. He let me know that Shutts need not sell the *Herald* because of him. He had never pressed Shutts to pay the note, and said he had no intention of doing so. But I told LeBlond of Shutts' circumstances—his age, his eye trouble, his other debts, and his desire to settle his financial affairs before his death. When I returned to see Shutts I could report that LeBlond was willing to trim $250,000 from the $750,000 principal and to forget the interest on the entire amount. This was a very important concession. It meant a considerable saving to Shutts."

Shutts was willing to reduce his asking price for the *Herald* to $2.5 million, but McDowell came up with another proposition. Knight would pay Shutts a salary of $12,000 a year as consultant for ten years if he would reduce the price to $2.25 million. This, McDowell convinced him, would be to his benefit. Shutts was agreeable. but he had to be shown, on paper, exactly how much he would have after his debts were settled.

"He had plenty to worry about," said McDowell. "His neighbors looked upon him as a millionaire, and he had lived like a millionaire for many years. He didn't want to leave his family penniless."

At one stage while Shutts was trying to make up his mind, McDowell and Davis rolled dice on the living room rug for nickels and dimes. Shutts watched with interest, despite worry wrinkles in his forehead, but never relaxed his reserve enough to join them.

The closing took place in New York, at the Waldorf-Astoria Hotel. Besides the Knight brothers, Shutts, McDowell, and Davis, lawyers from Shutts' Miami law firm were present, as well as Colonel Robert H. Montgomery, a partner in Lybrand, Ross Bros. & Montgomery, auditors of the *Herald's* books. A problem arose when Montgomery declared he could not be sure the audit was accurate. Because of Shutts' informal way of conducting his business, Montgomery suggested there might be debts that the auditors had failed to discover—debts that Shutts might have forgotten. Buying a newspaper without knowing the extent of liabilities would be risky, and Jack Knight had reason to be concerned. In order to cope with this unexpected complication, McDowell suggested taking a break. He then called Knight aside and suggested a possible solution—to ask Shutts to put $200,000 of the contract price in escrow to pay off any debts that might come up after the paper changed hands. Montgomery thought this was a practical solution and recommended it to Shutts, who nodded agreement.

The Knights took possession of the *Miami Herald* on October 15, 1937. They paid $2.25 million, a price Knight feared was high. How could he foresee, though, that the *Miami Herald* would become during his lifetime one of the most successful newspapers in America? Thirty years later John S. Knight would look back in amazement at the *Herald's*

COLONEL Frank B. Shutts, left, and John S. Knight, right, complete transfer of *Miami Herald* stock to Knight Newspapers on October 15, 1937. Shutts was sixty-seven, Knight within eleven days of forty-three.

growth. But the *Herald* was a sound newspaper when the Knights purchased it. Having grown with Miami from the time it was a frontier town of 5,500, the *Herald* by 1937 had won a dominant and permanent position in what was now an area of 250,000 population. The *Herald* went into virtually every home, and its influence was enormous. Its ability to more than meet the competition of the brightly written, smartly edited, and aggressively circulated *Miami News,* whose worldly publisher was a former vice-presidential candidate, is an indication of its prestige. Nor did it ever show the slightest signs of faltering in the face of withering attacks by the *Miami Tribune,* Annenberg's sensational tabloid. To appreciate how the *Herald* had achieved its important position in the community, you must go back to the beginning and observe its development during the twenty-seven years that Shutts was publisher. For the *Herald,* as much as any other American newspaper, was a product of the community it served as well as of the people who got it out. The quality of the paper was a reflection of the work done by those who produced it—those who wrote and edited the news stories, features, and editorials; who sold the display ads or promoted the classified section; who set the type, made up the pages, operated the presses, and distributed the final product. But above all, it was Shutts and his editor, Frank B. Stoneman, who established the foundation for the newspaper that the Knight brothers took possession of in 1937. It is Shutts and Stoneman, as well many of the colorful personalities who played a role in the growth of the *Herald* and the community, who set the stage.

Flagler's Invitation

FRANK BARKER SHUTTS arrived in Miami from Aurora, Indiana, on July 1, 1909, as federal receiver for a bankrupt Miami bank. Next day the *Miami Morning News-Record* carried a page-one story about him. "Frank B. Schultz/Is New Receiver," said the headline. Although the name was spelled incorrectly, the statement was factual—and prophetic for the newspaper. For, although Shutts had arrived to take over the receivership of the Fort Dallas National Bank, one year later he would be called upon to become the receiver of the financially troubled *News-Record*. A short time thereafter he would become its publisher. And on December 1, 1910, seventeen months after his arrival in Miami, Shutts would change the newspaper's name to the *Miami Herald*.

Shutts, a lawyer and a native of Indiana, had been receiver of the Aurora National Bank, which, like the Miami bank, had failed during a national recession in 1907. His success in closing out the affairs of the Aurora bank resulted in his being appointed receiver of a Denver bank. After Denver he was sent to Miami. Shutts was thirty-nine, moderately successful, and a bachelor. Nothing about this slender, homely man with prematurely graying hair suggested he had the ability to build a brilliant career in a frontier town, heading one of Florida's leading law firms and publishing the state's most influential newspaper; that he was destined to mix socially with the nation's top financial, business, and political figures, including presidents of the United States, and become a millionaire. But E. W. Bebinger, a young bank clerk who accompanied Shutts to Miami, noted half a century later that the Hoosier lawyer had qualities that made him popular among Miami's mixed population—a rough exterior, a sharp mind, and nimble wit.

"Mr. Shutts had another thing—ego," added Bebinger. "He believed

FORT DALLAS National Bank was located at the northwest corner of Miami Avenue and Flagler Street. The ornate building was knocked down in the 1930s to make room for a drugstore.

he could do anything, and he wasn't afraid of the biggest big shot in the world."

Shutts' father, Abram Shutts, was the postmaster of Cochran, then a village on the outskirts of Aurora, and supplemented his income as a cobbler to help support his large family. Young Shutts delivered newspapers and worked part-time for a druggist, John Ullrich, earning money to buy clothes and books so he could attend school. Ullrich, observing that the boy was bright, encouraged him to attend college and advanced him funds to enroll at DePauw University. Earning a law degree from DePauw in 1892, he returned to Aurora to practice.

Shutts had become an able and respected lawyer by 1907 when a recession—the "Bankers' Panic—swept the country. The recession brought about rapidly changing national events—events that would bring changes also for Shutts, and with them new fortunes and a new way of life, including marriage. At the same time that the Aurora bank was in trouble the Fort Dallas National Bank in Miami was having difficulties, too. A federal bank examiner, J. K. McDonald, closed the Miami bank's doors on July 3, 1907. McDonald remained to tackle the job of liquidating the Miami bank's assets and distributing the funds collected among the depositors, but he ran into difficulties. The officers and directors of the Miami bank were hard-headed men, many of them Florida Crackers with little education or wide business experience. Moreover, a good percentage of the depositors were illiterate. McDonald was unable to gain the confidence of these people, and in 1909 he was replaced as receiver by Shutts.

Although Shutts found the affairs of the Miami bank discouraging, as soon as he began talking with the officers, stockholders, and depositors he sensed the reasons for the complications. He called a meeting of the directors and major stockholders, which included Dr. James M. Jackson. Jackson, a physician and native of rural north Florida, had arrived in Miami in 1896, the year of the city's incorporation. He had developed a reputation as a leader and wielded considerable influence. The quality of his character was to be reflected several years later in the naming of Miami's Jackson Memorial Hospital in his honor. Enlisting Dr. Jackson's help, Shutts succeeded in clearing the first hurdle, winning the confidence of the suspicious pioneers. He could then go to the next hurdle, Henry M. Flagler. The builder of the Florida East Coast Railway and founder of Miami held a note on the Fort Dallas National Bank for $47,000. The note not only was overdue, but the Flagler System was demanding payment. Flagler was the only person with authority to extend the note, so Shutts on his return to Aurora went by way of New York to see the millionaire. The man who had helped John D. Rockefeller build the Standard Oil empire listened while the lawyer explained the muddled situation, how Miami's development was being affected, and, indirectly, Flagler's interest, too.

"You own half the city down there," said Shutts. "You own the railroad, the major hotel, a steamship line, and thousands of acres of valuable property within and near the city. It is to your advantage for Miami to get back to normal so it can continue its progress. The prospects are good for an early liquidation of the bank's assets, but at the moment we are in a mess. It is essential that the note you hold be allowed to ride a few months longer."

Flagler agreed to recess the loan temporarily, but in the meantime he had become impressed with the convincing way Shutts had presented his argument. To have a petitioner of such confidence and ability appear before him was a rare experience. Shutts was preparing to leave when Flagler detained him.

"Mr. Shutts," said the seventy-nine-year-old industrialist, "I need a lawyer in Miami. How would you like to represent me down there?"

Shutts, who had a good practice in Aurora, thanked Flagler but said he would have to turn down his offer, whereupon Flagler offered him a flat $7,500-a-year retainer if he would move his practice to Miami and represent him in southern Florida. That was a lot of money in 1909. It was an opportunity of a kind Shutts might never encounter again. He told Flagler he would consider his offer.

Flagler's offer occupied Shutts' mind throughout the train ride from New York to Indiana. He was well fixed in Aurora, and he was not fond of Miami, which he found hot in July and plagued by mosquitoes. But Miami seemed to have possibilities of growth that Aurora could never have. Its growth, from the three families who lived on the Miami River in 1895 to 5,000 persons in 1909, had been phenomenal. Moreover, the Everglades were being drained, with the prospect that a million acres of rich soil would become available for farming. Miami's importance as a winter tourist resort seemed less apparent to Shutts, for the city's two major tourist hotels, the sprawling Royal Palm and the Halcyon, were closed for the summer. Shutts also had a personal reason to consider leaving Aurora. He had been going with the same woman, Fannie Folk, for twenty years. They had postponed their marriage from year to year because of Miss Folk's devotion to her ailing mother. It seemed that the elderly Mrs. Folk would live indefinitely, and Shutts felt hooked. But if he moved to Miami he would leave this problem in Aurora. By the time Shutts' train reached Indiana he had decided to accept Flagler's offer.

Shutts began closing his practice in Aurora, and by the spring of 1910 was almost ready to move to Miami. The one thing he regretted was having to leave his secretary, Agnes John, an attractive young woman of whom he had grown very fond. In those days, a man did not take a young woman to a distant place as his secretary. The only way Shutts could take Miss John was to marry her. But how did a man propose to his secretary, with whom there had been only a formal employer-employee relationship? Time was passing rapidly. Shutts had boxed his books and papers for shipment and had very nearly wound up his law practice when he stopped by Miss John's desk to talk. Soon he would be on his way to Miami, he said as he rested his slender frame against her desk. He was going to miss her, he was going to be lonely, he found himself saying. Miami was a frontier, with new people and new ideas, so different from Aurora; he would have to make the acquaintance of an entirely new group of people. The opportunities, however, were great—so great he could not turn them down. Miss John remarked that the idea of a frontier appealed to her. Old Aurora was so dull. She, too, would like to go to a new place where the faces were new and the ideas new.

"Then, why don't you come with me to Miami . . . as my wife?" asked Shutts.

Miss John looked up into the lean, angular face of the gray-haired man and saw that he was serious. Reaching for the handle that controlled the typewriter well of her desk, she closed it as she rose to her feet.

"Let's go!" she said.

This story, together with recollections of his childhood, his parents, and his college years, was related by Shutts to the city editor of the *Miami Herald,* John Pennekamp, in 1931 during a trip to Tallahassee in the publisher's chauffeur-driven car.

Shutts and Miss John were married on June 8, 1910, and left for Atlantic City on a honeymoon before heading for Miami. Sixty years later Mrs. Shutts would recall that what struck her most about the southern Florida frontier was that all the adults she met had been born elsewhere. Many of them were Floridians, mainly from the northern part of the state. They had come to Miami after two severe freezes in the winter of 1894-95 destroyed most of the state's citrus groves.

"People dated events as happening before the freeze or after the freeze," she said. "It reminded me of being back in Indiana, where people dated events as happening before or after the Chicago fire."

Shutts formed a law partnership with Henry F. Atkinson, a native of Georgia and ten years his senior. Shutts & Atkinson took in another partner in 1911, William Pruden Smith. Atkinson left the firm in 1912 to become a circuit judge. That same year Crate D. Bowen arrived from Indianapolis to join the firm, which then became Shutts, Smith & Bowen. Smith left the firm in 1920, after serving as mayor of Miami. Shutts and Bowen, of about the same age, had been friends for several years. Both were members of Knights Templar and traced their friendship to meetings at state Masonic conventions. Although Shutts would become the major force behind their law firm, Bowen would remain in the office, getting the work done. Shutts involved himself less and less with the practice of law and increasingly more with the promotion of the law firm, the *Miami Herald,* and himself. Bowen did not complain, for together they prospered far beyond the dreams of either when they formed their partnership.

Publishing a newspaper would have been one of the last things to occur to Shutts when he arrived in Miami. He had been in Miami less than two months, however, when the owners of the *Miami Morning News-Record,* A. L. LaSalle, president, and Frank B. Stoneman, editor, called on him. Their paper was in financial trouble. The debts were greater than they could pay, and the creditors, the Flagler System being the major one, were pressing them. They had no choice but to put the company into the hands of a receiver. Because of the reputation Shutts had gained as receiver for the Fort Dallas National Bank, and perhaps because he

THE MIAMI HERALD was begun in this building, at the southwest corner of South Miami Avenue and Southwest Second Street on December 1, 1910. It formerly had been the home of the *Miami Morning News-Record,* published by A. L. LaSalle and Frank B. Stoneman.

FIRST DAILY newspaper published in Miami, the *Miami Evening Record,* was delivered by horse and buggy. Sign hanging from buggy shaft claims the largest circulation in Miami. (State Photographic Archives)

represented their most important creditor, they had come to him. Would he take over the paper, see what he could do to put it back on its feet, or liquidate the property and settle with creditors? Shutts could not have known that the nod of his head would embark him in a new and unfamiliar career, but one that would bring both riches and fame.

Frank B. Stoneman, like Frank B. Shutts with whom he was soon to join in an association profitable to both, was a native of Indiana. He was born in a Quaker colony at Spiceland, near Indianapolis, in 1858, but after the Civil War the family moved to Minneapolis. Young Frank attended Carleton College, where he came under the influence of an activist classmate, Thorstein Veblen, who later became a leading American socialist. It was during this period that Stoneman was converted to the Episcopal Church, more liberal than the Quakers. He was for a time a member of the Socialist Party. Stoneman entered the University of Minnesota, but the death of his father, a surgeon, ended his formal education. He taught school for three years, worked part-time on a newspaper, then joined a friend and journeyed to Billings, Montana, a fast growing frontier town, where they opened a grocery store. During idle hours the studious Stoneman read extensively in history and law. At night cavalry officers rode into town to join Stoneman and his friend at checkers. Stoneman frequently played against Bean Belly Brown, veteran Indian fighter. That was the only name Stoneman would remember, but he never forgot that Bean Belly always won.

"Stoneman," said Bean Belly at the end of an evening of continuous winnings, "I admire your courage, but damn your judgment."

Stoneman's business acumen was no greater than his ability at checkers, and in the middle 1880s he returned to Minneapolis. A construction boom was underway, and Stoneman got a job with a building and loan association. Within a short time he was doing well and his future looked good. He met a young woman, Lillian Trefethen, from Taunton, Massachusetts, whom he married in 1889. The following year a daughter, Marjory, was born.

Many years later the daughter, Marjory Stoneman Douglas, who had become a widely known writer, would recall that life had been good to her parents in those years. By 1894 Stoneman had enough money to take his wife and small daughter on a cruise to Florida and to Cuba. By the time the Stonemans returned home, however, a depression then sweeping the country—the Panic of 1893—had reached Minneapolis. Out of a job and unable to find work, Stoneman moved his family to Providence, Rhode Island, a short distance from his wife's parents at Taunton. The best job he could find was selling lubricating oil to factories and machine shops. Meanwhile, Mrs. Stoneman, reacting to the unexpected reverses in their lives, developed a serious mental illness. Unable to provide for his ailing wife and their child, Stoneman left them at Taunton and boarded a train for Florida, winding up at Orlando. Stoneman was to remain in Florida for the rest of his life. His wife lived until 1912 without regaining her health.

Stoneman was in his early forties when he arrived in Florida to begin a new career, this time as a lawyer. But he had never given up his ambition of one day publishing a newspaper, and in 1901 that opportunity came when he formed a partnership with a printer, A. L. LaSalle, to found the *Orlando Daily Herald*. Orlando was still suffering from a recession caused by the great freeze of 1895, so in 1903 Stoneman and LaSalle moved their press to Miami, where they began the town's first daily, the *Miami Evening Record*. In 1904 Flagler began the extension of his railroad to Key West, bringing thousands of workmen into the area. Stoneman and LaSalle were soon doing so well they could buy a two-story stucco building at the southwest corner of what is now South Miami Avenue and Second Street.

The *Evening Record*, published six days a week, proved to be a strong competitor of the *Miami Metropolis*, an afternoon weekly which had been started in 1896 with the help of a loan from Flagler. The pro-Flagler *Metropolis* was forced to become a daily. Flagler's side was unpopular in the early 1900s, and Stoneman, as editor of the *Record*, took advantage of the situation. He could go only so far, though. Like the *Metropolis*, the *Record* ran the time schedules of Flagler's railroad and steamship lines, which appeared in both papers as sizeable display ads. So Stoneman, taking editorial pokes at the Flagler System, embroidered his criticism with praise for Flagler the man. But three things happened that were to change the fortunes of Stoneman and LaSalle. They did so well during their first four years in Miami that in 1907 they bought out a failing newspaper, the *Miami Morning News*, and merged it with the *Record*. Giving the afternoon field to the *Metropolis*, they changed to morning publication. In the process they incurred a heavy indebtedness to the East Coast Company, or Flagler System. Unfortunately, LaSalle and Stoneman chose a recession year to plunge into debt. But worst of all, the *Metropolis* was turned over in 1909 to a fire-eating editor, S. Bobo Dean, who was destined to leave an indelible mark on the history of Florida journalism. Reversing the newspaper's editorial policy, Dean began attacking both the Flagler System and Flagler himself. Although he lost the Flagler System's advertising, Dean turned the attention of Miami readers to the evening paper.

Dean, a native of Gadsden, Alabama, became a reporter on the *Knoxville Journal* at nineteen, and two years later headed for Florida, where, in 1898, he started a paper that was later to become the *Palm Beach News*.

Dean was then an admirer of Flagler, whom he looked upon as a great man. Despite a rigid moral outlook, he supported Flagler in 1901 when his friends in the State Legislature pushed through a bill that permitted him to divorce his second wife, Alice Shourds Flagler, who was insane. Flagler was then free to marry Mary Lily Kenan of North Carolina. Eventually Dean became disenchanted with Flagler. For despite his support of churches and preachers, Flagler was far from being a paragon of virtue. While Flagler was frequently pictured in newspapers as a generous and lovable old capitalist, the Flagler System was callous and uncompromising. Nothing was permitted to stand in the way when the Flagler System wanted something.

In 1905 Dean moved to Miami and became a minority owner and editor of the *Metropolis*. While he sought to steer the paper away from its praise of Flagler, his hands were tied by B. B. Tatum, the majority owner

FRANK B. STONEMAN

and one of Miami's leading real estate developers. Tatum, growing weary of the intractable Dean, sold his ownership in the *Metropolis* to A. J. Bendle, a wealthy northerner. Given free rein, Dean tore into the Flagler System so fiercely that he soon became known as "the Bobonic plague." His campaign reached a climax with a series of articles on the city waterworks, also owned by Flagler. After tasting what he thought was an unusual flavor in the water, Dean sent a reporter into the streets to ask others if they had noticed anything wrong. They had, and Dean ran a story. The flavor grew worse, and Dean ran daily stories complaining about the worsening situation. But the Flagler people, accustomed to Dean's attacks, shrugged off the stories and made no effort to check the water system. Businessmen, fearing the attacks would have an adverse effect upon the upcoming tourist season, asked Dean to lay off Flagler for awhile. The requests were ignored, and a few days later the body of a man was found floating in a water tank.

When Dean was not battling the Flagler crowd he was building a fire under the coattails of his competitors. Stoneman, now fifty-one, lacked the wit, the vituperation, and the hard experience to match the onslaughts of the fiery Dean. Despite his age, Stoneman was still growing as a newspaperman, but he had the disadvantage of having never worked under the wing of an experienced, driving editor. Dean taunted Stoneman for having been a Socialist and poked fun at him whenever editorials about morality appeared in the morning paper. A teetotaler, Dean was strongly against saloons, while Stoneman was one of the saloons' best friends. The high watermark in Dean's attacks on Stoneman was a limited edition of the *Metropolis* with a page-one cartoon of the *News-Record* editor sitting drowsily drunk on a bench outside the Ben Hur Saloon. A spider was depicted spinning a web between Stoneman's bulbous nose and nearby objects. To draw further attention to the cartoon, the *Metropolis* staff dabbed red ink on Stoneman's nose.

By the summer of 1910, when Miami's seasonal economy was at its lowest ebb, the *Miami Morning News-Record* was in serious trouble. Not only had circulation declined, many of the advertisers were not paying their bills. Stoneman remembered for the rest of his life what a relief it was when Shutts took over as receiver on August 22, 1910, and assumed responsibility for the business operation.

During the weeks ahead Shutts had a chance to study the paper's records, to talk with Miamians about its strengths and weaknesses, and to reach a conclusion about its future possibilities. He decided that the paper, if well managed, could be made to pay. Furthermore, it could be turned into a useful force to counteract the harmful effects of Bobo Dean's attacks against his client, Flagler. So, in the fall of 1910 Shutts made an appointment with Flagler and, with a pass, boarded a Florida East Coast Railway passenger train for New York.

To the eighty-year-old Flagler Shutts made his appeal: to pay off the other creditors of the Miami morning newspaper and take over its operation, installing a publisher sympathetic to the Flagler System, together with an experienced business manager. He presented a picture of a revitalized newspaper sympathetic to Flagler's plans and aspirations in Miami. After listening to Shutts, Flagler informed him he was not interested in owning the *News-Record* or doing anything to counteract criticism in Miami. Explaining his reasoning, Flagler recalled a decision he and his partner, John D. Rockefeller, had made years before in connection with the operation of the Standard Oil Company. He said:

John and I long ago decided that if we were going to be successful—as we have been—we had to expect this kind of handling on the part of newspapers. We ignored newspaper criticism . . . and I have continued to ignore newspaper criticism in connection with my Florida operations."

Shutts, more promotion-minded than Flagler, was not easily dissuaded. He replied:

"Mr. Flagler, you need somebody down there to tell your side of the story; to counter the attacks of the *Metropolis*. And if you don't acquire the *News-Record,* it could fall into undesirable hands."

Flagler was firm. He informed Shutts he had no intention of acquiring the Miami newspaper.

"But, Mr. Shutts," added Flagler in the tone of one to whom a new thought had occurred, "if you want to publish the newspaper yourself, then I might consider acquiring it."

The possibility of becoming the publisher himself Shutts had not considered. But now, realizing the empire builder had made his final statement on the matter, he quickly agreed to Flagler's suggestion. Flagler directed Shutts to pay off the other creditors of the *Miami Morning News-Record* and reorganize it as a Flagler System company.

Shutts reorganized the *Miami Morning News Record* under the *Miami Herald* and on December 1, 1910, began publishing under a new masthead, with himself as publisher and Frank B. Stoneman as editor.

Shutts Employs a Chauffeur

ONE OF THE major news breaks in the *Miami Herald's* early history sent its circulation soaring ahead of that of its fierce competitor, the *Miami Metropolis*. It occurred on the evening of April 15, 1912, when news of the *Titanic* disaster, which had occurred nearly twenty-four hours earlier, reached Miami. Breaking on the *Herald's* time, the story of the greatest maritime disaster in peacetime history gave the new paper a decided advantage, and the *Herald* made the most of it. In August, just four months later, the *Herald* could claim to be the "largest newspaper in Florida south of Jacksonville and east of Tampa." Its circulation soared past 2,000, and the flatbed press Shutts had acquired when he took over the defunct *News-Record* was near the limit of its capacity.

Shutts had launched the *Herald* seventeen months before. There is no reason to believe that Miamians were very excited about the new paper. Except for a change of names, the *Miami Herald* was little different in appearance from its predecessor. Like the *News-Record,* it ran eight pages six days a week, but in a few weeks a Sunday edition was added, which ran twelve to sixteen pages. Readers of a later day would consider the front page, which changed little from day to day, very dull. Reflecting the conservative tastes of its Hoosier publisher and editor, the front page had carried no streamer before the sinking of the *Titanic,* and seldom a headline of more than one column.

Shutts, a mature and patient man, was satisfied to see his paper make progress slowly. Although aware that news sold newspapers, he realized that a newspaper was a business and must be sound to survive. So the first thing Shutts did was set up a financially sound organization. As general manager he hired Oscar T. Conklin, a bright New Yorker who had risen from a menial job in the circulation department of the

Metropolis to editor within a four-year period. It did not worry Shutts that the raid on the *Metropolis* was to make a lifelong enemy of Bobo Dean. The publishers had too many opposing views to get along anyway. Conklin proved to be an efficient manager of the business and production operations of the *Herald,* relieving Stoneman of responsibilities outside the editorial department. Although working twelve to fourteen hours a day, writing editorials when he wasn't reading reporters' copy and composing headlines, Stoneman couldn't have been more pleased. He could do the work he loved most without having to concern himself with selling advertising, trying to collect bad bills, and holding off irate creditors.

The *Herald's* first major improvement came in late 1911 when it became Miami's first newspaper to receive the news service of the Associated Press. Circulation made a noticeable gain that winter, and so did advertising. The daily *Herald* often went to twelve pages, while the Sunday *Herald* hit twenty to twenty-four pages. But the circulation was still below 2,000 when Shutts early in 1912 hired Harry O. Huston, an able newspaperman, as night editor. Huston was in charge of the newsroom on the night that a news flash stirred the *Herald* staff with a report of the *Titanic* sinking.

The *Titanic* had hit an iceberg just before midnight Sunday, April 14, and two hours and forty minutes later the 883-foot "Queen of the Seas" upended and sank. Of the 2,224 passengers and crew 711 survived, mostly women and children who were put into lifeboats by armed officers. The Titanic was not merely the largest ship in the world on its maiden voyage from Liverpool to New York, it carried the cream of American society, as well as giants of banking, investment, and industry. The ship had been promoted by the White Star Line, its owner, as unsinkable. Many of the American passengers had journeyed to England to make the trip. Among them were John Jacob Astor, A. B. Widener, Isador Straus, and J. Bruce Ismay, whose combined wealth exceeded half a billion dollars. No similar disaster that took the lives of so many important people had happened in peacetime.

One Monday morning the *Herald* carried a one-paragraph item on page one reporting that the *Titanic* had hit an iceberg and had requested assistance. The Associated Press had filed the brief out of Montreal shortly after 2:30 a.m., when a report was received from the steamship Virginia, which had intercepted a call for help. No other details were available, but the possibility of serious damage to the big ship was discounted. It was not until late Monday, when rescue ships began picking up survivors, that the story broke with full impact. The *Metropolis* had finished its press run of the Monday afternoon paper long before, and, like most Miamians, the staff was now home and in bed.

THE MIAMI HERALD.

NEWS OF THE WORLD EVERY DAY BY ASSOCIATED PRESS

THE WEATHER
Fair today, Wednesday showers

VOL. 2. No. 108.   MIAMI, FLORIDA, TUESDAY MORNING, APRIL 16, 1912.   PRICE FIVE CENTS.

Steamer Titanic Goes to Bottom With Over Fifteen Hundred Souls

IF EARLY REPORTS ARE TRUE THE DISASTER IS GREATEST IN WORLD'S MARINE HISTORY

Four Hours Before Making the Plunge, Giant Liner Had Crashed Into an Iceberg Off Newfoundland

ONLY 675 OF 2200 PASSENGERS SAVED

The Great Flood and Two Scenes as a Result Along the Mississippi River

THIRTEEN PARISHES AND TWO COUNTIES NOW FACE UNPARALLELED DISASTER

From Deluge of Flood Now Sweeping Over Many Miles of Territory in Arkansas and Louisiana

ILLINOIS DEMOCRATS WERE CONTROLLED BY POLICE AND MILITIA

WALL OF WATER FROM SIX TO TWENTY FEET

FOUR HUNDRED AND TWO NEW VOTERS

Miami Council, Knights of Columbus, Was Formally Organized Sunday Afternoon

Wealth Aboard Titanic Was Over Half Billion Dollars

Total Number of Dead May Reach to Eighteen Hundred

Some of the Monetary Losses

HISTORIC FRONT PAGE of the *Miami Herald* which sent its circulation soaring ahead of its evening competitor, the *Miami Metropolis*. This shocking headline gave Miamians the first news of the world's greatest peacetime maritime disaster.

It was a time, before radio and television, when the public depended entirely on newspapers for news. Disasters brought people flocking to newspaper offices, as did ballot counting after important elections, or outstanding sports events. But the news of the *Titanic* broke so late in the evening that most Miamians did not get the electrifying news until they opened their Tuesday morning *Herald*. The first streamer the paper had ever carried, "Steamer *Titanic* Goes to Bottom/With Over Fifteen Hundred Souls" blared at readers in the largest black typeface that could be fitted in two lines across the top of the page. The story, transmitted by Morse telegraph over Western Union wire, was received in bits and pieces by *Herald* staffers, who pasted it together, frequently rewriting to improve continuity and clarity. In a page-one box Huston could inform readers that the *Herald* was giving them the same details about the *Titanic* that the big New York dailies were carrying, since they all got their report from the same source, the Associated Press. Later in the morning an extra was published, giving more background and a revised survivor count. But in the first edition were all the grim details, leaving nothing for the *Metropolis* that was new. The disappointed *Metropolis* editors made the mistake that countless other editors have made before and since: they handled the disaster like a second-day story, as though presuming the paper's readers already knew the details. The *Metropolis* never quite caught up in the days after as survivors began to give eyewitness accounts to reporters, but continued to take a "second-day-story" attitude. It was one of the few beatings the *Herald* gave the usually very-wide-awake *Metropolis* during those early days of intense competition. But what made the beating so significant was that the *Herald* jumped ahead of its competitor in both circulation and advertising.

During the days immediately following the *Titanic* sinking, more large blackface type appeared on page one of the *Herald* than the paper had used during the previous seventeen months. Shutts then allowed his editors freedom to continue using bold, attention-grabbing headlines long after the *Titanic* story had been laid to rest. At times the front page looked like someone had stood back and thrown a variety of large type at it. Shutts tolerated this extravagant display until the United States' entry into World War I, when he and Stoneman restored the austere image they had agreed upon when the *Herald* was launched. So well was the *Herald* doing in 1912, however, that Shutts did not want to argue with success. In fact, the paper was making so much money that Shutts bought a new Franklin automobile and charged it to the *Herald's* account, and he used an employee from the classified advertising department, Ben Field, as his chauffeur. When the Flagler System's auditor examined the

THIS VIEW of Miami Avenue, looking north toward Flagler Street, could have been shot from the Miami Herald building at about the time Frank B. Shutts began publication of the *Herald* on December 1, 1910.

paper's books, Shutts was called on the carpet to explain why he needed an automobile and a chauffeur.

Henry M. Flagler and Frank B. Shutts had only three meetings. Such was the prestige of Flagler that decisions made at each of these meetings were to have a profound influence on Shutts' career—as a lawyer, as a publisher, and as a wealthy person of importance in his community. Although Flagler was showing the effects of physical decline at their last meeting, the millionaire's mind was sharp, and he was still directing his Florida empire with the efficiency that many years earlier had impressed John D. Rockefeller. Now eighty-three, Flagler figured his time was short, and he was trying to get his affairs in final order. He had willed his empire to his wife, the former Mary Lily Kenan. This included the Florida East Coast Railway, hotels, steamship lines, utilities, and two million acres of Florida land. The operation of this empire would fall to the responsibility of trustees after his death, and he was studying auditor reports carefully in an effort to catch any flaws in the operations of the Flagler System. Such was the state of his mind while studying an audit of the *Miami Herald's* books—when his eyes caught the inclusion of an automobile for the publisher and a chauffeur's salary. Flagler immediately dictated a letter to Shutts, asking him to justify such an expenditure of funds.

With great faith in his persuasive ability, Shutts caught a train to Palm Beach and took a horse carriage to Flagler's mansion, Whitehall. Flagler listened attentively as Shutts explained that a newspaper publisher must constantly expose himself in a community, moving about in business, professional, civic, and social circles.

"This means going out frequently at night," said Shutts. "I'm often called on to make speeches, or serve as master of ceremonies at dinners, all of which make me as publisher better acquainted with subscribers and advertisers. And driving at night—especially after I have had a cocktail or two—does not appeal to me. Mr. Flagler, I need a car and a chauffeur, and I hope you agree with me. The rapid growth in circulation and advertising indicate how successful the *Herald* has been under the kind of management I have been giving it."

"I'm inclined to agree that perhaps you do need a car and a chauffeur," replied Flagler, "but I have made it a rule to follow the recommendations of my auditor in matters like this—and he informs me that a car and a chauffeur are not necessary in connection with the operation of the *Miami Herald*. You'll have to remove these from the books."

"Mr. Flagler, I don't see how I can do that," replied Shutts. "I am unable to operate an automobile."

"Then we are at an impasse," snapped Flagler.

"No, sir," said Shutts in a conciliatory tone. "With your permission, I would like to buy the *Miami Herald.*"

Flagler was agreeable. Apparently he let Shutts have the paper for what he had in the property, $29,000. Shutts paid $10,000 down and signed a note for the $19,000 balance.

Although Shutts had bought himself a gold mine, it would prove a costly one to develop. His first major expenditure, $15,000 for a new Goss Comet flatbed press and a third typesetting machine, had to be made a few months later. By 1917 the circulation had gained so rapidly, passing 4,000, that Shutts had to replace the flatbed press with a second-hand high-speed rotary press. With such monetary growing pains, he was unable to finish paying off his debt to the Flagler System until 1919. Never in the twenty-seven years that Shutts published the *Herald* was he free of debt—not until he sold the paper to John S. and James L. Knight in 1937.

(4)

The Flagler Era Passes

M IAMI HAD TWO hangings in 1914. The second hanging was rushed in order that Sheriff Dan Hardie could swing both men from the same scaffold. To give the impression Miami had no favorite color when it came to hanging, the first victim, Clarence Daly, was white, the second victim, Joe Brown, black. Daly, an ignorant and mad laborer, had been found guilty of raping an eighty-year-old woman, Brown of slaying another man. A pioneer would remember half a century later that on the morning of the hangings a "depressing pall" hung over the city. A *Herald* reporter who covered the hangings failed to mention anything unusual. The only "local color" the reporter noted appeared in the story about the hanging of Daly. After the sheriff "tripped the trap door and Daly's bulk dropped to the end of the rope," the reporter added:

"In the distance the bell of a locomotive clanged and the horn of an automobile sounded. Someone struck a match and lit a cigar."

If a pall existed in spring and summer of 1914, it had to hang over the entire world. A bloody revolution was being fought in Mexico, and war clouds were gathering over Europe presaging the beginning of World War I in July. While the hanging stories were put inside, the *Herald* played the Mexican Revolution in bold headlines. Mexican bandits, as the *Herald* called the revolutionists, were slaying American citizens and destroying American property. The handling of the Mexican Revolution by the *Herald* reflected the temper of the era. Feelings were influenced by a strong nationalism, and Miami's pioneering citizens took the acts of the Mexicans as a personal affront. They wanted President Wilson to slap down the "bandits." Shutts and Stoneman felt as strongly about the Mexican situation as did the readers of their newspaper.

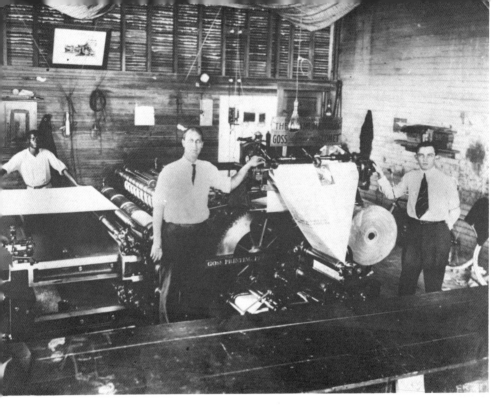

SO RAPIDLY did the young *Miami Herald* grow after beating its competitor, the *Metropolis,* on the sinking of the *Titanic* story that in 1915 a new press and a third typesetting machine were needed. But by 1917 the Goss Comet flatbed press, above, was inadequate and had to be replaced by a high-speed rotary press.

ENTIRE STAFF of the *Miami Herald*—nineteen, but not including the publisher—posed in front of the Miami Herald building about 1912 for this group photograph. Editor Frank B. Stoneman is fifth from left, but Publisher Frank B. Shutts was unavailable. Others identified are William Stuart Hill, reporter, number one, left; Charles Bates, in charge of advertising, two; Oscar T. Conklin, general manager, eleven; Harry O. Huston, night editor, fourteen; and Ben Field, eighteen. (Courtesy of Miss Dallas M. Conklin)

The *Herald's* front page must have been irresistible to readers at a time when the newspapers were the only source of world news. The interminable fighting in Mexico and the worsening political situation in Europe got big play. But it was the Mexican Revolution that got the most attention. The stories, mainly about battles or threats of battles, were exciting and full of tension but without any background on the Mexican events or interpretive articles attempting to explain the nature of the revolution. Stoneman's editorials about the Mexican conflict reveal a glaring ignorance about the political, social, and economic background of Mexico. Although well educated, Stoneman's reading had been mainly in the classics and in history that reflected a world from the Yankee and English-Victorian viewpoint. Despite Stoneman's early interest in the theories of socialism, his editorials reveal little appreciation of the effects of economic and political conditions upon the revolution, which the *Herald* viewed as being no more than a fight between leaders ambitious to seize power. Editorials often reflected a feeling that the world might be doomed and that the end of time was close at hand. Stoneman seemed to be turning more and more to religion in search of a solution for the world's problems. The *Herald* since its founding had carried on Monday morning a sermon that a Miami pastor had delivered on Sunday. On April 6, 1914, the following three-column, three-line headline announced a sermon delivered the day before in a Miami church: "If God Is Not With Us,/Days of Republic are Numbered/Despite Wealth and Pride."

The world seemed mad indeed after war began in Europe. But the Continent must have seemed more remote to Shutts and Stoneman than the moon would be to later generations. Neither publisher nor editor had been to Europe, and they had no first-hand knowledge of what that part of the world was like. The *Herald's* editorial viewpoint was that the United States should remain neutral but should insist on complete freedom of the seas. This meant the right to sell arms to both sides. The morals of this were not discussed, nor did there appear to be any fear it might get this country involved in war. Even after the sinking of the *Lusitania* by a German submarine in 1915, with the loss of 128 American lives, the *Herald* failed to reflect concern that the United States might become involved by its insistence on trading with the belligerents. The *Herald* preferred to see the United States go to war rather than give up its "freedom of the seas." While giving lip service to the dovish efforts of William Jennings Bryan, Secretary of State and a Miami winter resident, the paper backed Wilson's military preparedness program and warned Imperial Germany and her allies that if they knew what was good for them they would avoid trouble with the United States. America, now becoming prosperous because of the war, was feeling a growing national pride and power.

Meanwhile, Miami's population passed 15,000 in 1915. But for a time after the death of Flagler in 1913, which marked the passing of an era of big spending, an atmosphere of uncertainty followed, resulting in a local recession. Long freight trains rattled through Miami bound for the deep-water port of Key West, with cargo for Cuba, the Canal Zone, or South America. Northbound trains carried pineapples from Cuba, bananas from Central America, together with seafood, including live green turtles strung out on the bottoms of gondola cars on their backs with their fins nailed down. Although Miami had become increasingly important as a tourist town, the "Season" was restricted to several weeks during the winter. During the summer Miami's unpaved, white limestone streets were nearly deserted. Miamians became increasingly aware of the end of the Flagler era. Hundreds were out of work. Money was tight. The Dade County government had no funds in the bank. County employees were paid by check but had to pay banks a ten percent discount to get them cashed. The bankers' excuse was that they were unsure when they would receive their money from the county. But just as Miami's economy was about to go from bad to worse, another "sugar daddy" arrived to fill the void left by Flagler. He was James Deering of Chicago, vice-president of International Harvester Company. In 1914 a trainload of construction equipment arrived in Miami, and soon a thousand Miamians were employed at Villa Vizcaya. The building of Vizcaya, on Biscayne Bay between Miami and Coconut Grove, took nearly three years. Deering imported Italian stonecutters and Scottish gardeners. The cost of the mansion and its magnificent gardens has been estimated variously at between $7 million and $15 million, but the lesser figure would have been a very large amount at a time when a carpenter received two dollars a day for ten hours of work. Deering moved into his mansion just before Christmas, 1916. A story in the *Herald* on December 17 stated that Deering had arrived in his private railway car, but little else was said. It was at a time when wealthy capitalists enjoyed a freedom from reporters that amounted to an immunity almost equal to that accorded a prince. But William Jennings Bryan, who arrived the same day, was interviewed and a lengthy article about him appeared in the *Herald*. Bryan, three times the Democratic Party's choice for President of the United States, thrived on attention and courted the press. He had been Wilson's Secretary of State from 1913 to 1915, when he quit after a disagreement with Wilson over the handling of the *Lusitania* sinking. Because of his political prestige and his image as the "Great Commoner," any story about Bryan was sure to be widely read; but there could hardly have been greater curiosity about him among Miamians than about the mysterious and silent James Deering.

During the years immediately preceding the United States' entry into World War I, Miami, like the rest of the nation, was involved in morality campaigns to close the saloons, to close the houses of prostitution, and to stop all unnecessary work on Sundays. Believing the world was out of joint, many felt that only through a renewed moral dedication could people regain their sanity and stop senseless killings, crime, and debauchery. While the *Herald* supported back-to-church campaigns, it resisted pressures from the anti-saloon group as well as from those who wanted to impose Sunday blue laws on the city. A delegation of churchwomen called on Stoneman, demanding that the *Herald* observe the sabbath by discontinuing its Sunday paper. After greeting the ladies courteously, Stoneman explained that if they wanted to protest against Sunday-produced newspapers, their concern should be about the Monday *Herald,* since the Sunday *Herald* was mainly produced on Saturday, while the Monday *Herald* was mainly produced on Sunday. This was too confusing for the ladies. Changing the subject, they sought to induce Stoneman to cut out the comics, which, the ladies thought, had a corrupting influence on Miami's children. Stoneman thought this decision should rest with parents, who could remove the comics if they did not want their children to read them.

Although the *Herald* condemned prostitution, it continued to support Sheriff Dan Hardie, who had failed to carry out his promise to close the houses. A wandering soldier of fortune before discovering Miami, Hardie was a cocky, hard-muscled man who had made himself widely popular, but particularly with the newspaper reporters to whom he catered. But he was less popular with the county physician, Dr. E. K. Jaudon, whom he left locked in the county jail for three hours. The physician had entered the jail to give the inmates a routine health check, expecting to be there only briefly. Hardie forgot, and by the time he regained his memory he had to face a crimson-faced medical examiner who greeted him in shouting anger. In the meantime the prisoners had held kangaroo court, had tried Dr. Jaudon on charges of "breaking and entering" the jail, and had fined him twenty-five cents.

Another Jaudon, James F. Jaudon, is given credit for suggesting the Tamiami Trail across the Everglades, but it was a *Herald* reporter who planted the idea. Cap'n Jaudon, county tax assessor, was a person of energy and enthusiasm whose word was highly respected. A hard-muscled man of the outdoors like Hardie, Jaudon also was a favorite with reporters. Reporter William Stuart Hill, who covered the county courthouse, and Jaudon were good friends. A native of Tennessee, Hill had come to Miami in 1904, and, after serving as a peace justice for a time, acquired the title of judge. Judge Hill was a tall man whose white hair, heavy black mustache, and bushy black eyebrows made him an impressive figure. Although Stoneman did not consider him an outstanding reporter, his southern manners and Tennessee drawl helped to win friends for him at the courthouse and city hall. One day the reporter and the tax assessor were talking.

"Jim," said Hill, "I wonder if it wouldn't be possible to build a highway across the Everglades and Big Cypress Swamp, from Miami to the Gulf coast. You've spent a lot of time in the backcountry. What do you think of the idea?"

"I don't see why it couldn't be done," replied Jaudon, who had hunted and fished in the wilderness west of Miami for several years. "There's a solid rock foundation all the way across southern Florida. To build a road, all you'd have to do is dig a canal and pile the spoil alongside. You level the spoil and you've got a road. I guess I've thought about it, but never seriously."

"Say, could I quote you?" asked Hill, fingering for his notebook and pencil.

The nearest highway across the state in 1914 was at Titusville, nearly 200 miles north of Miami. Moreover, the Everglades was being drained by several canals that had been opened within the past two or three years, and it appeared that the rich muck country would be developed for agriculture.

"Sure, go ahead and quote me if you like," said Jaudon, with growing enthusiasm. "A road across the Everglades not only would give us a short route across the state, but would make the Everglades accessible for farming—and beyond the Everglades, in Big Cypress Swamp, is the greatest hunting in the world."

Hill wrote the story, and Stoneman backed the idea with an editorial. Miami's perennial booster, E. G. Sewell, secretary of the Chamber of Commerce, liked the idea, too. So did the *Tampa Tribune,* which picked up the story. D. G. Gillett, secretary of the Tampa Chamber of Commerce, visualized a road connecting Tampa with Miami. He suggested the wedding of "Miami" with the first two letters of "Tampa," and the name "Tamiami Trail" was born. By June 1915, surveyors were staking a route across the wilderness, and in October, Dade County freeholders voted 325 to 43 in favor of a $275,000 bond issue to begin work on the Miami leg of Tamiami Trail. A short time later Lee County voters approved a $325,000 bond issue to build the trail south from Fort Myers to Naples and across Big Cypress to the Dade County line. But the building of Tamiami Trail would prove to be a tougher construction job than Cap'n Jaudon had imagined. Forty thousand pounds of dynamite was used for each mile. Beneath the saw grass and muck was hard limestone. A dredge, straddling the canal it dug, removed the rock pulverized by the dynamite and piled it alongside to be leveled as a road bed. After many starts and stops, the Tamiami Trail was completed in 1928, thirteen years after work was begun—four years longer than it had taken Flagler to build his Overseas Railroad from the Florida mainland to Key West.

MIAMI'S WATERFRONT in 1917. Dredges have just begun to deepen the shallow Biscayne Bay for the city's first major seaport. A county causeway was built to Miami Beach on the spoil deposited alongside the channel that was dredged between the port and the ocean. After World War II the name was changed to MacArthur Causeway. In the distance is the wooden Collins Bridge, opened in 1913 as the first connection between the mainland and the Beach. It was replaced in the 1920s by the Venetian Causeway. (Richard B. Hoit)

5

War and Disillusionment

THE *Miami Herald* was but a small town newspaper in 1914 when World War I began in Europe. Yet its front pages, read today, give a stirring picture of that bloody conflict in a way no history book could portray. There are the daily headlines of successes and failures and stalemates. You sense the bitterness of the defeats and the emptiness of victories. A battle won means only that another battle must be fought. On and on, month after month of trench warfare, with enemies facing each other across a no-man's land of barbed wire, land mines, and shell holes, the *Herald's* front page records it all. A photograph of the first tank, a continuous tread tractor with gun and armor to protect the driver and gunner, appeared on page one. You also see a photograph of the first use of gas. Clouds of gas, released by men wearing masks, spread out across no-man's land in the direction of enemy trenches, but as the caption suggests, no one could be sure the direction of the wind would not change. Through rain, knee-deep mud, and snow the fighting continued, with constant artillery fire against opposite trenches, underground forts, and supply routes. A battle to gain 500 yards made headlines in 1916 because its cost was 5,000 lives. In the Battle of Verdun 400,000 lives were expended. The fighting and the dying on a dozen fronts seemed interminable. Names of battles and fronts became household words for Miamians—the Marne, the Meuse, Ypres, Verdun, Dardanelles, Pepit Marshes. A whole new geography was learned by *Herald* readers. The names of battle heroes appeared in bold headlines—Joffre, Petain, Ludendorff, von Hindenburg, Beatty, Jellicoe—names that would be meaningless to future generations burdened by World War II and the Korean and Vietnam wars.

But the nation was prospering from its trade with the belligerents, and so was Miami, which in 1916 experienced a building boom. Miami Beach had been incorporated in 1915, and the work of clearing the island's mangrove swamps and raising the land level by dredging and filling was in progress. Plans for a county causeway between Miami and Miami Beach, together with the deepening of the ship channel and the improvement, of the harbor, were being pushed. Work on Miami's first high-rise, the McAllister Hotel, was begun. But as 1916 passed the nation was closer to becoming involved in the war. Wilson was insisting that American ships had the right to travel anywhere on the high seas, and he warned Germany to sink no more ships carrying American citizens. Wilson correctly guessed the temper of Americans. While they wanted peace, they did not want it at "any cost." Meanwhile, Washington announced new defense preparations, and Miami was selected for a Navy seaplane flight training base to be built at Dinner Key, a decision that signaled the beginning of Miami as an important aviation center.

In December of 1916 Wilson made a plea to the belligerents to end the war, calling for "peace without victory." Germany's reply was to announce on January 31, 1917, a policy of unrestricted naval warfare against the ships of all neutral nations found in belligerent-controlled waters. A hue and cry went up from newspapers, including the *Herald*. Wilson severed diplomatic relations. The public was ready for war. One can almost hear the trumpets of war sound from the *Herald's* front page. On April 2 President Wilson asked Congress to declare war against Germany "to make the world safe for democracy." Miami, too, went to war. So did the *Herald*. Under the heading of "Declaration Inevitable," Stoneman wrote that this country was ready to descend into "the very hell of war" to defend its flag and pride.

When the Wilson government asked newspapers to impose a censorship on news that might be of aid or comfort to the enemy, the *Herald* went far beyond the guidelines. In an editorial the paper announced it would refrain from criticizing the government or the military until after the war. Moreover, the *Herald* changed its format to one of severe austerity. The liberal typography Shutts and Stoneman had permitted since the sinking of the *Titanic* in 1912 disappeared overnight. Despite the major events taking place during the first three months after the United States entry into the war, no streamer appeared on home-delivered papers until June 28, when a story was received reporting the landing of the first American troops in France. The paper reflected its patriotism in its news coverage, in editorials, and in makeup. The war was to Shutts and Stoneman both noble and of deep religious significance. They felt the war had to be fought to save the world from its own destruction. Readers were urged to ignore rumors and show faith in the government.

FIRST WOMAN reporter on the *Miami Herald,* Marjory Stoneman Douglas, joined the paper in 1915.

ARMISTICE DAY, November 11, 1918, brought out all of Miami to celebrate the end of World War I. You are looking east on Flagler Street, and the incomplete structure in the distance is the McAllister Hotel.

Miami's building activities and population growth speeded up as the war progressed. By late 1917 Dade County had three air stations where Army, Navy, and Marine Corps fliers were being trained. The city was now getting a new kind of visitor, parents of young men in flight training. They came in the summer as well as in the winter, because there was no "Season" for parents who wanted to see their sons before they were sent overseas.

Meanwhile, Stoneman lost his daughter and the *Herald's* first woman reporter to the war effort. Mrs. Marjory Stoneman Douglas had come to Miami in 1915 after a brief and unhappy marriage to join her father, who himself had recently remarried. Marjory was assigned first to cover meetings of the Linger Longer Society, the Booklovers' musicale, the Merry Matrons of Allapattah, the Ladies Auxiliary of the Brotherhood of Railway Trainmen, and the National Association for Woman's Suffrage. She was soon covering a variety of assignments, and despite some unkind remarks she since has made about her writing at that time, she became a proficient reporter. Her fluency in the use of "purple prose" gives some hint of the talent she would develop later to make herself a well-known author. But in 1917, soon after the United States declared war on Germany, Marjory went far beyond the call of duty when she was sent to a Navy recruiting vessel, docked at the foot of Flagler Street, to do a story on a group of twenty-four Miamians who had enlisted in the Navy. Returning to the newsroom, Marjory wrote her story and handed it in. The editor noted that "twenty-four men and one woman" had enlisted. The woman was Marjory Stoneman Douglas, who had signed up as a yeoman, the first woman in Florida to enlist in the Navy.

While waiting to be called to duty, Marjory was assigned to accompany a committee of woman suffragetes to the state capitol at Tallahassee to lobby for women's right to vote. Several states had passed such a bill, and the committee, headed by Mrs. William Jennings Bryan and including the widows of two former Florida governors, sought to induce the Legislature to give women equal rights in Florida. Such was the influence of the committee that a joint meeting of the Senate and House of Representatives was convened to hear Mrs. Bryan and other speakers. And so carried away was Marjory, herself an ardent worker for woman's suffrage, that she abandoned her reporter's role, got to her feet, and made a speech. The committee lost, of course. Believing that a woman's place was in the kitchen when she was not rocking the cradle, those Cracker politicians were not about to give women the right to vote.

While the *Herald* professed to be in favor of individual states giving women the right to vote, it was strongly against a constitutional amendment, which is what the women were fighting for. The paper also opposed the prohibition amendment, which was proposed in December 1917, "while the boys were in the trenches," as critics said. Both Shutts and Stoneman liked to drink and they shared the belief that drinking should be an individual choice.

A record eight editions were published on Armistice Day, November 11, 1918. Wilsonian idealism oozed from editorials in the days following the war's end. Stoneman believed that the war had been one to "end all wars," in the full meaning of the phrase coined by the President. Said Stoneman editorially: "America has won all the things for which she fought." Disillusionment was to follow. The *Herald,* however, took a little time to break out of the straightjacket of censorship and austerity it had imposed upon itself during the war. Eighteen months of involvement with an overwhelming patriotism had dulled the paper's newspapering instincts. But the dream era passed and the editor was shocked by the awakening.

Repercussions of the explosion of Russian Communism in 1917 were beginning to be felt throughout the world by the end of 1918, and by 1919 the *Herald* was running streamer headlines about the threat of Bolshevism. The idealism and hope that had guided the *Herald* during the war faded from its pages. Confusion and fear took command. This was reflected not only in editorials but in the scare stories and headlines that began to appear on page one. On March 22, 1919, this eight column headline screamed across the top of page one: "Bolshevik Army of Million to Invade Europe." Two stories from Paris by *New York World* correspondents reported that "unfavorable weather" was the only thing delaying a powerful army, under the command of Leon Trotsky, from marching on the west. There was no follow-up, but on April 4 a bold streamer announced: "United States May Recognize Bolshevik Regime." It was just another unfounded report. The *Herald* was now falling for the rumors it had urged its readers during the war to ignore. At that time an American expeditionary force was in Siberia fighting the Reds alongside soldiers from Great Britain, Czechoslovakia, and Japan. Lenin and Trotsky had proclaimed worldwide revolution and were calling upon the workers to unite, "throw off their chains," and set up "dictatorships of the proletariat." With the unrest and strikes of labor in western Europe and the United States following the war, it appeared to Stoneman that revolution was at hand.

Waging war against Bolshevism and atheism, the *Herald* conducted go-to-church drives and called upon Americans to reexamine their conscience and get right with God and country. The drive to save souls and rebuild "basic American values" culminated in March 1919 with the most unlikely coverage of a religious event ever attempted by the *Miami*

THE MIAMI HERALD

VOL. 8, NO. 342   MIAMI, FLORIDA, MONDAY MORNING, NOVEMBER 11, 1918   PRICE FIVE CENTS

THIS NEWSPAPER IS AN AUTHORIZED FARM LABOR AGENCY, NO. 226, OF THE U. S. EMPLOYMENT SERVICE, DEPARTMENT OF LABOR.

THE WORLD WAR ENDS TODAY

ARMISTICE GOES INTO EFFECT AT SIX A. M. WASHINGTON TIME

Representatives of the German Government Sign Epoch-making Document at Midnight and News is Immediately Flashed to Washington and Given to the People of the United States by Sec. Lansing through the Associated Press; the Announcement Was Made by the State Department at 2:05 This Morning.

KAISER FLEES TO HOLLAND WITH GEN'L STAFF AND CROWN PRINCE

Berlin is in the Hands of Revolutionists Who Proclaim a Republic; New Government Issues a Proclamation Saying, "This Day the People's Deliverance Has Been Fulfilled"; Councils of Workmen and Soldiers Are in Control of the Situation.

Peace has come to the hard-tried world after considerably more than four years of strife such as the annals of history have never before recorded.

A new order of things prevails in Berlin and a new government is in control. Dispatches are sent out by the councils of workmen and soldiers and they are in full control of the situation. The former emperor has fled to Holland, accompanied by the crown prince, the former empress of Germany and the entire general staff of the German army.

Hindenburg, the much heralded great genius of the German military organization, has fled to Holland, close on the heels of the fleet-footed Wilhelm Hohenzollern.

Reports coming out of Germany through the neutral capitals tell for most part of the seizure of the government in various cities and states of the German empire by peaceful means, and in some instances the princes are co-operating with the soldiers' and workmen's councils in establishing the new order.

In some instances the incensed soldiers and marines have turned their war-stained weapons against those who sought to oppose them and blood has flowed freely; in others they have attempted to murder their former rulers.

Another attempt has been made against the life of Prince Henry, brother of the former kaiser, and the hand of the soldier has been raised against the wife of Prince Adelbert, one of the former emperor's six sons.

News of the signing of the armistice was flashed to the United States immediately and given to the people by Secretary Lansing through the Associated Press at 2:05 this morning.

Washington, Nov. 11—(By Associated Press)—World

war will end this morning at six o'clock, Washington time, eleven o'clock Paris time. Armistice signed by German representatives at midnight. This announcement was made to the state department at 2:05 this morning.

The terms of the armistice, it was announced, will not be made public until later. Military men here, however, regard it as certain that they include: Immediate retirement of the German military forces from France, Belgium and Alsace-Lorraine.

Disarming and demobilization of the German armies.

Occupation by the allied and American forces of such strategic points in Germany as will make impossible a renewal of hostilities.

Delivery of part of the German high seas fleet and a certain number of submarines to the allied and merchant naval forces. Disarmament of the German ships and supervision of the allied and American navies which will guard them.

Occupation of the principal German naval bases by one forces of the victorious nations.

Release of allied and American soldiers, sailors and civilians held prisoners in Germany without such reciprocal action by the associated governments.

Forty-seven hours had been required for the courier to reach headquarters and unquestionably several hours were necessary for the examination of the terms and a decision.

(By The Associated Press)

William Hohenzollern, the abdicated German emperor and king of Prussia, and his eldest son, Frederick William, who hoped some day to rule the German people, are reported to have fled to Holland.

The revolution which is in progress throughout Germany, although it seemingly has a peaceful one, probably threw fear into the hearts of the former kaiser and the crown prince and caused them to take refuge in a neutral state.

Wilhelm II, reigning king of the monarchy of Wurttemberg, is declared to have abdicated Friday night, and reports have it that the grand duke of Hesse, ruler of the grand duchy of Hesse, has deemed the formation of a council of state to take over the government there. Every dynasty in Germany is to be suppressed and all the princes exiled, according to Swiss advices.

(Continued On Page Two.)

Members of Allied War Council Who Decided Germany's Fate

GENERAL PERSHING — LLOYD GEORGE — PREMIER CLEMENCEAU — COL. E. M. HOUSE

V. E. ORLANDO — SIR DOUGLAS HAIG — GENERAL FOCH — SIR ERIC GEDDES

GENERAL BLISS — ADMIRAL BENSON — ADMIRAL SIMS

WAR WORK DRIVE TO BEGIN TODAY

Plans Complete For Whirlwind Campaign To Raise Dade County's Quota Of $95,000 For Seven United Organizations' War Relief

AERIAL STUNTS A FEATURE OF THE WAR-WORK CELEBRATION IN MIAMI

Parade, Mass Meeting, Music, Songs And Addresses Usher In The Week's United Campaign For War Work Funds Here

EIGHT EDITIONS were published on Armistice Day, November 11, 1918, the end of World War I.

Herald. It was day-by-day, page-one report on a revival conducted in Saint Augustine by evangelist Billy Sunday. Before the war the *Herald* had been a frequent critic of Sunday, classifying him with the crackpots. Now he was looked upon as the possible savior of mankind. Billy Sunday stories appeared for two weeks, most on page one, and some under bold headlines. According to the *Herald,* thousands flocked to Saint Augustine to hear the "man of God." The stories told of cripples being saved, throwing away their crutches and walking normally again; of men long cursed by the possession of the devil breaking their chains; of the dissolute becoming shining moral images again. A windup story on page one told of Sunday saving more than 400 souls.

Under the pressure of the moralists' campaign in the spring of 1919, the Florida Legislature passed blue laws designed to close all businesses, including drugstores, on Sunday. In the beginning, the blue laws went unnoticed in South Florida, despite pressure from church groups. The *Herald,* publishing on Sunday, made no comment. But in the spring of 1921 the pressure had become so great that County Solicitor Fred Pine ordered the closing of all businesses and all recreation activities in the county. Sheriff Louis A. Allen announced he would arrest anyone breaking the law. Closed were golf courses, movie houses, and beaches. The playing of Sunday baseball was stopped. Even busses and streetcars were ordered to stop running. Pine announced he was considering filing charges against a preacher to make a court test to determine whether Sunday church services broke the law. The *Herald* quietly continued to publish, and while it carried stories about the Sunday closings no editorial comment appeared. However, the strict enforcement of the blue laws made a laughing-stock of the legislative act, and few complaints were heard when enforcement was relaxed.

The *Herald* began 1920 with a new masthead, "The Miami Herald" being changed from plain, light-face type to Old English—"The Miami Herald." Prices were soaring. Labor was impatient for higher wages. And the government was cracking down on radicals. On January 2 a *Herald* streamer reported the first major roundup, largest in America's history. The raids were carried out "from Portland, Maine, to Portland, Oregon," said the story. Between 700 and 800 were arrested in New York City alone. A new word for radicals—Reds—appeared in the *Herald* for the first time. An editorial lauded the arrest of the "Reds," whom the editor referred to as "AntiChrists".

Miami's 1920 population was 30,000, compared with 5,500 in 1910. Warren G. Harding and Calvin Coolidge, the Republicans' choice for President and Vice-President, were elected in 1920 over James M. Cox, governor of Ohio, and Franklin D. Roosevelt, under-secretary of the

ACTIVE MIAMI was beginning to feel the rise of boom-era fever in the early 1920s when military and patriotic groups marched in this Armistice Day parade, in celebration of the end of World War I. Miamians loved parades, and thousands gathered along Flagler Street to watch.

Navy during the war. The *Herald* had supported the Democratic candidates guardedly, but appeared pleased when the Republicans won. The editor hoped the Republicans would provide a stabilizing influence at a time when there was an increase in drug traffic, particularly opium, and a decline in morals and patriotism. The editor also hoped the Republicans would do something about the record high cost of living. A short recession in 1921 took care of the high prices but had little effect upon prosperous, expanding Miami. County building permits, which had set a record of $4.4 million in 1920, set another record in 1921, of $5.4 million.

Daily *Herald* circulation gained from 9,350 in 1921 to 13,560 in 1922, while Sunday circulation gained from 11,980 to 16,670. The Sunday *Herald* ran to thirty-six pages. Classified advertising ran four pages, and for the first time full page display ads promoting real estate ventures were beginning to appear regularly. Shutts purchased an adjoining three-story building. Doors were cut through the fire wall separating the buildings, permitting an expansion of the cramped newsroom and the composing room. New typesetting machines were added, bringing the total to eight. Carpenters' Hall occupied the third floor, and the carpenters continued to meet there until the space was needed for the expanding advertising department. There had been no slowdown in growth since Shutts began publishing the *Herald* in 1910.

Meanwhile, the *Herald* began backing away from its preoccupation with national confusion and international strife to concentrate on the problems confronting rapidly growing Miami. Among the goals set by the paper for the community were improving the harbor, building a railroad to Florida's Gulf coast, and completion of the Tamiami Trail as well as such prosaic necessities as improving sewage disposal and acquiring the municipal waterworks, which were still owned by the Flagler System. And to improve South Florida's image, the *Herald* urged that the name of the Everglades be changed in order to keep people from associating southern Florida with a wilderness. During the twelve years Shutts had lived in Miami he had seen the Everglades pushed back several miles from the city's outskirts. James Bright's new subdivision, Hialeah, was going up in what was formerly flooded saw grass country. And the Curtiss-Bright Flying Field, destined to become part of the Miami International Airport, likewise had been a wet glade before drainage. Shutts, foreseeing the eventual development of the entire backcountry, believed that the present name of Everglades was a misnomer and actually did harm because people in the North associated the name with "Indians, rattlesnakes, and alligators." So the *Herald* in May of 1922 began a campaign to change the name. Many readers fell enthusiastically for the idea and began sending in suggestions. Among those published include Florida Prairies, Prairie Meadows, Great Prairie, Florida Nile, Grandeur, and Majestic Gardens. The campaign never got off the ground and the name Everglades was retained. In a later era the word Everglades was to become associated with the image of a unique wilderness that would bring people to Florida rather than repel them. And the *Miami Herald* would become a leading advocate of its preservation forever as part of the Everglades National Park.

6

Boom and Bust

THE FLORIDA LAND BOOM was the greatest local story the
Miami Herald had covered—as big as any local event it was likely
to cover for a long time. Although the mad part of the boom
lasted but a few months, from late 1924 until the fall of 1925, its beginning may be traced to World War I. Population growth increased rapidly
after the war, and by 1923 Miami was experiencing a prosperity which, in
any ordinary sense, could have been described as a boom. But if Miami
was booming in 1923, no word exists to describe 1925.

So rapidly did Miami grow after 1920 that it was difficult for construction to provide enough residences, apartments, and hotel rooms. By the
end of 1922 the population was estimated by the *Herald* at 45,000, a gain
of 15,000 in two years. The city grew to an estimated 70,000 by the end of
1923, and to 102,000 by the end of 1924. But the greatest gain was recorded in 1925, when, according to the Chamber of Commerce, Miami's population soared to 177,000, far exceeding housing facilities. To provide
sleeping accommodations, warehouses and other large buildings were
filled with closely spaced cots. Still the demand became so great at the
height of the boom that the "hot bed" system was devised. A cot was
rented to two persons, each on a twelve-hour basis. One used the cot during the day, another at night. Five years later, in 1930, federal census
counters could find only 142,739 permanent residents in all of Dade
County, with 110,600 living in Miami. But that was long after the
boom—after Miami had suffered two major disasters, the 1926 hurricane
on top of the "bust."

In the summer of 1924 the tallest building in Miami was the ten-story
McAllister Hotel. Twelve months later Miami had a skyline in varying
stages of completion. By the fall of 1924 boom fever was spreading
throughout Florida. Miami was the heart of the boom, the *Miami Herald*

its nerve center. Developers ran full-page ads and sought to induce the editor to run stories about their projects. The extent of real estate operations made thorough investigations impossible, and some extravagant stories were run. Releases from credible sources sometimes turned out to be fanciful. An example was a release by Cornelius Vanderbilt, Jr., who appeared in the *Herald's* newsroom in late 1924 to announce that Barron G. Collier, streetcar advertising magnate who had purchased a million acres on Florida's lower Gulf coast, would build a railroad from Fort Myers to Miami. Two hundred miles of rails and six locomotives had been loaded on a train for delivery to Collier's Florida Navigation & Railroad Corporation in Florida, according to Vanderbilt. The story got big play. Like a hundred other announced multimillion dollar projects, the Collier railroad was never started, but young Vanderbilt, who had ingratiated himself with the *Herald's* staff, induced the editor to run a story about his plans to start a third newspaper in Miami. The *Illustrated Daily Tab* began publication January 12, 1925, and lasted through the rest of the boom. But it took no business from the *Herald,* which was getting more advertising than it could handle.

For thirteen months in 1925 and 1926 the *Herald* was the largest newspaper in volume of business in the world, topping the great papers of London, New York, Chicago, and Los Angeles. It set a world's record in 1925 with 42.5 million lines of advertising, 12 million more lines than any newspaper had ever carried in a year's time. The peak was reached in January 1926, however, when the *Herald* did twice as much advertising as it had done any month of the previous year. But the *Herald* could not match the 504-page issue which the *Miami Daily News* published on July 26, 1925, in a dual celebration of the paper's twenty-ninth anniversary and the opening of the new Miami News Tower on Biscayne Boulevard. The *Herald,* its two old presses running twenty-four hours a day, lacked facilities to publish special editions. The daily *Herald* ran sixty to eighty-eight pages, while Sunday editions ran 160 pages and more. Advertising Sales Manager Charles "Pop" Bates turned down as many as fifteen pages of advertising every day. The *Herald* was caught unprepared for the boom, as were the railroads, steamship lines, and utilities. For the boom, which had blossomed with increasing speed, burst upon Miami with an immense explosion. For a time the Magic City appeared to be a little mad. So did the *Herald.* And after it was over, blown away in a massive hurricane on the morning of September 18, 1926, the boom was like a psychotic's dream—and Miamians would be a little paranoiac for a decade afterward.

In January, 1924, the *Herald* was being printed on a one-unit rotary press capable of delivering a twenty-four page paper. Eight typesetting

A GLAMOROUS TOWER in Miami's skyline, the Miami News building, was completed in July, 1925, at Biscayne Boulevard and Northeast Sixth Street. After the *News* moved out in 1958 the building became a temporary headquarters for the handling of Cuban refugees and acquired the name of Freedom Tower. (State Photographic Archives)

machines were in operation. The paper was growing, but there was no indication yet of the explosion that was to come. Fortunately, Shutts had made a change in 1923 that would provide the editorial leadership and experience for the unforeseen days ahead. He made Olin W. Kennedy managing editor, and by the beginning of 1924 the *Herald* for the first time in its fourteen years had the appearance of a newspaper produced by professionals. The addition that year of a second press, which had printed the *Denver Post* for twenty years, provided the *Herald* with its major production facilities for riding out the boom. Even this was not enough. During the height of the boom a daily insert was printed on the presses of Vanderbilt's *Daily Tab*.

Kennedy, in his late forties, was a native of Ohio. Although he had received little formal education, Kennedy entered the newspaper profession at an early age and found he had a flair for it. He worked first on Cincinnati papers, then on Saint Louis, Denver, and Washington papers before Shutts hired him in 1919 as city editor. Kennedy was slightly smaller than average, blondish, with blue eyes and white skin that was seldom exposed to the sun. He wore rimless, pinch-type glasses similar to the kind worn by President Wilson. Kennedy signed memos and bulletin board notices with his initials, O.W.K., and behind his back was known

MANAGING EDITOR Olin W. Kennedy in 1923 changed the image of the *Miami Herald* from that of a small town sheet to a professional-appearing newspaper.

FIRST NEWSPAPER in Miami was the *Miami Metropolis,* founded in 1896. It was located at 70 West Flagler Street, next door to the downtown fire station. The name was later changed to the *Miami News.* (State Photographic Archives)

to the staff as the "Great Owk." None dared call him Great Owk to his face, because Kennedy, sensitive as a result of his lack of college training and what he assumed to be the refinement that went with it, was not the kind of person with whom an underling became familiar. He did not smoke and seldom drank. His vices were concentrated into gambling. During the nine years he worked at the *Herald* Kennedy was a patron of virtually every gambling club in Miami. He had arrived in Miami in 1919 broke, and he departed broke in 1928. But he had more influence over the publisher than anyone who had worked on the *Herald* before him, including Stoneman. Under Kennedy's direction the format of the paper changed—the headline typeface, the makeup, and the use of pictures. Shutts wanted a paper that resembled the *New York Times.* While Kennedy was unable to turn the *Herald* into a southern version of the *Times,* he could at least produce a paper with a similar format—the image of conservatism, dependability, and permanency. So pleased was Shutts that he gave Kennedy an additional title—assistant publisher. This not only put him over Stoneman but also over the general manager.

During the same year Kennedy became managing editor, James M. Cox, former governor of Ohio and onetime presidential candidate, purchased the *Herald's* competitor, the *Miami Metropolis.* Short and egotistical, Cox wore a derby tilted to one side, giving him a "bantam" image. Also publisher of the Dayton, Ohio, *Daily News,* Cox was an able newspaperman. He changed the name of the *Metropolis* to the *Miami Daily News* and began to make improvements in its appearance and content. Shutts had reason for concern, now that he had a competitor with as much wealth and prestige as Governor Cox. But Shutts had a title, too. Governor Carey Hardee of Florida had made him an honorary colonel on his staff, and Shutts outfitted himself with the colorful dress uniform of a staff colonel, which he wore on official occasions. Stories in the *Herald* that mentioned Shutts now referred to him as Colonel Shutts, and he became known as Colonel Shutts to everyone who greeted him or mentioned him in conversation, a practice which would last the rest of his life.

Shutts early in 1925 began making plans for a new production plant at the *Herald.* In midsummer work was begun on a four-story building, at the rear of and tied onto the old buildings that faced Miami Avenue. With presses and other new equipment, the investment was to exceed one million dollars. In the meantime, the two old presses were operating at top speed day and night, never being shut down except to change plates or to replace lost bolts. For many years afterward those who had worked on the *Herald* during the boom would look back with painful recollection: the new facilities did not become available until the boom was over, when the daily *Herald* was down to twenty-four pages again.

The sale of the *Miami Metropolis* to Cox was not all bad news for Shutts. At last he had the "Bobonic Plague" off his back. Dean not only had been a dogged competitor since the beginning of the *Herald* in 1910, the moralistic Alabaman had seized upon every opportunity to attack the vulnerable Shutts, whose law firm represented the Flagler System and whose newspaper had been "on the side of the godless" in its stand against prohibition. What one publisher wanted the other was sure to be against. Although he lived within the city limits, Dean kept a cow. The surplus milk was sold to neighbors by the Dean children. Shutts sought in vain to force Dean to dispose of his cow. The rows between the publishers not only hurt the credibility of both newspapers but proved costly to the community. An example was the battle between Dean and Shutts over the purchase by the city of Biscayne Bay waterfront for the development of Bayfront Park. The waterfront property was owned by the Flagler System, which as a result of Shutts' influence offered it to the city for $415,000. Dean blew up the deal into a major political issue and killed it. When the city did purchase the property, in the 1920s, it had to pay $1,340,000.

Another issue the publishers disagreed on was horse racing. Shutts wanted a thoroughbred racetrack for Miami, and he frequently discussed horse racing with Mayor Ed Romfh, president of the First National Bank and one of a five-member commission of bankers elected to run the city of Miami during that mad period. While the mayor was no more of a sportsman than Shutts, he agreed that a horse track would be good for Miami. A winter track would draw many sportsmen and big-time bettors who made summer racing popular in the North. The publisher and the banker discussed horse racing with James Bright, who owned 17,000 acres in the "Humbuggus-Pokeymoonshine" section of the Everglades northwest of Miami, which included the new community of Hialeah. Bright was more than a little interested. He was a cattleman and a lover of horses. He told Shutts he would consider providing the land in exchange for stock in the venture. Although wagering was illegal under Florida law, the governor at that time was disinclined to interfere in the affairs of the counties, so long as scandal and his political neck were not involved. Casino-type gambling had been operated for years in Miami and at Palm Beach without interference from the governor. Not even Bobo Dean was able to get the governor involved. But Dean could be depended upon to create a scandal if any group tried to open a horse track. But Dean had sold his newspaper when, early in 1924, Joseph M. Smoot, an impeccably dressed Virginia gentleman wearing two-toned

MIAMI's city commission in 1925 was composed of five bankers who helped to complete the city's image as the capital of the Florida Boom. They are, left to right, C. D. Leffler, James H. Gilman, Mayor E. C. Romfh, J. E. Lummus, and J. I. Wilson. In the economic depression that followed the Boom, all these bankers except Romfh saw their banks go bankrupt.

PROMOTED by the *Miami Herald* and its publisher, Frank B. Shutts, Hialeah Park opened early in 1925.

shoes, a flat straw hat, and carrying a cane swaggered into the office of Banker Romfh. Smoot, who liked red convertibles, blondes, and thoroughbred horses, had just sold a brokerage firm in Buffalo for $300,-000. A compulsive gambler, he was on his way to Havana to play the horses at Oriental Park, but had stopped off in Miami, he told Romfh, to "look for some investment opportunities." Romfh had a knack for sizing up a man. While Smoot's loud clothes may have made the conservative banker a little suspicious, Smoot had a flair that he liked. Reaching for a telephone, Romfh called Shutts.

"Frank, I've found the man we've been looking for to promote that horse track," said Romfh. "He's right here, in my office. Come down and meet him."

Shutts, whose law offices occupied two floors of the bank building, came down immediately. He was as much impressed by the quick-thinking, smooth-talking Smoot as Romfh had been.

"We need a horse track in Miami," said Shutts, "and you're the man to put it over."

Smoot was introduced to James Bright and to Glenn Curtiss, pilot and aircraft manufacturer who recently had become a partner of Bright. And by the time Smoot left for Havana, a decision to build a horse track at Hialeah had almost reached the stage of signing a contract. Nor did the talks cease while Smoot was in Havana. Shutts and Romfh brought Val Cleary, a businessman, into the picture, and by the time Smoot returned the group was ready to organize the Miami Jockey Club and begin work on a racetrack and grandstand. A couple of weeks later James E. Donn, Sr., owner of Exotic Gardens, a florist and landscaping firm, was asked to meet with the group. Donn recalled forty-five years later, when he was owner of Gulf Stream Race Track, that the meeting took place on a sandy prairie, the present site of Hialeah Park. Before the draining of the Everglades the area had been under water much of each year. Donn was offered the landscaping contract, provided he would accept preferred stock in the track as payment.

The opening of Hialeah Park on January 15, 1925, got more space in the *Miami Herald* than any other sporting event up to that time. And it is doubtful that any sporting event since has received so much space on the front page. Virtually every important person in the Miami area was present. The Florida East Coast Railway, which had built a spur line to the race track, put on a special train from West Palm Beach. The cream of Palm Beach society was on board. Hialeah's clubhouse and grandstand, built for 5,000, were overwhelmed by a crowd exceeding 17,000. People came from as far as Jacksonville, Orlando, and Tampa. All of the *Herald's* top writers were there. "They're off!" was the way Doris Stone, feature writer, began her page-one story. Miss Stone followed this shouting lead with two thousand words of vibrant description—about the excited crowd, the swift horses, the new racing plant, the prominent visitors. Sportswriter Walter St. Denis sought to outdo Miss Stone in extravagant description. Wrote St. Denis:

"Never in the history of the opening of any track, not even the famous Belmont Park or of Saratoga's picture track, was there such a glittering assemblage."

Although only 300 horses arrived, Hialeah, with the help of *Herald* promotion, enjoyed a profitable fifty-one days of racing in January, February, and March of 1925. So large were the daily crowds and so great was the play that the investment in Hialeah was paid off in the first seventeen days.

"At the end of the season," said Donn, "I not only was paid the $25,-000 the track owed me, but I was given ten shares of common stock as a bonus."

When John D. Pennekamp arrived in Miami in the summer of 1925 to write a series of stories for the *Cincinnati Post* about Ohio capitalists who were involved in the boom, the *Herald's* newsroom resembled a madhouse more than it did a newspaper office. Desks of reporters and editors occupied every usable foot of space on the second floor, with barely enough room in the aisles between the desks for a person to walk. The clackety-clack of typewriters, the buzz of conversation, and the ringing of telephones filled the air. After accustoming his eyes and ears to the scene, Pennekamp asked a copyreader where he could find Olin Kennedy.

"Who?" asked the young man, looking up wide-eyed.

"Mr. Kennedy, the managing editor," replied Pennekamp.

"Oh, him," replied the man. "You mean the Great Owk. In there," he added, pointing to an office in which sat a pale-pated man bent over a cluttered desk.

Pennekamp was to learn that new editors and reporters came almost daily, sometimes working only a week, seldom longer than a month. Most of them put on golf knickers, a popular style of the time, and became real estate salesmen. To get a license all you had to do was give your name, age, and address, and pay a small fee. Miami had issued over 5,000 real estate salesmen licenses during the first six months of 1925. The turnover in the editorial staff of the *Herald* was so great that it was almost impossible for the city editor, Stuart Gorrell, to keep up with the names of reporters or junior editors, so he referred to them as "Hey, You." Upon entering Kennedy's office, Pennekamp stood for a few moments before catching the attention of the intent managing editor, faced with the mind-dulling task of going through stacks of stories, letters,

DURING THE BOOM Miami acquired a skyline within a period of eighteen months, in 1925-26. This photograph, made by G. W. Romer in late 1925, shows the Columbus, Colonial, and Everglades hotels under construction on Biscayne Boulevard. Frame work behind the three-towered McAllister hotel is the Meyer-Kiser Building.

memos, and expense vouchers. Finally Kennedy looked up and studied Pennekamp momentarily through his pinch glasses.

"You looking for a job?" he asked. Most strangers who entered his office were, unless they were real estate promoters. But Pennekamp, a settled, confident man in his late twenties, lacked the effervescence of a promoter.

Introducing himself, Pennekamp explained his mission. He wanted information about the activities of such Cincinnati capitalists as Richard K. LeBlond, president of the Myers Y. Cooper Construction Company (who later became governor of Ohio); Charles Hirsch, president of the Fifth-Third National Bank of Cincinnati; and Charles Williams, founder and president of the Western Southern Life Insurance Company. LeBlond also headed the American Builders Corporation, which he and his Cincinnati associates had organized. The firm had entered into a $75 million contract with George E. Merrick, founder of Coral Gables, to build 1,000 homes, many of them in the $100,000 class. All of these capitalists had been the subject of stories in the *Herald*. They were also personal friends of Shutts, who was associated with LeBlond and Cooper in downtown investments. Kennedy was glad to open the newspaper's files to a fellow Ohioan.

Getting the background he needed, Pennekamp interviewed his subjects and wrote his stories. But before leaving Miami, he returned to the *Herald,* this time to do a story on Kennedy, the former Brown County, Ohio, boy who was now managing editor and assistant publisher of the "largest newspaper in the world."

After the interview, it was Kennedy's turn to ask a question: Would Pennekamp consider taking the job as *Herald* city editor?

It was a tough job, and the present city editor, Stuart Gorrell, had been ill and wanted less strenuous duties. Kennedy was looking for a top-notch executive-type editor who could take over full responsibility, including the organizing of his own staff. It was an intriguing offer. Pennekamp promised to return in September to begin work.

Attendance at Hialeah Park in the early part of 1925 gives but a partial picture of the affluent crowd the boom was drawing to Miami. Miami had entered 1924 very much an overgrown small town. When newcomers got off a train at the dinky depot, a block from the old courthouse, a two-story structure built in 1912, he would look around, rub his eyes and ask: "Where's Miami?" The Magic City was far from the image outsiders had of it. When a newcomer got off the train in 1925 he would know he was in Miami, for a new skyline was rising downtown. During those hectic months, passenger trains were rolling into Miami in four and five sections. The Florida East Coast Railway was being double-tracked, and civic leaders were urging S. Davies Warfield, president of the Seaboard Airline Railroad, to hurry the extension of his line from central Florida to Miami. All the county business was being done in the old courthouse, but in late 1925 a twenty-seven-story courthouse was started. Its steel framework was erected around the old building, and after completion of the sixth floor, the original courthouse was dismantled. But like the *Herald's* new production plant, the double-tracking of the F.E.C., and the extension of the Seaboard to Miami, the new courthouse would be completed after the boom was over.

In January 1925, Miami's gates were thrown wide open and whatever innocence the twenty-nine-year-old community had vanished forever. By March, according to a boom watcher, Florida had "run out of land" and real estate brokers were "selling lots over and over," often to one another, each time at a marked-up price. By April not only had the swamps of Florida been platted into subdivisions—all on paper—but the subdividing extended to the Okefenokee Swamp in southern Georgia. Developers might not have seen the property they had bought, although their offices were lined with maps of subdivisions, even cities, laid out in streets and lots. Promoters ran incredible ads in the *Herald* and in the *News.* The more ridiculous the claims the better they fitted the image of Florida. Royal Palm Estates, in the middle of what is now the Everglades

National Park, claimed in a full-page ad that it soon would be connected with ten railroad tracks from Jacksonville. The demand for property grew stronger every week, and anyone who held a thirty-day binder on a lot, for which he had made a ten percent deposit, had no trouble selling the binder for a profit. Binders were worth more than money; you could always sell them for more than you paid for them. And, so, by April the "Binder Boy" era was well under way. The era lasted only a few months, but it produced the wildest land speculation the United States had ever seen.

"A composite picture of the binder boy," wrote Kenneth Ballenger, a *Herald* reporter who covered the boom and later wrote a book about it entitled *Miami Millions,* "possibly would reveal an individual slightly under normal height, never very clean or neat, bending every effort to make a lot of money in a hurry without the slightest pretense of remaining in Florida once that was done. He was attired in golf knickers, because they didn't need pressing or the addition of a coat."

Hardly fitting Ballenger's composite was William D. Pawley, who arrived in January 1925, to have a look at the boom. Pawley, twenty-eight, was a slender man just under six feet tall. The boom had been tailored for a person of his boundless energy, drive, mental sharpness, and self-confidence. A few days after his arrival Pawley went into the real estate office of "Doc" E. E. Dammers, onetime auctioneer who had turned developer, and bought the first piece of real estate he had ever owned. It was a residential lot in the vicinity of Red and Bird roads, costing $1,-000. Pawley paid $250 down. He mentioned to a fellow hotel guest that he had purchased the lot, and the guest immediately offered him $500 for his contract, or binder. Returning to Dammers' office, Pawley bought two additional lots and quickly sold them. Within a month Pawley had peddled $100,000 worth of lots. Now he teamed up with another salesman and bought twenty acres on LeJeune Road between Flagler Street and Southwest Eight Street. Subdividing, they sold out in seventeen days, making $400,000 on a $200,000 investment. By this time the boom was entering its mad phase. Pawley, going it alone, bought another twenty acres, which he subdivided, and began his own construction company.

"It was fantastic," said Pawley, years later recalling that period after he had won fame as organizer of the Flying Tigers of World War II and had served as ambassador to Peru and to Brazil. "I was making $25,000 to $30,000 a day. Between January and September, 1925, I made $1.2 million."

On September 7, Pawley's twenty-ninth birthday, he rented the Coral

Gables Country Club and threw a party for 300 people, including 100 salesmen who worked for him, and announced his retirement.

"They begged me to stay until January first," said Pawley. "I weakened and stayed. In the meantime the boom busted and I dropped $800,000 in four months."

Pawley was more than a binder boy; he became one of the movers and sakers of the boom and remained to supplement his fortune after the bust.

The boom was nearing its peak in July when William Jennings Bryan left Miami for Dayton, Tennessee, to assist in the prosecution of a high school science teacher, John T. Scopes, who was charged with teaching Darwinism in violation of a state law. Bryan had taken leave from the highest paying job of his life, selling Coral Gables real estate for George E. Merrick. The thousands drawn to the Coral Gables Venetian Pools by Bryan's silver-tongued oratory found his sales talk irresistible. For his name and his tongue Bryan was paid $100,000 a year. The Coral Gables that Merrick had visualized was now under construction—its downtown, residential sections, and the Miami Biltmore Hotel and Country Club. Plans for starting the University of Miami, on 160 acres donated by Merrick, were being completed. Miami's affluent, most of them new millionaires, had pledged $10 million toward the construction of the university. Meanwhile, Miami's skyline grew daily, while at Miami Beach several hotels were under construction, including the Roney Plaza. Five miles north of Miami, Hugh M. Anderson and Roy C. Wright were investing millions in Miami Shores. In May they had set an all-time high during the boom for undeveloped property by paying $6.5 million, or $30,600 an acre, for the 212-acre estate at Buena Vista that Charles Deering had started in the early days of Miami but had abandoned for a site at Cutler, twelve miles south of Miami. By July, Anderson and Wright were talking about connecting Miami Shores and downtown Miami with a 100-foot wide boulevard. Twenty miles north of Miami, Joseph W. Young was building Hollywood and dredging Port Everglades, which he expected to compete with Miami's port. He also was finishing plans for the Hollywood Beach Hotel. Fort Lauderdale had several major subdivisions in progress, including dredging operations to create a Venicelike residential area on Las Olas Boulevard. But forty miles north of Miami the Mizner brothers' Boca Raton was getting the greatest ballyhoo of all.

With the backing of General T. Coleman duPont, one of the nation's wealthiest men, and Charles G. Dawes, Chicago banker and vice-president of the United States, the Mizners planned to spend $200 million to create a community for "rich" millionaires. The flamboyant Addison

Mizner, who had become famous for his extravagant design of Palm Beach estates, had laid out Boca Raton about a twenty-lane boulevard, Camino Real, and was building the 100-room Cloister Inn, costliest hotel in the world for its size. While Addison did the planning and the building, his brother Wilson, known for his wit and the role he had played in the Alaskan gold rush, ran the business side. Within six weeks after the Mizners opened their project on May 1, 1925, sales reached $9 million, and within four months sales hit $25 million. Wilson, more at home with the characters in the dives of San Francisco than with the rich he had to deal with at Boca Raton, grew bored with success. When his secretary shoved a $10,000 check before him for his signature he growled:

"Quit bringing me this chicken feed; bring me a million-dollar check to sign."

The Scopes trial, in progress in Tennessee, competed with developers for space in the *Herald*. To cover the trial, the *Herald* sent Dr. J. Delman Kuykendall, a Congregational minister whose column, "Sunday Sermon," appeared on the editorial page. Although asserting that the paper held no brief for Darwinism, the *Herald's* editor sympathized with Scopes. The paper's editorial outlook had changed immensely since the days immediately after World War I when the news pages and editorial page reflected a hysteria resulting from political, economic, and social upheavals. The editor was now siding with the modernists to the extent that he was backing women's right to bob their hair and to shorten their dresses. Moreover, the editor defended the independent young women whom moralists had given the name of "flappers." He thought the flapper was delightful. So it was no surprise when the modernist editor took a slap at the fundamentalists who were after the hide of the Tennessee science teacher. One sees the influence of sixty-seven-year-old Judge Stoneman, who was spending his mornings conducting city court, his afternoons writing editorials. The *Herald* called the Scopes trial "the inquisition revived" to persecute a person "for his beliefs." Although Bryan won a conviction, he lost the moral issue in the withering debate with Scopes' defense lawyer, Clarence Darrow. Bryan collapsed in his Dayton hotel room on July 26 and died.

The boom took off little time to mourn the passing of the Great Commoner. During that week James M. Cox and N. B. T. Roney paid $3 million for Seminole Beach, 115 acres of palmetto-covered sand along the ocean just north of the Dade County line. After quickly platting the property and planting a rumor that Seminole Beach was to become a rich seaside resort, it was "quietly" put on the market. In a wild crush a frantic mob bought every lot in six hours for $7,645,000. Within a week the buyers resold Seminole Beach for $12 million.

PHILOSOPHER, poet, and promoter most frequently identified with the Boom was George E. Merrick, developer of Coral Gables.

The high water mark of the boom may have been reached on September 3, when 400 acres of Miami Shores waterfront lots went on sale. Near-rioting customers threw cash and checks totaling $33,734,350 at salesmen, leaving it to the developers to select their lots. Five days were required to catch up with the paper work. But, alas, most of the buyers did no more than make a deposit. Thirty days later, when the time arrived to close out, the boom was on the skids and purchasers were having second thoughts about paying fabulous prices for property. The sellers were forced to lower prices, but still a majority of the once enthusiastic buyers sacrificed their deposits. By the end of September the binder boys were leaving Miami by freight train as well as by passenger train. Unlike Wall Street bears, they could not ride the boom downward.

But in the *Miami Herald's* editorial, advertising, production, and circulation departments there was no evidence in the fall of 1925 that the boom was on the skids. Advertising volume was as great as ever, and daily circulation, below 20,000 in 1924, had soared above 33,000—all the old presses could accommodate. In 1926, with new presses, circulation reached 43,000, while Sunday circulation hit 50,000. The *Herald,* because of its advertising volume, had become the daily index on which the real estate dealers based their activities. If you wanted to sell or buy real estate, you consulted the *Herald.* With the *Herald* maintaining its enormous advertising volume and Miami's skyline growing daily, how could the editors suspect that the wildest peacetime event in Florida's history was coming to an end? Shutts, however, had reason for concern. He was involved in downtown real estate developments and at the same time was a member of another group of speculators, including C. Bascom Slemp, former secretary to President Coolidge. The group had paid $1.5 million for fifty thousand acres in the Everglades, far out on the uncompleted Tamiami Trail. As head of the largest law firm in Florida, Shutts must have been aware that the boom was on the skids, but perhaps he considered the falling prices merely a market fluctuation.

Miami's mayor, Ed Romfh, could not believe the boom was over. Although he had been a cautious banker during the boom, refusing to lend money on inflated land values, Miami's prosperity appeared to him to be going strong. The immense construction program then under way

MILLING PEOPLE and sounds of the rivet hammer dominated Miami during the Boom years. Photographer Ralph Willits stood at the intersection of North Miami Avenue in late 1925 and aimed his camera east, in the direction of Northeast First Street. Under construction at left is Cromer-Cassel's, now Richards. At right is the Seybold Building, while in the distance is the frame of the Meyer-Kiser Building.

would keep Miami prosperous for a time. Romfh's major concern was a breakdown in rail transportation. More than $100 million worth of construction was in progress in the Miami area, with only one rail line and ships to bring supplies. The Drake Lumber Company alone had demands for seventy-five carloads of lumber a day. In San Francisco, entrepeneurs had taken old sailing schooners out of "Rotten Row," loaded them with lumber, and sent them on a one-way trip to Miami. By the fall of 1925, when Mayor Romfh was contemplating Miami's economic scene, Biscayne Bay looked like a dead forest, so many were the masts of these schooners. Because of the insufficient dock space, ships were headed into the shore, holes cut in the bows for unloading. But still the builders were crying for more lumber, cement, steel, hardware, and furnishings for newly completed homes, hotels, apartments, and office buildings. The Flagler System complained that more cars were being delivered to Miami than were being unloaded, with the result that cars were backing up on sidings all the way from Miami to Jacksonville. Faced with a hopeless situation, the Flagler System slapped an embargo on new freight and served notice that no more cars would be accepted for delivery at Jacksonville until the mess in Miami was cleaned up. Within a week freight cars filled yards north of Jacksonville as far as Savannah and Columbia, waiting delivery to the Florida East Coast Railway.

Miami was in the midst of its freight embargo problems when John Pennekamp reported for work as city editor at the *Miami Herald.* An efficient copyreader, Pennekamp edited a lengthy, overwritten story and trimmed it in half, then passed it to the copy desk for a headline. News Editor Ellis Hollums saw the story and returned it to Pennekamp.

"We don't trim stories on the *Herald,*"said Hollums. "We have a tough time getting enough copy to fill the paper."

Pennekamp settled down to the routine of getting out the monstrous daily and Sunday *Herald* with the help of mostly fly-by-night reporters and a small nucleus of dependable staff.

In past years the summers had been dull, with lethargy settling over the community, but in 1925 Miami residents had seen little difference between January and July from the standpoint of activity. Downtown was a perpetual traffic jam every day except Sunday. H. H. "Honk-Honk" Arnold, traffic control officer, installed traffic lights, then made some streets one-way. This helped. But it failed to keep pedestrians from overflowing the sidewalks into the streets, at times bringing automobile traffic virtually to a halt, despite the constant "ah-OO-ga" of 1925-vintage horns. To cope with the pedestrian problem, Arnold banned jaywalking. Unfortunately, his traffic policemen were new and untrained. What he had were mainly plowhands, recruited from Georgia by the police chief, H. Leslie Quigg. One day a new patrolman became so incensed with a knicker-clad pedestrian who disobeyed his order to remain on the sidewalk until the light changed that he drew his revolver and fired at the lawbreaker. He missed, but half a block down the street the zinging bullet wounded C. F. Mowery.

In January, 1926, Miamians could look back on the most fabulous year they had ever seen. Construction included 481 hotels and apartment houses, together with thousands of individual homes. Coral Gables had sold $94 million worth of property and Miami Shores $75 million. To provide housing for his employees, Shutts purchased two apartment houses and began construction on fifty residences in Hialeah. By now it was obvious that the peak of the boom had passed, but newspaper advertising had not yet been affected. The Flagler System had lifted the freight embargo and now vast quantities of building supplies were moving into Miami daily, by rail and by ship. Not only was Miami's harbor filled with ships, either unloading or waiting to be unloaded, but off Miami Beach other freighters and schooners waited their turn to enter Government Cut. Then, on the night of January 10, the steel hulk of the Prinz Valdemar, a ship brought to Miami to be converted into a hotel, capsized in the harbor channel. Six weeks were required to open the channel and return shipping to normal. By the middle of February those left of the "boomers" were sobering up and regaining their balance. Major sources of funds that had been supporting the boom were cut off. While most of the steel and concrete structures in Miami's new skyline would be finished, the wild activities of 1925 had vanished. Against this background, with many paper millionaires going broke, the average Miamian continued to enjoy a prosperity he would remember in the lean days ahead.

The *Herald's* editor took the viewpoint that "the readjustment" was good for the economy. The "wild, speculative era" was over and now Miami could enjoy normal growth and prosperity. The editor foresaw that in a few years Miami would be a metropolis of a million. But as 1926 progressed advertising fell off, then slumped badly in summer. By August the paper was down to twenty-four pages. It was like a normal summer in the years before the boom. Neither Shutts nor his advertising manager, "Pop" Bates, worried. They looked for a return of volume advertising in the fall, as always had happened in the past.

On Thursday, September 16, the *Herald* reported a tropical storm north of the Virgin Islands. A statement by Richard W. Gray, Miami Weather Bureau forecaster, was interpreted to indicate that the storm posed no threat to Florida. A routine story was run under a one-column headline, "Storm to Miss/Florida Coast." On the morning of September 17 the *Herald* reported the hurricane, off Turk's Island, was of "great intensity," but readers were assured that the storm posed no threat to Florida. At the time readers were scanning this story over morning coffee, the hurricane was approaching George Town, Great Exuma Island, 300 miles southeast of Miami. Of monstrous size and destructive power, the storm continued its course toward southern Florida, a course it had not changed for a thousand miles. But Miamians went about their plans that Friday morning with little or no concern that the destructive killer, swirling through the Bahamas, might disregard the *Miami Herald's* assurance and hit Florida.

BOOM FEVER had subsided by the end of 1925 but money for construction of Miami's rising skyline was still pouring in. Then, on the night of January 10, 1926, the *Prinz Valdemar* capsized and sank in the channel, blocking Miami's port. By the time the channel was cleared six weeks later the capitalists were withdrawing their support and many buildings under construction would not be completed for several years. (Richard B. Hoit)

7

September 17-18, 1926

IF FRIDAY, SEPTEMBER 17, 1926, was different from any other day to Henry Reno, night police reporter for the *Miami Herald,* it was just duller. Nothing had happened since his arrival at the Miami Police Station at five in the afternoon. Now it was eleven and time to go to the *Herald* and man the city desk telephone until two. A squall was blowing out of the northeast as Reno left police headquarters. He slipped into his raincoat and as he headed east on Flagler Street he bent his head to keep the flying rain out of his eyes. By the time he had walked the block to Miami Avenue the squall was over and the wind had settled down to a light breeze. Reno was vaguely aware that a hurricane was blowing in the Atlantic. He had read in the *Herald's* early edition that the storm was crossing the Bahamas, traveling in the direction of Florida, but was expected to turn northward and avoid the mainland. Another hurricane had followed that pattern a month before. Richard W. Gray, the Miami weather forecaster, had been quoted repeatedly in the *Herald* during the last three days that the present hurricane, which had originated far out in the Atlantic doldrums earlier in the month, also should avoid Florida. The *Herald* had reassured Miamians they were in no danger. Reno, who could not recall of Miami ever having been hit by a hurricane, assumed that Miami was immune to these big storms.

Statistically Reno was almost right. Miami had been hit by only one hurricane in its thirty years of existence, and that was in 1906. The city then had a population of about 3,000, and only one person now working on the *Herald* had witnessed that storm. He was Judge Stoneman. Few of Miami's 1926 residents had ever seen a hurricane or knew anything about the mechanics of one—a doughnut-shaped monster whirling counter-clockwise around a calm center. Winds circling the center of a full-fledged hurricane could reach 100 to 150 miles an hour, or more, accompanied by blistering rain. This great doughnut of wind and rain moved forward at five to twenty miles an hour, preceded by squalls and falling barometer. The barometer hit its lowest level as the center passed over an area and began to rise toward normal as the storm moved on. No less ignorant of tropical storms than the public was the *Herald's* publisher, Frank B. Shutts, the managing editor, Olin W. Kennedy, and the city editor, John D. Pennekamp. None had hit Miami during the sixteen years Shutts had lived here, and he reasoned that it was unlikely any of the several reported in the Atlantic, Caribbean, or Gulf of Mexico each year would hit. Shutts wanted Miami to have a good image, and he insisted that the *Herald* be devoted to this aim. Kennedy had virtually banned stories and headlines of a sensational nature that tended to put Miami in a bad light or to cause "undue alarm."

Reno arrived in the newsroom to find no more activity than he had left at the police station. Pennekamp had departed at eleven. Only two persons were in the news room, Nate Noble, the news editor, and a copyreader.

"I'm glad you got here," said Noble. "The telephone's been ringing—people asking about the storm."

Seating himself in the city editor's chair, Reno picked up the latest edition, scanned the storm story, and found nothing new. Gray was still hopeful the storm would veer away from the coast. The telephone rang. A boat owner wanted the latest forecast. His boat was tied up at the Royal Palm Hotel docks at the mouth of the Miami River. Should he bother to take it up the river at this late hour?

"According to the weather bureau the storm's going to veer to the north," replied Reno.

This reassured the unidentified boat owner, who thanked him and hung up. A few moments later the telephone rang again. It was Mr. Gray of the weather bureau. He had an announcement. Reno reached for copy paper, took a pencil from his shirt pocket. The Washington Weather Bureau had just ordered hurricane warnings hoisted, at eleven o'clock, Gray said.

"Does that mean we're going to get the hurricane?" asked Reno. At this Noble's head popped up straight.

"No, Henry," replied Gray, "but the new advisory warns everyone in South Florida to take precautions against dangerous winds. The storm's still traveling in a northwest direction, which would bring it directly over Miami if it continues its present course. Storms traveling in the pattern of this one have a tendency to veer northward as they approach the coast. But if this one doesn't recurve to the north, the center could pass over Miami."

As soon as Reno hung up Noble was on his feet.

"What did he say?" asked Noble.

Reno began reading his notes.

"Don't give me all the horrible details; are we going to get the hurricane?"

"The storm's still heading toward Miami and the barometer's dropping," replied Reno. "Hurricane warnings have been ordered."

"What's the wind velocity?"

"Twenty-five miles an hour is the highest so far."

"Humph, that's not much wind," muttered Noble as he walked to a window from which he could look down into Miami Avenue. A light rain was falling, but the gentle swinging of a sign, illuminated by the dim street lights, was the only indication that the rain was accompanied by wind. Returning to his chair, Noble reached for the latest edition. Studying the storm story, in the first column of page one, he realized a new lead was needed for the city edition. But how would he handle it? Would the storm hit or not? Midnight, deadline for making changes in the final edition, was approaching. He would have to make a decision soon. And, for the next several moments, Noble sought to resolve a problem faced by countless editors before and since—how to handle an important, developing story of possible disaster in a way that would satisfy a management which ruled out "sensational" stories and headlines that might cause "undue alarm" to readers. It might seem to an editor that a storm of such dimensions, heading toward Miami for a week, presented a dangerous threat. But suppose the *Herald* should come out with a "scare story" and the storm then veered to the north and missed the area altogether? A *Herald* editor of later vintage would have had no trouble making a decision. He would have "sensationalized" the story to match the sensational episode that appeared to be developing. He would have put a streamer across the top of page one, "Hurricane Alert," in the boldest type that would fit. But in 1926 an editor's indoctrination forbade this kind of thinking. If the hurricane missed, the *Herald* would be made to look like a fool and the editor probably would be fired. His only choice was a middle-of-the-road position.

Rising, Noble walked over to the city desk, picked up the notes Reno had typed, and studied them as he returned to his desk. He ran a sheet of copy paper into his typewriter and stared for a moment at the blank paper before he began to type:

"Miami stood on the fringe of a rushing gale at an early hour this morning as the edge of a hurricane centered close to Nassau swept through the city and up the east coast of Florida as far as Jupiter."

Ambiguous, the epitome of saying nothing, the lead was nevertheless readable. Noble then wrote a one-column, three-line head: "Storm's Edge/Brings Strong/Winds to Miami." Rising, Noble headed toward the composing room with the new storm story lead and new headline, together with the advisory that Reno had finished typing. He could have sent the copy by the young reporter. In fact, most news editors would have assigned Reno to write the lead, then turned the story over to the copyreader for a headline. But Noble, quick-witted and aggressive, must have felt that he knew better than they what he wanted to say. He liked Miami, a vigorous, interesting, and fast-growing city. If he expected to rise on the *Herald* he would have to satisfy the publisher, a lean, gray-haired man he had seen but had never spoken to. His feeling of responsibility weighed heavily.

Two o'clock came, time for the newsroom staff to go home, but a gale was blowing outside, driving a drenching rain and buffeting the building with blasts that clattered the windows. And all the while the velocity of the wind was increasing. At two-thirty Noble said to Reno:

"Henry, call the weather bureau and see if the storm's here."

"The telephone's dead," said Reno, holding the receiver to his ear.

By three the wind had increased to an awesome roar, slamming against the old building so hard it creaked and trembled. Rain was beginning to stream down the walls from the windows and form puddles on the dark wooden floor. Noble strode into the production building, where he could hear the hum of the presses above the roar of the storm. The city edition was being run. There was still time to get a bulletin on page one. He strode back to the newsroom.

"Henry," said Noble in a commanding voice, "run over to the weather bureau and find out what in the hell's going on. Get a statement from Gray. And hurry back, so we can get something in the paper."

"Yes, sir," replied Reno, jumping to his feet and slipping on his raincoat. With flashlight in hand, he bounded down the stairs. Pressing his shoulders against the door and bracing his long legs on the floor, he managed to crack it enough to squeeze himself outside into Miami Avenue. The wind slammed past his ears in a thunderous roar, tugging fiercely at his lanky form as he held onto the door handle. Bracing himself against the onslaught, he crossed the avenue and followed the lee side of buildings until he reached Flagler Street. He could go no farther. Signs were crashing in the streets and being carried away to smash against buildings with fearsome bangs and crunches. Awnings over the sidewalk were giving away, their tattered ends popping in the wind like the crack of a hundred whips. Streetlights were blinking on and off and electric wires overhead were arcing in eerie blue flashes. Groping along the north side of Flagler Street, Reno found a protected alcove in the

A HURRICANE was needed to convince everyone that the Boom was over. The September 17-18, 1926, storm was one of the severest Florida had experienced, leaving 372 dead, thousands injured, and property damage in the millions of dollars. The wreckage above is that of a Hollywood school. At left, Miami's seventeen-story Meyer-Kiser Building, badly twisted, had to be reduced to six stories. Below, ships and barges were tossed into Bayfront Park and Biscayne Boulevard by the storm tide.

Seybold Arcade, to which he retreated, his drenched body shivering from cold. Here Reno crouched in total darkness, for a time broken by the flashing of arcing power liens in Flagler Street. As the wind grew fiercer even the arcing stopped; the power had been shut off.

For the first time in his life Reno felt genuine fear, which grew with the wild roar of the ever-mounting wind, the crashing of glass, and the banging of flying objects. His body became numb and his ears hurt. He was both trembling from cold and sweating. An hour passed. Two hours passed. He was beginning to think the storm would never end until, increasing in its fury, it destroyed everything, including the buildings over the arcade where he had found refuge. Like tens of thousands of other Miamians, Reno's worst fears sprang from his ignorance of hurricanes. He had no idea about the shape, size, or intensity of a tropical storm. Hurricanes had not been discussed at home or in his high school science class. Hurricane had been only a word, a synonym for a big storm; but the big storms always blew somewhere else, and neither he nor anybody he knew had taken hurricanes seriously.

After what seemed an eternity, a lead-gray light began to filter through the storm and creep into the arcade. Reno slipped from his alcove and sought to look outside into Flagler Street, but all he could see was the white monster. The flight of a large object through the arcade sent him in rapid retreat to his alcove. But shortly thereafter the wind suddenly eased, then, releasing a great sigh, stopped. Stunned by the unexpected silence, which left his ears ringing, Reno remained frozen for several moments. Then, cautiously, he slipped out and waded through the ankle deep water in the debris-strewn arcade to Flagler Street. For a moment he had the fearsome feeling that he might be the only person alive in Miami. The destruction was beyond belief. As far as he could see, east and west, the street was piled with rubble, broken glass, and litter from buildings. Human forms among the debris added to his fright, until he realized that they were manikins blown out of display windows. Stores on the unprotected south side of Flagler Street appeared to be only shells. He looked at his watch. It was 6:15.

Picking his way through the rubble, Reno waded toward the Federal Building, conscientiously aware of the mission Nate Noble had sent him on more than three hours earlier. He began to see other people—people who had left their hotels and apartments to survey the destruction. They seemed ghostly, with taut, pale faces, fixed eyes, zombielike. Reno was approaching the Federal Building entrance when the door opened and out came Richard Gray in shirt-sleeves. An intent expression was fixed on his face as he dashed past the reporter.

"The storm's not over! The storm's not over!" shouted Gray at the people in the streets. "We're in the lull! Get back to safety! Protect yourselves! The worst part is yet to come!"

The people, most of whom had never seen the slightly built, gray-haired forecaster, gawked at him in wonder. Reno watched in equal awe. He, too, thought the storm was over. He had never heard of a "lull." Suddenly, he turned on his heels and hastened toward the *Herald*. As he picked his way through the wreckage he wondered at Mr. Gray's statement. Glancing at the sky, now covered by thin clouds with patches of blue showing through, he saw sea birds flying lazily about, several being of a kind he had never seen before. As he turned his head his eyes caught the new seventeen-story Meyer-Kiser Bank Building. The structure had been twisted and great patches of the outer walls had torn loose, leaving floors exposed.

Reno was surprised to see the old office building of the *Herald* still intact, rising from the wreckage strewn about it. As he approached the building the sky began to darken, and beyond the Miami Avenue bridge, two blocks south of the *Herald*, he saw what appeared to be a gray cloud moving rapidly toward him. As it grew closer he could see that it was a mass of debris being driven before wind and rain. Reno made the front door and got inside just before the monster passed, roaring and rattling like a freight train. The lull had passed, and now Miami was being lashed by the "other side" of the hurricane. Almost immediately the wind was hurricane force, seventy-five miles an hour, and within five minutes it was blowing more than 125 miles an hour. How much greater velocity was attained no one would know for sure, for the highest reading was 128 miles an hour before the last wind gauge was blown away. Gray estimated the velocity at 140 to 150 miles an hour. But Russell Pancoast, an architect who went through the hurricane, several years later estimated the wind reached 200 miles an hour. He made his estimate from the destruction, compared with that left by many other hurricanes he studied during his long career. Thousands of people, including many of those downtown who gawked at the excited Richard Gray, were caught outside. Some perished on the causeways between Miami and Miami Beach.

As soon as the wind changed direction it began to push the water in shallow Biscayne Bay northward, but the flow was temporarily blocked by two causeways. The result was a piling-up of water that overflowed the shore on both sides of the bay, and eventually rose above the causeways to sweep northward. Meantime the water rose over the south end of Miami Beach until bay and ocean met, while on the mainland side the water, driven higher and higher by the fierce wind, formed a bore that shot up Miami River eleven feet above mean tide, wrecking hundreds of boats that boat owners had taken upstream for protection. Boats tied to

The Miami Herald

FLORIDA'S MOST IMPORTANT NEWSPAPER

VOL. 16: NO. 298.   HERALD TELEPHONE 5-131   MIAMI, FLORIDA, MONDAY MORNING, SEPTEMBER 20, 1926.   HERALD TELEPHONE 3109   PRICE FIVE CENTS.

75 ARE DEAD IN MIAMI STORM, 60 LIVES ARE TAKEN IN HOLLYWOOD

TWO RELIEF TRAINS ARE SENT TO MIAMI AREA

PROPERTY LOSS IS $13,000,000 IN MIAMI DISTRICT

10,000 Homes Are Unroofed or Otherwise Damaged as Hurricane Strikes

THE DEAD.

THE INJURED.

PROCLAMATION

MEDICAL AID IS RUSHED TO THE STRICKEN CITY

Corps of Doctors and Nurses Are Sent from Lake Worth and West Palm Beach

26 OF HOLLYWOOD DEAD HAVE BEEN IDENTIFIED

THANK YOU, MR. CONKLING.

FRONT PAGE of the *Miami Herald* on September 20, 1926, second day after the hurricane. Most of the type was set by the *Palm Beach Post*.

flimsy docks were lifted, docks and all, and deposited on the shore. Boats tied to strong docks were sunk at their moorings. By now the bay was sweeping over the causeways. Persons who had sought to drive across Biscayne Bay during the lull were caught, to be carried away in their cars by the hurricane-driven tide. Now sweeping through the Miami port, the water lifted barges, yachts, and schooners as though they were skiffs, carrying them into Bayfront Park and beyond to Biscayne Boulevard. Among them was the *Rose Mahoney,* a four-masted schooner that was deposited on the boulevard near the News Tower.

Henry Reno, meanwhile, had taken refuge in the *Herald's* new four-story production plant. He had abandoned the newsroom, which was drenched by rain that came in through the shattered windows. The old building trembled, groaned, and creaked. He feared it would go. In the new production building he felt safe, but beyond the poured concrete walls thousands of terrified people sought to save themselves, many of whom had abandoned their flimsily constructed houses to seek sturdier shelter. For nearly a quarter of a million people in southeast Florida it was a terrifying experience. Scores lost their lives, thousands were injured, and countless others were reduced to numbed horror by a fury they did not understand.

It was early Saturday afternoon, after the wind had died to squally gales, before people could safely leave whatever shelter they had found and view the destruction about them. Streets were covered with a massive tangle of telephone and power lines, together with the wreckage of houses, overturned cars, and treetops. Trees that remained standing had been stripped of their leaves and most of their branches. Coconut palms stood like poles, stripped bare of their fronds. It would be two days, however, before people could read newspaper accounts of the widespread destruction. Neither the *Herald* nor the *News* had electric power and therefore could not publish.

In the meantime, linemen from the Florida Power & Light Company, whose main power plant was located on the Miami River, began stringing a temporary line to deliver power to the *Herald.* The decision had been made at a conference between power company officials and Miami political leaders. This was the quickest way to inform the public of the extent of destruction and of efforts being made by the rest of the nation to send help. While the power line was being installed on Sunday, *Herald* employees were getting out a newspaper for Monday morning—an eight-page edition without advertising except for three columns of legal notices left over from Sunday. Across the top of page one was a two-line, eight-column streamer: "75 Are Dead in Miami Storm, 60/Lives Taken in Hollywood." The story nourished hope among survivors by reporting that two trains were on their way from the North with doctors, nurses, Red Cross officials, and supplies of food and clothing. Martial law had been declared, and National Guardsmen and Marines patrolled to halt looting. The Florida death toll was set at 300 by the Associated Press, which estimated the homeless at 28,000. The *Herald* put a ridiculously low figure of $13 million on damage. Pennekamp had passed the AP's estimate of $100 million in damages without question, figuring that it was conservative. But before the story got past the copy desk, Kennedy saw it. He took it back to the city desk.

"Look, we can't run a figure like this," said the Great Owk. "People will get the idea that nothing is left of Miami. Cut the losses to $10 million."

Pennekamp, who could look across the Miami skyline and see $10 million in damages, replied, "Yes, sir." Kennedy was the boss. Compromising with his conscience, Pennekamp set the estimated damage at $13 million, reducing the original figure by $87 million.

As the week passed it became obvious that Florida had suffered the most severe damage ever done by a hurricane on the United States mainland. Although the loss of life, 372, was small compared with the loss of 5,000 in the Galveston hurricane of 1900, more than 800 were hospitalized in Miami alone, while thousands suffered lesser injuries. More than 4,700 homes were destroyed and another 9,100 damaged in Dade and Broward counties. President Coolidge called upon the American people to open their pocketbooks to help Miami. The early response was great. The American Red Cross released virtually all of its national facilities to take care of the destitute. National Red Cross headquarters announced a $5 million goal for Miami. Chicago alone set a $1 million goal. Several northern newspapers sent $5,000 to $10,000, while many wealthy individuals sent $15,000 to $25,000.

In midweek Mayor Romfh released a statement to newspapers and to the Associated Press in which he played down the severe damage. Although thousands of small homes and small businesses had suffered, and the plight of the destitute "could not be exaggerated," he said, Miami's "famous tourist facilities" had come through "with little damage." He stressed that these facilities would be ready to open for the winter season of 1926-27 as usual. Northern newspapers pounced on the statement, accusing the mayor of being more concerned with tourism than with the distress of the poor devils who had lost everything but their lives. Romfh's reluctance to admit that paradise could suffer disaster had the effect of making it difficult for the Red Cross to raise the funds it needed to carry out the massive relief that was required to get southeast Florida back to normal. Red Cross Director John Barton Payne struck out at those who "sought to suppress the extent of destruction." Payne, having inspected the Miami area, was aware of the extent of the disaster. The *News* sided with the critics. The *Herald* stayed out of the controversy while tending to emphasize the sunny side of the picture. Editorially, it took an opportunity to swing at the *News* for "sensational journalism."

On October 20 the *Herald* carried on page one a short item about a hurricane in the Caribbean south of western Cuba. "Hurricane Not Likely," said the headline reassuringly. Forecaster Gray was quoted as saying it was "physically impossible" for the "hurricane in the Caribbean to reach Miami." He added that "all the indications now are that the hurricane will spend its force in the Gulf of Mexico."

That evening Miamians must have wondered whether Gray was out of his mind. For the storm barely missed Miami, passing a short distance to the east and lashing the city. Next morning the *Herald* reported the passage of the hurricane under a three-line, one-column head on page one: "Storm Center/Turns to East,/Avoiding Miami." Contrary to Gray's forecast, the hurricane had crossed Cuba, leaving 650 dead and great destruction, to move northeast through the Florida Straits. According to the weather bureau, Miami got seventy-mile-an-hour winds. According to the *Herald* damage was small. Both the wind velocity and the *Herald's* report of little damage were to remain challenged by those who went through that frightening storm. Veterans of the September 18 hurricane insisted that the wind of the October 20 storm reached 100 miles an hour and that damage was extensive, particularly at Miami Beach.

Buried in the low-key *Herald* story was a paragraph about "nearly 20,-000 storm-wise people" seeking shelter in buildings stronger than their homes. A large crowd pressed against the ticket windows of the Florida East Coast Railway depot, seeking to buy tickets on northbound trains. Every seat on the trains was sold. Miami was a madhouse that day, according to eyewitnesses, with citizens boarding up their homes and storefronts, and thousands of frightened people seeking refuge in strong buildings. But you get no such impression from the *Herald's* coverage.

The *Herald* management was yet to learn that readers did not mind being "unduly alarmed" about hurricanes and other possible disasters when the newspaper did an honest job of reporting. In later years when the *Herald* sought to give complete coverage of hurricane movements, along with precautions to be taken against possible dangerous winds and rising seas, no readers called to blame the editor for "crying wolf" if the storm went elsewhere. All readers wanted was the truth, which they thought a newspaper should provide as a public service.

8

Miami's Booze Heroes

AFTER MIAMI SUFFERED two disasters, the collapse of the boom and a major hurricane, a third disaster, financial collapse, was to come. Fortunes built on paper foundations during the boom would vanish. Banks would fail. And on top of this would come a national depression following the stock market crash of 1929. Miami would lose nearly half of its boom-time population, dropping to 110,000. Things might have been a lot worse had it not been for illicit liquor. Thanks to liquor-running, the speed of locally built boats, and the unpopularity of the prohibition act, Miami became one of the nation's important entry ports for whiskey in the 1920s. The era was not without its tragedies, but there were some laughs, too; and in the meantime a good many Floridians became wealthy from running liquor between the Bahamas and the mainland. Moreover, this highly illegal industry—and it was big enough to be classed as an industry—made it possible for a lot of people to eat who might otherwise have gone hungry.

For a brief period after the 1926 hurricane Miami enjoyed a reconstruction boom. Several million dollars in Red Cross and other relief funds were distributed to the owners of homes and businesses to repair storm damage, or, in many instances, to rebuild entirely. Hotels and office buildings required extensive repairs, too. The upper floors of the Meyer-Kiser Building had suffered such major structural damage that the building had to be cut back to six floors. Lobbies of hotels along the oceanfront at Miami Beach were filled with sand almost to the ceiling. Work was still in progress on the building of Biscayne Boulevard, started in 1925 by the developers of Miami Shores, while workmen were laying track and building a new train station and yards for the Seaboard Air Line, which was being extended to Miami. The boom was over, but those who decided to stay in Miami could, for a while, find jobs.

Miamians would long remember the energy with which people worked to clean up, rebuild, repaint, and redecorate. Spirits were boosted, too, by a unique display of nature. Trees, stripped of their leaves and most of their branches by the high wind, soon were covered by bright new growth, giving Miami the appearance of spring. Most residents, who had never witnessed nature's response to a hurricane, looked upon the spectacular change as a phenomenon akin to a miracle, while the more religious viewed the display as the work of God. Morale could not have been higher. The Magic City was coming back faster than anybody could have believed. By the middle of November the major scars left by the storm had been healed, and people arriving in Miami for the first time since the hurricane wondered where all the damage was they had read so much about.

This expectation of visitors to find great damage two months after the storm worried Miami's leaders. It appeared obvious that the rest of the nation thought Miami had been virtually destroyed. This could be fatal to Florida's tourist season. With the boom over, the area depended heavily on tourism for survival, and if the upcoming season proved to be a flop Miami and its neighboring communities would face bankruptcy. A committee headed by *Herald* publisher Shutts, and including Mayor Romfh and Judge Stoneman, took a train for Philadelphia to see an old friend, Cyrus H. K. Curtis, publisher of the *Saturday Evening Post.* Curtis was a vain little man with a white beard that he kept trimmed in a style befitting the dignity of a commodore. He spent his winters in Miami aboard his 110-foot yacht and was well acquainted with the members of the delegation. All but Stoneman were members of the Cocolobo Cay Club, an exclusive club for millionaires at Caesar's Creek in south Biscayne Bay. Like many of Shutts' friends in the publishing business, Curtis often gave advice on the contents, the editing, and the format of the *Herald.* One morning in 1925, at the height of the boom, Curtis appeared at the *Herald* building, mounting the creaky stairs two at a time, until he reached the newsroom.

"Where's Colonel Shutts?" he demanded imperiously, brandishing a copy of the *Miami Herald.*

The editor, recognizing Curtis, explained that Shutts spent his mornings at his law office and afternoons at the *Herald.*

"Well, there's an error in this morning's paper," said Commodore Curtis, pointing to a story he had circled in bold pencil. "Look, this story gives the length of my yacht as 105 feet. The length is 110 feet. This is important, a matter of prestige. I want this error corrected."

A correction that the *Herald* ran may have been worth millions of dollars to South Florida. For when the Miami delegation appeared in

Curtis' office the chairman of the Curtis Publishing Company couldn't have been more cordial. He sent a top writer, Kenneth Roberts, to Miami to do a special story for the *Saturday Evening Post,* then the most widely circulated magazine in America. The result was that Miami had a lively tourist season in January, February, and March of 1927. But behind the lively scene, including the spirited attendance at Hialeah Park, economic disaster was facing many Miamians who had been looked upon as bulwarks of their community. Of the five banker commissioners who had run the affairs of Miami during the boom, all but one, Mayor Romfh, would see their banks fail. George E. Merrick, developer of Coral Gables, and Carl Fisher, angel of Miami Beach developers, would go broke. So would the once rich and powerful Florida East Coast Railway. At Boca Raton the Mizner brothers, Addison and Wilson, already were broke.

"We had fun while it lasted," said Wilson as the Mizners signed over their multimillion dollar development, including the fabulous Cloister Inn, to creditors.

The *Miami Herald* might have gone into receivership, too, had it not been for the friends of Shutts, particularly Richard K. LeBlond. Together they lent Shutts a million dollars to pay off impatient creditors. But few could boast of such friends. Like the Mizners, the developers of Miami Shores lost everything, turning over what assets they had left to creditors. In 1925 the wealthy Phipps family of Palm Beach had lent the company $9 million to build Biscayne Boulevard from Miami Shores to downtown Miami. The cost of the 100-foot wide roadway, extending for forty blocks, including twenty-three blocks of residences, was much greater than had been estimated, and the company ran out of money. But for the Phipps family, the project would have remained incomplete, a boulevard that went nowhere.

The Phipps family consisted of three sons and two daughters of Henry Phipps, onetime partner of Andrew Carnegie. Not only were they immensely wealthy as individuals, they owned interests in Bessemer Securities Corporation, one of the richest family investment enterprises in America. How much money the Phipps family plowed into Biscayne Boulevard the offspring of that generation could never determine accurately. The *Herald* later referred to Biscayne Boulevard as a $100 million development. Perhaps the value of the family holdings along the boulevard, together with the cost of building the six-lane route, might have added up to this much at a later date, but Michael Phipps, a family spokesman, estimated the original investment at closer to $16 million. The Phippses also advanced the City of Miami funds to extend the boulevard southward from Northeast Thirteenth Street to Southeast

First Street, a distance of fourteen blocks. But the Phippses managed to stay so well in the background, with their names submerged in Bessemer Properties, a firm set up especially for the Miami operations, that a *Herald* story about the ceremonies opening Biscayne Boulevard in 1927 failed to mention the Phipps family.

Although the *Herald's* business held up well during the fall and winter of 1926-27, display and classified advertising were but a dim shadow of the boom era linage. The daily paper averaged twenty-four to thirty-two pages, while the Sunday paper reached seventy-two pages. In severe contrast to the boom, hardly any real estate advertising appeared. Among the employees in the classified advertising department was Joseph Cotten, a Virginia youth who spent his evenings at the Mayfair Art Theater, where he was getting experience as an actor with the Miami Civic Theater Group. Cotten was a handsome and personable youth who enjoyed doing favors for his friends. When George Mangus, *Herald* artist, submitted a classified ad, Cotten wrote "no charge" across the top. The business office was loosely run. It would have taken more than a Joseph Cotten personality to survive such a breach of the rules after the Knight brothers acquired the *Herald* in 1937. But by that time Cotten was long gone, his acting talents having led to a brilliant career in Hollywood.

Another young man who would become famous in the entertainment field also worked at the *Herald,* in the studio of Radio Station WIOD, then located on the fourth floor of the new production building. He was Rudy Vallee, who, with his saxophone, had his own program. Eddie Cantor came to Miami to appear at the Olympia Theater. Vallee gave him a plug, and, in exchange, Cantor strode over to the *Herald* to appear as a guest on Vallee's program. Something went wrong. As they came down from the studio they were arguing, about what nobody knew except themselves. But as they walked through the newsroom they were virtually fighting, and as they started down the stairs toward the street they began to exchange blows. Disappointingly, the fight broke up as the editors and reporters gathered to watch. Everyone agreed it would make a terrific story—a fist fight between Eddie Cantor and Rudy Vallee—but it never made the paper.

Shutts, strapped for money, saw his competitor, James M. Cox, buy WIOD and remove it to the News Tower. Upon moving out, WIOD took only the microphones and other electronic equipment, leaving the expensively decorated studio intact—thick carpet, heavy drapery, even a grand piano with a vase of pussy willows standing on the tasseled scarf that covered it. Jefferson Bell, eccentric reporter and cooking editor for the *Herald,* took over the studio and set up a kitchen to test recipes. There she allowed a cat to raise a litter of kittens, which she did not clean up after, and when you opened the studio door you retreated quickly, for you could not take the aroma of food cooking together with the odor of a cat outhouse.

Snowbirds the Great Owk had hired for the winter of 1926-27 were paid off in late spring, for advertising had declined sharply and the size of the paper had shrunk. Business did not pick up very much in the winter of 1927-28. Despite the Coolidge prosperity in the rest of the nation, Miami's economy suffered. And for the first time in the eighteen-year history of the *Miami Herald* its circulation dropped below that of the previous year. Tourists came that winter but because the racetracks were closed by order of the governor, the sporting crowd went to Havana. A group of Jacksonville ministers had gotten a dog track operator convicted of "conducting a resort for the purpose of gambling." This forced the governor to act, and Miami's tracks and jai-alai fronton were kept closed during the winter of 1927-28. Shutts and his friends realized that without racing Miami stood little chance of regaining its prestige as a smart winter resort. Before Shutts left for his summer home in Massachusetts in June 1928, he sat down with officers of the Miami Jockey Club, including President Joe Smoot, to thrash out a plan to reopen Hialeah in January 1929, without open wagering. The track would sell shares in horses. You would buy shares in your favorite horse and if it won, the management would declare a dividend, the amount depending on the odds that came out of the parimutuel pool.

About the only thing that kept the tourist season of 1927-28 from being a complete flop was the supply of good whiskey. Clubs, protected by law enforcement officials with the consent of the establishment, served liquor as freely as though it had been legal. The only law enforcement people the clubs had to fear were the federal agents, but most of them were too busy chasing the big boys who were transporting liquor from the Bahamas, by plane as well as by fast boat, to bother the clubs.

Although the National Prohibition Act had been responsible for the creation of a highly profitable industry, because of hijackers, or "liquor pirates," liquor-running could be dangerous. And once a runner got past the hijackers, he still had to elude the Coast Guard, customs officers, and federal prohibition agents. But the returns were so great that countless adventurers were willing to take a chance. South Florida's heroes during the latter half of the 1920s were liquor-runners—people like Duncan "Red" Shannon, Johnny Campbell, and Troop Horn. Liquor running was looked upon as a daring kind of adventure. Runners like Campbell became veritable phantoms who outdistanced Coast Guard cutters and shot it out with hijackers. People said Campbell made a million dollars from booze running. At the height of liquor running an estimated ten million gallons of alcohol was being transported each year from West End, Grand Bahama, and Bimini to the mainland. Boat building for booze runners became a specialized industry in Miami. Forrest Johnson, who had a boatyard on the Miami River, designed a thirty-foot boat in which he installed a Liberty airplane engine that was capable of doing fifty miles an hour, a high speed for boats in that era.

Respect for the law reached an all-time low. It was difficult to get a liquor runner convicted, unless he was caught with the goods. This seldom happened because the liquor was packed so that it could be easily tossed overboard, where it sank immediately. Scotch was packed in four-quart bundles, the bottles separated by straw and sewn in burlap bagging. A runner could lighten his load by tossing several gallons of liquor overboard, and, if his capture became imminent, he tossed the entire cargo overboard. The Coast Guard, however, was not averse to firing on a fleeing runner, as it did on Red Shannon, fatally wounding him before the eyes of several thousand people who had lined the Miami Beach side of Biscayne Bay to watch a regatta. Many recognized the *Goose,* Shannon's fast boat, and Shannon himself, his red hair flying in the wind. But most thought the gunplay was part of the show until Shannon's limp body was taken from his boat and laid upon the lawn of Carl Fisher's Flamingo Hotel, where Father Francis J. Finn, a Jesuit priest, uttered the last rites. A public furore was raised against the Coast Guard. Prohibition had become unpopular, and public sentiment was on the side of the lawbreakers.

The era did produce its bad characters whose acts won them no sympathy. One such character was James Horace Alderman, the "liquor pirate" who, in August 1927, shot and killed three federal men in a Gulf Stream battle. Alderman was a hardened Cracker fisherman who had turned to liquor running and alien smuggling. He had spent a year in prison some years before after being convicted of slugging and robbing an intoxicated Seminole medicine man, Josie Billie, of $185 he had received from the sale of otter skins in Fort Myers. Alderman vowed he would never go to prison again. When a Coast Guard cutter stopped his liquor-filled boat thirty-five miles east of Miami, Alderman got the drop on his challengers and disarmed them. While Alderman was lining up the Coast Guardsmen and a secret service agent to force them to "walk the plank," pirate fashion, one of the crew lunged at him and a shoot-out ensued. Slain were Boatsman S. C. Sanderlin, Seaman Victor A. Lamby, and Secret Service Agent Robert K. Webster. Coast Guardsman J. L. Hollingsworth lost an eye in the fracas, which ended after Alderman had been stabbed several times with a icepick and beaten into un-consciousness by the survivors.

Taken to Miami, along with a companion, Robert Weech, Alderman recovered to be convicted of murder. Appeals by his attorneys delayed his walk to the gallows for two years. Meanwhile, Weech pleaded guilty to a lesser charge, in exchange for his testimony against his partner, and had served his time before Alderman's hanging was set for August 17, 1929.

News coverage of the hanging, to be carried out in a Coast Guard hangar in Fort Lauderdale, was banned by Federal District Judge Halstead L. Ritter of Miami. It had been only two years since a New York *Daily Mirror* reporter, with a camera strapped to one of his legs, snapped a picture of Ruth Snyder in the Sing Sing prison electric chair. The picture, showing Mrs. Snyder in her death paroxyms, made the front page of the *Mirror*. Judge Ritter was determined that no such photograph would be made of Alderman, or any lurid stories written, either. So strict were federal officers in carrying out Ritter's orders that a *Herald* photographer who attempted to get a shot of Alderman while he was being transferred from the Dade County jail to the Broward County jail the day before execution was so roughed up that hospital treatment was required for his lacerations.

Ritter, a classmate at DePauw University of Frank B. Shutts, had been appointed to the federal bench by Coolidge just before turning over the presidency to Herbert Hoover. No person in Florida less influential than Shutts could have landed so important a post for Ritter, who had lived in the state only a couple of years.

A *Herald* reporter nevertheless witnessed the hanging of Alderman. He entered the hangar as the driver of a hearse owned by the Miami under-taker who had been awarded the contract of preparing the hanged man's body for burial. A couple of nights before the execution, John Pennekamp received a call from Frank J. McGhan, manager of the King Funeral Home. McGhan, who thought Ritter had acted in a high-handed manner in forbidding the press to witness the execution, wanted to help the *Herald* "put one over" on the judge. If the *Herald* had a reporter who could drive a hearse, he could witness the hanging. McGhan had thought about offering this opportunity to his friend, Henry Reno, but knew Reno would be recognized. Pennekamp liked McGhan's idea, but who would he send? He could not send any of his regular reporters, George Kenney, Arthur Peavy, or Cy Berning. Somebody would recognize them. Looking across the news room, his eyes fell upon Eddie Hay, amusement columnist. He called Hay over.

"Eddie, can you drive a hearse?" he asked.

"I guess so," replied Hay. "But why drive a hearse?"

"I want you to cover the Alderman hanging and this is the way you would have to do it as the driver of a hearse."

"Why pick me, Penny?"

"Because I don't have a reporter who wouldn't be recognized."

Hay consented. Pennekamp called Shutts and got his permission. He, too, thought that Ritter had acted in a high-handed manner. And, so, Eddie Hay appeared at the King Funeral Home just before two o'clock on the morning of August 17, and, with a companion—a mortician—left for Fort Lauderdale in a black hearse. As they approached the entrance to the Coast Guard station, flanked by barricades of barbed wire and uniformed Coast Guardsmen armed with submachine guns, Hay became so uneasy that the mortician noticed it.

"Don't let them scare you, Eddie," he said. "Drive right up to the gate. We're official, you know."

The guards swung the gate open and ushered the hearse into the hangar, where an officer directed Hay to park. As Hay slipped from the driver's seat and looked about he saw the scaffold looming into the high-raftered space of the hangar. On the concrete apron in front were white uniformed guardsmen armed with rifles and fixed bayonets. But Hay found the discipline within the hangar relaxed. A young man in uniform soon engaged him in conversation.

"I asked for this duty," said the guardsman. "I want to see the sonofabitch hang. He killed my buddy."

As the first light of gray dawn began to filter through the hangar door, Alderman was escorted inside, the door closing behind him. The condemned man wore starched white duck trousers and a white shirt. After pausing at the gallows, he calmly walked up the dozen steps without assistance. On the platform with two officials was the one-legged sheriff of Palm Beach County, Bob Baker, selected as hangman because of his experience. One of the officials stepped forward and fitted the hood over Alderman's head. He was led to the trap door where Baker pulled the noose down over the hooded head and slipped it taut about his neck, while an official tied the condemned man's legs together. Feeling the noose, Alderman began to murmur a hymn, falteringly, in an unnatural, strained tone: "Jesus, Here I'm Coming."

The words sounded hollow through the black hood. The sun was rising. Hay, looking about, could see that much of the hangar was cluttered with the hulls of liquor-running boats, trophies captured by the Coast Guard in its relentless but futile drive against the violators of the National Prohibition Act.

" . . . Then, goodby," Hay heard Baker say above the doleful hymn, "and may God have mercy on your soul."

There was a snap as a bolt shot back, followed by a dull bang and shattering crack as the trap fell, and the black-hooded figure plunged feet-first through the floor to thump at the end of the manila rope. The doleful hymn had stopped. The time was 6:03 a.m. Alderman hung for twelve minutes, gurgling, kicking, strangling, before his body relaxed. A doctor stepped forward and pronounced him dead. Hay was almost too stunned to move when the mortician nudged him, saying:

"O.K., Eddie, now we take over."

As Hay drove through the gate he was surprised to see a photographer aiming a camera at the hearse. Suddenly Hay was no longer the mild-mannered, good-natured person his friends knew. Pressing on the accelerator and turning the steering wheel, he headed the hearse at the photographer. Now he recognized the man, Pop Willets, veteran *Miami News* photographer. The agile Willets escaped with his life. That afternoon the *News* carried the picture on page one, but Hay was relieved that the driver could not be recognized.

After delivering the hearse to the King Funeral Home, Hay braced himself with coffee and cigarettes, then went to the *Herald* to write an eye-witness account. But, alas, the account never got into the paper. Shutts had a change of mind and called Pennekamp and ordered him to kill the story. He did not want to risk conflict with his old friend, Ritter. Meanwhile, reporter Jefferson Bell hunted down Alderman's widow and daughters, whom she found living in a shabby house in Miami's northwest section. Everything Alderman had made from liquor running had been used to pay defense lawyers; the family was now living in the meanest poverty. But Alderman, dead, got plenty of attention. More than eight thousand filed through the King Funeral Home to see the body of the erstwhile liquor pirate, and his funeral had the largest attendance of any funeral to that date in Miami's history.

Judge Ritter later learned that a reporter had witnessed the Alderman hanging, and he sought for a long time to obtain his name. The judge promised Cy Berning, who covered the federal court, that he intended to give the reporter a jail sentence, as well as the responsible editor who sent him.

9

Miami Attracts All Kinds

ONE EVENING EARLY in February 1928, a chubby-faced, broad-shouldered man dressed in an expensive business suit and wearing a derby entered the *Miami Herald's* newsroom and stopped at a desk where a shirt-sleeved editor was bent over a stack of copy.

"Could you direct me to Colonel Shutts?" asked the stranger.

Vernon Collins, who had started to work the week before, looked up.

"Shutts? Shutts?" he mused. "Don't know him."

"Could I use your telephone?" asked the stranger.

"Sure, help yourself," replied Collins, shoving his telephone across the desk and returning to work.

A few moments later the stranger offered the telephone to Collins.

"Colonel Shutts would like to speak to you," he said.

On the telephone the impatient publisher identified himself.

"The gentleman inquiring for me is Mr. Herbert Hoover, Secretary of Commerce and a candidate for the Republican presidential nomination," snapped Shutts. "I want you to contact the garage and have him driven to my home right away."

Collins, coming awake, recognized the name. He informed the city desk and soon a Model-A Ford from the *Herald's* garage drew up in front of the building to take Mr. Hoover to the publisher's home.

Next day Hoover continued to Key West by way of the Overseas Railway, accompanied by columnist Mark Sullivan, the leading press agent for the Republican Party. Meanwhile, Managing Editor Ellis Hollums called Earl Adams, the *Herald's* stuttering Key West correspondent, and delivered a message from Colonel Shutts. Adams was to call on Mr. Hoover at the Casa Marina Hotel and offer his services to make the secretary's vacation pleasant. Shutts knew that Adams, a Conch, as native Key Westers are known, was acquainted with the top fishing guides and was likely to know where the best fishing was to be found. Adams did as directed, but Hoover was being well taken care of by the island's Republicans. Seeing that Hoover was cordial, Adams asked for an interview. Hoover promised to have Sullivan do a special piece for the *Herald.* After some pressure, Sullivan did prepare a release, delivering it just before he and Hoover departed from Key West. It purported to be an announcement by Hoover of the states in which he planned to enter the primaries. In the story was a very unusual statement: that should it appear Florida would go Democratic in November, the Republican administration would counter the trend by spending more money in the state. The excited Adams rushed to his typewriter, where he put a Key West dateline on the story and wrote a lead paragraph indicating that Hoover had made the announcement after winding up a Florida fishing vacation. He then hastened to the Western Union office and sent the story to the *Herald,* where it not only was run on page one but was picked up by the Associated Press.

By the time Hoover's train reached Savannah the repercussions began reaching him by telegram. The announcement had proved to be badly timed, and many Republican leaders were offended. Hoover reacted in the best tradition of the politician. He wired Shutts, denying the story, and asserted it had been fabricated. The *Herald* ran an apology, together with an announcement that the reporter had been fired. Adams, in the meantime, was on his way to Miami with the original copy of Sullivan's release.

"If I-I were capable of writing such a st-story myself," stuttered Adams to Shutts, "I-I wouldn't be wo-working for the lo-low sa-salary th-the *Herald* has been pa-paying me."

The chagrined publisher sent his secretary, Harold Wells, to Key West to investigate, and Adams was rehired at a higher salary. The *Herald* was happy to get him back because, in the meantime, Key West had been closed to the paper as a news source. Nobody in town would talk to a *Herald* representative until fellow Conch Adams was reemployed.

While Hoover went on to win the Republican nomination and to be elected president in November, with the promise of two cars in every garage and a chicken in every pot, 1928 was one of Miami's roughest years. A tourist economy was not sufficient to support the large population that had managed so well during the boom. The construction period was over and the jobless were leaving to seek employment elsewhere. The *Herald's* declining circulation reflected the economic conditions and steady exodus. Circulation dropped from 47,600 in 1927 to 46,200 in 1928, the beginning of a decline that would not stop until the bottom was reached in 1934 when circulation dipped to 38,200. Moreover, the area was beginning to suffer an increasing number of bankruptcies. An uneasy and uncertain mood permeated Miami. Thus the vaguest kind of rumor was all that was necessary in February 1928 to start a run by depositors on the Southern Bank & Trust Company.

For two days the long lines continued. It mattered not that the pioneer J. E. Lummus, a symbol of financial soundness and dependability, was president. On the third day the doors failed to open to the block-long line. Only then did the *Herald* tell its readers that the bank was in trouble. The paper failed to record any of the drama—the long lines of worried depositors, the busy cashiers, and the harassed officers, including the tall, slender and serious Lummus. The article was more of an editorial apology than a news story, castigating rumor-mongers and assuring readers that the bank was sound and "would reopen by March 15." For the rest of the week the *Herald* carried articles and display advertising to convince the public that Miami's surviving banks were sound.

The Southern Bank & Trust Company did not reopen, but Miami's other troubled banks held out until 1930, after the stock market crash of 1929. The major blow fell when the Bank of Bay Biscayne failed. President Jimmie Gilman, looked upon as Miami's stalwart prince of finance, could only stand by helplessly as depositors swarmed about the stone lions guarding the impressive edifice to demand their money. After it was all over Gilman was ruined. Like Lummus and several other bankers of the boom era, Gilman had lent vast sums to his friends, accepting as security property whose value was inflated a dozen times beyond its real worth. The boom was now over, the friends broke, and the property on which Gilman had lent money was hardly worth the unpaid taxes. Next to fail was J. C. Penney's City National Bank, despite a pledge by Penney, made in a *Herald* display ad, guaranteeing depositors' money. A sister bank at Miami Beach also closed. Penney gave up his mansion at Miami Beach and left Florida. But the First National Bank managed to stay open despite the long lines of depositors demanding their money. Ed Romfh had securities to cover the withdrawals, not just signatures on worthless pieces of paper. Even so, cash got embarrassingly low. At the height of the boom deposits had bulged to $66.7 million, $56 million of which was retained in cash and marketable securities. At the bottom of the toboggan ride, Romfh's bank had less than $12 million in deposits. Depositors were withdrawing money from the First National and walking a block to the post office to buy postal savings certificates, then a popular means of saving. The money went directly back to the First National. Romfh deposited United States government bonds with the post office as security. Meanwhile, Romfh, who parted his hair in the middle like Hoover and had almost the same chubby cheeks, frequently stepped to a balcony to address depositors lined up before the tellers' windows.

"Could I have your attention?" he would say. "I am E. C. Romfh, president of this bank. All of you down there who do not have confidence in me or in the First National Bank, I want you to get your money, and I want you to get out of this bank and don't come back."

Romfh, who had been described as stingy and unimaginative during the boom when he refused to accept notes or mortgages not backed by what he considered sound security, survived.

"Banks are 'busted' from the inside, not the outside," Romfh told the *Herald.* "A bank with a board of directors of ordinary intelligence and with an honest desire to obey the law does not fail."

Banking laws during the boom era were not nearly so stringent as they later would be. It would not be until after Roosevelt became president in 1933 that Congress authorized federal insurance on bank deposits. So the little person who had scrimped and saved, depositing his money in Miami banks, lost virtually all when banks failed, just as did big shots who had lost millions in paper wealth when the bottom dropped out of land prices.

Miami had a final fling before the stock market crash which triggered the great depression. Yankees riding the crest of Coolidge era prosperity came down early in 1929 to seek the sunshine and to play the game of "buying shares" in the horses at Hialeah. The "world's greatest sports promoter," Tex Rickard, was in Miami in January for the opening of his new Miami Beach dog track and to get ready for the fight he was promoting between Jack Sharkey and W. L. "Young" Stribling, contenders for the world's heavyweight championship, voluntarily relinquished by Gene Tunney. Rickard got to see neither the opening of his track nor the fight. Stricken by appendicitis, he was taken to a hospital to die of peritonitis after an operation. The *Herald's* front page wept copious tears of printer's ink, which flooded over onto the sports pages. Jack Dempsey, whose fights Rickard had promoted, wept too. So did other sports toughs. But the sportswriters wept most—through their typewriters. The *Herald* gave Rickard's death more coverage than it had the death of William Jennings Bryan.

Nevertheless, it was a record winter season for Miami. On February 26, 1929, a headline over the lead story on the *Herald's* front page said: "Record Made/As Thousands/Enter Miami." Travelers filled the steamships, and railroads added special trains. Hotels were 100 percent filled. For a time it was like the boom. Many of the thousands had come to see the Sharkey-Stribling fight. Held on the night of February 27 in Flamingo Park, it drew a crowd of 40,000. Among the spectators was Al

Capone, spending his second winter in Florida. Despite the interest in the fight, the *Herald* next morning reported it under a one-column headline, although the story got ample space. Sports Editor Jack Bell, who liked to write succinct leads, started like this:

"Sharkey wins!

"Sharkey whips Stribling."

Capone, a onetime prize fighter himself, sat with his cronies in hundred-dollar ringside seats. With his darkly tanned skin, he looked robust and delightfully pleased with himself as he followed the footwork, feinting, parrying of blows, punching, and swinging of the two opponents. Chewing an expensive cigar, he frequently turned to one of his underworld buddies to make a comment, with the air and confidence of an *aficionado,* Capone had come down in January, bringing with him a severe cold from the raw climate of Chicago. He soaked up the Florida sunshine while disregarding the shrill cries of those who sought to rid the Miami area of the nation's top gangster. Meanwhile, Capone's cold turned into pneumonia. Or so said his doctor. And for several days the king of the underworld was confined to bed, with a fever that touched 104 degrees. His illness was long past, however, when on February 17 a deputy United States marshal served him with a subpoena that ordered him to appear before a Chicago federal grand jury. Capone's doctor submitted an affidavit that stated that he was in no condition to travel. Capone's appearance before the grand jury was postponed until March 20. But before that date the federal district attorney charged Capone with contempt of court. A number of people had seen Capone everywhere but in bed during most of January and February, when his doctor said he was ill. They saw him at the racetrack, a pilot flew him and a party of hoodlums to Bimini for drinks and a picnic, and a merchant on Flagler Street sold him expensive silk shirts, ties, and other clothes. They all reported that Capone appeared to be in robust health, swaggering, and leaving a wake of ten dollar tips.

Capone had first arrived in Miami in 1928, taking over the entire top floor of the Ponce de Leon Hotel on Flagler Street. Parker Henderson, who owned the hotel, became a close friend and confidant of the gangster as well as a front for him in banking and business transactions. It was through Henderson, son of a former mayor, that Capone purchased a home at Palm Island, in Biscayne Bay. Miami's two newspapers displayed opposite reactions. The *Herald* ignored Capone, while the *News* attacked him constantly. Shutts as a lawyer realized that so long as the gangland lord kept the peace, Miamians could do nothing. Capone hired lawyers who went to court and got an injunction that stopped harassment by the county prosecutor, the American Legion, the Chamber of

Commerce, and a host of other guardians of Miami's morals. Moreover, the court hearings proved to be an embarrassment and indictment of the Miami area. Capone's lawyers, cross-examining witnesses who appeared to testify against him, made them admit that Miami had gambling, prostitution, and illegal liquor traffic, just like Chicago had; that while the establishment was trying to run Capone out of town it was permitting the operation of a swank gambling casino, the Palm Island Club, within dice-clicking sound of the gangster's residence—a casino where the area's leading citizens went to drink, eat and gamble.

Although Capone made a semblance of obeying the law while in Florida, his hoodlum nature surfaced at the horse tracks. Flashing a roll of greenbacks, he established a first-name friendship with Hialeah president Joe Smoot and, through his henchmen, began fixing the races he wanted to win. John C. Clark, who was to become president and principal owner of Hialeah in 1940, would never forget a chilling experience he had with the Capone gang. One day he was approached by an olive-skinned hoodlum who sought to induce him to "pull" his horse in a forthcoming race.

"Al Capone has a horse in that race, and he expects to win," said the hoodlum.

"If my horse runs, he'll run to win," replied Clark, seeking to hide his nervousness behind a little braggadocio.

"That's not being smart, with Al Capone interested in that race, mister," sneered the hoodlum.

If Clark felt uneasy as the time for the race approached, he had more reason to feel uneasy afterward. His horse won. But, as it turned out, he had nothing to worry about. Capone had decided to bet on Clark's horse.

Capone in 1931 was convicted of contempt of court in Chicago and sentenced to six months in jail, and, while he was waiting for his case to be appealed, a federal grand jury indicted him on charges of income tax evasion. Convicted, he was sentenced to eleven years in prison, which he began in 1932. Released after seven years behind the bars, Capone returned to his Palm Island home in 1939. But World War II began in Europe that year, and the gangster was small potatoes compared with such names on the wanted list as Hitler and Mussolini.

In 1930 Miami attracted another personality who, although he did not make the stir that Al Capone did, was to leave a more durable imprint on Florida. He was Joseph E. Widener, Philadelphia horse racing enthusiast and a collector of Rembrandt paintings. Of aristocratic pretensions, Widener believed strongly in himself and had immense faith in what money could do. And only such a person who had no doubts could have believed that the Florida Legislature, dominated by politicians from the state's Bible Belt, could be induced to pass a bill legalizing wagering on horses. Widener purchased Hialeah Park, fired the flamboyant Joe Smoot, and set out to get a parimutuel bill passed. With Widener's backing, Miami Representative Dan Chappell introduced a bill which offered to divide the spoils of racing—the taxes collected from parimutuel betting—equally among the state's sixty-seven counties. This bone to Christian conscience worked. The only hitch was that Governor Doyle E. Carlton, Sr., of strong Cracker moralistic tradition, vetoed the bill.

Widener, who hated greyhounds, had managed to keep any mention of dog racing out of the parimutuel wagering act. But after the governor's veto, the dog people had their day. And so the dogs rode to victory on the backs of the thoroughbreds when the Legislature overrode the governor's veto. So did jai-alai.

In the summer of 1931 Widener left plans for a new racing plant with James Bright, with orders to make Hialeah Park the "most beautiful horse track in America," and departed for Europe. The seven-year-old grandstand and stables were knocked down. A new clubhouse of French architecture was built. Hundred-foot royal palms were removed from the wilds of Big Cypress Swamp to give the landscape a spectacular character. Costs meant nothing.

But while Widener was in Europe, plans were being made for two additional horse tracks in Dade County. William "Big Bill" Dwyer, millionaire promoter with friends in the underworld, had taken over Tropical Park, a defunct dog track, while Joe Smoot was seeking a permit to fill a part of Biscayne Bay and build a track adjoining the new Seventy-Ninth Street Causeway. Widener, upon hearing of these plans, was upset. Dwyer, who had managed to win Widener's friendship, suddenly was an enemy. Dreaming of getting into Florida racing as Widener's partner, Dwyer had thrown a $100,000 champagne party for him in the spring of 1931 at the Biltmore Hotel in New York. Widener's friends were present, and, at the propitious moment during the lavish banquet, in walked three of Widener's best horses ridden by jockeys wearing the colors of the Widener stable. Widener was touched. Tears filled his eyes. After the party was over Widener and Dwyer embraced and protested everlasting friendship. But the gregarious Dwyer was mistaken to think he now had the introspective Widener in his pocket. For when he approached Widener with a proposition to operate Hialeah and Tropical parks as a joint venture, Widner haughtily turned him down. And when Tropical opened on December 26, 1931, twenty days before the grand opening of the new Hialeah plant, Widener let horsemen know that if they raced at Tropical they could not race at Hialeah.

Smoot, meanwhile, failed in his efforts to build a horse track because of opposition to his plan to fill so large an area in Biscayne Bay. He departed for California where he promoted legalized parimutuel wagering, then helped to found Santa Anita Park. Smoot reappeared in Florida in 1937, this time to promote Gulfstream Race Track.

While the rest of the nation was plunging further into economic chaos as the Hoover administration drew to a close, Miami was beginning to enjoy brief flushes of prosperity. The declining population was becoming stabilized. Legalized betting on horses, dogs, and jai-alai was bringing winter crowds to Florida, despite the depression. It was a mixed picture, but behind it a revolution was taking place—in merchandizing, aviation, freight transportation, banking, and industry. Chain stores were growing. Trucking firms were beginning to take business away from railroads. Airline travel was on the increase. Bankers and industrialists who had had their way during good times were being challenged by young leaders with new ideas. Despite the bankruptcies, the millions of unemployed, the breadlines, and the melancholy atmosphere that pervaded much of the nation, there was a great vitality. You noted a restlessness among people, almost like wartime. People moved about the country, swarming onto freight trains, or hitchhiking and walking, looking for work, searching for new opportunities. Many persons, finding it impossible to obtain work in the North, began drifting to Florida early in the 1930s. There was a saying that if you were going to starve, you might as well starve in a comfortable climate and among pleasant surroundings. You could starve cheaply, too. Although wages had plummeted to a record low since World War I, so had prices and rents. Luncheons at the Dinner Bell in downtown Miami cost fifteen cents, yet included meat, vegetables, coffee, and dessert. Dinner, from soup to dessert, cost twenty-five cents. Steak or Florida lobster cost thirty cents, and you could eat Maine lobster for fifty cents.

A noticeable expansion in the aviation industry began in Miami during the late 1920s and early 1930s. Pan American Airways moved its operations from Pan American Field on Northwest Thirty-Sixth Street, from which it had been operating land planes and amphibians, to Dinner Key, from where its flying boats were charting new routes that would soon make Miami one of the world's foremost international air travel centers. Meanwhile, Eastern Air Lines in 1931 began using Pan American Field—eventually to become a part of the vast Miami International Airport—as a terminal for flights between Miami and other mainland cities. To promote Miami as an aviation center, in 1929 the city began the annual Miami All-America Air Meet, which attracted fliers from all over the country to participate in races and to do acrobatics for the large crowds the event drew. Miami became an international center for fliers, not only because of the city's image but because of the ideal flying weather much of the year. It was a period when aviation had many heroes, the greatest of them being Charles A. Lindbergh. Nearly all of them got to Miami at one time or another. The "Lone Eagle" was employed by Pan American to open new routes between Miami and the Caribbean and Latin America.

Among the fliers who found their way to Miami in those years was a swashbuckling Englishman, a former Royal Air Force pilot, Captain William Newton Lancaster, and an eighty-five-pound Australian flier, Mrs. Jessie M. Keith-Miller. The pair had met in 1927, the year Lindbergh soloed across the Atlantic. Lancaster was looking for someone to finance a flight from London to Australia. Mrs. Keith-Miller, a widow with some money, agreed to back Lancaster provided he let her go along as copilot. Called "Chubbie" by her friends, she was twenty-five and, although no exceptional beauty, was personable and attractive in a petite way. They teamed up and on October 14, 1927, took off from London. Although they did not arrive in Australia until March 19, 1928, the five months' trip, beset by hardships that had to be overcome by great courage, patience, and endurance, proved to be one of the most publicized in aviation during that period. By the time the pair reached Australia they had attained worldwide fame—and they had fallen in love. They would have been married except for the fact that Lancaster's wife refused to give him a divorce. Still they remained together and for the next couple of years took advantage of their fame, flying together or individually to find glory wherever they went, including the United States. Among Chubbie's feats was to beat the famous aviatrix, Laura Ingals, in setting a national record for women in a cross-country flight from coast to coast. Eventually, however, the popularity of Lancaster and Chubbie cooled. The feats they performed had become old hat. They wound up in Miami in 1931, taking a house in Coral Gables. It was a convenient arrangement for Lancaster, who was now broke. But at Christmas time, a second man entered the picture. He was Charles Haden Clarke, a thirty-year-old newspaperman from New Orleans. Clarke, out of work and living temporarily with his mother, an English professor at the University of Miami, suggested doing a book on the diminutive Chubbie. Moving in with the pair, he began taking notes for the projected book. A few weeks thereafter Lancaster was offered a job in the West, flying air freight between the United States and Mexico. The job did not pan out, and Lancaster returned to discover that Clarke and Chubbie had fallen in love. Several drinks were downed that evening by the three as they sought to settle an insoluble problem—how Chubbie could be faithful to two men who professed to love her and whom she

MIAMI became an international aviation center in the 1930s, with Pan American Airways flying boats taking off from Dinner Key for flights to Latin America and the Far East. Miami also was a center for the coming and going of personalities—and some of them worked on the *Miami Herald.*

professed to love. The problem was still unresolved when the three went to bed—Chubbie to her own bedroom, the two men to beds on a sleeping porch. In the middle of the night Chubbie was awakened by Lancaster.

"A terrible thing has happened!" he blurted. "Haden has shot himself!"

The evidence at Lancaster's trial on a murder charge should have made it difficult for a jury to doubt his guilt, but the flier had as his defense attorney James M. Carson, one of Miami's ablest lawyers. His image in the courtroom was that of a simple, conscientious man who would have been unable to defend a guilty person. His method of questioning was simple and direct, but his arguments were persuasive. Putting Lancaster on the witness stand, Carson asked:

"Did you kill Haden Clarke?"

"I did not," replied Lancaster firmly.

If Lancaster did not kill Clarke, then Clarke had to kill himself, and Carson proceeded to convince the jury that Clarke, neurotic and unstable, was the kind of person who could have killed himself under the circumstances. And Carson was able to sway the jury despite the fact that Lancaster admitted writing a suicide note and forging Clarke's name to it; despite the absence of powder burns; despite the fact that the gun belonged to Lancaster, and despite Lancaster's motive for killing Clarke and the absence of a motive for Clarke killing himself. And so the handsome Lancaster went free, to be deported as an undesirable alien. Chubbie followed.

It had been one of the most intriguing murder trials ever held in Miami and, because of the names involved, was one of international interest. Never had so many foreign reporters been attracted to Miami. Wire services carried long accounts of the testimony that revealed the relationship between Mrs. Keith-Miller and her two lovers. Arthur Peavy covered the trial for the *Herald*. An excellent leg-man type of reporter but not gifted as a writer, Peavy got the information down and John Pennekamp put together the lengthy accounts that ran each morning in the *Herald*. It would be many years before the paper was again to give so much space to a murder trial.

Several months after gaining his freedom the restless Lancaster took off from London in a single-seated plane for Cape Town in an attempt to set a new record and to regain some of the international renown he formerly had enjoyed. He was last seen alive in Algeria, where he made a refueling stop before taking off at night over the desert. Twenty-nine years later, in February, 1962, a French camel corps found the almost perfectly preserved body of Lancaster, where he had died beside his plane. A diary he kept indicated he had survived seven scorching days and seven bone-chilling nights after making a forced landing because of engine trouble. Upon hearing that Lancaster had kept a diary while waiting for rescue or death, the *Herald* was anxious to learn if the flier might possibly have admitted slaying Haden Clarke. But his daily jottings did not mention Clarke.

Miami was attracting a wide variety of people in the 1930s—rich and poor, restless and adventurous, talented and mediocre, normal and unstable, honest unemployed and bums looking for an easy way of life. Among the unemployed and unstable was Guiseppe Zangara, an Italian-born bricklayer who arrived about the same time as did Captain Lancaster and Mrs. Keith-Miller. Finding no work, Zangara left for a year, then returned. Still there was no work for a bricklayer, so he turned to doing odd jobs, including gardening. Zangara was a bit of a man, five feet one inch and weighing 105 pounds. He was a loner and antisocial. Thirty-three, he had been in the United States ten years and spoke understandable English. But he had no close friends. The people with whom Zangara came in contact looked upon him as an eccentric who frequently complained of a "pain in da belly," but he was hard-working and appeared to be harmless.

Zangara awakened early on February 15, 1933. He had no work that day, and it was a good thing because he had that chronic "pain in da belly." He made coffee, gnawed on some hard bread, and nibbled on some white cheese. The pain persisted, however, and he brooded. And when Zangara brooded he thought of the rich, their mansions and big cars, and how easy life must be for them. It was not right for some to be so rich while he was so poor. For this he blamed the kings, the dictators, and the presidents. If he could kill these leaders this would right the wrongs. How, he was not sure. His pain kept him from thinking that far.

By mid-morning Zangara's pain had become so intense he could stay in his room no longer. The only way he could get relief now was to walk. So, he left his room. In the street he stopped to read the headlines of the *Miami Herald,* on sale in front of a shop. His eyes caught a headline that excited him. "Miami Awaits/Visit Tonight/Of Roosevelt," said a three-column head. "Plans are completed for reception here to next president," said a subhead, and beneath that was still another subhead: "Will be heard from motor car." Zangara bought a paper. Roosevelt, to be inaugurated president on March 4, had been on a fishing trip for twelve days aboard Vincent Astor's yacht *Nourmahal* which would arrive in Miami that evening. "Mr. Roosevelt will speak briefly in Bayfront Park before boarding the ten p.m. train for New York," said the story. The yacht would dock at nine-fifteen, at Pier One, "the hour set for a motorcade to escort the president-elect to the park." After Roosevelt spoke to the crowd assembled there, without getting out of his car, said the story, he would rejoin the parade to the Florida East Coast Railway station, eight blocks distant.

Zangara must have been clutching the paper tensely by this time, and one can imagine him muttering to himself as he quickened his step: his step:

"I keel, I keel."

Ten years before in Italy Zangara had bought a gun with the intention of killing King Victor Emanuel, but his plan was thwarted when the pressing crowd prevented him from getting near the monarch. This time, however, he would not fail. On Miami Avenue he stopped in front of a jewelry store that also sold guns, cameras, binoculars, and musical instruments. In a display window were two double-barreled sawed-off shotguns.

"I lika buy shotgun," said Zangara to Harry Rubin, the proprietor. "How much you get?"

Rubin studied the little man, noting his bulging eager eyes and the tense muscles in his neck. He had bought the guns to sell to the police, or to operators of gambling casinos who were being harassed by holdup men. But the sale of sawed-off shotguns was regulated by a federal law and required a permit. So Rubin told Zangara he could not sell him a shotgun.

"Then you sell me peestil, a peestil for about seex dollar?"

"I can't sell you a gun." said Rubin. "You'll have to go somewhere else."

And so Zangara left Rubin's store, walked across Miami Avenue, and entered a pawnshop operated by Gordon Davis. Davis had known Zangara for two years and, knowing nothing against his character, sold him a hammerless thirty-two caliber, five-shot revolver. He also sold him ten bullets.

That evening Zangara put the revolver in his right front pocket and walked to Bayfront Park. Thousands already had gathered, occupying the seats close to the spot where Roosevelt would speak. As Zangara got closer to the bandshell, where important guests were to sit, he encountered some resistance, but, biding his time, he inched forward. By nine o'clock 25,000 persons had gathered in Bayfront Park and along Biscayne Boulevard where the president-elect would pass in an open car with Miami Mayor R. B. Gautier. Roosevelt, meanwhile, had finished a press conference on the *Nourmahal,* and reporters had dashed to telephones or to typewriters. In the *Herald* newsroom Pennekamp waited nervously as reporter Tom Smith, who had attended the press conference, pecked out his story. He had no reporter to send to Bayfront Park to cover Roosevelt's talk. Although he had an advance copy, there was always the chance Roosevelt might stray from the text or add something bright or witty; and, too, there was the reaction of the crowd and the color which Pennekamp thought should be in the story. Looking around, he saw Arthur Peavy sitting at his desk. Peavy, who covered the county building and circuit court, had finished work an hour before but, having a reporter's "premonition" that something might happen, had remained at his desk. Pennekamp asked him if he would mind "running down to Bayfront Park" and "get a couple of paragraphs of color" to go with Tom Smith's story.

Peavy arrived at the park moments before he heard cheers in the distance. A little before nine-thirty the parade came into view, led by Miami motorcycle policemen. As the president-elect arrived at the bandshell, riding beside Mayor Gautier in a four-door green convertible, he smiled and waved a hand to the crowd, now reaching a peak of elation. While being introduced, Roosevelt spotted Mayor Anton J. Cermak of Chicago sitting among the dignitaries on the platform of the bandshell, and the two gave each other high signs. Roosevelt rose carefully and, using his crippled legs to push himself into a sitting position on the back of the

ASSASSINATION attempt on President-elect Franklin D. Roosevelt, February 15, 1933, in Bayfront Park, ended the open-car parades through Miami's streets by the nation's chief executives.

WOUNDED by bullet meant for Roosevelt, Mayor Anton Cermak of Chicago is assisted by W. W. Wood and L. L. Lee. Cermak was rushed to Jackson Memorial Hospital in Roosevelt's car. He died on March 6. At right is Guiseppe Zangara.

convertible's seat, took a microphone proffered him by Fred Mizer of Radio Station WQAM, and began to talk, not only to the crowd but to a South Florida radio audience. His speech lasted less than five minutes. All he said was that he was glad to be in Miami again, that the weather and the fishing had been excellent, and that he had gained weight, which he didn't need. It was not the place or the time to discuss grand strategy for ending the worldwide depression, and the happy crowd expected nothing like that. His talk over, Roosevelt handed the microphone back to Mizer, smiled and waved a hand at the cheering crowd, then slipped down into the seat beside Mayor Gautier. At that moment Cermak reached the car to shake hands with Roosevelt. It was a politician's handshake, four hands, together with smiles and enthusiastic greetings. Roosevelt had just released his hands and Cermak was straightening up when a shot rang out, then a second shot. Roosevelt turned to see part of the crowd in confused motion a short distance away, and in the middle of the confusion was a man with a pistol. Hands reached for the man, and the pistol was jerked this way and that way as it popped again and again until five shots had been fired.

"There seems to be some little excitement here," said Mizer into his microphone. "Somebody's shooting some firecrackers . . . Well, that's all, folks, good night, added Mizer, signing off to a South Florida audience and missing an opportunity of making history with one of the great eyewitness accounts of the century.

Screams followed, mixed with shouts of excited policemen, officials, and secret service men.

"Don't let him kill Roosevelt!" someone shouted.

"Kill him! Kill him!" another shouted.

Secret service men were throwing themselves between the president-elect and the man with the gun.

"Get out of here!" shouted a secret service man to the uniformed policeman driving the convertible. "Get the president out of here!"

Starting the motor, the policeman stepped nervously on the accelerator, and the car shot forward as excited motorcycle patrolmen, their sirens screaming, began racing their motors and clearing a way. At this moment Roosevelt saw two men holding Cermak. One of the men was Miami's assistant city manager, L. L. Lee, formerly a *Miami Herald* reporter, the other a policeman.

"Stop!" ordered Roosevelt. Cermak was assisted to the car, where Roosevelt helped to get the mayor of Chicago into the seat beside him, into which the wounded man collapsed.

"Get going!" shouted a voice. "To the hospital!" The driver, knowing Flagler Street already was crowded with parade watchers who, at this moment, were not aware of the assassination attempt, turned north up Biscayne Boulevard, the direction from which he had just come. With his motorcycle escort he drove to Fourteenth Street and turned west toward Jackson Memorial Hospital. The trip took less than ten minutes, but Roosevelt, in recalling the experience next day aboard his northbound train, said it seemed like half an hour.

Zangara, meanwhile, after being hammered with fists, knees, and elbows, was subdued. The many police officers and secret service men rescued him from the angry crowd without difficulty, and he was taken to jail by Sheriff Dan Hardie, escorted by deputies and other lawmen. Six persons had been hit by Zangara's bullets, including Cermak, the most seriously injured.

Arthur Peavy witnessed it all and heard the radio announcer Fred Mizer utter the unbelievable report of firecrackers exploding and sign off. Instead of waiting to obtain further details, Peavy sprinted two blocks to the Urmey Hotel, where he knew a telephone was available, and dialed the *Herald.*

"There's been an assassination attempt . . . on Roosevelt" shouted the winded Peavy into Pennekamp's ear. "A wild man fired from the crowd. Roosevelt apparently wasn't hit. Mayor Cermak of Chicago was shot. Don't know how serious. He's on the way to the hospital, in Roosevelt's car. I heard five shots. Others hit, too, one of them a woman."

That was all Peavy knew, except that as he departed the crowd was subduing the little man who had fired the shots. Pennekamp wheeled to his typewriter, dashed off a lead, and followed with the meager details supplied by Peavy. Then he jerked the copy from the typewriter and dashed to the composing room. The timing could not have been more perfect. Page one was at that moment being closed for the run of an up-state edition. Pennekamp ordered it held while the copy and a banner headline were set. In a matter of minutes an extra was in the streets. Two additional extras were published as more of the details reached the news-room. Next morning the final edition carried several accounts, including a long running story that contained interviews with eyewitnesses, not too well written and containing countless repetitions, but nevertheless the kind of material that everyone would read through the full five columns of unbroken type. The sharpest, most concise account was written by the assistant city manager, Lee, who was standing beside Cermak when he was hit. But the most colorful story was written by Jack Bell, the *Herald's* sports editor. It was an interview with Zangara, arranged through Sheriff Hardie, a close friend of Bell. The Italian talked freely, admitted he intended to kill Roosevelt, but showed no remorse except for having missed his target. Zangara told Bell he liked Roosevelt as a person, but wanted to kill him because he was a leader. He wanted to "keel" all leaders. He also told Bell about his "pain in da belly."

On February 17, two days after the shooting, Zangara was arraigned on four counts of attempted murder. Going to trial on February 20, after a weekend in jail, he pleaded guilty and was sentenced to eighty years in prison. But Cermak died of peritonitis early in the morning of March 6. A grand jury was impaneled that afternoon and by five o'clock had indicted Zangara on a charge of murder. The court appointed three attorneys to represent the prisoner. On March 9 Zangara, accompanied by his attorneys, was led before a circuit judge. He pleaded guilty, and, while his defense attorneys watched in respectful silence, the judge announced he would defer sentence until the next day. On March 10 Zangara was sentenced to die in the electric chair. In the absence of an appeal by his attorneys, the condemned man was removed from jail that same day by Sheriff Hardie and taken to Raiford State Prison in north Florida. On the morning of March 20 Zangara was led from his cell and strapped into an electric chair. As a metal cap was fitted over his shaven head he was asked if he had any last words.

"Pusha da button!" he replied.

And Hardie threw a switch that sent the mentally sick little Italian into eternity.

Only one newspaper in Florida saw anything unusual or possibly wrong in railroading a man to the electric chair nine days after his trial and only fourteen days after the death of his victim. The paper was the *Alligator,* the student publication at the University of Florida. A staff member who was studying law had the audacity to suggest in an editorial that justice had not been served, that Zangara possibly was insane. Reaction was swift. In the face of wholesale public demands that the student be expelled, the president of the university ordered an investigation. The student was forbidden to write again for the *Alligator.* When he was appointed during the summer session to be editor of the *Alligator,* university authorities locked the doors to the editorial offices. The *Gainesville Sun* made its pages available to the students.

Melvin J. Richard was the student. His stand split the faculty at the university and made his life so difficult that a less determined student would have transferred to another law school. But Richard stuck it out and was graduated, to become a successful lawyer at Miami Beach, as well as to be elected a city councilman and mayor.

The *Herald* was among the newspapers that played the Zangara trial and execution straight. And with the public's mood being what it was, to have taken a different attitude would have been running the risk of losing thousands of subscribers. A Tampa newspaper had, in fact, suggested that Zangara be boiled in oil.

10

Reporter Kidnaps a General

DaVERGNE BARBER was tall and portly, but also handsome and dynamic. He had worked on a score of big city newspapers and claimed to know the great and the mighty. He had a line of convincing gab that got him through doors that other top-notch reporters failed to open. Moreover, he was an airplane pilot and claimed he had taught Lindbergh to fly. John Pennekamp hired Barber in 1933 from a New Orleans newspaper. Barber had done an outstanding job for the *Herald* in covering the capture at New Orleans of a Miami jewel robber who had escaped from a Florida prison camp. At the end of the story, filed through Western Union, Barber added that he was looking for an opportunity to change positions; did the *Miami Herald* have an opening? Although Pennekamp had no opening, he did not want to risk losing an excellent newspaperman, so he hired Barber by return wire.

Barber arrived in the *Herald* newsroom two weeks later, bubbling with personality and impatient to begin work. Pennekamp was impressed by Barber's energy and enthusiasm. His talents were put to use immediately, and to Pennekamp's satisfaction he continued to write fresh and imaginative stories. He was a fast and brilliant writer, and when Pennekamp ran out of ideas, Barber would come up with some of his own, such as fishing from the Goodyear blimp or interviewing a celebrity whom he "happened to know." He had a way with important people, and soon the city editor was using Barber almost exclusively to interview the great who visited Miami. Barber was good at conning these people, making them seem more important than they were, and obtaining from them quotes—which he may have put into their mouths—that equaled the output of the highest paid promoter.

In early 1934 President Roosevelt visited Miami on Vincent Astor's yacht *Nourmahal* as he had done the year before. One day the president, who had an eye for publicity and a way of keeping on friendly terms with the press, invited the White House press corps to fly out on a Coast Guard flying boat and spend a day fishing with him. DaVergne Barber was assigned to go along. But when Barber appeared at the Dinner Key Coast Guard base, White House Secretary Louis McHenry Howe refused to let him go.

"Only accredited White House reporters are invited," said Howe in a tone that rankled Barber.

"I'll get even with you," spluttered the furious reporter. And he was even more furious after returning to the *Herald* to explain to Pennekamp why he had not made the Coast Guard flying boat. For Pennekamp was the kind of editor who gave excuses a cold reception even when he privately sympathized with the reporter. Moreover, this was the first time Barber had failed. The city editor had begun to believe that his reporter was capable of surmounting every obstacle.

A couple of days later an announcement came from Howe that Roosevelt had summoned General Hugh S. Johnson, head of the National Recovery Act (NRA), from Washington to confer with him aboard the *Nourmahal.* The NRA had been set up in 1933 by Congress to bring the nation out of the depression. Roosevelt had appointed Johnson, also known as "Old Ironpants," to head it. Johnson had taken the job with a braggadocio pronouncement that he would create five million new jobs. This and other newsworthy statements gained him frequent headlines throughout the country. He had become a prime news source, second only to the president. Pennekamp assigned Barber to meet Johnson's train at West Palm Beach and interview the NRA chief before he reached Miami. Barber met the train and succeeded in conning Johnson immediately.

"My father soldiered with you in World War I, General," said the persuasive reporter. "He was in the Eighth Division."

"That so?" mused Johnson, who was proud of his record as commander of the Eighth Division in France. And so he not only granted Barber's request for an interview, but shooed away members of his retinue from the compartment. The train had journeyed but a short distance southward when Barber said:

"General, I thought I ought to tell you that there's a big crowd waiting for you in Miami. I know you don't want to get caught in a crowd like that."

"Hell, no," growled the general, "not if I can get out of it."

Barber forthwith offered a plan to avert a confrontation with the mayor, commissioners, civic do-gooders, the American Legion Drum and Bugle Corps, and an assortment of others who hoped to shine in the glare of publicity created by the great man's presence, not to mention the array of newsmen who would be there to ply him with questions. When the train stopped at the village of Little River, five miles north of downtown Miami, Johnson left with the reporter. They walked a short distance to Little River, where Barber had a rented motorboat waiting. The general had agreed to a bizarre plan—to buzz across Biscayne Bay to Miami Beach where Barber had a car waiting. From there they would drive to the Roney Plaza Hotel, where a suite had been reserved for Johnson by the White House staff.

Barber's skiff had gone about half the distance when the motor spluttered and died. Checking the gas tank, Barber discovered it was empty. Somebody, during that depression-ridden period, had siphoned out the tank. Johnson was furious but helpless. The two overweight figures managed to exchange places in the boat without mishap, and Barber applied himself to the oars. But they still had a long way to go, and, furthermore, Barber was rowing across a tide. A red wintry sun was rapidly dropping behind the shoreline in the west when a yacht owner trained a pair of binoculars on the skiff. Turning to friends who had come aboard for cocktails and an evening cruise, he said:

"I know you'll say I've had one too many drinks, but the man sitting in the stern of that skiff looks exactly like my old friend, General Hugh S. Johnson."

The general and the reporter were rescued and delivered to Barber's waiting car, a Model A Ford drawn from the *Herald's* car pool. They reached the Roney Plaza to discover that White House Secretary Howe, fearing General Johnson had been kidnapped, was on the verge of sounding an alarm to the FBI and local police. All that the members of Johnson's retinue had been able to tell Howe was that he had left the train at Little River in the company of an impressive looking man who said he was a newspaper reporter.

Publisher Frank B. Shutts was as angry as Howe was frustrated. He ordered Barber fired. Shutts, a lawyer, was not impressed by the reporter's explanation that he was after an exclusive and different kind of story. So, instead of writing his story, Barber called Norfolk and got a job there, charging the call to the *Herald.* Next day he went to a private airport, taking with him a German Shepherd dog he was keeping for Pennekamp, and sought to rent a plane and charge it to the *Herald.* In the absence of what the airplane owner thought was sufficient identification, Barber was asked to provide security.

"Well, you can keep my dog," he said. "You can be sure I'll be back for him."

And so Barber took off and flew to Norfolk. Pennekamp never got his dog back. The owner of the plane, having become attached to the dog, refused to give it up, claiming he had not been paid in full for the cost of returning the plane from Norfolk. So Pennekamp lost both a good reporter and a fine dog.

While Colonel Shutts had a sense of humor, it was reserved for talks he was frequently called upon to make at conventions that were coming to Miami in increasing numbers, or for his peers whom he met at exclusive places like the Surf Club or at the Cocolobo Cay Club. But Shutts usually only listened while having a drink with Arthur Brisbane, a Hearst columnist who had a winter home on Brickell Avenue two blocks from Shutts' home. So much did Shutts respect Brisbane that his column was moved to page one in 1932, and no editor dared to change a word. On occasional evenings the publisher and the columnist would get together for cocktails. Brisbane not only was the highest paid newspaper writer in the world but was described by the Hearst syndicate as the "greatest living editor." He had spent all of his life newspapering, and now in his upper years he liked nothing better than the company of someone interested in newspapering and talking over drinks in the evening after he had written his column and delivered it into the hands of a Western Union messenger. Although a publisher, Shutts was not himself a newspaperman in the sense that Brisbane was, and so Shutts listened, with the attention of a disciple, while the editor-columnist expounded on what was right or wrong with the *Herald*. Sometimes Brisbane thought the paper was running "too tight," meaning the ratio of advertising to editorial content was too great for reader appeal. At other times Brisbane thought that the paper appeared to be a little "too open," and that, for economic consideration, the pages could be "tightened" a bit with additional advertising. Kenneth Robson, who did the page layouts for the *Herald* each day, could tell when the publisher had been talking shop with Brisbane the evening before. Shutts always stopped by Robson's desk, usually on his way home, to discuss the layout of the paper and the advertising linage for the next morning. If he had been talking with Brisbane he was likely to say:

"Robbie, don't you think the pages have been a little too tight lately? Maybe we should open them a bit. We must think of our readers, you know."

"Yes, sir, we can," replied Robson.

And if Shutts suggest the pages be tightened a bit, Robson gave him the same answer, "Yes, sir, we can." The truth was that the ratio of editorial content to advertising remained virtually the same day after day, but Robson knew that the best way to get along with the boss was to agree with him rather than to make an attempt at explaining. The result would be embarrassing to Shutts and would mean a lengthy conversation

The Miami Herald

FLORIDA'S MOST IMPORTANT NEWSPAPER

THAN THAT OF ANY OTHER FLORIDA NEWSPAPER

ADVERTISING AND CIRC IN THE MIAMI TERRI

VOL. XXIV; NO. 233 — MONDAY MORNING, JULY 23, 1934 — TEN PAGES TODAY — PRICE FIV

Today

3 Shapiros, All Dead
Ambition Drives
Abraham Lincoln Said People

By ARTHUR BRISBANE

TOP RANKING U.S. ARMY AIR CORPS ASKED

Aviation Committee Recommends Making It Second To None

WOULD ACQUIRE 1,000 NEW PLANES

Predict First Clashes of Next War Will Take Place In Air

BULLETS END DESPERADO'S CAREER

JOHN DILLINGER

PLAY BRIDGE DESPITE 110-DEGREE WEATHER

12 BURNED TO DEATH AS BUS PLUNGES OFF ROAD EMBANKMENT

26 Others Are Injured As Vehicle Is Enveloped In Flames

NEWS SUMMARY

ONE IS KILLED, 3 WOUNDED IN PRISON BREAK

Three Others Escape In Dash From Texas 'Death House'

CONVICT CAUGHT HERE FLEES CELL

Companion of Late Clyde Barrow Among Those Making Getaway

BUSINESS INCREASE IN AUTUMN IS SEEN

Figures of NRA Experts Indicate Decline of Summer Months Below Normal

WOMAN'S DEATH LAID TO PEEPERS

Shot Fatally While Sitting In Indianapolis Park

GEORGIAN KILLED IN CAR MISHAP

Wiley P. McNair of Macon Was Brother of Miamian

MARATHON BIRTHDAY CELEBRATION STARTS

Dillinger Shot To Death By Federal Agents As H Leaves Chicago Thea

15 CRACK MARKSMEN PUT END TO CAREER OF NOTED DESPERADO

Outlaw Had Been Watching Picture Titled 'Manhattan Melodrama'

HIS EXIT AWAITED WITH DRAWN GUNS

Residents of Northwest Side Throng Street To Watch Shooting

FATHER AND SISTER 'KINDER EXPECTING IT'

U.S. WILL CON MAN HUNT F OF MIDWES

AGENTS CAN COLLECT R

Attorney Gene Is 'Only Inci Crime W

DEATHS REACHED 267 FROM SIEGE OF HEAT

Southwest and Midwest Are Hardest Hit By Extended July Scorcher

BANDIT FIRES UPON MIAMIAN AT HIS HOME

GEN. JOHNSON LEAVES ON TRIP TO SAN DIEGO

TYPICAL FRONT PAGE of the *Miami Herald* in the 1930s reflected the conservatism in make-up of the *New York Times,* which pleased Colonel Frank B. Shutts, the publisher. The *Herald* in 1934 had a circulation of 44,206 daily and 44,550 Sunday, and led all other newspapers in Florida in circulation and advertising. On this day, July 23, the *Herald* was only ten pages, reflecting the depressed condition of the times. Note that Arthur Brisbane's column, "Today," appears in the first column.

at a time when Robson was extremely busy with last-minute layout problems. Moreover, Robson knew that Shutts was more interested in the linage of the *Herald's* classified advertising—and that question was yet to come. Shutts had never forgotten what the late Henry "Marse" Watterson, walrus-mustached publisher of the *Louisville Courier-Times* and a frequent Miami visitor, said to him several years before: "You can judge the confidence readers have in a newspaper by the size of its classified advertising section."

Every day Shutts wanted to know the linage for the following morning, the percentage of increase or decrease from the same date last year, the predicted linage for the month, and the predicted linage for the year, together with percentages of increase or decrease. And he wanted also to know how much the *Herald* was leading its competitor, the *Miami News*. Although Robson could have prepared a memo containng this information and put it on Shutts' desk, which he had suggested, the publisher preferred this informal contact with a favorite employee. There was something reassuring in Robson's calm and even voice.

After Brisbane's column was transmitted by Western Union to Universal Service headquarters in New York, the original copy was delivered to the *Herald.* Sometimes, however, the original was so nearly unreadable, having been changed by penciling and overlining, that the copy desk waited for the column to appear on the Universal Service teletype machine. The original was then tossed into a wastepaper can. One night soon after the first edition came out, Shutts called the newsroom.

"Who edited Mr. Brisbane's column?" he demanded.

Charlie Ward, the editor, was put on the telephone. "I did, sir," said Ward, nervously.

"And who gave you authority to cut Mr. Brisbane's column?"

Ward explained that he had used the wire copy out of New York and had made no changes whatever.

"Oh," said Shutts in a relieved tone. "Here, you tell Mr. Brisbane."

Brisbane came on the telephone, and Ward repeated his story. The world's highest paid columnist hemmed and hawed, thanked Ward, and hung up. Half an hour later Shutts was on the telephone again, asking for Ward.

"What did they cut out in New York?" asked Shutts, his curiosity reflected by the impatient tone in his voice.

Ward, as curious as Shutts, already had gone through the wastepaper can and retrieved the original copy. He read to Shutts a short paragraph that did not appear in the wire copy. It was about an "excellent meal" Brisbane had been served at the Roney Plaza Hotel.

"Hmmn," mused Shutts, who then thanked Ward and hung up.

Most of the *Herald's* employees looked upon Shutts as aloof, but the publisher was by no means a cold person. He would have liked to be closer to his employees, but his background as well as the customs of the time combined to inhibit him and to make it impossible for him to display the warmth he felt. The deference with which his executives treated him did nothing to reduce the barrier between the publisher and his employees. He knew few of the *Herald's* people below the administrative level, and to most of the underlings he was virtually a myth. The executives competed among themselves for Shutts' attention, and, although he could not have cared less about the choice of a favorite, the jealousy and infighting did much to keep the publisher distant and aloof. It was not until he had worked on the paper for six years as city editor that Pennekamp had a chance to meet Shutts personally. That was in 1931, during the biennial session of the Florida State Legislature. Shutts had been asked by Governor Carlton to confer with him over the selection of a state racing commission, authorized by the Legislature to license and regulate the operation of pari-mutuel wagering. It was a two-day trip each way in Shutts' chauffeur-driven car, and an unforgettable experience for Pennekamp. The publisher had taken Pennekamp along because he wanted company, and because, as he suggested to Managing Editor Hollums, Pennekamp deserved a vacation. Pennekamp found Shutts to be warmly human; a man who liked to talk—to talk so much, in fact, that after the trip he apologized for "blabbing too much." The publisher's oldest daughter, Marion, was at that time in love with a young man of whom he strongly disapproved, and this bothered him so much he felt compelled to tell his city editor. But he talked mostly about other things, including how John Ullrich, the druggist of Aurora, Indiana, assisted him to get through DePauw University; how a meeting with Henry M. Flagler had resulted in his moving to Miami in 1910; how, through Flagler's assistance, he had acquired the *Miami Morning News-Record,* then founded the *Miami Herald;* even how he had proposed to his attractive secretary as he closed out his law practice in Aurora. So important did these details seem to Pennekamp that in the evenings he jotted down notes on everything he could remember that Shutts had told him that day. Many years later these notes and Pennekamp's memory would be the only record of many small but important details in the life history of Frank B. Shutts.

In the business offices, newsroom, and mechanical departments of the *Herald,* however, Shutts had little opportunity to display his warmer side, and when he did it could be embarrassing if a lowly employee was the object of any notice whatever from the publisher. Hoyt Frazure, a young advertising department employee, had an uncle, Robert H. Seymour, who was a well-known Miami attorney. Seymour had befriended Shutts when he first arrived in Miami in 1909, and Shutts had not forgotten. When Shutts encountered Frazure, on the stairs or in the advertising offices, he was likely to stop him.

"How is your uncle doing, Hoyt?"

"Fine, sir," replied Hoyt.

"Well, tell Mr. Seymour to drop by when he's passing this way," said the publisher. "I'd like to see him again."

"Yes, sir, I will," said Hoyt.

This informal contact between Shutts and a beginning employee aroused the suspicion, jealousy, and ire of the executives. No sooner had Shutts disappeared into his office than the curious executives were plying Frazure with questions.

"What did he say?" asked Advertising Director Charlie Bates.

"What did he say?" asked General Manager George Harper.

Although Frazure's ego was not hurt by these experiences, he felt his job was in jeopardy. After being called into Shutts' office one day he was glad to learn a few hours later that his new assignment would keep him out of the *Herald* in the afternoons, when Colonel Shutts was there.

At least one *Herald* employee was insufficiently impressed by the severe reputation of the publisher to be afraid of him. Reporter Cy Berning, hunting hurriedly for a telephone, rushed into Shutts' office, empty at the time. Dialing his party, he flopped into the publisher's chair, leaned back, and cocked his feet on the desk. Berning, sometimes a windy conversationalist, was still sitting there thirty minutes later when the slender, gray-topped figure of Colonel Shutts entered and glared at him. Berning dropped his feet, jumped up, ended the conversation, and hung up.

"Who are you and what are you doing in my office?" stormed Shutts.

Berning, who was equal to most situations, sought to explain.

"Well," said Shutts, now more calmly, "whenever you enter the boss' office, you never sit in the boss' chair."

Shutts, nearing his middle sixties, had much less interest in the news and editorial content of the *Herald* than he had shown in the early years of the newspaper, particularly prior to the boom years. In those early years, through Editor Frank B. Stoneman, the editorial policy had been set. Judge Stoneman was still editorial writer, although past seventy-five. It did not appear to matter to Shutts that the editorials had become increasingly bland over the years, losing much of the intellectual flavor and pungency that had made them so readable in the pre-World War I years. The buildup of the boom and the flop that had followed had done something to Stoneman. He was no longer quick to want to show through the display of editorial wisdom how wrongs could be righted, and now appeared to share the viewpoint of Shutts that all the cleverness in the world could not "alter the course of the planets or change the twinkle of a single star." Helping Judge Stoneman to write editorials during the 1920s and early 1930s were H. Bond Bliss, Grace Norman Tuttle, and W. Bob Holland. Of the three, Bliss wrote with the greater flair and showed more imagination. All three wrote columns that appeared on the editorial page, a great, gray expanse of type with never a photograph or a cartoon to relieve its dullness. Mrs. Tuttle signed her "Echoes of Miami," as did Holland his "Sidelights." But Bliss' "In Today's News," which appeared in the first column beneath the masthead, was never signed. Bliss delighted in short sentences, often of two or three words, following each other in a staccato and ungrammatical way. The writing was effective, however, for Bliss attracted a great many readers. The column had a special appeal to those who had a feisty outlook toward the world; who were angry and impatient with the unimaginative leadership of the conservatives as well as with the harebrained schemes of the liberals. Bliss' column was infinitely superior to those of Mrs. Tuttle and Holland, which were dull. But Mrs. Tuttle and Holland were suitable for the *Herald* at a time when editorials were confined to flatulent comment about the state, the church, and the rights of individuals, but avoided controversy. What was needed most in the world were leaders with wisdom, who governed with justice and concern for all, and the editorials called upon people to have greater faith in their leaders, as well as greater faith in themselves—they should work hard, practice thrift, and cultivate patience and tolerance until the nation could recover from the economic and social crisis of the 1930s. This line of vacuous reasoning appeared to set well with the publisher.

Colonel Shutts did not interfere with the newsroom any more than he did with the editorial writers. Olin W. Kennedy had created the kind of newspaper that Shutts liked in format and content. Not only was the appearance conservative, like that of the *New York Times,* which Shutts admired, but so was the handling of stories. Neither Shutts nor Kennedy cared for the sensationalizing of stories. Day after day the front page of the city editor looked virtually the same as the previous day, and this format continued after Kennedy resigned in 1928.

Kennedy, broke as a result of habitual gambling, had to borrow money to get to Cleveland where he was to head an organization set up by competing publishers to bargain with labor unions. But the organization folded, leaving Kennedy without a job. And so, the Great Owk, broke as ever, went back to newspapering in the depth of the depression, working variously as a copyreader or in any other position that paid him enough to live. He died at Little Falls, New York, in 1944 at sixty-eight. Kenneth Ballinger, Kennedy's nephew and a former *Herald* reporter, arranged to have the body sent to Miami, where a handful of old acquaintances attended services and burial in Woodlawn Park Cemetery.

The Alabama-born Hollums moved into Kennedy's office as managing editor. He soon discovered his chief talent—that of a wheeler and dealer in the political scene. It was like a vacuum waiting to be filled, and Hollums, shrewd in the ways of southern small town politics, found that he fitted perfectly. Shutts was withdrawing more and more from the political scene. His setbacks due to the end of the boom, together with his developing eye difficulties, now tended to dampen the ardor that had driven him during his early years in Florida. Hollums, in an attempt to fill the void, was soon wielding more political influence, particularly in City Hall, than Shutts had ever attempted to wield. But up the boulevard, sitting in his luxurious office in the Miami News Tower, was the greatest wheeler and dealer of his era—Daniel Mahoney, son-in-law of James M. Cox. Mahoney, handsome and gregarious, had an Irishman's flair for politics. He considered himself a king-maker in local and state politics. He sought to dictate to mayors and to governors in exchange for the support of his newspaper, and, although he suffered many setbacks, still, with his Irish personality and display of optimism, he made countless friends and became a person of considerable power, both for good and for evil in Miami. He liked to think of himself as having influence to get the gravy for people with whom he associated politically and socially, making himself more respected and more powerful over the years. The governor, members of the Florida Legislature, United States senators, and congressmen were as close to him as the telephone. He used his influence for good, too, raising millions of dollars for the University of Miami.

The *Herald's* influence was greater than that of the *News,* and Hollums was quick to take advantage of this. While he never attained anything like the prestige of the incomparable Mahoney, who moved in circles of establishment society denied to Hollums, he did become a behind-the-scenes boss who had to be reckoned with. City commissioners soon saw the wisdom of checking with Hollums in order to see how the *Herald* "felt" about activities in City Hall. Through the influence of Hollums, the *Herald's* former government reporter, L. L. Lee, became Miami city manager. In 1935 when the Miami police chief was almost certain to be fired by an angry commission, Hollums sought to have "one of my boys" named to the job. He sent word to police reporter Henry Reno he wanted to see him. Always suspicious of big-shot editors who called him in, Reno wondered what was up now. Entering Hollums' office, he remained standing until asked to be seated, and then he sat uncertainly on the edge of his chair.

"Henry," said Hollums, leaning back in his swivel chair and studying the bespectacled police reporter, "Henry, how would you like to be chief of police?"

"No, sir," replied Reno promptly, "I'm not qualified to be police chief."

"If you want to put it that way, neither is the man the city commission is considering," snapped Hollums, irritated at Reno's reply.

Reno knew that the man being considered was H. Leslie Quigg, who had served as police chief during most of the 1920s. Although Quigg might not have been outstanding material for police chief, he was capable of the political maneuvering the job required. Reno was not.

As a newspaper influential with its readers, the *Herald* was affected but little by the politics of Hollums. Every morning the *Herald* presented the same conservative front page to its readers when they opened the paper to read it over toast and coffee. The headlines, the way the stories were presented, and the absence of catchy nonsense and sensationalism seemed to inspire dependability and generate hope in its readers at a time when the future economic and political conditions of the nation and the world were very much in doubt. This doesn't mean that the *Herald* was without critics among its readers, some of whom disliked its ultra-conservatism in politics and its defense of old-fashioned economic policies. But after its declining circulation became stabilized in the 1930s, the *Herald* began a steady growth, while the *Miami News* grew at a lesser rate. And the *News* lagged despite its being the brighter-looking paper, which played its stories in bigger headlines, used more illustrations, and carried editorials that were more significant and meaningful than the *Herald's*. Although a good newspaper—probably a better newspaper than the *Herald* during that period—the *News* failed to elicit the confidence given to the morning paper. And this was discernible particularly in advertising. The *Herald,* in front as the 1920s closed, maintained an increasing lead during the 1930s, growing at a faster pace after Jack Knight succeeded Colonel Shutts as publisher.

REPORTER Henry Reno was offered job of Miami police chief by Managing Editor Ellis Hollums, Sr., but turned it down.

11

Sunshine Rediscovered

T HE DISCOVERY OF Florida's winter sun by Colonel Henry L. Doherty, founder and chairman of Cities Service, proved to be worth infinitely more to the Miami area than would have been the discovery of an oil field on Flagler Street. Doherty early in 1929 suffered an illness that undermined his health, and on the advice of his doctor he and his wife came to Florida to the Miami Biltmore Hotel. Doherty was impressed by the beauty and magnificence of the Mediterranean style structure in its setting in the piney woods countryside of Coral Gables, together with its luxurious country club and golf course. His health recovered quickly, for which he credited the Florida sunshine, and he fell so deeply in love with the area that he and his wife went house hunting. They found a gem on Main Highway in Coconut Grove—El Jardin, then the finest example of residential architecture in Miami outside of James Deering's Villa Vizcaya. Designed by Richard Kiehnel in the Mediterranean tradition, with Moorish overtones, the mansion was built in 1919. Doherty found it convenient to purchase the ten-acre property in the name of Cities Service. Now with an anchor in Florida, he purchased the Miami Biltmore, the Roney Plaza Hotel on Miami Beach, and the Key Largo Anglers' Club on Key Largo. To integrate his properties for the convenience of hotel guests, he formed the Florida Year Round Clubs, with the Miami Biltmore Country Club, Roney Plaza Cabana Club, and Key Largo Anglers' Club as members.

Colonel Doherty—the "Colonel" was honorary—was a feisty little man with white hair and a white goatee. With his cold eyes and horn-rimmed glasses he resembled Leon Trotsky. More than once Doherty was taken for the sharp-witted Russian, and, although the capitalist professed to be mortified, he privately enjoyed the thought that he might possess energy and leadership comparable to the revolutionary, then in exile in Mexico. Doherty was sixty-two when he began acquiring Florida hotels. With Trotskylike directness he sought to put them on a paying basis. And to promote his hotels and sell Florida sunshine, he hired one of the nation's top public relations men, Carl Byoir. Operating with virtually a blank check, Byoir invited newsmen, columnists, and magazine writers to stay at the Miami Biltmore for a dollar a day. Among the first to accept Byoir's offer was liberal columnist Heywood Broun, who, while attacking the economic royalists of the 1930s, found it convenient to ignore Colonel Doherty. Westbrook Pegler, labor union-baiting columnist, paid one dollar a day for a luxury vacation at the Biltmore, then went away to attack Doherty not as an economic royalist but as a conniver and swindler. Byoir, however, did not care what Pegler called Doherty if he mentioned the Biltmore, which he did. And so Byoir succeeded so well in his promotion that for a time during the middle 1930s "Miami Biltmore" was used as a dateline for stories filed by wire services. For half a dozen years the Biltmore was virtually a wintertime extension of the White House. While the hotel may have been "in the sticks," as one columnist described it, the location proved ideal for the New Deal brass like James A. Farley, postmaster general and political mastermind for President Roosevelt, and Harry Hopkins, trouble-shooting head of the president's "brain trust." For a time the Biltmore also was the wintertime "in" place for wealthy social climbers as well as for New Deal personalities; and they frequently rubbed shoulders with tuxedo-clad big-time hoodlums around the gaming tables of the hotel's plush gambling casino.

To provide communication between the Biltmore and the Roney Plaza, Doherty operated a fleet of Aero-cars, a trailer type bus drawn by an automobile. One of the drivers was young Bebe Rebozo, who years later would become a close friend and confidant of President Richard Nixon. But the Aero-cars were slow; it was a twelve-mile trip from the Biltmore to the Roney, through downtown Miami's traffic, while the boat trip to Key Largo was nearly thirty miles. So Byoir got the idea of adding service by autogyro, a forerunner of the helicopter, for those who wished to travel faster. Doherty lost money on his hotel operations, particularly the Biltmore, whose 500 rooms were seldom filled, but he may have considered the satisfaction he received worth the cost. His association with the New Dealers paid off handsomely. It was at a time when many of the nation's big-time capitalists were under federal investigation in connection with alleged stock manipulations. Congress was seeking scapegoats to blame for the depression, and Colonel Doherty was among those under suspicion. When a federal marshal sought to serve Doherty with a summons to appear before a hearing in Washington, he retired to a suite in the Biltmore tower. There he remained day after day while a

PROMOTER extraordinary, Carl Byoir, at John Pennekamp's urging, raised funds to make Miami's first Orange Bowl game possible.

CITIES SERVICE chairman Colonel Henry H. Doherty kept to his tower apartment in the Miami Biltmore Hotel while a federal marshal, waiting to serve a warrant, cooled his heels in the lobby, with reporters and photographers for company.

process server waited in the lobby, together with bored newsmen and photographers. Doherty invited his friends up to play bridge or have drinks, and outlasted the process servers until the Washington hearings were over. Byoir went to work on a project that would prevent anything like this from happening again; he promoted the annual Franklin D. Roosevelt Birthday Ball, the proceeds going to fight infantile paralysis. For this Doherty forked over $75,000, after which the federal investigators stopped investigating him.

To Doherty must go the credit for helping Miami to launch its annual Orange Bowl parade and football game. He gave $5,000 to bring the University of Manhattan football team to Miami in 1933 for a New Year's game with the University of Miami Hurricanes, and he put up the visiting team in the Biltmore. Money was scarce. The city of Miami was broke. George E. Hussey, official greeter for the city and athletic director for the Florida Power & Light Company, went to John Pennekamp with the problem of raising money. Pennekamp called Carl Byoir. Byoir went to Doherty and got the money. The unexpected defeat of the northern team by the Hurricanes boosted the spirits of the depression-ridden area, and from this small beginning grew the annual Orange Bowl game and its attendant festivities.

Doherty spent large sums to promote and advertise Florida. The tourist business during the winter season of 1932-33 increased fifteen percent above that of the previous year at a time when travel and tourist trade were declining elsewhere. Despite the depression a few had money, and Miami, with its horse and dog racing, casino gambling, and warm sunshine in January and February, was made highly attractive by Byoir's promotion. But during the summer the town was virtually dead. The resort hotels, none air-conditioned, closed, and most of the wealthy and influential left for the summer. The *Herald* was dead in summer, too. Desk men below news editor and city editor, together with virtually all the reporters, were asked to take an extra month's vacation without pay. The "vacationing" men sought outside jobs. Charlie Ward got a job one summer doing publicity for the Reverend C. Roy Angell, pastor of Central Baptist Church. Despite the publicity Ward was able to get into the *Herald,* there was no appreciable increase in church attendance or in collections. Nor did Ward receive the compensation he was expecting. Eventually he went to Dr. Angell.

"But you haven't earned anything—and furthermore you were doing God's work," said Dr. Angell.

Ward eventually received his pay, but before he did he decided that preachers could be the devil to work for.

The editorial department and the advertising department had exchanged floors in 1930—the editors and reporters moving up to the third floor, the advertising salesmen moving down to the second. Summer brought hordes of mosquitoes that entered the unscreened windows. Copyreaders and reporters wrapped their ankles with newspapers and made smudges in wastepaper cans to discourage the pests. Still the mosquitoes bit reporter Henry Cavendish until he would jump up from his chair, cursing them in his tenor voice and denouncing Colonel Shutts, who spent the summer in the Berkshires and was unaware of the mosquito plagues. Cavendish partly solved the mosquito problem by wearing spats.

Miami's metropolitan area began to grow in the middle 1930s, with Miami Beach setting the pace. The *Herald's* circulation set a new record in 1935, with daily circulation passing 50,000 for the first time. In 1930 the population of Miami Beach had been only 6,500, in spite of the fabulous 1920s. But the Beach quadrupled its population in the 1930s, growing to 28,000 by 1940. And this growth was made while economic depression was wracking the rest of the nation. Two important things happened during the decade: Jews discovered Miami Beach, and the construction of oceanfront "hotel row" north of the Roney Plaza was started.

Until the middle 1930s Miami Beach had been widely promoted as a winter vacationland where beautiful bathing girls displayed their charms under coconut palms growing along the beach. But the brochures of most hotels included a warning that the clientele was restricted to gentiles. Some hotels brazenly exhibited "No Jews" signs on registration desks. The Beach did have a few Jewish hotels and apartment houses in the early 1930s, but they were clustered about the south end of the Beach. "High class" Jews were welcome in the anti-Semitic strip north of Lincoln Road; these were the wealthy Jews with money to spend. These Jews kept coming and spending their money, and many came to live the year round. By 1935 the population was twice that of 1930. Then construction began on a new string of high-rise resort hotels during the last half of the 1930s.

It was the Whitman Hotel, opening in 1935, that served as a pacesetter for hotel row. The builder, W. F. Whitman, Sr., owned a hotel in Chicago that had been designed by architect Roy F. France. While in Miami in the winter of 1932 spending a golfer's vacation at the Miami Biltmore, France called on Whitman, who had a winter home at Miami Beach. Whitman told him he was thinking about building a hotel there. This was enough to induce France to pack up and move from Chicago to Florida.

"I wasn't doing anything in Chicago," said France, "and living was cheaper at Miami Beach."

By the time France settled in Florida, Whitman told him to go ahead on plans for a hotel. The Whitman proved to be an immediate success. The country wasn't broke after all, and the Whitman was packed during January, February, and March of 1935. After that France was kept busy designing resort hotels for the next several years; these included the Edgewater Beach, Patrician, Shoremede, Ocean Grande, Sands, White House, Cadillac, National, Sea Isle, and Versailles. Miami Beach's skyline was changing rapidly. Thousands of new tourists were coming every winter, a high percentage of them New York Jews. Most of the Jews were business people who had money to invest as well as to spend on a Miami Beach vacation. They began going into the hotel business in a big way. So many Jews moved to Miami Beach during the latter half of the 1930s that of the 28,000 population in 1940 nearly 6,000 were Jewish, their number practically equaling the city's 1930 population. Visitors, meanwhile, were far more numerous than the permanent residents, exceeding 50,000 in 1938, the *Herald* noted. But hotel owners worried as they watched the skeletons of new hotels rise. Here was a boom in the midst of depression, and it didn't make sense. One morning in the spring of 1938 a delegation of hotel owners, merchants, and investors—most of them Jewish—called on Claude A. Renshaw, Miami Beach city manager since 1925.

"Mr. Renshaw, you've got to find a way to prevent the construction of any more hotels," said a member of the delegation. "Miami Beach is overbuilt."

"We'll all go bankrupt," said another.

"You've got to stop issuing permits," demanded a third.

Finally the explosions of concern ended, and Renshaw looked at the semicircle of faces waiting for him to make the next move.

"Gentlemen," said the city manager, speaking for the first time, "I can't stop the construction of new hotels at Miami Beach."

Renshaw waited for a new flurry of squalls to pass.

"But the Beach is already overbuilt," they said. "What are we going to do?"

"I don't agree with you about Miami Beach being overbuilt," replied Renshaw. "When you increase the number of hotel rooms the next thing to do is increase the promotion and advertising—and fill the rooms."

Miami Beach's promotion and advertising budget was increased, the number of winter visitors increased in proportion, and the new hotel rooms were filled. By 1940 Miami Beach was drawing 75,000 visitors a year—and across Biscayne Bay the city of Miami was becoming a bedroom community for the thousands employed by the tourist industry. Miami Beach pride was expanding rapidly, too, and the island's leaders began talking about getting out of Dade County and founding a new county. This kind of talk grew out of the high taxes hotel row was paying to the county, for which the owners felt they received little in return. Moreover, the Miami Beach establishment wanted to exercise more control over vice, particularly gambling, rather than have to share the pie, in graft payments, with the sheriff's department across the bay.

But the sheriff and his deputies were not the only ones taking graft. The prohibition era and the permissiveness of South Florida's leaders toward a "little sin"—gambling, prostitution, and associated evils—had done something to the area's moral fiber. The "little larceny in every man's heart" was beginning to show in the middle 1930s. And it affected not just the lowest and the meanest in society, but touched the great and the mighty, the most respected and stalwart of the area's citizens. Even Miami's Judge of Criminal Court, E. C. Collins, was accused of soliciting a bribe. But who would have expected to find larceny in the federal judiciary? The larcenous federal judge was Halsted L. Ritter, Frank B. Shutts' classmate at DePauw University.

Ugly rumors had spread among members of the judge's profession that all was not right with Ritter's record. The rumors reached United States Congressman from Florida J. Mark Wilcox of West Palm Beach. Wilcox initiated an investigation that quietly went into Ritter's private affairs, with the result that the judge of the Federal District Court in Miami was haled before Congress, where he was tried on seven counts of misconduct in connection with his handling of bankruptcy cases, including the allowance of huge fees to lawyers and the alleged acceptance of a $4,500 kickback. Ritter's impeachment shocked Shutts, who was responsible for his appointment as federal judge, and his friends in suburban Coconut Grove where he lived. Many of them Republicans would never believe in Ritter's guilt but would blame the Democrats, whom they accused of framing the venerable judge. Ritter's neighbors were among the elite of the Miami area. They looked upon the judge, a man of great charm when off the bench, as a person of unquestionable honesty and respectability. Ritter was a white-haired, easy going, and scholarly man; as a judge, was patricianlike, remindful of a Roman senator. A social lion, Ritter was seldom home in the evenings when the city desk asked a reporter to call and get his comment on some story about the federal court. But Cy Berning, after covering the court for several years, got to know pretty well what Ritter would say anyway. And so, when he couldn't reach a source—Berning would make up a quotation. Although he worried about the judge's reaction next day, it was always good.

"Couldn't have said it better myself," said Ritter, leaning back in his swivel chair and pressing the tips of his long fingers together.

Berning and Ritter developed an easy friendship, although one far from cronyism. Whenever the reporter dropped into the judge's office on quiet days he would frequently sit for thirty minutes while they engaged in relaxed conversation. One day the judge produced a photograph of a mural that soon was to be hung in the courtroom of the new federal building, then nearing completion. Done by artist Denman Fink under the auspices of the WPA, the painting depicted the development of the law, from the earliest times to the present. Berning noted the figures of Egyptians, Jews, Greeks, and Romans, as well as early Christian monks. Most of the monks were bent over tables recording the laws in Latin, but one monk represented the Spanish Inquisition, and his eyes glared villainously from the mural. If Berning had been a Protestant or a Hebrew this might not have disturbed him, but he was a Catholic and very sensitive to pictures of villainous-looking monks. As Berning departed, Ritter reminded him that the photograph had been shown to him in confidence and that nothing was to be written about the mural until its unveiling. But Berning worried. A few days later, in answer to his conscience, he went to Gesu Catholic Church, near the Federal Building, and related to a priest with whom he was acquainted the horrible picture he had seen in Judge Ritter's chambers. Two weeks later, after complaints had cleared first the Catholic hierarchy and then the federal bureaucracy in Washington, all hell broke loose. The mural was withdrawn before the public had a chance to see it, and Fink was ordered to do another. But Judge Ritter never sat beneath the new mural, having been impeached before it was completed. He did not miss much, for the substitute is a noncontroversial, highly idealized representation of South Florida's people working together in various industries. At the apex of a compositional triangle is a federal judge administering justice. Reporters who covered the federal court after Ritter's departure used to study the judge in the mural and shift their eyes to the figure of Ritter's successor, John W. Holland, to note the unquestionable likeness.

Just before the investigation that would result in the trial and impeachment of Ritter, Miami got a new newspaper, the *Miami Tribune*. Its publisher was Moses L. Annenberg, who controlled a nationwide race wire service. At the time Ritter was haled before Congress, the tabloid was riding at the height of its glory and claiming a circulation of 100,000. The *Tribune* saw that Ritter's trial created more than a scandal in the federal judiciary; the tabloid used Ritter as ammunition to strengthen its attacks against the *Miami Herald* and its publisher, Colonel Shutts. Ninety witnesses for and against Ritter were heard by the Senate. The trial was in progress for several days, providing a constant flow of sensational headline material for the *Tribune.*

The trial brought out what appeared to be a sorry connivance between federal judges and lawyers in the handling of receivership cases, which were numerous during the depression. Fees sometimes equaled the value of a bankrupt firm's assets. Lawyers not only claimed and were allowed exorbitant fees, they received one hundred percent on the dollar in payment, while bondholders and preferred stockholders might be lucky to receive anything after a bankrupt firm's assets had been liquidated. In the years ahead many other scandals involving depression-time bankruptcies would be uncovered by federal prosecutors, but such investigative work by reporters was uncommon in the 1930s. Few reporters were sufficiently trained to examine the complicated records of firms in receivership or to recognize suspected thievery. But a newspaper like the *Tribune* needed to do no investigative work to come up with sensational stories.

The Senate found Ritter guilty by the exact two-thirds majority required by the Constitution for impeachment. All three Miami newspapers missed an ironic turn in the Senate voting. The decisive ballot was cast by Senator Sherman Minton of Indiana. Minton had been a friend of both Ritter and Shutts, and between 1925 and 1928 had been a member of the law firm of Shutts & Bowen. Leaving Miami because of a decline in legal work, Minton returned to Indiana, his home state, and went into politics.

Through the influence of his friend Shutts, Ritter was saved the embarrassment of having to face possible disbarment proceedings, thus providing additional ammunition for *Tribune* attacks. Eventually Ritter set up a law practice in Miami. He lived until 1951, dying at eight-three and claiming to the end that he was innocent. But innocent or not, Shutts never forgave his onetime classmate for the gross mismanagement of his affairs that brought about his impeachment.

12

Yellow Journalism
at its Best

MOSES L. ANNENBERG may have been looked upon by Shutts as being only a cut above an underworld character, but for a three-year period in the 1930s he wielded through a sensational morning tabloid an influence in Miami that seldom has been surpassed in journalism. The *Miami Tribune* was dismissed by its competitors, particularly the *Miami Herald,* as a scandal sheet and an example of yellow journalism at its worst. But under an aggressive, suspicious, and cynical editor, Paul G. Jeans, the *Tribune,* within a few months after its inception in November 1934, experienced an explosive growth that gave it the largest circulation in Florida. And while it was giving its competitors the equivalent of a journalistic hotfoot, the *Tribune's* effect upon the local scene was virtually traumatic.

Although the *Tribune's* nosy reporters may not have uncovered as many scandals in City Hall as the paper claimed, its way of handling stories, with bold, screaming headlines, gave them a shocking quality that the *Herald's* more conservative presentation lacked. Jeans, given free rein to pursue his kind of journalism, recognized no sacred cows. The paper tackled the mayor, commissioners, city manager, police, and pompous bigwigs with equal energy, puncturing egos by revealing their shortcomings and misdeeds. Had the *Tribune* been in the hands of a less erratic, more mature, and fair editor, as seriously concerned with the building of a community as he was in tearing it down, this scandalizing tabloid possibly could have become Miami's dominant and most influential newspaper. But the *Tribune* was an anachronism in journalism. Published by a man whose reputation was only slightly better than that of Al Capone, the daily tabloid could hardly have been expected to be honest and, like Caesar's wife, above suspicion. Although the *Tribune* did give a proper play to scandal, constantly revealing an unholy alliance between the establishment, public officials, and the police, it was the kind of newspaper you could not bring yourself to respect. And as you read it you felt embarrassed, glancing over your shoulders to see if anyone was looking.

Although the *Tribune* constantly lost money, Annenberg could well afford it. Despite a depression, Annenberg was enjoying an income as great as anyone else in America—about $5 million a year. And, as was to be revealed later in his trial on charges of income tax evasion, he was pocketing most of it. Annenberg had nationwide control of racing information, and his services went to horse bookmakers in every major city. In Dade and Broward counties he was reported to have more than 100 subscribers for his service, which gave instant results from horse tracks. He also published the *Racing Form,* printed in eight major cities, including Miami. And he published the more respectable New York *Morning Telegraph,* which covered the theater as well as horse racing and other sports.

The son of an immigrant Jewish junk dealer in Chicago, Annenberg at seventeen started tending bar in a tough West Side saloon. In 1899, when

MOSES L. ANNENBERG

MIAMI TRIBUNE Editor Paul Jeans, far right, and reporter Shannon Cormack, second from left, pose with their lawyers on the courthouse steps after their acquittal in 1935 of criminal libel charges. The attorneys are K. D. (Pete) Harris, far left; James M. Carson, center; and, to Carson's left, M. Victor Miller. Jeans and Miller were killed in an automobile accident, April 18, 1937.

twenty-one, he began working in the circulation department of Hearst's *Chicago American,* quickly rising to circulation manager. The circulation wars ignited by Moe and his brother, Max, circulation manager of Hearst's *Chicago Examiner,* became a scandalous chapter in the newspaper business. Leaving Chicago for Milwaukee, Annenberg, in addition to controlling the circulation of Chicago papers in that area, invested in restaurants, drugstores, pool halls, and bowling alleys, becoming a millionaire before he was thirty. In 1920 Annenberg moved to New York as head of circulation for newspapers and magazines for the entire Hearst empire. Although many times a millionaire, money wasn't coming in fast enough, nor had he attained the respectability for his family that was with him a driving ambition. In the meantime, he had met Arthur Brisbane, the great Hearst editor. Annenberg identified publishers and important editors with the elite, as lions of respectability in a field where fortune, fame, and influence were synonymous. So now, through Brisbane's influence, he ventured into the publishing field.

Annenberg's first venture can hardly be identified with the ultimate in respectability, yet it proved to be the beginning of a vast new fortune. In 1922 he bought the *Racing Form,* a new publication. By 1930 Annenberg was printing the *Racing Form* in more than half a dozen major cities, while his racing information wire service had grown to be one of American Telephone & Telegraph's biggest customers. In the fall of each year he moved his family from his Long Island mansion to Miami Beach, to the respectable Family Jacobs Hotel Alamac. Daily he drove across Biscayne Bay to Miami, where his *Racing Form* was printed in a ramshackle building at Northwest First Avenue and Twenty-First Street. During the winter of 1933-34, in an agreement with a group of resort acquaintances, Annenberg printed a tabloid, the *Miami Beach Tribune.* The paper folded after three months. Annenberg in the meantime had sought to buy the *Miami Herald.* When rebuffed by Colonel Shutts, Annenberg launched his own paper.

Neither Annenberg nor his editor, Paul Jeans, could have foreseen the splash the *Miami Tribune* was to make. When first hawked in the streets for two cents a copy, it made little stir. But then the *Tribune* got a break, a gangland style killing. In order to appreciate this break, however, one should know what the Miami area was like in the middle 1930s.

Both Miami and Miami Beach were wide open to gambling and prostitution, with the assent of the establishment. You could walk into any pool hall in downtown or into almost any Miami Beach hotel and place a bet on your favorite horse. Not only were horse bets being taken openly within a block of the *Miami Herald,* but slot machines could be heard whirring as you passed along the sidewalk, and you could walk into any cigar stand and take your chances on a variety of punchboards. Bolita was run openly, too, but in the 1930s was confined mainly to the black districts. In the evenings you could take your wife or your girlfriend to any of several clubs on either side of Biscayne Bay, dine, see a floor show, and then wind up the evening by strolling into gaming rooms to roll dice, play blackjack, or bet on the turn of a roulette wheel. In the better places the costs were high and men were required to wear tuxedos to be admitted. Miami's established newspapers, the *Miami Herald* and the *Miami News,* gave silent approval of the permissive attitude toward a "little sin." Fred Pine, the county solicitor, had been elected on a platform that promised "liberal" law enforcement. Outsiders, such as the hoodlums of New York and Chicago, were discouraged, and the newspapers could point with pride to the absence of gangland type warfare such as northern cities were experiencing.

Then, just after Christmas in 1934, a dapper, tough-minded gambler and bookmaker, George "Skeets" Downs, was taken for a "ride" into the edge of the Everglades northwest of Miami. Downs' bullet-riddled body, with a powder-burned *coup de grace* in the head, was found by a hunting party. It had been the second similar killing in less than two months. On October 30 a Miami Beach bookmaker, Leo Bornstein, was slain by a hail of bullets after he was called to answer a telephone in the hall of the apartment building where he lived. Although that story broke before the *Tribune* began publishing, the slaying of Downs made it page-one material again. Blaming the killings on the underworld, the *Tribune* played the stories in screaming headlines. A grand jury was convened. Although it failed to indict anyone in connection with the two slayings, an indictment was returned that proved to be sensational. Judge E. C. Collins of Criminal Court was indicted on charges of accepting a bribe of $465 from an illiterate farmer of Jemison, Alabama, John W. Davis, in exchange for the release of his son, who was in jail on a charge of stealing an automobile. While the *Herald* stuck with its one-column head policy—"Miami Judge/Named By/Grand Jury"—the *Tribune* spread headlines and story all over its tabloid front page.

Judge Collins was a staunch pillar of Miami society, prudish, and a stickler for decorum in his court. Nobody—except for a few close to him—had ever questioned his integrity. He also was a severe judge. If you were found guilty you could expect no mercy. He was an ardent churchgoer and was head of the Men's Bible Class at Miami's First Baptist Church. Miamians, including the editors of the *Herald* and the *News,* were dubious about the charges. But the *Tribune's* editor, Jeans, read the text of the indictment with the firm conviction that Collins was a rascal. The illiterate farmer who had given Collins the money, which the indictment said the judge pocketed, was too guileless to lie, Jeans reasoned. Jeans' instinct told him that Collins, while flouting his religion and morals, was, underneath, a shyster judge and a cheap crook.

"City Hall is filled with crooks," shouted Jeans to a group of reporters after the final edition of his paper had gone to press with the Collins story. Jeans leaned back in a swivel chair, propped his feet upon a makeshift desk made by laying a door over two sawhorses, and puffed on a cigarette at the end of a long holder that he held between his teeth. "We're going to clean up this town, men," he said to the group, which included a woman reporter, Jeanne Bellamy. "We're going to fire all our big guns."

On January 29 another highly respected Miamian, Joe H. Adams, manager of El Comodoro Hotel, was arrested on federal charges that he helped to harbor Alvin Karpis, notorious outlaw and partner of Fred Barker in the kidnaping of Edward G. Bremer, Saint Paul, Minnesota, banker whose family paid $200,000 ransom for his release. Only three days before Adams' arrest a task force of Federal Bureau of Investigation agents had slain Barker and his mother, Kate "Ma" Barker, in a hideout at Oklawaha, in northern Florida, after a five-hour gun battle. The *Herald* had played down the Oklawaha battle under a headline saying "5 Are Killed/In Three Battles/With Outlaws." This big Florida story, containing all the drama one could imagine during the period of John Dillinger, Baby Face Nelson, Bonnie Parker, and Clyde Barrow, was grouped in a story with the slaying of three outlaws in other states, while the *Tribune* came out with extra editions that sold as fast as news-hungry people could buy them. The news of this gun battle topped off three days later with the arrest of Joe Adams, who was one of the leaders in the local American Legion, sent *Tribune* reporters to the dictionary in search of new adjectives to describe the rapidly unfolding sensational events. The *Tribune* sensationalized the story further by connecting, through association, the names of other prominent Miamians, including Robert "Bob" Knight, Adams' father-in-law and owner of El Comodoro Hotel and Biscayne Kennel Club; his brother, John C. Knight, a former city commissioner whom the paper described as "one of the powers behind the throne in the City Hall Gang," and Sam McCreary, Miami public safety director, onetime employee of Adams. The *Tribune* intimated Bob Knight's involvement because he had put up Adams' bond. McCreary's dismissal was demanded because of his previous association with Adams. So many were the story breaks that the *Tribune* was pressed to find space for them. At the time of Adams' arrest the front page not only was still occupied with the Collins indictment but also with one of the most sensational jewel robberies in Miami's history.

On the night of January 26 two bandits had followed wealthy Mrs. Margaret Hawksworth Bell and Harry Content, suave New York stockbroker, from the horse races at Hialeah Park to their adjoining suites in the Miami Biltmore Hotel. Gaining entrance to Mrs. Bell's suite on the pretext of delivering flowers, the masked men tied up their victims and slipped away with jewelry insured by Lloyds of London for $185,000, together with Content's platinum watch and $200 in cash. The robbery and the fantastic developments that followed gave the *Tribune* headline material for weeks and months. Six days later Miami Beach police arrested Charles Cali, whom they had caught dismantling a stolen bicycle. Searching his room, police found Harry Content's platinum watch. Cali admitted his part in the holdup and implicated Nicholas "Little Nicky" Montone, who was arrested in New York. He talked, too, but said the jewels had been turned over to a man in Miami. Meanwhile, an insurance company detective, Noel Scaffa, had been in Miami huddling with police and prosecutors. On March 18, Sergeant E. C. Bryan of the Miami Beach police reported he got a call from a man who directed him to be at the desk of the Flamingo Hotel at 6:15 p.m. Bryan went to the hotel, accompanied by a private detective, Charles Harrington, who represented Scaffa. Nobody at the hotel desk knew anything about a call, but when Bryan and Harrington returned to their car they found the Bell jewels inside, wrapped in black paper, Bryan reported.

Although both bandits had admitted the robbery, at their trial in Criminal Court Cali denied knowing Montone. Allowed to plead guilty to unarmed robbery, Cali got eight years and Montone went free. It had not mattered to Prosecutor Fred Pine or to Judge Ben C. Willard that the holdup victims had identified the suspects and had testified that both were armed. It looked like somebody had been paid off, and the *Tribune* said so. Meanwhile, Henry L. Doherty, owner of the Biltmore, had hired his own lawyers and detectives. They arranged to have Chief D. E. Sox of the Coral Gables police swear out a warrant for Cali and Montone, charging them with armed robbery. The pair was arrested as they left the courtroom. On that same day J. Edgar Hoover released a statement in Washington which implicated Scaffa, Harrington, and Sergeant Bryan in an insurance payoff. The *Tribune* already had a confession from Bryan, but was holding the story at the request of the FBI until Hoover could release his statement. Now the *Tribune* published the payoff arrangements—$15,000 to police, lawyers, and insurance company representatives involved in the case. The money was never paid, of course.

Cali and Montone, tried on the new charges, were found guilty of armed robbery and sentenced to long prison terms. Sergeant Bryan was fired.

Scaffa was convicted in New York on charges of transporting stolen jewelry and of perjury, and was sentenced to prison. In a transcript of testimony, Scaffa was quoted as remarking:

"You talk about fixing prosecutors down there (Florida) just as you talk about taking a drink."

No further charges were filed, and the lesser figures went free. But this only gave the *Tribune* more ammunition to fire at Pine, whom the paper nicknamed "The Vindicator" because he appeared so often to be on the side of the defendant. But the *Tribune* had by now declared open season on the majority of Miami's public officials, including Mayor E. G. Sewell, nicknamed "Windy Ev"; Safety Director Sam McCreary, called "Crooked Sam"; and the city manager, L. L. Lee, referred to as "the *Herald's* boy." City Hall, the county prosecutor's office, and the police were linked by the tabloid with the underground—with thieves, robbers, gamblers, and murderers. The *Tribune's* attacks against local officials had the sound of a shrill cry. To the officials, particularly the mayor, the attacks were intolerable. Sewell was cartooned with a woodpecker pecking at his shock of iron gray hair, which he let grow to hide an ugly wen on the back of his neck. Having enjoyed a sacrosanct position in Miami for more than a quarter century, Sewell was accustomed to a toadying attitude by the *Herald* and the *News.* So upset did he become over the tabloid's attacks that he frequently interrupted commission meetings to rant at *Tribune* reporters present.

Meanwhile, the public was eating up the *Tribune's* stories and laughing at the cartoons. So much dirt had been uncovered in City Hall that people were beginning to wonder whether the *Tribune* was the only courageous paper in Miami. Meanwhile, Judge Collins was tried on several counts of embezzlement, but the case ended in a hung jury. The next morning the *Tribune's* headlines shouted "4 Fixed Jurors Save/Collins From Chains." At his next trial Collins preferred not to face a jury and threw himself on the mercy of the court. After a conference with Collins' attorneys, he was let off free in exchange for his resignation. Although his guilt was indicated in a letter he signed, Collins was not required to plead guilty. Instead of being kicked out of the Florida bar, he was allowed to resign. This permitted him to return to his former home in Ocilla, Georgia, to practice law and teach Bible in the Baptist Sunday school. But while Pine was helping his friend Collins to get off, he was not forgetting the jury-fixing accusation by the *Tribune.* He filed criminal libel charges against Jeans and Shannon Cormack, the reporter who had written the story.

Jeans employed attorney James M. Carson. Although the *Tribune* came up with such alleged "jury fixers" as H. S. "Homebrew" Kelly and C. H. Robertson, the "Mayor of Ojus," the testimony at the trial was nonproductive, other than that the court got to hear Robertson described as being "more evil in Broward County than in Dade." The *Tribune* lacked evidence other than heresay to back up its accusations of jury fixing in the Collins case, and only Carson's clever handling of the case got Jeans and Cormack off the hook.

Although not quite six months old, the *Tribune* in 1935 put up its own candidates for the Miami City Commission. Among them was one of Miami's better known citizens, R. C. Gardner, a well-to-do but politically naive groceryman. "The Three Musketeers," as the *Tribune* dubbed them, made a surprisingly good showing, but none got elected. Still, the close voting showed the meteoric influence of the tabloid. It was about this time that the wily editor, Jeans, cocked his feet upon his desk, lit a cigarette, and called for one of his investigative reporters.

"I want you to go down to City Hall and look up the records of George F. McCall, the clerk of Criminal Court," he ordered the reporter. "I think he's a damn crook."

Jeans had received a tip that McCall was missing and that there was a shortage of funds in his office. The *Tribune* soon had new headline material, giving the other papers a beating. A state auditor took over the missing clerk's office and soon confirmed the tabloid's charges. McCall, penniless, was arrested several months later in San Diego. He was returned, tried, and sentenced to ten years in prison, much to the injury of Jeans' conscience. The clerk obviously lacked the influence of his former boss, Judge Collins. The *Tribune* remarked editorially that McCall may have been the first Dade County official to be sentenced to prison for stealing.

A short time later City Clerk Harold Ross was fired after a $20,000 shortage was discovered in his office. Ross admitted a shortage but said the money had gone to pay campaign workers for various city commissioners he had been ordered to employ but was unauthorized to add to the city's official payroll. But Ross never had to face criminal charges. Too many City Hall "big-wigs would have to be implicated," explained the *Tribune.*

The *Tribune's* attacks on public officials caused tempers to flare, with threats of violence to reporters and photographers. A series of articles accusing the police of brutality and lumping all of them as Cossacks sent them into quick action. Detective Eddie Melchen, upset by a story written by Charles Davis, punched the reporter in the face while Miami's new safety director, Andrew J. Kavanaugh, recently named to replace Sam McCreary, whom the *Tribune* had succeeded in getting fired, looked on approvingly. When the reporter fled to escape further beating, the detective shouted at a pair of uniformed policemen standing nearby:

"Get that man and lock him up, he's drunk."

Jeans sent a doctor to examine Davis, who was found to be sober, whereupon the police dropped the intoxication charge but retained a disorderly conduct charge. The next night burly Detective J. H. Williams attacked photographer Tommy Kane, and the following day Detective Chief L. O. Scarboro smashed the camera of photographer Weston Haynes. But no policeman shot a *Tribune* reporter; an irate lawyer did that. It happened after the operator of a Tamiami Trail juke joint, The Windmill, was slain on June 11, 1935. He was William Estas, an Everglades character who might have been slain by any one of a dozen enemies. At an inquest it was revealed that a client of a well known Miami lawyer, O. B. White, had paid Estas and his wife to board a young woman for several weeks. The *Tribune's* reporter, Shannon Cormack, slept through the testimony. By the time he awoke the hearing was nearly over, and he found himself having to check with reporters from the *Herald* and the *News* for notes.

"Boy, you really missed it," said Steve Harris of the *News.*

"What was that?" asked Cormack as he readied his pencil. Cormack was a slender, bony man whose suit hung on him like a sack. He had a prim mustache that gave him a personality that matched his arrogant disposition.

"The testimony brought out that O. B. White was keeping a wench at the Estas joint," said Harris. "White and Estas had some trouble over the girl. It really looks bad for the lawyer."

Cormack swallowed the story, which Harris told in a tongue-in-cheek manner. Without further checking, Cormack hastened to the *Tribune* and wrote the racy kind of story that was his specialty. Jeans put it on page one, under a streamer: "O. B. White Named As/Estas Foe At Inquest." Upon seeing the headline in the early edition, White became furious. It was not until late evening that he was able to reach Cormack on the telephone. By this time he was intoxicated and carrying a pistol.

"I'm coming over and kill you, you dirty, lying son-of-a-bitch," shouted White over the telephone.

Fifteen minutes later White appeared at the *Tribune.* Upon entering the grubby building, White spotted Cormack working over a typewriter. Rushing to him, White began beating the reporter with his fists, then seized him. Cormack picked up a heavy spring that lay on his desk and struck White, who released his grip. Free, the reporter sprinted toward the composing room. White whipped out a .38 caliber revolver, dropped to one knee, and, holding the gun with both hands, aimed and fired. The first bullet missed, penetrating a photographic darkroom and barely missing the head of a photographer. The second bullet hit Cormack in the back, near his left shoulder blade. The injured reporter got through a door into the composing room where he fell beneath a typesetting machine. The newsroom staff grabbed White and disarmed him.

The *Tribune* exploited the story for all its worth. The lawyer was pictured as a bold, would-be murderer, while Cormack, recovering in a hospital, was made to appear as an innocent newspaperman fulfilling his obligations in reporting testimony before a coroner. Jeans pressed the prosecution of the lawyer, who was tried on charges of assault with intent to kill. He was found guilty, and Judge Willard sentenced him to seven years in prison. White appealed to the Florida Supreme Court, and a new trial was ordered. This time the lawyer pleaded guilty to a lesser charge, aggravated assault, and Willard fined him $500. The ironic part of the story was not reported by the *Tribune*. Cormack recovered to find himself without a job, Jeans having hired a reporter who could be counted on to stay awake during inquests.

Normally, during the doldrums of Miami's depression time summers the *Herald* and the *News* slipped into a placid, noncompetitive coexistence. But during the summer of 1935 the *Miami Tribune* gave the established newspapers no rest. The editors of both papers frequently discovered their reporters had missed stories or that they had underplayed stories that the *Tribune* ran under bold headlines. It wasn't because the *Tribune* got all the breaks; the hard-driving Jeans merely made his reporters do more digging and work harder for longer hours. As a result, the *Tribune* was claiming record circulation growth, leaping ahead of both the *Herald* and the *News*. But the *Tribune's* reputation as a "scandal sheet" was growing, too. Although this image might have been all right with Moe Annenberg, whose avowed aim was to force Frank B. Shutts to sell him the *Miami Herald*, it caused some anguish for Jeans, who wanted to develop a prestigious tabloid on a model of the New York *Daily News*. Jeans' big chance to prove that the *Tribune* could do more than report scandal came on September 2, 1935, when the most violent hurricane to date in the Western Hemisphere swept across the Florida Keys, leaving 500 dead and almost total destruction in its wake.

On the day before the hurricane hit, the Miami Weather Bureau predicted that the storm, located between Cuba and the Bahamas, would continue a westerly course through the Florida Straits and into the Gulf of Mexico. But the storm changed its course, and, in the late afternoon of Monday, Labor Day, began crossing the upper Florida Keys. Lacking the sophisticated storm investigating facilities that would be common thirty years later, the Weather Bureau was unable either to pinpoint the storm or to suggest its unusual ferocity. Both the *Herald* and the *News* played the storm low-key; there was no reason to think that the small storm was much more than hurricane strength. There was sufficient concern among public officials on Monday afternoon, however, that the Florida East Coast Railway was requested to dispatch a passenger train to the Keys to evacuate those wishing to flee to the mainland. At the last minute the Associated Press dispatched a reporter on the train, but none of the three newspapers felt the situation was critical enough to send either reporter or photographer. The train did not return that evening, and, as all communications with the Upper Keys had been cut, there was no way to know where it was. The *Herald's* editors talked about a "lost train," and they sat in the newsroom throughout the night waiting for reports they hoped would come through. None did, except an SOS from the passenger liner *Dixie,* which, caught in the storm, was tossed onto the Florida Reef with 400 passengers aboard. At the mercy of mountainous waves that washed over it, the ship appeared to be in imminent danger of destruction.

Paul Jeans, eager to get a beat on his competitors, early Tuesday dispatched two reporters, William Freeze and Robert Quinn, and a photographer, Harold "Red" Willoughby, southward on U. S. Highway One, which at that time extended only to Lower Matecumbe Key. They encountered little destruction until they reached lower Key Largo just before dawn. At Snake Creek they found both highway and railroad bridges washed away, and a tidal torrent was rushing through the Snake Creek channel with such force that no one could hope to get across by any means. Dawn came, one of those traditionally beautiful dawns that follow hurricanes, this one no less spectacular in Miami than in the Keys. Across the channel the *Tribune's* men could see human figures moving about. Reporter Freeze climbed out as far as he could on what was left of the railroad trestle and yelled across.

"What happened?" asked Freeze.

Eventually he heard a reply above the roar of the furious current.

"Five hundred . . . Five hundred dead . . . We are the only survivors."

The *Tribune* hit the streets at 7 p.m., after the street edition of the *Herald,* with a report of "500 dead" and "total destruction" in the Upper Keys south of Snake Creek. The *Herald* continued to give the storm low-key coverage, reporting on Wednesday morning a "possible death toll" of twenty-five. By that time the *Tribune* had raised the estimated toll to 700. It was not until Thursday morning that the *Herald* leaped into action with a five-column, two-line head: "Hundreds of Bodies Are Found/In Wreckage on Florida Keys." By this time refugees from the liner *Dixie* were arriving in Miami. There would be little rest for editors, reporters, or photographers on any of the three papers or the press services for the next forty-eight hours. By now the Labor Day Hurricane had become a national story.

Although small in diameter, the hurricane was one of the fiercest storms ever reported. Its winds exceeded 150 miles an hour, with gusts up to 250 miles an hour. For a twenty-mile stretch water levels rose eleven to eighteen feet, sweeping across Lower and Upper Matecumbe keys with such destructive force that virtually every building and every tree was smashed and washed away. Even the steel coaches of the passenger train stranded at Islamorada on Upper Matecumbe Key were carried several hundred feet from the track, and would have been carried into the Gulf of Mexico but for the debris against which they lodged. The Associated Press reporter and several companions spent a hectic night standing in the seats of a coach to escape drowning. The heavy steam engine remained on the track, although the tide rose into the cabin to threaten the lives of the frantic engineer and fireman. Most of the railroad along a ten-mile stretch was washed away, including the bridges. Because the cost of rebuilding would have been prohibitive, the Overseas Railway was abandoned. The state would later use much of the roadbed, including the long bridges, to support the Overseas Highway to Key West.

As it turned out, the *Tribune* was more nearly correct in its first estimate of the loss of life than it was in the second. Jeans had based the figure of 700 on the number of World War I veterans who were at that time working on a highway project in the Upper Keys as part of a depression-time federal relief project. Fortunately for most of the veterans, the storm hit on a holiday while they were in Miami or Key West. But the natives were home, and the toll among them was so great that in many instances only one or two of a family survived.

Among those who lost their lives was a well known madam from Miami, Mabel Gray, who had followed the veterans to the Keys. With her girls she had set up a house in a fishing camp at Lower Matecumbe Key. Her girls drowned with her. On Mrs. Gray's body was found $1,000 in greenbacks.

As a result of its hurricane coverage, the *Miami Tribune's* circulation soared by 10,000 daily. Jeans loaded editions with pictures of the destruction, distraught survivors, and funeral pyres. So many were the deteriorating bodies that a state health officer had ordered them burned. On Sunday, September 8, the *Tribune* came out with a sixteen-page supplement filled with the best hurricane photographs. Photographer Red Willoughby became famous. Unfortunately, his fame was short. Two months later he was killed in an automobile accident.

Few other newspapers ever had so many breaks or played the breaks better than did the *Miami Tribune* under Paul G. Jeans. While the news was often slanted and distorted, in the context of its time the *Tribune* was no mediocre newspaper. Certainly no other newspaper ever gained greater attention within so short a time. Whether the influence the tabloid wielded was for good or for evil has been much debated. Most certainly its enemies thought of it as evil. Among them could be counted Colonel Shutts. So incensed did Shutts become as a result of the tabloid's attacks on him and his newspaper that he ordered copies of the *Tribune* banned from the *Herald* building. But while Shutts may have suffered personally as a result of the *Tribune's* attacks, the *Herald* continued to enjoy a prestige that the tabloid never attained in spite of its soaring circulation. For the *Herald,* as well as the *News,* sought to reflect some of the hopes and aspirations of the community, while the *Tribune* drove on with its negative approach, attacking the "City Hall gang," prominent personalities, and even the foundations of Miami's frontier society. While much of the *Tribune's* criticism may have been well-founded, a great deal of it was nonproductive. As time passed, Miamians bought the *Tribune* to see who was "catching hell now." Whenever a Miamian wanted to sell something, or offer a room for rent, he chose not the *Tribune* but one of the other papers, more often the *Herald.* Thus, despite its higher circulation, the *Tribune* was fighting a losing battle. With the other papers getting the majority of the advertising, Annenberg continued to operate at a loss reputed to be a quarter million dollars a year. Still, in 1937 he opened a new $300,000 publishing plant, and from all appearances he intended to keep the *Tribune* going. But on April 18, 1937, Paul Jeans lost his life in an automobile accident near Saint Augustine. The car, moving at high speed, swerved, presumably to avoid cows crossing the highway. Skidding across the median strip, the car crashed head-on into a vehicle driven by Edward Morr of Cincinnati. Jeans and his companion, lawyer M. Victor Miller, were killed instantly, as was Morr.

Jeans' death proved to be traumatic for the *Tribune.* Prior to Jeans' death, Annenberg visited the new plant daily. After the editor's death he was seldom seen in his office again. But Annenberg found himself another interest that was more intriguing than the losing *Tribune.* He purchased the *Philadelphia Inquirer,* paying a reported $15 million.

The *Tribune* continued publishing nevertheless, and in the spring of 1937 was influential enough to elect three candidates to the Miami City Commission. One of them, Robert R. Williams, a political novice, became mayor. Its candidates, once they got into office, were dubbed the "Termite Administration" by the *News,* and the Tribune's commissioners eventually were recalled. But by that time Moses L. Annenberg could hardly have cared less about Miami politics, having sold his *Miami Tribune* to John S. and James L. Knight.

13

Pigeon Loft

J OHN S. KNIGHT took possession of the *Miami Herald* as its president and publisher on October 15, 1937. His younger brother, James L. Knight, whose name appeared on the masthead as secretary-treasurer, had arrived three weeks earlier—"to see that nobody tried to walk off with the plant." Upon arriving, Jim wondered "why in the hell I was sent; there wasn't anything worth walking off with."

The old buildings that housed the administrative, advertising, and editorial departments were run-down, dirty, almost firetraps. There was no elevator except in the four-story mechanical building that Publisher Frank B. Shutts had erected in the 1920s. The usually affable Jim Knight had good reason for apprehension. The Knight brothers had just emerged from four years of financial hardship. Their father, Charles Landon Knight, owner and publisher of the *Akron Beacon Journal,* had died in 1933, leaving an estate of $515,000, but also leaving debts and inheritance taxes totaling $800,000. The elder Knight's death had occurred in one of the worst years of the depression, when few newspapers were making a profit. Moreover, the *Beacon Journal* had a strong competitor, the *Times-Press,* a Scripps-Howard paper. Taking command of the *Beacon Journal* as publisher, Jack Knight had audaciously tackled his competitor, at the same time freezing family earnings until the paper's indebtedness could be paid. This he managed to accomplish within four years, although not without hardship for the Knight family. Jim, who had married Mary Ann Mather of Akron in 1934, received so little income that he and Mary Ann had to postpone starting a family until 1937 when Barbara, the first of four daughters, was born. But during the belt-tightening period not only were the Knight family's creditors paid off, the *Beacon Journal* became Akron's leading newspaper.

If Jack Knight had been audacious as the publisher of the *Beacon Jour-*

nal, he was more audacious in agreeing to pay $2.25 million for the *Miami Herald.* But in 1937 when he became publisher of the *Herald* he was within eleven days of being forty-three, and he was confident that he knew something about newspapers and the newspaper business. Born on October 26, 1894, at Bluefield, West Virginia, Jack grew up at a time when his ambitious Georgia-born father, C. L. Knight, was driving for success. The father had become publisher of the *Beacon Journal* in 1907 and its owner in 1915. A brilliant and colorful personality and writer, "C.L.," as he was widely known, hoped to train a son to carry on after he was no longer around. C.L.'s aspirations were concentrated on the first son, Jack, fifteen years older than Jim. So at an early age Jack was put to work in the *Beacon Journal,* variously as a printer's devil and copy boy, in the advertising department, and as a budding reporter. Jack also was groomed for college and law school. Having practiced law himself before entering the newspaper field, C.L. felt that the study of law was an essential part of a publisher's background. Moreover, the father hoped to see the son enter politics, as he had done. C.L. had been elected to Congress in 1920 on the Republican ticket and had run unsuccessfully for governor of Ohio.

World War I interfered temporarily with C.L.'s plans for his elder son. Jack left Cornell University in 1917 just before graduation to enter the military service. Going in as a private, Jack went overseas with an Army motor transport corps, but early in 1918 he applied for infantry officer's school at Langre, from which he was graduated as a lieutenant. He was sent to the Alsace-Lorraine front, but before seeing much action was transferred to the fledgling Army Air Corps where he was in training as an artillery observer and aerial gunner when the war ended.

After being discharged from the military service, Jack loafed for several months while deciding whether to finish college and attend Harvard Law School or to go to work. He was twenty-five. Four years of law school did not appeal to him. But it took courage for a son to work for C. L. Knight, and Jack felt this keenly. As the publisher's son he would be on trial not only with his father but in the eyes of everyone in the newspaper plant. So he delayed, spending the $5,000 he had won shooting craps with his buddies in France. Then, when his father offered him a job in the newsroom of the *Beacon Journal,* he accepted. But he accepted on two conditions. First, if he lacked ability, if he had no flair for writing or editing, he could quit; second, if he lacked ability but was unable to recognize it, he was to be fired. Under no circumstances did he want to be carried on the payroll merely as his father's son.

C.L. owned two smaller Ohio newspapers in addition to the *Beacon Journal,* the *Springfield Sun* and the *Massillon Independent.* Jack worked

C. L. KNIGHT (*left*), publisher of the *Akron Beacon-Journal,* controversial editorial writer, colorful personality, and the founder of Knight Newspapers.

JOHN S. KNIGHT (*right*) is shown as an infantry officer and aerial observer in World War I in France.

THIS CONGLOMERATION of buildings at 200 South Miami Avenue was the home of the *Miami Herald* in 1937 when purchased by John S. and James L. Knight from Frank B. Shutts. The publisher's office was located in the near corner of the second floor. The four-story building in the rear, far right, housed the production department and presses. It was built in 1925-26.

on both papers. In 1925 C.L. made him managing editor of the *Beacon Journal,* a job he held at the time of his father's death. Jack was a careful watcher of the better newspapers in other cities, and, as a result of his observations, was able to make a number of improvements in the *Beacon Journal's* appearance, as well as in the selection of feature material, including comics. Sometimes C.L. resisted the changes. "What in the hell is that?" he would ask when a new feature appeared. "Well, I think it's got potential," the son would say. "Let's try it for awhile." The feature usually stayed and in time the son would add another. After Jack became publisher and had complete freedom he sought to make the *Beacon Journal* stand out as Akron's leading newspaper. To do this, he carried more news and a greater number of features than did his competitor, the *Times-Press,* which, like the *Beacon-Journal,* was an afternoon paper. Owned by Scripps-Howard, the *Times-Press* had unlimited funds behind it, but Knight knew its editors had limited authority, having to operate by formula—so much space for news and features to so much advertising. Unhampered by formula, Jack sought to "swarm" over his competitor by giving his readers large quantities of news regardless of the amount of advertising. He also sought to publish a gutsy newspaper, with the needs and aspirations of the people of Akron on its editorial conscience.

Jack Knight's first great test as a publisher came in 1936, during a long and bitter strike in the Akron rubber industry. Since rubber manufacture was Akron's principal industry, the city felt the strike keenly as it dragged on week after week. Money became virtually nonexistent, and many businesses, including the *Beacon-Journal,* had to pay employees in script, which was accepted by local stores. Newspaper advertising dropped virtually to nothing and both papers suffered, but while the *Times-Press* cut back sharply to reduce its losses, Knight ignored the losses and increased the space allotted to news and features. The people of Akron were especially hungry for local news. Moreover, the men on strike had plenty of time to read. Knight insisted that his reporters leave nothing uncovered, while concentrating on news about the strike. It was a gamble that cost the *Beacon Journal* a lot of money. But the biggest gamble was yet to come.

The longer the strike dragged on, the more unreasonable both labor and management appeared to become until the people of Akron wondered if the strike ever would be settled. Bitterness began to increase on both sides, but, except for a few minor fracases, bloodshed was averted. In the midst of this tension the mayor of Akron began to promote an organization of vigilantes, which he promised to lead through picket lines and open the rubber plants for those who "wanted to work." Realizing that such a desperate act could only result in bloodshed and in bitterness Akron would be many years forgetting, Knight wrote a page-one editorial under the heading of "No Room For Vigilantes," in which he condemned the mayor and "other promoters of violence." The editorial caused a furore, but soon the strike was settled and the *Beacon Journal* blossomed into the strongest position in its history. The prestige of John S. Knight soared. Even his competitor, the *Times-Press,* was impressed enough to boom Knight for governor of Ohio. He smiled and declined. His father's activities in running for public office had been evidence enough of the incompatibility of newspapering and politics. The flattering gesture of the *Times-Press* editors did not mean they were backing off from competition. Had Knight fallen for the suggestion that he run for governor, much of his energy would have been diverted. Instead, the *Beacon Journal,* now irresistible to Akron readers, forged ahead and soon smothered the *Times-Press.*

Jim Knight's background had been much different from that of his brother. He was in his early twenties at the time of his father's death, having reached his teens after C.L. had passed the prime of life and no longer was driving for such lofty goals as governor of Ohio and possibly the presidency. The result was that Jim grew up without having to contend with the constant pressures of an ambitious father, as Jack had done. Thus Jim reached adulthood with a more relaxed and placid personality than Jack, who tended to be the more intense and impatient of the two. Jim's friendly, outgoing personality would prove an advantage in the business side of newspapering—the "nuts and bolts department," as he liked to call it. Joining the business department of the *Beacon Journal* under John H. Barry, he developed into one of the most capable newspaper managers in the country. And in the years ahead he proved to be just as audacious as his brother.

Barry was fifty-one at the time of C. L. Knight's death. He had been general manager of the *Beacon Journal* since 1911. Barry not only knew the business and production side of a newspaper but was shrewd in sizing up men, and he could deal with forceful personalities like the flamboyant C.L. A poker player, C.L. on occasions would go into the *Beacon Journal's* cash register and take out a couple of hundred dollars. It created a major bookkeeping problem, but who was going to complain? Nobody did until Barry arrived. He went to the boss after witnessing the first invasion of the cash register.

"Whenever you take money from the cash register, Mr. Knight," said Barry, "would you please leave a chit? We need the information for our bookkeeping." Thereafter C.L. left a chit.

Jim Knight was twenty-two in 1931 when C.L. turned him over to

Barry with instructions to teach him the "business and production side of newspapering." He had just dropped out of Brown University. It was depression times. Banks were failing, companies were going bankrupt, and millions were jobless.

"It was something I didn't understand," said Jim, "and somehow I didn't see how I was going to gain very much understanding in the halls of learning."

But young Knight did understand work, and he told his father that's what he wanted to do—go to work on the family newspaper, in the business department.

"I never fancied myself as a word weaver," said Jim. "That just wasn't my line. But I knew it was the editorial content that sold the paper; I always appreciated that."

Working under Barry, however, was not very productive. Barry was not the kind of manager who used assistants. Therefore he was a poor teacher. Much of what Jim learned was on his own, "snooping around," observing, and asking questions. Nor did things change much for Jim after his father's death. Jack jumped from managing editor to publisher, but for Jim there was no place to jump to—or from. However, Jim's "snooping around" and observing had taught him a lot about a newspaper plant. And as he walked through the *Miami Herald* for the first time, accompanied by Shutts' business manager, George Harper, he was far from being impressed. He and his brother had bought a name. He didn't know how much the name was worth, but certainly the plant itself was not worth anything like $2.25 million. Jim had followed Harper through the newsroom and they were about to inspect the wire room of the Associated Press when his nostrils caught a whiff of an odor he had never smelled in a newspaper plant before.

"Humph, what's that I smell?" asked Jim, stopping in his tracks. "Smells like a hen house."

It wasn't a hen house, but a carrier pigeon loft on the roof of the two-story business office that adjoined the third-story newsroom. There was no airconditioning, and the odor from the pigeon coops, accentuated by the warm and wet September weather, wafted through the open windows.

"Who owns those birds?" asked Jim.

"Why, they're part of the *Herald* operations," replied Harper.

Knight looked at Harper in disbelief, but the big surprise was yet to come. Harper kept the pigeons, at *Herald* expense, while waiting for the big story to break when the birds could be used to bring in news sent by reporters from some remote place. The idea of using carrier pigeons in connection with news coverage had occurred to Harper after the 1926 hurricane, which destroyed communications through South Florida.

Harper explained how the pigeons were to be used. Reporters sent to cover a story where conventional communications were nonexistent would take along a cage of pigeons. The pigeons would be used, one by one, to file the story.

"Each pigeon, after its release, would fly directly to the *Herald*," said Harper.

"How do you know that, Mr. Harper?" asked Knight.

"These are high-bred birds, Mr. Knight," replied Harper with growing enthusiasm. "We test them frequently. Several of these birds have won trophies in carrier pigeon contests."

"What kinds of stories have you covered with the pigeons?"

Harper admitted that an opportunity to use the pigeons had not occurred.

"We're keeping the pigeons on hand while waiting for that opportunity," he added.

"Well, Mr. Harper, I don't believe we'll require pigeons for our news coverage operations," said Knight.

"But they're part of the inventory . . . "

"I don't care about that, Mr. Harper," said Knight bluntly. "As far as I'm concerned the pigeons belong to you—and the sooner you can remove them from the building the better."

It was Jim Knight's first decision in connection with *Miami Herald* operations, and it was one of the easiest he would ever have to make. But during the remaining three weeks while "snooping around" the *Herald's* plant he gathered evidence to help him make another decision. It concerned Harper. He not only sensed Harper's incompetence, but what disturbed him most was the thorough dislike of him among the people who had to come in contact with him. Jim's suspicions were confirmed by John Barry, who arrived a few days before the October 15 closing date to familiarize himself with the paper's business procedures.

Harper had started in the *Herald's* circulation department in 1917, rising to circulation manager a few months later. In 1924 he was elevated to business manager. Harper, a cigar-smoking man with a rough exterior, appealed to Shutts, who himself had a rough exterior. And as Shutts grew older he turned over to Harper more of the publisher's responsibilities. Harper had as a secretary an officious, ambitious young woman who was as thoroughly disliked as the business manager by the other employees. The glass in the windows of Harper's office and the transom over the door had been frosted. Employees reported to Barry and Knight that Harper kept the door locked while dictating to his secretary, who spent an inordinate amount of time in the office. A well used couch added credence to rumors. So did the secretary's domination of her boss. She considered her authority equal to that of the business manager and treated other executives as underlings. The real purpose of the couch, however, was a sleeping place for Harper after too much bourbon.

"His name should have been I. W. Harper," wisecracked Jack Knight.

Except for an elderly sister of Shutts, who managed a small, inefficient morgue on the first floor, Harper and his secretary were the only persons let go after the Knights took over. And to end for all time any suspicions among the employees of what might happen between executives and secretaries behind frosted glass, Barry had the walls of the offices in business and advertising departments cut down to four feet. Meanwhile, Jack Knight made no immediate changes among editorial personnel, except to elevate Judge Stoneman to editor-in-chief.

"I had a great deal of respect for Judge Stoneman," said Knight. "He was an outstanding personality, a great and honorable old newspaperman, and I wanted to do as much as I could to honor him."

Hollums, Shutts' managing editor and confidant, was retained. Experience had taught Jack Knight to avoid making hasty changes in a newspaper, either in policy or in the staff. A mistake he had made as a young editor he remembered painfully, although the lesson had been of great value to him. Soon after joining the staff of his father's newspapers, he was appointed editorial director of the *Springfield Sun,* a competitor of James L. Cox's *Springfield News.* Twenty years later Knight and Cox would become competitors in Miami, with Knight as publisher of the *Herald* and Cox as publisher of the *Miami Daily News.* But Knight was inexperienced when he became editor of the *Sun,* although he lacked nothing in audacity. He soon found himself facing an important editorial decision. Through contacts, he had obtained a list of Klu Klux Klan members in Springfield. As he read through the list he saw names of several prominent persons, outstanding of which was the son of United States Senator Sidney D. Fest. And so the young activist editor rushed into print with the list.

"I can tell you that the publication was not received with the greatest enthusiasm," said Knight. "We won no friends."

Jack's decision hampered his efforts to bring about needed changes in Springfield. Instead of being welcomed as a new and promising editor who could be counted on to help build a better community, he was looked upon with suspicion and distrust. He had telegraphed his punch; he had made a bad tactical mistake.

"I was a hurry-up boy; I couldn't wait," he said. "But I learned a valuable lesson. I learned that when you enter a new community you shouldn't begin telling people what you're going to do, but wait and size up things and then proceed in order of priorities, I brought that lesson with me to Miami."

When Shutts turned the *Miami Herald* over to Jack Knight in 1937, he had been its publisher for twenty-seven years. Shutts had guided the development of a paper with an editorial and news policy, as well as format, that was in keeping with his conservative political philosophy and personal outlook. The *Herald* reflected an image of comfortable permanency and credibility that had won for it a respect among its readers which would have been the envy of many other newspapers more smartly produced. Jack Knight may have had some reservations about the quality of the *Herald,* but he couldn't say that it was unsuccessful.

Miami was by no means a strange city to Knight, but he did not pretend to understand it. Certainly Miami was different from Akron or any other northern city with which Knight was acquainted. Miami was to him anything but an average city. It was more like a large, overgrown frontier town—large enough to be a city but hardly developed enough to be called a city. Intellectually it was undeveloped, too. Moreover, its morals were loose and its establishment selfish and unconscionable. Miami's mayor, Robert R. Williams, was one of three city commissioners who owed their election to the support of Moses L. Annenberg's *Miami Tribune.* The other *Tribune*-supported commissioners were John W. DuBose, a lawyer, and Dr. Ralph B. Ferguson, an osteopath. A fourth commissioner, R. C. Gardner, owner of a large grocery, owed his election partly to *Tribune* support. In a previous election he had been a *Tribune* candidate, but, after his defeat, the editors had become disenchanted with him. So he ran with the support of gamblers and bookmakers, whom he later repudiated. "Sure, I accepted money from racketeers; that's the only way you can get elected in Miami," he said. "But that doesn't mean that I have to go along with the racketeers."

A few days after Jack Knight became publisher of the *Herald* Commissioner DuBose called upon him. He represented the Miami City Commission in an unofficial capacity. Judge DuBose, as he was known, had been judge of the county court in Duval County (Jacksonville) for eighteen years before coming to Miami in 1932 to practice law. DuBose was well acquainted with Shutts as well as with Hollums. It had been the practice of the commissioners to "feel out" the editorial attitude of both the *Herald* and the *News* before taking a stand on major issues. But what kind of man was this new publisher from Akron? Judge DuBose had come to find out. After the usual exchange of pleasantries, the publisher from Akron said:

"Well, Mr. DuBose, what can I do for you?"

"Well, Mr. Knight," replied DuBose, "I wanted to know what we have to do at City Hall to get right with you."

Knight, who knew politicians, was by no means floored. He could have laughed but chose to be serious. He said to the commissioner sternly: "Nothing, Mr. DuBose, except to be good public servants."

Knight was determined to divorce the *Herald* from involvement in local politics. But, being pragmatic, Knight decided to keep Hollums, figuring that he knew more about the dark closets of Miami politics and the roles played by the leading members of the establishment than did anyone else he could have hired. So, to make better use of Hollums' talents, Knight suggested that he write a column, "Behind the Front Page." The column proved to be a valuable addition to the paper. For Hollums, who had joined the *Herald* in 1922 as news editor, knew the community, its institutions, and personalities; he also was acquainted, and had been a party to, many of the machinations behind the front page. A native of Cherokee County, Alabama, Hollums had risen to news editor on the *Jacksonville Journal* at twenty-nine. Coming to the *Herald* to do the same job, he had an opportunity to work under Olin W. Kennedy until that editor left in 1928. Shutts then elevated Hollums to Kennedy's position of managing editor.

Knight's pragmatism also was responsible for his keeping another person, H. Bond Bliss, whose column, "In Today's News," occupied the first column on page one. Bliss was a little man, five feet six and weighing ninety-nine pounds. For so small a person he possessed an enormous ego. Born in Michigan, Bliss had joined the *Herald* in 1925. Bliss wrote a popular column that appeared on the editorial page. It was a compilation of local, national, and international news, accompanied by feisty comment.

A similar kind of column, Arthur Brisbane's "Today," previously had appeared on page one. The Brisbane column not only was fresh, but it was written succinctly, with a flair that carried great authority. Newspaper readers of later generations might, in retrospect, find Brisbane's writing and comment old-fashioned—even naive—but the syndicated column, for that period, was sound and clever to millions of readers. Brisbane was a person of immense prestige and self-confidence, which came through in his column. One day in the middle 1930s Brisbane was taken on a tour of the *Herald* by Shutts. The great editor was shown through the various departments and was introduced to the executives and to members of the editorial staff. In the editorial page office Brisbane met H. Bond Bliss.

"So, this is the man who writes the column, 'In Today's News,'" said Brisbane. "Well, Colonel Shutts," he added, turning to the publisher, "you are looking at my successor, the Brisbane of tomorrow. When I retire, Mr. Bliss is the one to take my place."

It was like a monarch naming a successor. Brisbane lived but a few months, dying on December 25, 1936. On January 1, 1937, Shutts ordered Bliss' column moved to page one. The Hearst syndicate signed a year's option to buy the column if Bliss turned out to be "another Brisbane," but the option was not picked up. Bliss, a kind of poor man's Brisbane, was by no means unpopular, though. He struck out at taxes, waste in government, the unemployed on relief, foreign nations that had not repaid their World War I debts to the United States, and at liberals such as Franklin D. Roosevelt, who, he said, were guiding this country toward communism. He predicted accurately that Roosevelt's policies would involve the United States in war. But generally there was little substance in the column, which Bliss wrote in a kind of "short jabs" style. Jack Knight thought the comment frequently was inane. Here is how he began one column:

"Random thoughts. Special weeks. The past one has been a humdinger. Foreign Trade, Cotton and Poetry and Debts. At least these are official. Probably others are crowded into it. Such as tip your hat week. Brush your nails. Spinach, Hogwash. And why write week. That's right. Why write? Because!"

Although Knight found this hard to stomach, he tolerated the column, as he did the daily horoscope, because a fair percentage of readers wanted it.

In 1937 the *Herald's* daily circulation was 55,000, compared with 43,-000 for the *News.* On the day the Knights took possession of the *Herald* a box appeared on page one that morning stating that the paper had carried 454,908 paid classified ads so far that year, which was "270 percent more than the *Herald's* closest competitor." The "closest competitor" was the *News,* but never again would the *News* enjoy a position in circulation and advertising so close to the *Herald.* In the years ahead, as the morning paper gained rapidly in circulation and advertising, the evening paper would fall farther behind, as the *Times-Press* had fallen behind the *Akron Beacon Journal.* While the slipping of the *News* may be attributed to a variety of causes, the most serious may have been the management's relaxed attitude toward competition from the *Herald* during the early period of the Knights' ownership.

Jack Knight did not look upon Annenberg's *Tribune* as much of a competitor. Carrying little advertising and depending mainly on street sales for its circulation, the *Tribune* was losing an estimated quarter of a million dollars a year. Although Annenberg could afford to keep the

Tribune going as long as he pleased, Knight suspected that Annenberg had lost interest in the tabloid since his purchase of the *Philadelphia Inquirer.* Two weeks after the *Herald* deal was closed, Knight had a visit from Smith Davis, the Cleveland broker who had introduced Knight to Colonel Shutts.

"Now that you own the *Miami Herald,"* said Davis, "you should buy the *Miami Tribune."*

"And how would I do that?" asked Knight. "I haven't heard any hints that Mr. Annenberg wants to sell."

"Why don't you go to Philadelphia and ask him?" replied Davis. "I know Mr. Annenberg. Why not let me call and tell him you're coming to see him?"

Knight thought about that for a moment.

"Well, all right," he said. "I'll go to Philadelphia and see Mr. Annenberg."

A few days later Smith Davis called Knight and told him arrangements had been made for him to meet Annenberg. The same week Knight was on his way to Philadelphia. Annenberg, in his office at the *Inquirer,* was most cordial. Annenberg took him on a tour of the plant, but they engaged in no serious talk until they returned to the office. Now as soon as they had sat down, Annenberg leaned back and looked at Knight.

"Well, young man, what is it?" he asked, turning the conversation to a get-down-to-business tone.

"Mr. Annenberg," replied Knight, "I know you are an extremely busy person, so I'd like to ask you three questions:

"Number one: Do you think there's room in Miami for three newspapers?"

"No," replied Annenberg.

"My second question is: Would you sell the *Tribune?"*

"Yes, I would sell," replied Annenberg.

"My third question is: How much do you want for it?"

"A million dollars," he replied.

"Well, Mr. Annenberg," said Knight, "I don't have a million dollars. As you know, I have just made a deal for the *Herald."*

"Well, what do you have?"

"I have a little paper in Massillon, Ohio."

"And where in the hell is that?"

Knight described where Massillon was, between Canton and Wooster, twenty miles south of Akron.

"Do you have any figures?" asked Annenberg.

"Yes, sir, I have last month's statement."

"Are you going to show it to me?"

"Of course," replied Knight, producing the statement from a coat pocket.

Annenberg required but a few moments to digest the statement. He said:

"That looks pretty good."

"Well, Mr. Annenberg," said Knight, "I'm not privy to your secrets, but we make about $50,000 a year in Massillon, and my understanding is that you may be losing as much as a quarter of a million dollars a year in Miami. Perhaps we could make a swap of some sort."

"What's your proposal?" asked Annenberg.

This started serious negotiations. In the beginning, however, Annenberg's asking price for the *Tribune* was so high that Knight said, partly in jest:

"But, Mr. Annenberg, how could I ever pay that price for your paper?"

"Oh, you don't pay for it, young man; the people pay for it," he said.

Knight asked him to expand on that. Annenberg replied:

"Well, you like that SOB, Governor Cox. I don't like him and I don't like Shutts, but if you buy the *Tribune*, go to Cox and show him how much an increase of five cents in home delivery prices would mean. Don't tell him what it would mean to you, but you just tell him what it would mean to him. If he agrees to your proposal, the people will pay for the *Tribune*."

This is what eventually happened. Knight went to see Cox. It was a time of rising costs, so Cox welcomed a chance to raise home delivery prices five cents a week.

Meanwhile, Knight turned the final negotiations for the purchase of the *Tribune* over to Blake McDowell, who had negotiated with Shutts for the purchase of the *Herald*. Annenberg agreed to sell the *Tribune* for $600,000, with the *Massillon Independent* as part of the payment. With the sale of the *Miami Tribune* went its new building and all the equipment in it. The building, a new press, and other equipment were later sold at prices considerably below their worth. Annenberg's final act as publisher was to run a swan song on page one of the *Tribune,* reminding Miamians how he had saved the city from "evil politicians" and had installed "able men."

"The city with its new commission is in good hands," wrote Annenberg. "Nothing remains but to go ahead."

Knight closed the *Tribune* down on December 1, 1937, and locked the building. But he did take half a dozen of Annenberg's top employees—three reporters, an editor, a photographer, and a circulation man. And, except for those thrown out of work, few mourned the passing of Miami's most sensational newspaper.

But Moses L. Annenberg was not to be forgotten. He soon was on the front pages of newspapers throughout the nation after his indictment on charges of income tax evasion. Found guilty, he was sentenced to three years in prison. He also had to pay $8 million in tax claims. His nationwide race wire services were closed down by federal order. Annenberg spent twenty-three months in prison. Released in 1942 because of broken health, he died seven weeks later at sixty-five.

Thirty-two years after Jack Knight purchased the *Miami Tribune* from Moses L. Annenberg, Knight Newspapers, Inc., purchased the *Philadelphia Inquirer* and *Philadelphia News* from his son, Walter Annenberg, ambassador to Britain, paying $55 million. Author Gaeton Fonzi, in *Annenberg, a Biography of Power*, describes the sale of the two Philadelphia papers to the Knights as Walter Annenberg's "finest contribution to American journalism." The father's sale of the *Miami Tribune* was, in the eyes of many Miamians, no less a journalistic contribution, overshadowed in importance only by the "extinguishing" of it by John S. Knight.

ADORED like a political saint, Everest G. Sewell was upset when newspapers disagreed with him. In 1939 he took on the *Miami Herald* in the bitterest battle of his career over the pasteurization of milk, the value of which he challenged.

14

Raw Milk and Fever

F EW NEWSPAPERS HAVE prospered like the *Miami Herald* under the ownership of John S. and James L. Knight. But in the beginning no changes were made in the paper's outward appearance. Morning after morning readers were greeted by the same conservative front page where only a national disaster got more than a one-column headline. Jack Knight had not wanted to offend long-time *Herald* readers by making precipitous changes. He wanted to retain the image of stability which the *Herald* reflected, but behind the front page he did make changes. Several new columnists were added, as well as new features, new comic strips, and more photographs. New columnists included Walter Winchell, Westbrook Pegler, Heywood Broun, General Hugh S. Johnson, Sidney Skolsky, and Eleanor Roosevelt, all obtained through the purchase of the *Miami Tribune*. Shutts already had Damon Runyan, who owned a winter home at Miami Beach, as well as Drew Pearson, Edwin C. Hill, George Matthew Adams, and Paul Mallon. Knight sought to obtain all the nationally known columnists available, reasoning that many of the *Herald's* readers—residents as well as visitors—came from all parts of the country and would want to follow the columnists they had read back home.

The gradual improvements were bound to remake the *Herald* in time. But two major news breaks in 1938, together with the paper's involvement in 1939 in the hottest political battle in its history, hastened a severance with the Shutts era. The first story was an accusation by the president of the Florida Power & Light Company that city officials had attempted to collect a bribe of one-quarter million dollars in exchange for the settling of a power rate case. The second was the kidnaping of toddler Thomas Bailey "Skeegie" Cash from his crib in south Dade County. The break with the past was made complete when the *Herald* put its news and editorial resources behind a campaign to stop the sale of unpasteurized milk in Miami.

The bribery story created a sensation when it broke in the middle of January, 1938. A grand jury was convened and indictments were returned against Miami's Mayor Williams and Commissioner Ferguson, as well as Thomas E. Grady, a rate consultant hired by the city, the city attorney and two assistants, and also a consulting engineer to Grady. The president of the Florida Power & Light Company, Bryan C. Hanks, broke the story to Jack Knight. But he had called upon the publisher primarily to get his advice about what to do. Hanks said Grady had approached him with a proposition that he considered an out-and-out bribe. In exchange for $249,300 the Miami City Commission would agree to settle a power rate controversy that could save the power company millions of dolars.

"I have worried about how to handle this," said Hanks to Knight. "I'm not about to pay a bribe. But should I forget about the proposal or should I make it public?"

Hanks shoved before Knight the copy of a statement he had prepared to run as a display ad in the *Herald* and the *News* in which he accused the city officials of trying to bribe him and his company, and offering to give the information to a grand jury. What did Knight think of the ad?

This was the kind of bold action Jack Knight liked. He advised Hanks to run the ad. Some changes were made at Knight's suggestion, and Knight wrote a headline to be set in bold type, "I Won't Pay A Bribe!" Hanks delivered it to the advertising departments of both papers. It appeared in the *Herald* on the morning of January 12 and in the *News* that afternoon.

The chain of events behind the alleged bribe attempt had its beginning in 1933 when Mayor E. G. Sewell pushed through a city ordinance that required the power company to reduce its rates by one-third. Although Miamians were paying one of the highest electric rates in the nation—twelve cents a kilowatt hour—the company chose to fight. A long court battle ensued. Mayor Sewell was defeated in 1937 after a smear campaign conducted against him by the *Miami Tribune,* which elected three of its own candidates. The problem of resolving the electric rate issue fell to the new mayor, Robert R. Williams.

Under Shutts the *Herald* had covered the issue in a routine way. Under Jack Knight the coverage tended to change little. The fight had been going on so long that the public had grown cynical over the prospects of a settlement. This may explain, in part, why the *Herald* chose to handle the bribe story in such a way that it appeared to be only a cut above the routine. The *Herald* did give the story a three-column head in light-face type. That afternoon, however, the *Miami News* went all out, giving the story virtually all of page one, with bold headlines, together with a dramatic cartoon showing Corruption with its octopuslike tenacles entwined about City Hall, and a sharply worded page-one editorial. The aggressive and distinctive coverage by the *News* won a Pulitzer Prize, the first to be awarded a Miami newspaper. The defendants hired James M. Carson to defend them. It was Hanks' word against theirs, and Carson had little trouble creating doubts in the minds of the jurors, who returned a verdict of not guilty. The defendants filed libel suits against Hanks and the power company totaling $3.25 million. The suits eventually were dismissed, but in the meantime the Florida Power & Light Company lost its rate suit in the United States Supreme Court and had to pay $4 million in rebates to consumers. This, however, did nothing to appease citizens who were angry over the performance of the *Tribune's* commissioners. In a recall election Williams, DuBose, and Ferguson were booted out, while among the commissioners selected to replace them was Sewell, who again became mayor. But while the stories about power rates, bribery, court trials, damage suits, and recall droned on and on, the Cash kidnapping story had the quality of an explosion.

The kidnapping of five-year-old Skeegie Cash occurred at a time when kidnapping for ransom was common. Most kidnappings were done by gangs with killer reputations. Victims usually were of wealthy families. The kidnapping of the Lindbergh baby had set the pace for public concern about kidnappings. When kidnappings occurred, newspapers carried countless columns, headlining stories with bold streamers. Every important development was an excuse for an extra edition. For days on end an entire nation agonized with families trying to make contact with kidnappers, and when a victim was returned alive, nationwide rejoicing followed. Kidnapping had come to be viewed as the most heinous of crimes, and Congress passed a law making it possible for the Federal Bureau of Investigation to enter kidnapping cases even where the crossing of a state line was not involved. Within twenty-four hours after Skeegie Cash was taken from his crib twenty G-men were working on the case. J. Edgar Hoover arrived to take charge, and within forty-eight hours an additional force of forty G-men was involved.

The Cash family, who operated a grocery store in Princeton, a farm community twenty-five miles south of Miami, had its living quarters in the two-story building. Only moderately well off, the family was far from the image of affluence that kidnappers usually preyed upon. However, when the kidnapper took the Cash child from his crib on Saturday evening, May 28, 1938, he must have figured that the father would be able to raise the $10,000 ransom demanded in a note. The baffled sheriff's office called the FBI. The local chief FBI agent phoned both Miami newspapers, the wire services, and radio stations, asking them to carry nothing about the kidnapping until the ransom was paid and the child returned. This the news media agreed to do, in return for the FBI's promise to keep reporters informed of developments so that they could prepare stories for eventual publication or broadcast. But despite efforts by the FBI to keep the public from learning of the kidnapping, the news spread rapidly throughout south Dade County. People began to mill about the Cash store in Princeton. In fact, so many showed up that Sheriff D. C. Coleman felt it necessary to organize large groups under leaders to search the countryside for some trace of the child. By the end of the second day Coleman had between 2,000 and 3,000 persons organized into searching parties. The presence of so many people created a problem in the delivery of the ransom money. The kidnapper became frightened and failed to appear at the planned rendezvous. Another note was expected, but where would it turn up?

Monday night, forty-eight hours after the kidnapping, a cleanly cut, handsome young man, Franklin Pierce McCall, drove up to a dark filling station next door to the Cash store. He roused the owner, living on the premises, who opened the station and turned on the lights. McCall informed him he wanted to buy three gallons of gasoline for his father-in-law's truck. Then he stooped over and picked up from the floor a crumpled piece of paper.

"Hey, look at this," said McCall. It was a note from the kidnapper directing the father of Skeegie Cash to meet him at 4:00 a.m. Tuesday. The note was immediately delivered to the child's father.

With $10,000 in a shoe box, the grocer drove to the appointed rendezvous, made contact with the kidnapper, and left the box. Meanwhile, the *Herald* had decided to go to press with the kidnap story a little after midnight on the morning the ransom was paid. Managing Editor John Pennekamp argued that nothing would be gained by waiting longer; that everybody in south Dade County, as well as thousands in Miami, knew of the kidnapping. Delaying publication any longer would make no difference so far as the life of the child was concerned, he contended. So, a little more than forty-eight hours after the kidnapping, the *Herald* published a full account, together with a large photograph of the child on page one. After the ransom was paid the *Herald* followed with an extra.

The child, however, was not returned. Hoover and his FBI agents blamed the *Herald*. But by this time no reporter cared a rap about what the FBI said. From the beginning, *Herald* and *News* reporters had been treated by the FBI with a "no comment" to every question asked. Whatever information the reporters got they obtained from Sheriff Coleman or his deputies. The tense relationship between reporters and the FBI is illustrated in conversation between Steve Harris, a *News* reporter, and a G-man.

"Could you tell me where I could buy a Coke?" asked the agent.

"No comment," replied the poker-faced Harris.

The activities of McCall, however, had caused the sheriff to become suspicious. Amid displays of unnatural anger, McCall had made threats of what he would do if he could get his hands on the kidnapper of "my little pal," as he called Skeegie Cash. McCall, who lived nearby, knew the Cash boy well. On one occasion he nudged Coleman and said: "It must have been a smart guy that pulled this job." McCall managed to bring under suspicion an old carpenter, M. F. Braxton, and tried to incite a group of searchers to lynch him as the kidnapper. Coleman arrested Braxton and McCall, turning them over to the FBI. Braxton was held but McCall was released.

Meanwhile, Albert Watson, a farmer, had studied the filling station where McCall said he picked up the crumpled ransom note and concluded that a wadded piece of paper could not have been forced under the door. Watson informed Coleman, who agreed. Coleman accosted McCall.

"Was that note you found in the filling station wadded up like this?" asked the sheriff as he balled up a piece of paper in his fingers.

"Yes, it was," replied McCall.

Again Coleman arrested McCall and turned him over to the FBI, which wrung a confession from him. Tried and found guilty of murder, McCall was sentenced to die in the electric chair.

Seldom in the *Herald's* history have its reporters covered a story matching the Cash kidnapping in drama and suspense. But the following year, in 1939, a low-key item inside the paper revealing an estimated number of Miamians who had contracted undulant fever from drinking unpasteurized milk ignited one of the bitterest political fights in Miami's history. Dairymen, politicians, businessmen, the public—even the medical profession—chose sides in a battle that lasted all summer and into the fall. Viewpoints were polarized to an extent that later generations living in a more enlightened world would find difficult to believe. But neither the *Herald* nor Miami would be the same after the newspaper's campaign against the sale of unpasteurized, or "raw" milk.

Today it would be impossible to buy a quart of unpasteurized milk in any retail store in Florida. But in 1939 raw milk not only was commonly sold in Miami, the chances were good that the milk you ordered in any restaurant would be raw. Moreover, the chances were fair that the milk would carry the organism that caused a debilitating and often agonizingly painful disease, undulant fever. Neither federal nor state laws guarded the quality of milk in 1939, nor did Dade County or Miami have any laws governing the sale of milk. Distributors were not even required to specify on containers whether milk was raw or pasteurized. The *Herald* began its campaign against the sale of raw milk after one of its writers, Marion

Shutts Stevens, daughter of the former publisher, contracted undulant fever from a glass of milk she drank in downtown restaurant. The disease was enervating, causing fever and extreme fatigue as well as pain and swelling of joints. The symptoms hung on for months, and Mrs. Stevens was some time in getting her energy back. What Mrs. Stevens learned from her doctor surprised her. Undulant fever was common in the Miami area. It was transmitted in raw milk, from cows suffering from brucelosis, a bovine malady known also as Bang's disease. When diagnosed in humans it was called undulant fever, from the characteristic of the fever accompanying the disease. A check among twenty doctors by Mrs. Stevens revealed they had, together, treated 210 cases during the first five months of 1939. Estimates by Dr. George N. MacDonell, county health department director, put the number of undulant fever cases in the area that year at 1,000.

Mrs. Stevens discussed her findings among her associates, but, although they thought it was a bad situation and sympathized with her because of her experience, no one suggested she might have a newsworthy story. While Mrs. Stevens was not a widely experienced reporter—she did a radio column, book reviews, the church page, and other specialty assignments—she sensed that she did have a good story, and she wrote to John S. Knight in Akron. Knight returned the letter to Pennekamp with the suggestion that Mrs. Stevens might have a story worth investigating. Pennekamp assigned her to it.

The result was the beginning of a *Herald* campaign for 100 percent pasteurization of all milk and all milk products sold in Miami, which at that time held two-thirds of Dade County's 275,000 residents. No other campaign the paper had waged up to that time was given so much space, both in news and editorial page coverage, together with editorial cartoons. Nor could an argument have been more convincing. Leading medical authorities were quoted, including the president of the Dade County Medical Association and the director of the Dade County Health Department. The experiences of several persons who had contracted undulant fever were related. Mrs. Stevens did a history of pasteurization, taking the reader back to the time of Louis Pasteur, to prove the soundness of her thesis. The stories were sufficiently scary to discourage anyone from drinking raw milk. For raw milk, the articles stated, not only was capable of carrying undulant fever but also typhoid, scarlet fever, septic sore throat, and tuberculosis. Undulant fever was itself a serious disease, sometimes accompanied by such complications as arthritis, meningitis, pleurisy, or abcesses. The *Herald* urged the city commission to pass an ordinance forbidding the sale of unpasteurized milk, and the city's attorney drew up such an ordinance for possible commission consideration.

But Miami's mayor, Everest George Sewell, was by no means convinced by the *Herald's* arguments. Although a person of integrity, Sewell had little formal education and, like many others of his period, was woefully ignorant about science. Moreover, he and dairymen were long time friends. Sewell had arrived in Miami in 1896, a short time before the city was incorporated. His brother John was one of Miami's first mayors, and both grew with the city as successful merchants and community leaders. Ev Sewell, as a leader in the Chamber of Commerce, which he founded, had developed as a staunch and able promoter of Miami, particularly of tourism, aviation, and the sea port. He had mastered the art of lobbying, learned his way about Washington, and was, to a large extent, responsible for many of the handsome favors bestowed on Miami by the federal government. During his previous two terms as mayor he had left an enviable record. Sewell was Miami's outstanding greeter, who had turned over the "keys of the city" to more important people, including Presidents Coolidge, Hoover, and Roosevelt, than any other Miami leader. Sewell's stature had become so great that not until his later years was he ever subjected to severe criticism in a newspaper, and that was from Annenberg's *Miami Tribune.* Over the years both the *Herald* and the *News* had treated Sewell with such respect that even when they criticized him they apologized, as did the *Herald* on December 11, 1936, when he was chided editorially for having sided with the hated *Tribune* on an issue.

"Down the years he strode, a Colossus of civic virtue," said the editorial, "basking in the beneficence of public favor, bestowing the benison of his smile upon all and sundry, but frowning always upon those evil forces which forever are striving to gain claw-hold upon the body politic." After that opening Sewell was given a mild slap on the wrist.

Such was the stature of Mayor Sewell when, in behalf of the dairymen, he took on the *Miami Herald* in one of the hardest fought battles of his career. He let it be known that as mayor of the city of Miami he would "not be dictated to by the *Miami Herald."* Who was John S. Knight to insist upon an ordinance requiring the pasteurization of milk? What was wrong with drinking raw milk, anyway? The mayor preferred to drink raw milk, as he had done all his life—and "without harm." Moreover, pasteurization removed the food value and flavor from milk, he said, and "made milk dead." He announced that a public hearing would be called to air the issue.

The majority of the mayor's fellow commissioners were by no means sure that 100 percent pasteurization of milk was necessary. Commissioner Fred W. Hosea, a hardware merchant, thought that the only value of pasteurization was "to keep milk from getting rotten." Commissioner R. C. Gardner, a grocer, likened pasteurization to "embalming bodies." Commissioner Alexander Orr, Jr., a contractor, wanted proof that "communicable diseases are carried by raw milk." Only Commissioner C. D. Van Orsdel, an undertaker and the best educated of the lot, came out publicly in favor of pasteurization. It was not until August, however, that Mayor Sewell called a public hearing, drawing the fight out as long as possible. Meanwhile, the *Herald* carried almost daily stories about the ravages of undulant fever. Eleven dairies in the county were disclosed to be selling raw milk. Several dairies were revealed to be selling raw milk that they claimed to have been pasteurized. Since 1935, the county health department revealed, over 11,000 dairy cows had been slaughtered in Dade County after tests for Bang's disease proved positive. Still, at the public hearing raw milk had its champions, including members of the medical profession. Topmost was Dr. John G. Dupuis, Sr., owner of one of the county's leading dairies. Dr. Dupuis' dairy sold raw milk, and he recommended it for children and adults in preference to pasteurized milk. He was in a position to influence hundreds of families, for he was a highly respected general practitioner who had lived in Dade County for more than thirty years. His lawyer entered a brief at the hearing in which Dr. Dupuis cited several physicians throughout the United States who favored the drinking of raw milk. Four other local physicians testified in favor of raw milk. Several citizens described their own battles with undulant fever, testifying that their doctors had told them the disease came from drinking raw milk. Mayor Sewell then read a statement. He said his Washington physician, Dr. William Gerry Morgan, a past president of the American Medical Association, saw no harm in raw milk. Pennekamp assigned a reporter to call Dr. Morgan, who denied the statement.

When Sewell finally called for a vote on the milk issue, the commission voted three to two to let the public decide in a referendum whether it wanted 100 percent pasteurization. Sewell took the milk issue to the voters in a vilification campaign against the *Herald* and particularly against Jack Knight. And, in a sense, Sewell was the victor.

On November 7 only 10,206 of Miami's voters turned out, and the proponents of raw milk won by 5,468 to 4,293, with 445 choosing to ignore the issue. Although the vote in favor of "raw milk and fever" may have been a great personal victory for Mayor Sewell, it was for the dairymen an empty one. As a result of the *Herald's* campaign just about everyone in Dade County was afraid to drink raw milk, demanding assurance from dairies that milk delivered to homes was pasteurized. Except for a couple of dairies that produced raw milk for food faddists, its sale soon ceased. And with the end of raw milk, the number of undulant fever cases in Dade County dropped to zero.

15

Phony Quintuplets

THE *Miami Herald's* circulation gained 14,000 during the first two years of the Knights' ownership, proof that readers liked the revitalized newspaper. The editors had broken away from the *New York Times*-like format that Olin W. Kennedy had established in the 1920s. The *Herald* was now more lively—the stories better written and better displayed. But the former publisher, Frank B. Shutts, was not altogether pleased with the changes. He preferred the more formal format and the reserved, conservative editorial policy that he had fostered. His friends agreed with him. Receiving a retainer of $12,000 a year as a consultant, Shutts felt obliged to advise Jack Knight.

"Mr. Knight," said Shutts, "my friends at the Surf Club don't like all the changes you are making in the *Herald.*"

"But, Colonel Shutts," replied Knight, "I'm not publishing a paper for the Surf Club."

It was an honest statement of Knight's policy. Independent, he had not permitted any special interests to get him in their clutches. And while he had not ignored the establishment, he refused to act like a publisher who keeps an ear to the ground listening for rumbles of dissatisfaction from the high and mighty who wield the power in a community. Nor would he accept favors that might put the *Herald* under an obligation. Shortly after becoming publisher of the *Herald* he was offered a free box at Hialeah Park. Knight declined the offer. At another time after he and his wife had dined in a swank night club he discovered that the house had picked up the tab. Knight asked to see the manager.

"I insist on paying," said Knight.

"You can't, Mr. Knight," replied the manager. "Your check already has been taken care of."

"All right, that's up to you," said Knight, "but if I can't pay I won't come back."

The manager produced a check. But Knight's example was not necessarily followed by his editors and columnists, several of whom continued to freeload. Bob Fredericks, flamboyant amusement editor and critic, insisted on being given a front table at nightclub shows. A robust eater, Fredericks ordered the most expensive steak. And when the show was over he would walk out without paying or leaving a tip. Nightclub operators feared to challenge him and forbade employees to do so, lest he tear the show apart in his column—although he usually did so anyway. Waiters hated Fredericks, but instead of poisoning his steaks, they spat on them.

By the fall of 1939, after two years of ownership, Knight had made virtually all the improvements in the *Herald* that a publisher could hope to make through personal efforts. To make additional changes, he sent Ben Maidenburg, a ten-year staff member of the *Akron Beacon Journal.* Six feet four, weighing 250 pounds, and confident, Maidenburg had a personality that bowled you over. Highly aggressive, he could be obnoxious. But he had a brilliant mind, and not only did he know the newspaper business, he had learned it under the trained and steady eye of John S. Knight. He respected Knight more than any other person in the world, and he could be counted on to carry out Knight's orders no matter what the cost in money, blood, and tears.

The son of Jewish immigrants from Czarist Russia, Maidenburg was born in Philadelphia in 1910, a short time before his family moved to Marion, Indiana. Maidenburg got his start in journalism while in high school, working on the *Marion Chronicle.* After a year in Butler University he went to the *Des Moines* (Iowa) *Register* where he worked for a year before being hired in 1929 by Knight, then managing editor of the *Beacon Journal.* He had worked in several departments of the *Beacon Journal* and had risen to Sunday editor at the time Knight called him into his office late one Friday in September 1939 and asked him if he would like to go down to the *Miami Herald* and set up the procedures for a new rotogravure section. The thirty-year-old Maidenburg looked upon a request by Knight to be the same as an order. Yes, he said, he would like to go.

"When can you leave?" asked Knight.

"Well, I could be there Monday," replied Maidenburg. He had no idea how far Miami was, but hoped the train would get him there in two days.

Knight had other plans for Maidenburg but did not at that time reveal them to him. He had watched the sharp-witted and able Maidenburg and knew his capabilities. Furthermore, he had done much to influence him,

BEN MAIDENBURG

with the result that of all his editors Maidenburg probably could be trusted most to do the job that the publisher wanted.

Maidenburg proved to be a time bomb. He had been at the *Herald* just long enough to get acquainted when Jack Knight put him in charge of the copy desk, with the title of news editor. He swarmed over the rest of the staff, including the city editor, Jack Clark, who had succeeded John Pennekamp after his elevation to managing editor. Pennekamp avoided possible conflict by going home early and leaving the newsroom decisions to "Jack Knight's big boy," as the staff referred to Maidenburg behind his back.

The weather was still uncomfortably hot in late September, and Maidenburg, who had spent Sundays roasting himself in the Florida sun, sat in the slot of the copy desk stripped to the waist, his face and massive torso as red as a beet. On such an evening a man and his wife, accompanied by two small girls, entered the newsroom. Just as the family reached the top of the stairs Maidenburg's tenor voice rang out at a reporter:

"Goddamn it, how could you write such a stupid piece as this?"

Without uttering a word, the father directed his family back down the stairs.

During slack moments Maidenburg would stretch a rubber band between the index and middle fingers of his left hand and send a paper clip zinging at some unsuspecting reporter or editor, or at George Mangus, the *Herald's* artist, bent over his drawing board in the nearby art department. Or he would slip under the copy desk, insert a match in the toe of a copyreader's shoe, light it, and wait for the painful hotfoot.

"Haw, haw, haw," was Maidenburg's reaction. "Haw, haw, haw."

One busy evening on the copy desk Maidenburg slipped behind a copyreader and poured ice water in the seat of his chair as he arose to reach copy that had been placed on purpose at a distance that would require his rising. "Haw, haw, haw," sounded Maidenburg as the copyreader splashed down in the ice water that had filled the hollow seat of the captain's type wooden chair. But it wasn't funny to the copyreader, who, spurred by surprise and anger, picked up the chair and threw it at the huge, towering form of the news editor. Maidenburg was agile enough to remove his bulk from the path of the heavy chair, which bounded on across the floor of the newsroom.

"You nearly hit me!" shouted Maidenburg at the copyreader. The copyreader sat at the rim of the copy desk for the rest of the night without anything to do. After work began piling up on the next night Maidenburg shoved a stack of copy across the desk under the copyreader's nose.

"You working here?" he asked.

"I hope so," replied the copyreader.

"Then, God damn it, get busy."

Maidenburg had been given full authority to fire anyone on the staff he felt did not come up to Knight newspaper standards, and on every pay-day he would sit in an office in the rear of the newsroom with the pay envelopes on the desk before him. If he handed you a single envelope you were sure of your job for another week, but if he handed you two envelopes, you knew your services were needed no longer; the second envelope contained two weeks' pay. Whatever might be said of Maidenburg's methods, the able members of the staff quickly learned that they had no reason to fear losing their jobs. Reporters like Allen Morris, Steve Trumbull, and Jeanne Bellamy thrived under the Maidenburg regime. So did Joe Dressman and Charlie Ward, who worked variously on the city, state, and copy desks. Jack Clark was a victim of the Maidenburg regime; he was let go by Pennekamp at Jack Knight's order. Henry Cavendish, an able but wordy writer, whom the city editor could assign to anything from reporting a murder to covering a concert, was another victim. Maidenburg stormed at him for the length of his stories.

"Look at that! Look at that!" shouted Maidenburg one evening as he stretched out one of Cavendish's stories that had been written by the yard rather than by the inch. "Where in the hell do you think we can put that much copy? What kind of paper do you think you are working for, anyway?"

Cavendish quit.

Maidenburg knew better than Hollums or Pennekamp what the publisher wanted, and let nothing stand in his way in achieving it. His major problem was insufficient staff, particularly on the copy desk, which consisted of a telegraph editor and two or three copyreaders, one of them in his eighties and another so badly crippled he had to work standing up. The telegraph editor, Erit Wilson, was so afflicted with writer's cramp he used his left fingers to guide the right hand that held his pencil. Stacks of wire copy grew higher and higher on either side of him as the evening progressed, and he was forever looking for a story or an add to a story that was somewhere in the stacks. So frustrated did he become at times that you felt he was going to pieces at any moment, throwing up all the copy and screaming like a mad man. Maidenburg stormed at Wilson, making him more confused. After Maidenburg had been in Miami about three weeks it occurred to him that he never saw any copy from the Universal Service wire, which he knew the *Herald* received. Checking, he found a teletype machine clacking away in a side room. On it was the entire day's report of Universal Service, the copy dropping unused into a wastepaper basket.

"Mr. Wilson," stormed Maidenburg, "why in the hell aren't we using Universal Service?"

"I don't have time to bother with it," replied Wilson. "We get more copy from the AP and the UP than we can use."

The ancient copyreader, Thomas Baird, was a native of Protestant Ireland. He had a strong dislike for Catholics, and Maidenburg had to watch the headlines he wrote to see that they were not slanted. As a younger man Baird had worked on the old Chicago *Inter-Ocean,* from which he had been fired. The story about his firing had become a classic and was known to everyone in the newspaper business who was acquainted with the history of journalism. Baird, telegraph editor, had just put the *Inter-Ocean* to bed and was preparing to go home when a flash came over the Western Union telegraph wire—"U.S. MAINE BLOWN UP IN HAVANA HARBOR." Baird studied the flash, then wadded up the copy and dropped it into a wastepaper can. Baird did not consider the story important enough to stop the presses for a make-over.

Erudite in the use of English and a facile copyreader and headline writer, Baird enjoyed almost an immunity to Maidenburg's temper. But the old man would sometimes write a trite headline that Maindenburg would catch and rewrite. Baird's worst fault was the use of time-worn phrases. His favorite was "Hits Snag." The city commission, chamber of commerce, legislature, or congress was always hitting a snag over some issue. One Saturday evening when the street edition of the Sunday paper came up Maidenburg blew his top when he found five "Hits Snags" in headlines throughout the paper.

"That stupid, Irish son-of-a-bitch," shouted Maidenburg. "The next guy who uses 'Hits a Snag' in a head just as well quit right then."

Fortunately, Baird was at dinner and by the time he returned Maidenburg had calmed down, but he got the word.

Probably the most competent copyreader was Ben Robinson, the cripple; but he was sensitive to criticism and frequently flared back at Maidenburg, much to the big man's frustration. Robinson was too good and too badly crippled to be fired, and in his favor, too, was a lack of fear of Maidenburg.

Maidenburg was frequently baffled by the motley staff, with its uneven talents and peculiar personalities. He learned to avoid some, like the cantankerous amusement editor, Bob Fredericks, while he handled the former publisher's daughter, Marion Shutts Stevens, with silk gloves. Pennekamp he dealt with as distantly as possible although with respect. He was bowled over only by one *Herald* personality, the farm editor, W. F. Therkildson. "Therk" had worked most of his life as a salesman for agricultural firms. As editor of the *Herald's* All Florida section, he was a promoter rather than a reporter. His section carried glowing accounts of Florida agriculture—citrus, winter vegetables, sugarcane, livestock. He claimed Florida was the first state in the production of beef cattle when at that time it was a poor fifteenth, and he lauded Florida's citrus as the best in the world. Therk covered the state, driving an old twelve-cylinder Cadillac. He was himself a thick-chested, impressively built man with a massive head. His conservative dress, knowledgeable conversation, and authoritative and confident manner seldom failed to win friends for the *Herald.* Jack Knight had acquired Therk when he bought the *Herald.* He thought that Therk wrote about the dullest stuff he had ever tried to read, but he kept him because he figured the All Florida section served a useful purpose. Therkildson also sold advertising for his section and managed to do better than break even.

Therk spoke with the same air of importance and authority to a copyboy as he did to the publisher or managing editor, being certain he left no one unimpressed. His meeting with Maidenburg was like an encounter of titans. But Maidenburg, who towered over the ample-sized Therk, was completely taken in. A city boy, what did Maidenburg know about rural Florida, or about agriculture at all, for that matter? He listened in awe as Therk pushed out his chest and expanded about Florida, with all its productiveness, wealth, and limitless opportunities. Christmastime approached. Therk arrived in the office with a crate of oranges, which he began distributing in small sacks. Maidenburg at this moment was sitting in the office of Pennekamp, who had departed. Therk filled a large sack with oranges, took them into the office, and set them on the desk before the news editor.

"By the way," said Therk, reaching into his coat pocket, "I want to show you how my friends think of me."

Producing a check for $1,000 he dropped it on the desk under Maidenburg's eyes. The check was from the United States Sugar Corporation and had been signed by Clarence Bitting, president.

"What's this for?" asked the surprised Maidenburg. He had never in his life seen a check for $1,000.

"That's appreciation," said Therk, expanding. "That's for the write-up I gave the sugar corporation recently."

"That's wonderful," said Maidenburg, remembering that Therkildson had done a special advertising section on the sugar corporation in recent weeks. It was mainly promotion of the large sugar firm, which had extensive acreage about Lake Okeechobee and a mill at Clewiston. "It's too bad you have to send this back."

"Send it back!" snapped Therk. "What are you talking about?"

"You can't keep a check like this," said Maidenburg. "It's unethical."

"I don't know why in the hell I can't keep it," said Therk, snatching back the check as his massive face glowed.

Suddenly Maidenburg realized he was dealing with a promoter who had never heard of newspaper ethics.

"Look, Therk, I'm not kidding," said Maidenburg firmly, "I want you to return that check."

Therkildson, who had put the check in his pocket, picked up the sack of oranges and strode angrily out of the office. Maidenburg never knew whether the check was returned. But the staff was to discover a lot more about the voluble Therk after his death from a heart attack. Some weeks before his attack he had gone around telling everyone, including the barber on the corner across from the *Herald,* that he had unexpectedly become a millionaire as the result of a will left by a relative. Upon Therk's death Pennekamp asked Cy Berning, courthouse reporter, to watch for the probating of his will. Two weeks passed, four weeks passed.

"Better check again," said Pennekamp to Berning. "Something's got to be filed by now. Therk was a millionaire."

A few days later Therkildson's widow appeared in Pennekamp's office. She said she was destitute. Her husband had left her nothing but two old twelve-cylinder Cadillacs. She had only a few dollars left, and now the rent on her house was due. What would she do? Would the *Herald* consider letting her succeed Therk as farm editor?

"You may not know it, but I've always done most of the writing anyway," she added.

Mrs. Therkildson continued writing the All Florida section until some years after World War II, when she was retired on a pension.

Shortly after the arrival of Maidenburg, the *Herald* got a new women's editor, Arletta S. Weimer. She may not have been as big a bomb as Maidenburg, but she was hardly less explosive. She had worked for the *Akron Beacon Journal* and had been women's editor for Scripps-Howard papers before coming to the *Herald.* Knowing her ability, Jack Knight gave her carte blanche authority to revamp the women's department. Blonde, thin, and rawboned, Mrs. Weimer was thirty-five and "tough as nails"—a description given her by Maidenburg. Like Maidenburg, Mrs. Weimer was dedicated to the newspaper business more than to anything else in the world, having given up a husband in the pursuit of her work. Mrs. Weimer moved into her position on the *Herald* directly, asking pointed questions, giving sharp orders, making drastic changes.

The women's section of a newspaper was vastly different in the late 1930s from what it would be a quarter-century later. Studio-posed pictures of striking brides or of sedate and prim society matrons looked out at you as you turned through the women's section, but unless you knew the women or you had some special reason to search for names in the society or club news you moved on. Like other newspapers, the *Herald* ran columns of names, the names being more important in the eyes of the editors than the activities in which the women were engaged. Prior to Mrs. Weimer's arrival the women's section ran little about Jewish women's activities, other than a paragraph or two to prevent the *Herald* from being called anti-Semitic. One day Mrs. Weimer asked the club editor to make a photographic assignment of a Hadassah meeting at Miami Beach in connection with a charity fund drive. The club editor looked at her in disbelief.

"We don't run photographs of Jewish meetings," said the club editor adamantly.

"We don't?" said Mrs. Weimer. "Well, we will from now on."

The club editor quit shortly thereafter; she couldn't get along with the new editor. Mrs. Weimer also got rid of another member of her staff, Jefferson Bell, the aged cooking writer. Jeff Bell, who was becoming senile, came to work wearing dirty white dresses over her sparse, angular frame. Mrs. Weimer, who wore stylish clothes and a hat while working, could not abide sloppiness. At her insistence the *Herald* retired Miss Bell on a pension.

Within a year, working from ten in the morning until midnight, Mrs. Weimer created an outstanding women's section, with splendid art and make-up. Her job, however, was a tough one because she had to fight constantly to get high quality pictures, as well as sharper, more colorful stories and smart displays. She wanted stories about what women were doing in charities, scouts, schools, business and professional activities, and civic affairs. She also ran articles on medicine and health, education, women in politics, and household tips. Her goal was a women's section of interest to all women as well as to men who cared to know something about the changes that were then rapidly taking place in the American way of life. Although she hired several new editors and writers, only one, Eleanor Ratelle, whom she acquired as a young woman and trained, stayed with the *Herald*. Mrs. Weimer remained long enough to establish a format for the women's section that would endure, with improvements, for the next thirty years. She left in 1943 to become women's editor of the

Washington Post. But the hard work, the constant driving for perfection, together with the frustrations of having to depend on people whose qualifications were far below her standards, took their toll. She died in 1950 at forty-six.

In the middle of March 1940, police reporter Henry Reno came in one evening with a report that a Miami mother was to give birth to quintuplets. Maidenburg almost went through the ceiling with enthusiasm. The famous Dionne quintuplets were just six years old. The birth of another set of five babies would put Miami in headlines all over the world. Reno had received the tip from Dr. A. W. Wood, a relative of his wife Jane. Maidenburg called Wood, who, wary of newspapermen, gave him no satisfaction. A family expecting quintuplets should not be subjected to the glare of newspaper publicity, said the doctor.

"If your wife was going to have five babies," said Wood to Maidenburg, "would you want it spread all over page one?"

Convinced that he had been given the runaround and that there was a basis for the report, Maidenburg wrote a short item from the notes Reno had given him, which appeared in the *Herald* next morning. Then the *Miami News* hit the streets with a similar story under an eight-column banner, "Miami Quints Expected Soon," together with a photograph of the expectant mother and her husband, Emory Callahan. An unidentified physician at Jackson Memorial Hospital, where Mrs. Callahan was receiving prenatal care as a charity patient, was given as the authority. The five babies, which had shown up in an X-ray, according to the story, were expected in two months. Electrified, Maidenburg swung into action. He bounded downstairs to the business office and drew $150 in cash, then drove to the furniture factory where Callahan worked. Bribing a foreman with a twenty-dollar bill, Maidenburg got Callahan into the car after giving him a new fifty-dollar bill, and they headed for the *Herald*. Relaxing Callahan in Jack Knight's office with coffee and a steak sandwich, Maidenburg sent Jeanne Bellamy to the dingy one-room apartment where the Callahans lived to return with the expectant mother. Meanwhile, Maidenburg called Frank B. Shutts and asked him to come over with a contract for the Callahans to sign. Mrs. Callahan arrived, "as big as a house," and trudged up the stairs to Knight's office. A deal was made. The *Herald* would pay the Callahans $125 now, pay for prenatal care, delivery, and for postnatal expenses. And after the quintuplets arrived, the Callahans would receive fifty percent of any profits from the sale of stories and pictures. Meanwhile, the Callahans would move into a modern, furnished cottage, whose rent the *Herald* would pay for a year. To make the contract binding, Jack Knight's signature was needed, but it was evening before the busy Maidenburg had a chance to look up the publisher, whom he found dining with his wife at the Surf Club. The contract could have waited until the next day, because the Callahans' names were already on the dotted line, but the impetuous Maidenburg would not wait. He was barred from entering the private club, however, and Knight, who was eating a spaghetti dinner, refused to leave his table. Maidenburg sent word that his presence was urgently needed, and out Knight came, unhappily, because in getting up from the table he had brushed the sleeve of his white dinner jacket in spaghetti sauce. But after hearing Maidenburg's story the publisher was pleased, and he signed the contract without quibbling.

Next morning the *Herald* came out with a big spread of stories and pictures about the Callahans. Unable to obtain a medical report on Mrs. Callahan, because the physician who had examined her was off duty and unavailable that day, the reporters had depended entirely upon the expectant mother for information—about her examination, what the X-ray showed, and what the doctor had told her. Just about every member of the news staff had been assigned to do some part of the coverage on the Callahans, who wound up with as much space in the paper as would have been given the visit of the king and queen of England. By noon the *Herald* was swamped by requests from wire services, magazines, and major newspapers who wanted to buy stories and pictures, while baby food companies wanted to buy the right to use the babies' pictures in advertising. Cash offers totaled $50,000. "You name the price," one baby food company executive said to Jack Knight.

In the meantime, Mrs. Callahan had been admitted to Jackson Memorial Hospital, not only to prevent the possibility of a miscarriage as a result of the excitement, but also to keep her out of the clutches of other news writers and photographers. By midafternoon Maidenburg had settled down enough so that he could take a more sober look at the *Herald's* investment, so he went to the hospital where he found Jeanne Bellamy keeping guard, along with Callahan, who had quit his job. Maidenburg then sought to find out something about the X-ray of Mrs. Callahan that had shown the heads of five babies. But the responsible nurse he asked knew nothing about it nor did the hospital radiologist who would have taken the X-ray.

"Well, could we make some X-rays of Mrs. Callahan?" asked Maidenburg.

Arrangements were made, and Mrs. Callahan was induced to put on her robe and ride in a wheel chair to the X-ray room. The pictures were made and Maidenburg was taken into a dark room where the radiologist held up a wet film before a light and began interpreting the picture:

"Now that's a head; this is a spine, and those are legs and arms; over there is a gas pocket and . . . . "

"Only one head!"

"One head, yes, and only one," said the radiologist.

"God damn son-of-a-bitch," screamed Maidenburg. He had never come so near fainting, and if he hadn't cursed he probably would have.

"Where in the hell did this quintuplet rumor get started?" he demanded to know. The people in the hospital vowed they knew nothing of any such rumor until they had read it in the newspapers. Well, who examined Mrs. Callahan? It proved to be an intern. Maidenburg found the intern and pounced upon him.

"I examined her and I told her I thought it would be a multiple birth," said the intern. "That's all I said."

"How did you examine her?"

"With a fluoroscope."

Crushed but not completely satisfied, Maidenburg got the name of Dr. Gerard Raap, said to be the area's best qualified radiologist, and asked him to come to the hospital. Dr. Raap confirmed the reading of the X-ray by the hospital radiologist, then explained to Maidenburg how in a fluoroscope examination gas pockets and internal organs could appear as "heads" to an inexperienced doctor, leading the intern to conclude that Mrs. Callahan would have a multiple birth. And Mrs. Callahan, hearing the word "multiple," immediately associated herself with Mrs. Dionne. But how did Dr. Wood hear the report that a Miami woman was going to have quintuplets? Maidenburg would never know.

Meanwhile, the editor was no little worried about how John S. Knight would view this blunder that would cost the newspaper a few thousand dollars before it got the Callahans off its hands. But after reading the publisher's "Notebook," which appeared every Sunday in the Knight Newspapers, Maidenburg knew he had no cause for further worry. Knight praised the way the editors and reporters had handled the story. The reaction of the rest of the world had pleased him. The name of the *Miami Herald* had been spread far and wide. Knight described himself as being, for a time, an "expectant' editor sitting on the rim of what might have been the greatest human interest yarn since the birth of the Dionne babies." Meanwhile, he continued, "we are glad that we have been able to play a part in the removing of all financial worries from the Callahans." And with that the Callahans, awaiting the birth of one child, returned to oblivion.

Maidenburg was to remain at the *Herald* but a short time after the "phony quintuplet story," as it became known in the newsroom. He was transferred to the *Detroit Free Press,* which the Knights purchased in 1940, as Sunday editor. Shortly after Maidenburg departed Pennekamp had a heart attack. It probably had nothing to do with Maidenburg. But the turmoil to which Pennekamp had been subjected for nearly a year, together with the confusion and the anxiety of having to accede his authority to an aggressive and often belligerent news editor who technically was under him, had taken their toll. From the standpoint of Pennekamp's career, however, it may have been the best thing that ever happened to him. He gave up smoking, concentrated more upon relaxing while at work, and soon recovered. First as managing editor and then as associate editor, Pennekamp in the years ahead played an important role on the *Miami Herald.* Maidenburg, in the meantime, rose in the Knight newspaper organization to become publisher of the *Akron Beacon Journal,* turning his explosive energy into activist leadership in his community, winning love and respect from the citizens of Akron that those who worked under him on the old *Miami Herald* found difficult to believe.

MIAMI'S SKYLINE in 1940 was little different from what it was in 1926 at the end of the Florida land boom. Only one important structure, the seventeen-story Alfred I. duPont Building, had been added to the skyline in the intervening fourteen years.

16

War and Cinderella

W ORLD WAR II, which had begun in Europe in 1939, was to change so many values that the world people had known would never be the same. But in 1940 Americans still believed in Prince Charming, Cinderella, and many old fashioned virtues such as true love. So when a pair who represented these images in real life, the Duke and Duchess of Windsor, appeared at Miami's doorsteps in August 1940—he as governor of the Bahamas—the *Herald* had in its hands the biggest love story the newspaper had ever covered.

You had to have lived in that era to appreciate the stir caused by the abdication in 1936 by Edward VIII of England so that he could marry a twice-divorced commoner, Bessie Wallis Warfield Simpson of Baltimore. Edward, once the debonair Prince of Wales, was the "world's most eligible bachelor." His abdication and marriage to Mrs. Simpson was one of the big newspaper stories of the 1930s. After the invasion of France by Germany in 1940 the duke and duchess fled to Bermuda. There was fear in Britain that the Germans might kidnap the pair and set them up as king and queen of the British Empire in exile. To prevent such an embarrassment, Edward was given the rank of major general and appointed governor and military commander of the Bahamas. In August 1940, the duke and duchess boarded a camouflaged ship bound for Nassau.

To be certain a reporter was on hand to cover the arrival of the Windsors, Pennekamp sent one of his star writers, Jeanne Bellamy, to Nassau a week ahead of time. She arrived to discover many reporters already there, including correspondents from London papers. In successive days other reporters arrived by plane and by ship. The reporters gathered in the shaded Royal Victoria Hotel patio to sip cool rum drinks. All except Jeanne Bellamy.

The first thing Miss Bellamy did was to investigate the facilities for filing her story after the Windsors' arrival. To her dismay, the chances of sending a story at all appeared dim, for the pressure by more than a score of reporters on the meager telephone and cable services would be overwhelming. So Miss Bellamy took her notebook and strode to the government center on Bay Street. She found decorations going up for a gala event and rehearsals in progress. Roles to be played by the honor guard, band, officials, police, leading citizens, many lackeys, and even the public were being worked out and rehearsed for both performance and timing. The duke and duchess would disembark at 9:00 a.m., to be greeted by a band playing "God Save the King." They would walk through flag-decorated Rawson Square, through a courtyard dominated by the statue of Windsor's great-grandmother, Queen Victoria, and wind up in the Legislative Council Chamber where the oath of allegiance would be administered by the chief justice. Miss Bellamy had virtually a complete story of the event. She sent it to Pennekamp, saying she would make any necessary corrections after the arrival of the Windsors. Here, in part, is what Pennekamp received:

"And so Prince Charming and Cinderella came to their sea-girt castle.

"The love affair that stirred the world more than any ever told in story books entered a new chapter Saturday when Edward, Duke of Windsor, and his American-born duchess reached their new island domain. All the pomp this colony could muster was summoned to welcome them."

And on the story went, describing the arrival of the Windsors' ship, its docking, the disembarkation, the cheers of several thousand Bahamians.

On the morning of Saturday, August 17, Miss Bellamy accompanied a horde of reporters and photographers to dockside to watch the welcoming ceremonies. Everything progressed exactly as she had written earlier in the week. Only one thing she had failed to include in her story: what the duke and duchess were wearing. When the ceremonies were over, Miss Bellamy hastened to a telephone while the other reporters headed for their typewriters. Knowing her time was limited and that she could be cut off by anyone with higher priority under wartime regulations, she hurriedly dictated her notes to a *Herald* rewrite man.

By the time the other reporters had typed their stories, Nassau's overseas telephone and cable facilities, idle during the festivities, were busy again by official use. And so Jeanne Bellamy had beaten the world, including the sophisticated correspondents from New York and London, and on Sunday morning the *Miami Herald* was the only paper anywhere outside of Nassau to carry a complete account of the welcoming ceremonies for the Duke and Duchess of Windsor.

But with a bloody war in Europe in progress and with the United States heading toward certain involvement, a story in 1940 about Prince

Charming and Cinderella arriving at their "sea-girt" castle could last but one day. The German air force had launched an all-out attack on England early in August. On September 3, President Roosevelt announced the trade of fifty destroyers—over-aged, he called them—to Britain in exchange for naval bases in British possessions. Two weeks later Roosevelt signed a selective service act which required the registration of sixteen million men of military age. And on December 13 the president, returning aboard the cruiser *Tuscaloosa* from a tour of American defenses in the Caribbean, paused off the Bahama island of Eleuthera to confer with the Duke of Windsor about the building of naval bases in the Bahamas. Jeanne Bellamy broke this story—another world scoop—while in bed recovering from pneumonia.

Nearly a month before, on November 16, Miss Bellamy had been assigned to do a color story on a football game between the University of Miami Hurricanes and the University of Florida Gators. It had been a warm day, and Miss Bellamy wore a lightweight dress to the game, played in the Orange Bowl. But a change of weather brought a cold wave to Miami, and a frigid northwest wind began to sweep through the grandstands. Miss Bellamy, without sweater or wrap, was chilled by the end of the intermission, but by now she had most of the details she needed for her story, so she climbed the steps to the press box and knocked on the locked door. A policeman opened the door and glared at her. She identified herself as a *Miami Herald* reporter and asked if she could enter, hoping to spend the second half of the game behind glass protection from the cold.

JEANNE BELLAMY beat the "best reporters in the world" in the coverage of the arrival at Nassau in 1940 of the Duke and Duchess of Windsor, where he was to serve as wartime governor of the Bahamas.

"I'm sorry, but women are not allowed in the press box," said the officer.

"But I'm a reporter, covering the game," said Miss Bellamy.

"I can't help that; it's against the rules," was the stern reply.

And so Miss Bellamy had to return to the stands, where she shivered through the rest of the game. Next morning she awoke with pneumonia, from which she was to remain in bed for six weeks. On December 12 she had a visitor, A. J. "Jack" Cleary. A Miami businessman and leader in charity drives, Cleary had just returned from the Miami Biltmore Hotel where the Duke and Duchess of Windsor were staying while the Duchess was having some dental work done in Miami. Cleary had gone to the hotel to ask the duke if he would attend a charity banquet for Miami's annual Empty Stocking Fund, which was to be held the next evening.

"Is he going to attend?" asked Miss Bellamy.

"He can't; he's flying tomorrow morning for a conference with President Roosevelt aboard the cruiser *Tuscaloosa*," replied Cleary.

"He told you that?"

"Yes," replied Cleary. "Apparently it's no secret."

Perhaps not, but after Cleary departed Miss Bellamy called Pennekamp and related what she had heard. Pennekamp knew nothing of the conference, and now the *Herald* had a top story for next morning, under Miss Bellamy's byline.

Step by step the United States was preparing for war. And as the year drew to a close, the president on December 29 declared the United States the "Arsenal of Democracy" and called for all possible aid to Britain short of war. In March 1941, Roosevelt signed a lend-lease bill providing virtually unlimited aid to Britain short of sending Americans to man the guns. John S. Knight was an outspoken critic of what he described as Roosevelt's determination to get the United States involved in the war, while at the same time repeating a pledge that no American would fight abroad unless this country was attacked. Although no pacifist, Knight failed to see how the United States stood to gain anything by becoming involved in a European war. He felt that Roosevelt's policies toward Germany and Japan were unduly provocative and at the same time deceitful where the American people were concerned. Knight said so repeatedly in his "Notebook." By the spring of 1941 Knight thought he could see proof of what he had believed for several months—that Roosevelt and Churchill had connived to get the United States into the war. By May Knight was convinced that the die was cast: that our involvement in the European war was inevitable. Roosevelt had led this country to the brink of war and now it had become too deeply involved to avoid conflict. And on Sunday, June 1, after Roosevelt announced in an address to the nation that the United States was involved in an "undeclared war" against Germany and her allies, Knight reluctantly made a switch from critic to supporter. It was one of the most significant decisions Jack Knight would make in his lifetime—and one of the most difficult.

"The *Herald* is glad to know where Mr. Roosevelt now stands," he wrote in a signed, page-one editorial. "His previous policy of 'saving England' while trying to avoid a 'shooting war' was a type of unrealism which we were never quite able to comprehend . . . .

"The *Herald* has opposed every step leading toward involvement in a war which was not of our making," but concluded that "NOW the die is cast. We are in this war quite as though our Congress had made a formal declaration of hostilities. There is no turning back."

And in a complete reversal of editorial policy, Knight pledged the full support of Knight Newspapers to Roosevelt as president and commander-in-chief of our armed forces. He made no promise he would not criticize what he thought were "shortcomings" in national defense or other matters involving national welfare. But he let *Herald* readers know there would be no more debating in editorials about whether we should be involved in the war against Germany. So far as the *Herald* was concerned we already were.

For the *Herald's* number-one columnist, H. Bond Bliss, the switch was not easy. While the *Herald* was now supporting Roosevelt, Bliss was hammering away at the "interventionists." Bliss may have been right in foreseeing the consequences of America's involvement in the war—the rise of communism and the weakening of democracy—but he was, in Knight's viewpoint, unrealistic. In November he ordered Bliss' column removed from the front page and put inside, accompanied by an editor's note to the effect that Bliss'. opinions were his own. Four weeks later the Japanese attacked Pearl Harbor. Bliss was as shocked and as angered as anyone else, but the editor's note at the top of his column remained. On Christmas morning, Bliss started his column with "Merry Christmas" beneath the bold face notice that "Mr. Bliss" opinions are his own and do not necessarily represent the editorial opinion of the *Miami Herald.*"

In the months ahead Bliss' opinions and those of the *Herald's* editorial page grew wider apart. His column had developed into the kind that served no purpose in a wartime atmosphere. Still Knight did nothing until August 1942, after Pennekamp called him in Akron to discuss a column he had found highly objectionable. Pennekamp had read only a few sentences when Knight cut him short.

"Don't run it; don't run any more of Mr. Bliss' columns," he said.

That column was not preserved, and neither Knight, Pennekamp, nor

Bliss could remember in later years what it was all about. All Knight could remember was that it was "inane."

The year 1941 was an eventful one in the history of the *Herald* as well as the nation. The *Herald* moved into a new office building, Judge Stoneman died, and Ellis Hollums resigned as executive editor. Stoneman, who helped to found the *Miami Herald,* had worked until a short time before his death on February 1, 1941, in his eighty-third year. Although never considered a brilliant and colorful writer and editor, Stoneman had become identified with great moral strength and character, and at the time of his death was the most highly respected newspaperman in Miami. To Knight, Stoneman was an impressive personality whose integrity was beyond reproach. He loved newspaper work, and Knight had encouraged him to work as long as he felt like it. And so Stoneman continued coming to the office, writing his somber editorials against a Quaker background colored by a classical education and Victorian ideals until a few weeks before his death.

The construction of the *Herald's* new office building was in progress at the time of Stoneman's death. Realizing he probably would not live to see the building completed, Stoneman expressed a wish in the presence of his daughter, Marjory Stoneman Douglas, that his ashes be incorporated with the building. Upon his death Mrs. Douglas went to Pennekamp with her father's request. After the building was dedicated, on November 16, 1941, the story about Judge Stoneman's ashes being incorporated with the building spread among the newsroom staff. But it amounted only to rumor; nobody seemed to know for sure. Yet day after day you went to work with a constant reminder that the judge was "watching you from the woodwork," as a copyreader put it. A bronze plaque was mounted on a wall next to the elevator in the lobby, containing the judge's solemn and thoughtful countenance and bearing the following inscription:

Frank Bryant Stoneman
1857-1941
Editor in Chief
December 1, 1910, to February 1, 1941
No storm ever broke the gentle strength of his tolerance
or deflected him from the truth as he saw it

Not until 1963, when the staff was preparing to move to the present *Herald* building on Biscayne Bay, would Pennekamp give up the secret. Columnist Larry Thompson, after getting only confusing information from the staff, went to Pennekamp, who told him the story. Stoneman's ashes had been dumped into the concrete that went into one of the sup-

BRONZE PLAQUE of Frank B. Stoneman, by Bemelmans, was installed in the lobby of the *Herald's* new office building on Miami Avenue. In 1963 it was moved to the *Herald* plant erected on Biscayne Bay between MacArthur and Venetian causeways.

FRANK BRYANT STONEMAN
1857 — 1941
EDITOR IN CHIEF
DECEMBER 1, 1910 TO FEBRUARY 1, 1941

NO STORM EVER BROKE THE GENTLE STRENGTH OF HIS TOLERANCE OR DEFLECTED HIM FROM THE TRUTH AS HE SAW IT.

NEW OFFICE BUILDING of the *Miami Herald* was dedicated on November 16, 1941, twenty-one days before the Japanese attack on Pearl Harbor, drawing the United States into World War II.

porting columns extending from the foundation through the third-floor newsroom. Pennekamp, to whom the can of ashes had been delivered by a funeral home, made arrangements with the architect and engineer, William Ginsberg, to deposit them. But word spread among workmen, and when Pennekamp and Ginsberg appeared with the ashes and prepared to pour them into the wet concrete, the workmen put down their tools.

"We ain't gonna work with no dead man," said one of the workmen, obviously expressing a consensus of opinion.

Discovering that reasoning with the workmen was impossible, Pennekamp and Ginsberg withdrew so that the pouring of the concrete could proceed. Ginsberg later deposited the ashes in a bucket of concrete, and when it was poured into the column form the workmen were unaware of the "dead man's" presence. And for twenty-two years, from 1941 until 1963, Judge Stoneman's ashes rested in a column standing in the midst of newsroom activities. The ashes remain in that column today, now surrounded by activities of Goodwill Industries, which occupies the old Herald building. But at the time those ashes were deposited neither Pennekamp nor Ginsberg could have guessed that anyone living at that time would see the *Herald* outgrow its facilities and move to another site. The bronze plaque bearing Judge Stoneman's likeness accompanied the staff to the new building, where it was mounted on the wall of a quiet hall leading to the editorial page offices on the fifth floor.

With the movement into a new office building in 1941 and publication of a special "Growing With Miami" edition to celebrate, Ellis Hollums quietly turned in his resignation. Knight immediately advanced Pennekamp into Hollums position, placing him in charge of the editorial page, together with the responsibility of doing the daily column, "Behind the Front Page." But no title was mentioned, and Pennekamp retained the title of managing editor for several months—until after the arrival of a new man on the *Herald,* a man who seemed to have been born wearing seven-league boots, Lee Hills. While Pennekamp's greatest years remained ahead of him, during which he would become known as "Mr. *Miami Herald,"* Hills would be quietly building the foundation for one of the nation's outstanding newspapers, as well as a career that would make him one of the top newspaper executives in American journalism. And it all began in 1942, during wartime and at a low ebb in staff morale, when prospects for the newspaper in a severely cutback civilian economy looked far from bright.

ENGAGING VISITOR, Georgelin Temby, six, stops to talk with Steve Trumbull, ace *Herald* reporter, during the dedication of the paper's new office building. Within a year Trumbull would be in the Navy, in which he served as a lieutenant-commander during World War II. After the war Trumbull was to travel the byways and backways of the state, writing about his experiences in salty and colorful language, and becoming known as Mr. Florida.

DEDICATING the *Miami Herald's* new office building in 1941, Florida Governor Spessard L. Holland stands between James L. Knight, left, and John S. Knight, right. Friendship between Holland and Jack Knight led to the *Herald's* promotion of the Everglades National Park.

17

In Seven League Boots

T HE ENTRY OF the United States into World War II caused Miami's tourist-oriented economy to take a nosedive, and the area faced early economic disaster. By the end of January 1942, Nazi submarines were prowling the Gulf Stream off the Florida coast, torpedoing ships within sight of the shore. With the Navy's meager anti-submarine forces needed elsewhere to guard North Atlantic convoys carrying war supplies to Britain and to Russia, as well as to guard ships carrying men and equipment to America's far-flung bases in the Pacific, the unescorted vessels using the Gulf Stream were like sitting ducks for sharpshooting submarine commanders. So brazen did Nazi commanders become that they often surfaced to inspect sinking ships. Civilians attempting to go to the rescue of seamen were ordered back ashore.

"Get the hell out of here before you get hurt," shouted a submarine commander at pleasure boat skippers who had dashed out to a sinking freighter. But no attacks were made on the unarmed civilians.

Twenty-five ships were torpedoed between Key West and Daytona Beach between 1942 and 1945, but most of the casualties occurred during the early part of the war, before the Navy had an opportunity to build defenses. All together, 111 ships were torpedoed in the Gulf of Mexico, the Caribbean, and off Florida's east coast. In early 1942 ships were hit within sight of the Key West Naval Station. The grim aspects of the war were brought to southeast Florida when a tanker was torpedoed off Miami Beach. The hulk drifted northward in the Gulf Stream, its cargo burning furiously. You could see the plume of black smoke from the *Herald's* newsroom windows, but no details could be carried in the paper because of wartime censorship. Nor could the *Herald* carry anything about the heroic efforts of civilians who went out into the Gulf Stream in all kinds of weather to pick up refugees from sinking ships. Likewise, the scores of bodies floating ashore went unexplained. Weeks after a torpedoing occurred newspapers were permitted to publish the barest details, but these releases contained so little information that readers could not always tell which incident a report referred to. Except for land-based sailors who began appearing downtown, the Navy seemed to be virtually nonexistent. The sailors had arrived to take over the seventeen-story Alfred I. duPont Building on Flagler Street as headquarters for the Seventh Naval District and for an antisubmarine center, the Gulf Sea Frontier.

Preparing for repulsing a possible landing by the enemy in the Miami area, a small army of volunteers under the Dade County Defense Council was formed, armed, and "trained" in defense deployment. To test Miami's defenses, writer Philip Wylie led a motley party ashore from Biscayne Bay. Storming vacant lots near the Miami Woman's Club just north of the Venetian Causeway, the party was met by an equally un-disciplined party of volunteers. The "battle" was indecisive, but the *Herald,* in order to warn the enemy that Miami was defended, reported the invasion was repulsed.

Tourism, on which Miami depended largely for its livelihood, was dead and without hope of revival so long as the war lasted. The manufac-ture of virtually all unnecessary civilian goods came to an end as industry was converted to the production of war materials. Rationing was started, beginning with gasoline and tires. Foreseeing a grim future for Miami, countless heads of families went elsewhere in search of wartime work, and thousands of younger men and women entered the armed forces. The *Herald* felt the effect of the war no less than did other businesses. Adver-tising and circulation declined, and the paper immediately began to lose its younger employees. Those going into the armed services continued to receive a percentage of their salaries, which, together with service pay, helped families to go through the war without grave financial problems. With declining circulation and advertising, the loss of a number of employees resulted in no immediate hardship. When the *Herald* was ordered to cut its newsprint use ten percent by a government rationing board, it appeared that the newspaper would be able to get along very well with the reduced supply.

But in 1942 two important decisions were made that had the effect of transforming the Miami area into a military camp. First, the Seventh Naval District headquarters together with the Gulf Sea Frontier were es-tablished in Miami. Second, the empty hotels in Miami and at Miami Beach were taken over by the military and transformed into barracks and schools for the training of thousands of Army, Air Corps (now Air Force), and Navy personnel. In addition, the Miami area was transform-

QUICK-THINKING, energetic, and a chain smoker, Lee Hills arrived in 1942 to take charge of the *Herald's* newsroom. He was to rise to publisher of the *Herald* and chairman of the board of Knight Newspapers, Inc.

ed into a major wartime aviation center. The Army Transport Command took over the Thirty-Sixth Street Airport and converted it into a terminal for overseas air transportation. After the war these facilities, valued at $100 million, would become part of the Miami International Airport. The Air Corps also began construction of a major base at Homestead, while the Navy was building a base at Richmond Field for submarine-hunting blimps. The Marine Corps established a training base for its airmen at the Opa-Locka Airport, now the site of the Miami-Dade Community College's north campus.

By September 1942, just nine months after the beginning of the war, Miami's economy was changing enormously. When Lee Hills arrived on September 27 as *Herald* city editor, he noted that the men and women in uniform were almost as numerous as civilians on Flagler Street. Things had changed on the *Miami Herald,* too. Not only had the paper regained the circulation lost in the early part of the war, but it was becoming virtually indispensable as a source of information about price controls, rationing, dimouts, and other wartime regulations, in addition to the routine coverage of the war's progress. The *Herald's* new role as a major public service newspaper had not been anticipated. The demands upon the paper for information had put an extra burden on the inadequate staff, which was becoming smaller month by month. The younger staff members were not the only ones going into the armed services. Old salt Steve Trumbull, one of the *Herald's* top reporters, went into the Navy at forty-four with a lieutenant's commission. Jack Anderson signed up in Navy public relations. The Evans brother, Luther and Lee, who had worked their way into the sports department through the copy boy route, went into the Army. Lee Evans, a paratrooper, would drop behind the German lines with his unit and receive more decorations than any other *Herald* employee. Sunday Editor Lester Barnhill got a second lieutenant's commission in the Army, while Real Estate Editor James Hodges went into the Navy as a junior grade lieutenant. Larry Rollins, news editor when Hills arrived, had received orders to report for a physical examination, first step toward induction. Hills was just getting acquainted with the city desk operations when he was elevated to news editor. And, so, with most of the better editors and reporters either in the armed forces or slated to go, Hills found himself with the task of building a new staff and of making better use of the overworked staff he already had. The morale of the staff was so low that many of the men who had failed to qualify for the services were talking about leaving Miami for civilian wartime jobs, as the recent city editor, Hy Aramstan, had done. To a less experienced, less capable editor than Hills the prospects of getting out a satisfactory paper with a marginal staff might have seemed hopeless. But despite the multitude of problems he faced, you immediately sensed the ability of Hills to overcome them. Within a week you began to notice an improvement in staff morale, mainly because of the confident leadership Hills displayed. But to appreciate how Hills was able to clear the air and to put new order into a confused and demoralized situation within so short a time, you need to know something of his background.

Thirty-six when he arrived in Miami, Lee Hills had been a newspaperman more than half his life, having started on a weekly, the *News Advocate,* at Price, Utah, when he was fourteen. Hills had done virtually every kind of job in the editorial department of a newspaper and, in the summer of 1942 when he journeyed to Akron, Ohio, to ask John S. Knight for a job, he was news editor of the *Cleveland Press.* "I had never talked with a newspaperman who had better credentials than Lee Hills," said Knight, recalling that interview.

The second of three sons of Louis Amos Hills and the former Lulu Mae Loomis, Lee was born on May 28, 1906, on a farm at Egg Creek, near Granville, North Dakota. His ancestors, mostly English, Welsh, and Scottish, had settled in the East in the early part of the nineteenth century. Although it was in North Dakota where his parents met and were married, both were born in Iowa. They had moved with their parents early in the 1900s to new land just being opened for settlement. But for a drought that made wheat growing unprofitable for a time, Hills might have grown up on the Egg Creek homestead. When he was three his parents moved to Salt Lake City where, for a time, they raised chickens. The chickens did not pay off, and the family moved to Price, where the father went into the insurance business. The boys sold newspapers and magazines, raised vegetables, and peddled them from door to door. Lee was eleven when the boys lost their mother, and then, with their father traveling a lot, they were virtually on their own. At fourteen Lee got a job on the *News Advocate,* doing whatever jobs came up, from sweeping the floor to writing school news, from helping print the paper to selling advertising. "We never had much; we were poor by today's standards," said Hills, "but we never thought of ourselves as poor. It seemed that everybody was always working and you worked yourself without considering an alternative." This attitude did much to shape the character of young Lee Hills. He worked on his job, he worked in school. He became a stringer for Salt Lake City's three newspapers. By the time he was eighteen he was editor of the *News Advocate* and was winning prizes for editing the best weekly newspaper in Utah. In high school he studied typing and shorthand. While in his senior year the court reporter at Price became ill at the beginning of an important court term. In a desperate search for a shorthand specialist, the court called upon the high school. Young Hills was recommended. For the next several weeks he sat through trial after trial as he took testimony in shorthand. That experience made shorthand as familiar to Hills as longhand, and he used it as a primary written language for the rest of his life. During college—he attended both Brigham Young and the University of Missouri—Hills took down lectures verbatim, and, being able to read his shorthand months after it was cold, he only had to refer to his notebooks when preparing for examinations. Among the lectures he took down verbatim were those given off the cuff by Walter Williams, famous dean of the University of Missouri's School of Journalism. Three years later, after Williams was elevated to president of the university, a professor who succeeded him wrote to Hills to see if he still had his shorthand notes. He did and was able to transcribe Williams' lectures exactly as they had been delivered. "Reading the shorthand was simple; it was all that typing that was a pain in the neck," said Hills.

Forced to leave college before getting his degree because of a lack of funds, Hills went to work as a reporter on the *Oklahoma City Times* in 1929. The owner and publisher of the *News Advocate,* a widow, had offered to sell the paper to Hills, allowing him to pay off the indebtedness out of profits. But he turned down this opportunity. "It would have been a way to make money," he said, "but I'd had a taste of metropolitan journalism by this time."

So he went to Oklahoma City. There he worked as a reporter and as a copyreader. He covered the state capitol and state politics. In 1932, looking for broader experiences, he went to work for the *Oklahoma City*

News, a Scripps-Howard paper. The years on the *News* were glamor years for him. He quickly became the paper's star reporter, covering the big stories—the "Machine Gun" Kelly and other sensational trials; the activities of outlaw Charles "Pretty Boy" Floyd, together with the Herschel kidnaping, and, in the meantime, the colorful doings of Governor William H. "Alfalfa Bill" Murray of Oklahoma. Managing Editor Bob Fredericks thought enough of Hills work that he raised his salary above his own in order to keep him. But by 1935 Hills felt like a "one-eyed man in the land of the blind." When Deke Parker, editor-in-chief of Scripps-Howard Newspapers, came to town one day to talk with him about his future, Hills was already doubting whether he measured up to all the praise he was getting.

"I felt a strong need for real professionals to show me how to be a better writer or editor, or whatever I was going to be," he said. He expressed this feeling to Parker, who himself had won his spurs as the first and most successful editor of the *Oklahoma News.* Parker gave him a choice.

"I came here," said Parker, "to ask you to go to Washington where we need a top political writer and perhaps a future columnist. But we also need editors. We have a spot on the *Celveland Press* leading in that direction."

"You decide," replied Hills. "Whichever you think I can do best and you need most." Parker chose Cleveland for Hills.

Hills, then twenty-nine, had experienced such self-questioning before. He loved newspapering. But in Oklahoma City, where he covered the courts, local and state government, and state legislature sessions, he became fascinated with the study of law. At twenty-three he realized that most of the newspapermen around him hadn't progressed beyond ordinary jobs even in their middle years. So he enrolled in what is now the Oklahoma City University School of Law, attending classes at night, and won himself a law degree. "I figured that by the time I was an old man of thirty if I had not made the grade as a newspaperman I would go into law," said Hills.

Law came easy. He liked it and did exceedingly well. And it's a good thing, because seventy percent of his class flunked the state bar examination. Oklahoma had just decided to raise its standards and it adopted the New York State tests. Hills finished in the top ten percent of the thirty percent that passed, with the result that he got some good offers from law firms. But, liking newspapering even more than law, he decided to stick with it for a while longer to see if he could "really make it."

At Cleveland he ran the gamut, beginning as an investigative reporter, to be followed by assignments to rewrite, copyreading, to the city desk, then to news editor. In 1936 there was a shakeup in the *Indianapolis Times* and Hills was invited to go there, first as chief editorial writer, then as associate editor. Meanwhile, a crisis was developing on his old paper, the *Oklahoma News,* which had been losing money for some time. Scripps-Howard became disenchanted with the newspaper's prospects and with its flamboyant editor, Bob Fredericks. Deke Parker told Hills that Fredericks was to be fired, and he asked Hills to take over. His assignment: to see whether the paper could be salvaged and if not to recommend a course of action. Within a year Hills had cut the losses in half, but reported that it would continue to be a marginal operation and recommended that the paper be sold or folded. He was given the job of liquidation, but before he left Oklahoma City he got new jobs for members of the staff who were willing to relocate.

Hills moved to Memphis for another tough assignment. Scripps-Howard published the *Press-Scimitar* and the *Commercial Appeal* in separate plants. Hills' job was to spark up the *Press-Scimitar* editorially in order to improve its image so that publication of both newspapers in the newer plant of the *Commercial Appeal* would be acceptable by the public. That job finished, Hills was transferred back to Cleveland as news editor to await a new top assignment. It was a slow period ·for newspapers, however, and Hills became restless. Louis B. Seltzer, Cleveland Press editor, prepared the way for a meeting of Hills and his friend, John S. Knight. Seltzer informed Knight, in nearby Akron, that Hills "might be looking." Seltzer said to Knight: "I told Lee that the only man he should work for is you."

A short time later, on a Sunday morning, Hills called upon Knight in his home in suburban Akron. Knight was impressed with the slender, well groomed, and quick-thinking Hills, and so was Mrs. Knight, who was present for part of the interview. Knight said he had no "top job" to offer but outlined the situation developing in Miami in that summer of 1942. He said Hills could start there as city editor.

"I'll take it," said Hills.

Knight talked freely about what Hills would find in Miami; about how John Barry, general manager of Knight Newspapers, and his brother Jim

ONE-ARMED and using a single finger to peck out his "Town Crier," Jack Bell was for twenty years Miami's most colorful columnist.

Knight, business manager of the *Herald*, had concentrated on cleaning up a bad business operation; about steps he had taken to improve the *Herald* editorially before he was diverted to Detroit where he had purchased the *Free Press* in 1940, and the big job that remained to be done. Knight was far from satisfied with the *Herald's* editorial department, particularly the news side. His preoccupation with the *Free Press*, however, had left him little time for the *Herald*. But Knight was pleased with a move he had made the previous year, the hiring of Jack Bell to write "The Town Crier" column. Bell was a personality, a decorated hero who had lost an arm in World War I, and it mattered little to Knight that Bell, onetime sports editor of the *Herald*, recently had been fired as sports editor of the *Miami News*. What did matter was that Bell could write with a style and a sensitivity that touched the hearts of readers. The flavor of the city and its people came alive in his columns—the bums, touts, confused tourists, do-gooders and no-gooders, prizefighters, jockeys, gamblers, evangelists, rabbis and priests, crippled children, old folks. In his column throbbed the pulse of Miami.

When Hills arrived at the *Herald*, with the title of city editor, he found Chuck Watters, son of the retail advertising manager, holding down the job. Watters, who himself was facing the draft, rose to relinquish the chair.

"Don't get up," said Hills. "I want to get acquainted with the staff and the paper before I take over."

Hills never did sit down to the job. The news editor, Larry Rollins, was on his way into the Army within a few days, and Hills moved into his job. Bob Fredericks, the *Herald's* amusement editor and onetime Hills' boss in Oklahoma City, had hoped to succeed Rollins, but Knight passed him over. News editor at that time was really equivalent to the position of managing editor. But Pennekamp still held that title, although he was chief editorial writer and preoccupied with the writing of a daily column.

Hills' first move was to recruit Ned Aitchison from the *St. Petersburg Times* as city editor. Aitchison was an able newspaperman who gave a new stability to the staff. Hills called reporters and editors he had known on other newspapers, offering them jobs. And he advertised in *Editor & Publisher*, the newspaperman's trade journal. He also hired all the qualified women copyreaders and reporters he could find, but the newspaper profession had not been very attractive to women up to that time and few trained newspaper women were available. A new staff was built, although it was one of uneven talent. However, Hills now had warm bodies that he could put to work, and he set out to improve the *Herald's* image as a wartime public service newspaper. In the meantime, he started making gradual changes to modernize the typography and format of the paper. He initiated the building of a servicemen's news file. Parents who had sons or daughters in the military service were urged to send photographs and biographical material to the *Herald.* Several filing cabinets soon were filled with such material, and whenever a report came of a South Floridian being killed or wounded or, happily, decorated for heroism, the *Herald* had only to go to the files to obtain a half-column cut of the subject, together with additional biographical information. And to stop the spread of insidious rumor, Hills started a "Rumor Clinic." He urged readers to call the *Herald* and report the rumors they had heard. A reporter was assigned to run down rumors, checking with the military or civilian authorities until an answer was obtained. More often than not the rumors were groundless, but occasionally a rumor would be true, or partly true. Whatever the answer, it was reported in the "Rumor Clinic."

Two months after Hills' arrival he figured he had things going satisfactorily under wartime conditions. Then, on Sunday morning, November 29, 1942, Hills experienced his first crisis on the *Herald.* It was over a wire story out of Boston, the Cocoanut Grove night club fire; the *Miami News* had clobbered the *Herald* on the story. In 1942 the *News* was a far more competitive paper than it would be in later years. It had a Sunday edition, home-delivered in direct competition with the *Herald.* And it was an excellent newspaper, challenging both editorial and business departments of the *Herald.* On that Sunday Hills had left the *Herald* about 1:00 a.m., when copy desk slotman Charlie Ward was ready to put the final edition to bed. Top play was given to the war news from Russia with an eight-column streamer, "Reds Rout Germans West of Moscow." A second, smaller streamer covered wartime regulations: "New Dimout Will Hit Homes, Stores Monday." Hills walked to his apartment, two blocks from his office, and fell soundly asleep. Recently separated from his first wife, he was spending the days and part of each night in the newsroom.

Early on Sunday he picked up both the *Herald* and the *News,* which had been delivered to the door of his apartment. The *Herald's* front page was the same one he had seen some hours before. But when he looked at the front page of the *News* he was greeted by two eight-column black banner lines: "At Least 212 Dead, Hundreds Injured/As Fire, Panic Sweep Boston Night Club."

Hills couldn't believe his eyes. It was incredible. Not a line in the *Herald* about the tragedy. He showered, went to the office, and called Charlie Ward, copy desk editor, and Erit Wilson, telegraph editor.

"I want you to get down to the *Herald* as soon as you can," he said. "I want to talk with you."

They arrived and Hills read them off.

"But, Lee," complained Ward, "there wasn't a thing we could do. The story didn't break until after the final edition had been put to bed, and after that only Bill Sandlin and Henry Troetschel can stop the presses—and they have to agree on stopping them."

Bill Sandlin, a cigar-smoking, pot-bellied, no-nonsense type boss, was head of the composing room, while Troetschel, a serious man who wouldn't dare disobey an order from Jim Knight, was circulation manager. Hills listened to Ward in disbelief. He had never heard of the composing room and the circulation department making such a vital decision as to whether the presses should be stopped for an important story.

"Well, they do here," said Ward, to which the nervous Wilson nodded his head in agreement. "Hell, I argued with Bill Sandlin last night until I was blue in the face. Finally, he called Troetschel and they agreed to let me get in a bulletin on the fly. But it was then so late we made only about 2,000 papers on the final run."

Hills apologized to Ward and Wilson and sent them back home to bed. But to him the matter was far from being closed. He was not sure he would remain on the *Herald*. Certainly he would not continue to work under what seemed to him to be impossible restrictions on an editor. On Monday morning, before he could confront Jim Knight and talk it out, Jim came by Hills' desk and paused.

"Well," said Knight, smiling sarcastically, "I see that the editorial department really got clobbered by the *News* on the Boston fire." (On Monday morning the *Herald* had carried an up-to-date account of the fire. By this time it appeared that deaths might reach 400. The death toll eventually was set at 491.)

"No," replied Hills, "it wasn't the editorial department that took a beating. The system around here took the beating; it was the composing room and the circulation department—which have the power to edit this newspaper—that got clobbered, not the editorial department."

"How's that?" asked Knight, now quite serious. He saw that Hills was in dead earnest.

Hills explained what had happened, then added: "Jim, if you're going to have the composing room and the circulation department make the editorial department's decisions on the *Herald,* you don't need an editor and I think your brother made a mistake in hiring me. I think it's a hell of a way to run a newspaper."

Knight agreed. Then he explained the reason for the rule. Some costly editorial decisions had been made in the past, and the restrictions had been imposed to make sure the paper got printed on time. But now Knight was ready to have this authority go back to the editorial department. And out of this incident grew the closest possible working relationship between Jim Knight and Lee Hills, which was to continue through the years.

A year after the Boston fire episode, Hills and Knight faced another major problem, this time together. It was a newsprint crisis. At the beginning of the war, when the *Herald* was ordered to reduce its use of newsprint by ten percent, it caused no problem. But by mid-1943 more than 150,000 servicemen were in the Miami area. Instead of the depressed economic conditions that Miami had felt at the beginning of the war, the area now was enjoying a surging economy. With servicemen's families following them to Miami, homes and apartments were scarce. The prices of homes had about doubled within a period of less than two years; merchants were busy, selling the things allowed them in a wartime economy. The *Herald,* as much as any other business, was feeling the wartime economic surge. The paper not only had regained much of its prewar advertising volume, but the circulation was reaching new records every week. By November of 1943 the *Herald* was facing a critical newsprint shortage. Efforts to obtain relief through newspaper rationing authorities in Washington had been of no avail, despite the wartime changes that had turned the Miami area into an armed camp. In late November Jim Knight told Hills the *Herald* would run out of paper in two weeks, long before the new January paper rationing allotments could arrive.

"I figure that if we're going to get through December we'll have to cut the paper to ten or twelve pages daily and to about thirty-six pages on Sunday," said Knight. But how would advertising and news space be allocated? That was the problem.

Hills came up with a suggestion: cut out all display advertising for the full month of December and restrict classified advertising to housing, employment, and a few other war-related and essential items.

"Let's continue full coverage of the war and what people at home need to know to support the war effort," he said. "We can also conserve newsprint by cutting off circulation outside our immediate territory."

Hills then proposed to give one page free to the *Herald's* display advertisers, prorating the space to each according to the amount of space these advertisers had been buying in the past. Knight agreed that there appeared to be no alternative, but the thought of losing so much money during a normally heavy advertising month was a little shocking.

"Maybe we should call Jack first," he said.

John S. Knight was at that time chief liaison officer in charge of United States censorship in London.

"No," replied Hills, "I think Jack would do the same."

"All right, we'll do it, then," said Jim.

It was the right decision. Although unhappy, merchants appreciated the situation and were pleased to take advantage of the opportunity to run without cost their ads in the single page set aside for this purpose.

Meanwhile, the *Herald* continued to publish a full budget of war news and local news. London's great editor and publisher, Lord Beaverbrook, whose paper was reduced to four pages daily, read copies of the *Herald* passed on by Jack Knight, and had the highest praise for the complete news coverage during this trying period.

It proved to be a major turning point for the *Herald*. Its aggressive competitor, the *News,* boasted that it continued to give full space to advertisers during this period, but its news coverage suffered by comparison. The *Herald* had been gaining in circulation and would continue to gain even faster in the years ahead. The *Herald* temporarily took it on the chin financially, but it stockpiled reader confidence to an extent that it steadily pulled far out in front in the competitive battle.

The experience with the newsprint crisis paid a special dividend to Jim Knight. After making that decision at the age of thirty-four, he never would have trouble in making another.

18

Editor Challenges Judge

T HE UNITED STATES had been in the war more than a year when John S. Knight received a call from Steve Early, President Roosevelt's press secretary.

"Jack," said Early, "I've just been talking with Byron Price. He asked me to call and see if you would do an important job for him."

Price was head of the Federal Bureau of Censorship.

"What is it, Steve?" asked Knight.

Knight was interested, even though he reacted guardedly. He felt it keenly that nobody in the government had called to ask his help in the war effort. Although forty-eight and too old for the infantry, he was still in the prime of life and in top physical condition. With his background, he felt there were many administrative jobs he could do, as a civilian or in uniform.

"We're getting quite a trimming in England, involving censorship," said Early. "The British are going through our mails to obtain information on America's postwar plans in Europe—particularly in banking and aviation. They do this through what they call 'intercepts.' Our mail is being intercepted, and experts extract pertinent information.

"Byron is looking for someone to serve as liaison officer between the United States and British censorship offices in London. This is an important but delicate job. The individual has to be hard-headed and decisive, yet he must not be someone without personal charm or lacking in diplomacy. Britain is our ally and we can't be brazenly offensive, yet these intercepts must be stopped. We must have a censorship office in London that is capable of handling all United States mail. Byron is looking for someone to handle this job, and I told him you would be the best I knew. He asked me to give you a call."

"Well, Steve, I know nothing about this sort of thing," said Knight. "I can't undertake anything I know absolutely nothing about."

"Don't worry about that; they'll train you in procedures," said Early.

"In that case I would be interested," said Knight.

After a visit to Washington for an interview with Price, Knight returned to Miami and signed up as a federal government employee at the lowest civil service rating—the pay then was $1,100 a year—and began to cram on censorship procedures. Miami was a good place to learn, because the censorship station here was one of the more important in the country. Many worked here who had skills in languages. Quite a few individuals in the West Indies and Latin America were working directly with the Nazis, and it was the responsibility of the Miami censorship office to see that no information left the country which might aid the enemy. After several weeks in the Miami office, Knight went to Washington for further briefing, and in April of 1943 he went to London.

Trim, a natty dresser, a little swaggering without being offensive, the self-confident Jack Knight was to the British the perfect image of an American. He stayed at the luxurious Park Lane Hotel where the top people came and went. Having money to spend—his own—he entertained at every opportunity. The British liked his direct manner and his earthy sense of humor. He also let them know that he had been an infantry officer in World War I and had seen action on the Alsace-Lorraine sector in France. And when the Nazi planes flew over, dropping blockbusters and fire bombs on the city, Knight coolly joined the British in underground shelters. Meanwhile, Knight stepped up the efficiency of the American censorship office, and, gradually taking care of more and more mail, convinced the British that his office not only could handle all United States mail but intended to do so. He was a year in London, going through the blitz and experiencing the agony of seeing so much of the grand old city destroyed by bombs and fire.

In 1944, just before returning to the United States, Knight gave a party at the Park Lane for American servicemen from the Miami area. Nearly all were with the Eighth Air Corps, who were at that time clobbering the Nazis. Among his guests were two lieutenant-colonels attached to Air Corps public relations, both of whom had worked for the *Miami News* before the war. One was Hal Leyshon, managing editor, the other Jack Kofoed, columnist. Leyshon, who had no intention of returning to the *News,* pressed Knight to think about buying the paper.

"Hell, I don't want to buy the *News,"* replied Knight. "Competition is healthy for the *Herald.*

"If you were to buy the *News,"* said Leyshon, "I'd like to work for you. Of course, for a time it would be a sixteen-hour-a-day job."

"Hal," said Knight, "I don't have any sixteen-hour-a-day people working for me. If you work for me, you've got to get your work done in eight hours."

The party was about to break up when Knight asked Kofoed if he intended to return to Miami after the war.

"I like Miami," replied Kofoed. "I don't think I'd want to work anywhere else."

"Well, how would you like to work for me?"

"There's nothing I'd like better."

Taking adantage of an armed forces order granting anyone over fifty a chance to leave the service, Kofoed resigned from the Air Corps a few months later and returned to Miami. He began his column, "Jack Kofoed Says," on November 11, 1944. Kofoed had a brilliant career as a sports writer and columnist on New York newspapers before coming to Florida in the 1930s. Possessing a keen memory for names, events, and details, Kofoed could produce his column around the calendar without missing a day, even while on vacation. This he insisted upon.

"The loyalty of a reader lasts but one day," he said.

Although a clever and facile writer, Kofoed did not attempt to express the warm sentiments that readers found in Jack Bell's "Town Crier." Bell, Irish-Catholic and a perennial do-gooder, was a favorite object of supplication by countless downtrodden Miamians. They came early of a morning—winos, abandoned women, men who claimed the police had beaten them, the cripples, the sick in mind and body. The one-armed Bell would peck away on his typewriter with one finger while listening. So many were his callers that he had been forced to learn to do his column while listening to the flow of stories. Watching him as his face grew longer, you got the idea that he really heard nothing; but somehow he did hear. For as soon as the relater stopped talking Bell had a solution. The person was sent to one of the charities that the *Herald* supported, or if the story was of sufficient interest he would jot down a few notes before dismissing the individual. If the caller was hungry Bell would write a note that was good for a meal at the Herald Grille across Miami Avenue. One day when a wino pushed the note back to Bell, saying he wanted money, not food, Bell looked up and said.

"Scram, and don't come back."

But when the wino decided to take the food order anyway, Bell relented and handed it back to him.

"You're a bum, you know it," said Bell.

"I know I'm a bum, Jack," said the wino. "Oh, come on, give me fifty cents so I can buy a bottle of Old Tank Car."

Softening, Bell dug into his pocket and got some change and planked it on the desk.

"Don't blame me if they pick you up and put you back in jail," said Bell.

"I don't mind," said the bum, inching away from the desk now that he had the money. "Jail's not that bad. They feed you and give you a place to sleep."

The bum shuffled off and as Bell proceeded to peck away on his machine another down-and-outer moved forward to take the warm seat. After continuing to peck away for a few moments, Bell, without looking up, growled:

"Well, what is it this time?"

And another story of hardships and misery started pouring out. But with the war in progress in Europe and Asia, Bell wanted to get away from the down-and-out and see some action, and he kept nagging Lee Hills until he was sent to cover General "Vinegar Joe" Stillwell's Burma campaign, and later to Europe.

Meanwhile, in Miami the war had accomplished what moralists had been unable to do; it had closed the town to police-protected gambling and prostitution. But 1942 and 1943 were dark years. Long years of belt-tightening and fighting seemed to lie ahead, and an atmosphere of austerity prevailed. By 1944, however, the picture was beginning to look brighter. Optimism prevailed among the military and the civilians, with the result that some of the restraint was relaxed and people sought to "live it up" in the style they could afford. In keeping with the trend, the military establishment permitted the opening of a few select gambling places, under the watchful eyes of the military and civilian police, while keeping the lid clamped on prostitution. Among the clubs permitted to open were the Little Palm Club and Frolics Club in Miami, the Brook Club in Surfside, and the Teepee Club on the Tamiami Trail.

The Brook and Little Palm were high-class dining places as well as elite gambling casinos, offering gourmet food, even with wartime rationing, in addition to games of chance at roulette, dice, and blackjack. Both places became popular hangouts for military brass, politicians, businessmen, shady black-market characters, and wealthy older residents who had not become involved in the war and were bored with the restricted kind of life imposed upon them. Miami's newspapers and its better citizens exerted pressure to have the clubs closed. But with orders from higher ups, the police and sheriff's deputies continued to let the clubs operate. The state attorney, Stanley Milledge, who had been elected on a reform pledge, sought to close the clubs through court injunctions. His efforts proved fruitless. Affidavits which he presented to the Circuit Court as proof that the clubs were operating were thrown out on technicalities. This was nothing new. It always had been virtually impossible to close Dade County's gambling places or to bring the casino operators and bookmakers to trial because of the technicalities that judges found in search warrants, affidavits, complaints, or indictments. The *Miami Herald* took note of these deficiencies editorially, and particularly the difficulty of preparing an unchallengeable search warrant. An editorial suggested that the judges get together and produce an example of the legally perfect paper. The suggestion was ignored. In early November 1944, after the efforts of the state attorney to close the newly opened gambling casinos had been thwarted by the Circuit Court judges, the *Herald's* argument with the courts came to a head. The first of two editorials, under a heading of "Courts are Established for the People," along with a provocative cartoon by *Herald* cartoonist Pat Enright, appeared on November 2. Written by Arthur Griffith, who had attended Oxford and the Sorbonne, the editorial was long, erudite, and pointedly cutting in its criticism of Dade County's courts and judges.

"Every accused person has a right to his day in court," said the editorial in part, "but when judicial instance and interpretive procedure recognize and accept, even go out and find, every possible technicality of the law to protect the defendant, to block, thwart, hinder, embarrass and nullify prosecution, then the people's rights are jeopardized and the basic reason for courts stultified."

Enright's cartoon depicted a judge handing a criminal his dismissal papers while a disturbed citizen, standing below the bench, cried out in protest, "But Judge!"

Five days later a second editorial appeared. Captioned "Why People Wonder," it was short and critical.

Two days after the second editorial appeared, John Pennekamp, who had ordered the editorials, was on his way to lunch when he encountered Judge Paul D. Barns of the Circuit Court. They greeted each other amiably, stopped, chatted.

"I'm on my way to a Rotary luncheon at the Urmey Hotel," said Barns. "Why don't you join me, Mr. Pennekamp?

Pennekamp accepted the invitation. The senior judge of the Circuit Court and the chairman of the *Herald's* editorial page had enjoyed a hand-shaking acquaintance for fifteen years. Barns had become a circuit judge in 1927 at the age of thirty-three. He was a bright and self-assured man of less than average stature. Proud of his record, he had not let his friends, or reporters, overlook his meteoric rise in the judicial profession at so early an age. Now at fifty, he had won a place of lofty esteem among his fellow members of the bar. Many years after that luncheon Pennekamp would remember that the judge was cordial, that the conversation was light and friendly, and that after the luncheon he and Barns shook hands and parted on friendly terms.

Next morning a deputy sheriff entered Pennekamp's office in the

Herald and served him with a citation for contempt of court. Critical statements made in the two editorials, as well as the cartoon itself, were listed as grounds for issuing the citation. Pennekamp and the Miami Herald Publishing Company were ordered to appear in Circuit Court on November 28 and show cause why they "should not be held and adjudged to be in contempt." Beneath this commanding paragraph were the signatures of Marshall C. Wiseheart and Paul D. Barns, circuit judges.

Pennekamp had two options. He could appear before the judges in an apologetic mood, obsequiously denying that the *Miami Herald* had any intention of embarrassing the courts or of doing anything that would "interfere with the judges" in the "administration of justice," as the citation charged the editorials had done. This would have been an easy way out. Pennekamp doubtless would have been lectured, threatened with a jail sentence if he should repeat the offense, then forgiven. An apology would have appeared in the *Herald* the following morning, and the case would have been closed. But Pennekamp chose to challenge the judges, and Jack Knight, who only recently had returned from London, backed him.

"Well, if you're sure you're right, then go ahead," said Knight.

Pennekamp appeared before the judges with the *Herald's* lawyers, together with Elisha Hanson, eminent Washington attorney assigned to the case by the American Newspaper Publishers Association. They asked that the contempt citation be quashed on the grounds that the court lacked jurisdiction to issue it, that the criticism was not contemptuous, and that it was legitimate within the guarantees of both the United States and Florida constitutions.

The judges had to be aware of the corruption in the Miami area. Lawyer and bondsman reached jail ahead of the lawbreaker, the first with a writ of habeas corpus, the second with bonding money. And thus behind a facade of proper judicial procedure and legalistic gobbledegook was operated one of the best greased and most cynical spoils system in the country. It was this system that Pennekamp was fighting when he decided to stand up in court and challenge the judge who had bought his lunch. Only in this way could a newspaper ever gain the right to criticize the courts, heretofore held so sacrosanct that few editors dared to point a finger.

On December 18 the judges handed down their decision, denying the motion to quash the contempt citation and fining both the *Herald* and Pennekamp—$1,000 for the *Herald,* $250 for Pennekamp. An appeal was made to the Florida Supreme Court, and what was to become a landmark case, defining the rights, of newspapers to criticize courts and judges, was on its way to the highest court in the land.

The editor who was making this challenge was a person of strong personality and independent mind. As a veteran city editor he had been direct and terse when dealing with underling editors and reporters. An able newspaperman, he expected a good performance by his staff, and none dared question his orders or his judgment. Young reporters feared his wrath. But Pennekamp really wasn't that tough. He only appeared to be because of his efficiency, his speed as a copyreader, and his ability to make quick decisions. He had been a no-nonsense city editor, cutting out frills, purple language, or padded stories. He belonged to the who-what-where-when-and-how school of journalism. He liked to get as many local stories into the newspaper as possible, and unless a story was important or highly entertaining it was sure to be cut. Pennekamp possessed a quality that a stranger was quick to notice—confidence. Having been a boss for most of his career, he had become accustomed to running an organization and giving orders.

Born in Cincinnati of German-Catholic parents on New Year's Day of 1897, Pennekamp began working on the *Cincinnati Post* as a copy boy at fourteen. Except for a hitch in the infantry during World War I, he had never worked in any other profession. He went through high school by attending night classes. Working his way as a reporter and as a copy reader on the *Post*, he became city editor at twenty-two and news editor in his middle twenties. He was hired as *Miami Herald* city editor in 1925 by O. W. Kennedy, who thought he had seen in Pennekamp the strong executive who could build his own city desk staff and operate with limited supervision from above. Although publisher Shutts never gave him a higher title, he looked upon Pennekamp as the editor who got out the paper. Some years after he had sold the *Herald* to the Knights, Shutts was quoted as saying: "I knew nothing about the newspaper business myself; I had Penny."

Jack Knight made Pennekamp managing editor after he became publisher in 1937, elevating Managing Editor Hollums to executive editor. But in the change Pennekamp's duties changed none; he had been doing the managing editor's job for several years. When Hollums departed in 1941, Pennekamp moved into the editorial page editor's chair. Having been in Miami sixteen years, he knew the area well, its bad side as well as its good. There was never any doubt how the *Miami Herald* stood on an issue. And when Pennekamp believed he was right, nobody could influence him to take a moderate stand. By the fall of 1944 Pennekamp was becoming widely known as "Mr. Miami Herald," having gained greater prestige than John S. Knight, who had spent little time in the city since 1940, the year he acquired the *Detroit Free Press*. Politicians—friends or enemies—wanted to know how Pennekamp felt about an issue before they became involved. They never asked how the *Herald* viewed an issue; they wanted to know what Pennekamp thought.

If Pennekamp had a major weakness it was an over-suspicion of politicians, business leaders, and law enforcement officials. Having been close to the Miami scene for so long, he could be quick to brush off do-gooders as charlatans or as self-seeking persons with ulterior motives. Pennekamp's attitude sometimes irritated Jack Knight, who tended to be more tolerant. But although publisher and editor did not always agree, there were no great differences between them. Knight had admiration for Pennekamp, a man of decision, of action, and, above all, integrity. His courage was never demonstrated more than in 1945 after the Florida Supreme Court upheld the Circuit Court's decision in the contempt case against him and the *Herald.* Vowing to carry the case to the United States Supreme Court, Pennekamp stated:

"We stand squarely on our right to bring the conduct of our courts to the attention of our readers at all times."

The decision of the Florida Supreme Court was not unexpected. Most of the seven members had been nurtured in the South where authority and institutions, particularly courts and judges, were looked upon as above criticism. Five of the judges sided with this viewpoint of judicial sanctity, and Justice Glenn Terrell, the court's ablest phrasemaker, wrote a scorching opinion, with the obvious intention of putting critical editors and newspapers in their places for all time. Terrell condemned both editorials and Enright's cartoon. He went on to say:

"Since Chief Justice Coke said to King James I, 'The King is under God and the law,' the judge has been the symbol of law and justice as familiar to the people of this country as the symbol of Uncle Sam. Speak the word 'Judge' and there arises the visage of Marshall, Miller, Holmes, Brandeis, Taylor, or Whitfield, the very symbol of justice and wisdom."

Although *Herald* lawyers found several errors in the court's finding, Pennekamp turned down an opportunity to ask for a rehearing. He said later:

"We stood by our original determination to avoid any technicalities or technical delays, not to labor incidental aspects, and to keep the focus on the question:

"Has a newspaper the right to inform its readers of what is going on in the courts without fear that an annoyed judge will use his contempt power to silence the newspaper or its editor?"

That question the United States Supreme Court answered unanimously on June 3, 1946. In reversing the Florida Supreme Court's decision, it threw out the contempt convictions, and the justices wrote four strong opinions upholding a newspaper's right to criticize a court. The high court had in no way weakened the judiciary; it merely had reduced judges from the level of saints to humans.

The *Herald,* meanwhile, had been able to keep most of the casino gambling clubs closed through a practice of reporting every one that opened. Before the war the paper had conducted sporadic campaigns against vice. Discovering that the gambling casinos were open, bookmaking flourishing, and the houses of prostitution active, the *Herald* would launch a headline campaign. Embarrassed operators closed and prostitutes ran for cover, while the sheriff and police chiefs made vigorous denials that they knew anything was going on. With nothing left to report, the editors assigned reporters to something else. The unlawful operations then resumed. But after the courts stymied State Attorney Milledge's efforts to close the casinos. Lee Hills adopted a policy of having the city desk keep up with gambling activities and report them routinely. Through Henry Reno, who had a wealth of contacts, it was possible to know the day and almost the hour when a gambling club opened its doors. A two or three paragraph story would appear next morning, noting that the roulette wheels were turning again at the Little Palm Club or that tuxedo-clad gentlemen were rolling dice at Club 86. The clubs closed, only to open a few nights later. But the reopenings were reported in a short item the next morning. With such harassment, the casinos were able to operate only spasmodically, and eventually most of them closed for good.

Fortunately for John S. Knight he had trustworthy management at the *Herald,* for in 1944 he succeeded the late Frank Knox as publisher of the *Chicago Daily News,* adding a fourth important paper to Knight Newspapers. Knox, who died in April of 1944, had directed in his will that his executors sell his majority interest in the *News.* The will suggested that a buyer be sought who, as publisher would preserve the character and traditions of the *News.* A score of bidders sought to buy the Knox stock. Knight was one of the bidders, and his bid was by no means among the highest. But as the list was narrowed down Knight's name was retained and eventually he was offered the Knox stock, for which Knight Newspapers paid $3 million and assumed $12 million of indebtedness. Knox had been Roosevelt's wartime secretary of the Navy, and the newspaper, feeling his absence, had lost some of its luster. Knight put Basil L. "Stuffy" Walters, crusty, prodding editor, in charge of the *News,* then began fielding criticism that resulted in the changes made by Walters. The *News* had acquired a reputation for devoting more space to foreign news coverage than any other Chicago newspaper. Knight, however, looked upon the *News'* coverage as merely voluminous and dull. He wanted a newspaper that would be read. This meant brighter, succinct writing and the discouragement of long, ponderous articles. In Walters he had selected an editor who could make the changes, and gradually they were made. Carl Sandburg was so offended that he refused to enter the *News* building.

"John S. Knight is guilty of so many sins that they add up to one big one," he said.

Knight made no reply to the poet's criticism but went on insisting that a story had to be readable before anyone would read it, and argued that if a story wasn't read, it did not inform anyone. When a foreign policy dilettante demanded to know why Knight no longer attempted to produce the kind of paper that Frank Knox had published, Knight snapped:

"If this paper had continued to be edited as it was, there wouldn't be any *Daily News.*"

Knight had just reached fifty when he acquired the prestigious *Daily News.* By March 1945, it was obvious that the war in Europe was rapidly coming to an end, while American forces were preparing to take Okinawa in order to set up a jumping-off place for the invasion of Japan proper. It had been a curious war for Jack Knight, who had fought strongly against Roosevelt's involvement in the political turmoil that had shaken Europe and the Far East during the 1930s. But after the United States was involved in the war there was no more determined fighter than Knight. And while he himself was too old to enter active combat, his oldest son, John S. Knight, Jr., had gone into the Army in June 1942, as a second lieutenant after graduation from Culver Military Academy. For a time he was stationed at Fort Bragg, North Carolina, where he trained with a field artillery unit. It was a dull kind of military duty, however, and in 1943 he asked to be transferred to Fort Benning, Georgia, for training as a paratrooper. At nearby Columbus young Knight met Dorothy Elizabeth Wells. They were soon married. After completion of his training, Lieutenant Knight was shipped overseas with the Seventeenth Airborne Division. He participated in the drive through France, and, in December 1944, just before the German counterattack which became known as the Battle of the Bulge, Knight was elevated to first lieutenant for his audacious performances. In January 1945, he won the Bronze Star. In the weeks ahead, after helping to blunt the desperate German counter-offensive, Knight joined in the pursuit of the fleeing Nazi army into Germany.

Some weeks later, early in April, Jack Knight was playing golf in a foursome at the Indian Creek Country Club. He had just driven off the tenth tee when his brother, Jim, reached his side.

"It's Johnny," said Jim reluctantly, then proceeded to inform his older brother of the death of his son in Germany.

Miami Weather		6 Star Service

The Miami Herald

—Florida's Most Complete Newspaper—

Monday, December 8, 1941   No. 5.   32nd Year   26 Pages   Price 5 Cents

Japan Wars On U. S.;
Planes Bomb Hawaii

Armed Force Is Mobilized At Top Speed

FDR Will Address Congress At Noon; Leaders In Line

By CLIFFORD A. PREVOST

New Theater of Action Opens In South Pacific, Making War Worldwide

Raid Guam, Philippines; Wake Seized

Invade Thailand; American Battleships Reported Sunk

BY THE ASSOCIATED PRESS

War's Impact Felt At Once In Miami Area

Angry Congress Unites In Demand For Action

By the Associated Press

Eyewitness Tells of Blow To Honolulu

By RICHARD HALLER

HONOLULU BOMBED TWICE

Lewis Wins Union Shop

Tojo Pledges Jap Victory

Miamian Reported Aboard Oklahoma

U. of M. Classes Canceled Today

Gasoline Is Rationed To Mexico City Drivers

America First Group Pledges War Support

Georgia Flier Killed

Code For Victory's 'V' Adopted By Herald To Mark Stories' End

---

TWO DRAMATIC FRONT PAGES of the *Miami Herald*—December 8, 1941, and August 15, 1945—mark the beginning and the end of World War II for the United States. But

The Weather

The Miami Herald

FOURTH EXTRA

Wednesday, August 15, 1945   No. 255   Florida's Most Complete Newspaper   X   12 Pages   35th Year   5 Cents

WAR ENDS

★ ★ ★ ★ ★ ★ ★ ★ ★

Japs Accept Allied Terms; End Of Fighting Ordered

'We Want Harry.' Wild Crowd Chants At White House

President Appears Three Times In Answer To Great Ovation

By United Press

WASHINGTON—Harry S. Truman of independence, Mo., wrote the words and directed the music Tuesday night as the wildest celebration this capital ever saw.

At the main gate of the mansion and happiest crowd that broke into cheers as the stars emerged from the White House as soon as she had...

GEN. DOUGLAS MacARTHUR WILL RECEIVE JAP SURRENDER

'Hopes Sentence Won't Be Executed'

Petain Is Convicted, Sentenced To Death

By the Associated Press

PARIS—Marshal Henri Philippe Petain was convicted and sentenced to death early Wednesday by three judges and a 21-man jury who deliberated almost eight hours.

By United Press

WASHINGTON—Peace came to the world Tuesday night when President Truman announced that Japan has accepted unconditional surrender and that Allied forces have been ordered to cease firing.

Gen. Douglas MacArthur, "the man who came back," was named supreme Allied commander to receive the formal Japanese surrender.

World War II—The bloodiest conflict in all of human history—was at an end, except for the formality of signing surrender documents.

V-J day will not be proclaimed until after the instruments of surrender are signed.

The three Allies in the Pacific war—Great Britain, Russia and China—will be represented at the signing by high ranking officers.

Mr. Truman proclaimed the glad tidings at 7 p. m. (Miami time), shortly after he received Tokyo's formal reply to the Allied surrender terms.

Summoning reporters to his office, he read a statement which said:

"I deem this reply a full acceptance of the Potsdam declaration which specified the unconditional surrender of Japan.

"In the reply there is no qualification."

Truman Declares Holiday

WASHINGTON—(UP)—President Truman Tuesday night declared a two-day legal holiday, Wednesday and Thursday, for all federal employes in Washington and throughout the country. He told a press conference that the reason for two days was the employes had not had a chance to celebrate the last surrender on V-E day.

Announcement

'Cease Firing'—Nimitz

GUAM—(AP)—Orders have been issued to the United States Pacific Fleet and other forces under Fleet Admiral Chester W. Nimitz to cease offensive operations against the Japanese. The communique, read from Nimitz' headquarters at noon, Wednesday, Guam time, followed President Truman's announcement that Japan had accepted the Potsdam surrender declaration by three hours.

Turn To Page 4

---

the dates would be relegated to minor importance by youths involved in the Korean and Vietnam wars.

Jack's companions, likewise stunned by the news, wanted to end the game, but at his insistence played on. The remaining nine holes were played in grim silence. Knight blew the par-three tenth hole, shooting a five, but got hold of himself and finished the game only a few strokes off his usual game. "I just had to keep going," he told a friend later.

Young Knight was leading a reconnoitering party, two miles ahead of the main body of troops, when the party encountered a German unit. All but one in Knight's party were slain.

Jack Knight could not go near his office for three weeks. Then, on April 22, he wrote one of the most inspired and touching columns of his career—about the thousands of "Johnnies," who, like his own son, had given their lives. For anyone who has known Jack Knight the column is still touching to read more than a quarter-century after it was written. There is, however, a postscript to this story which was to compensate somewhat for Knight's loss of his son. A week before he wrote that column a grandson was born to the young widow. He was appropriately named John Shively Knight III.

19

Fire in the Wind

XCEPT FOR THE land boom of 1925, no other event in Miami's
history had done so much to change the city as World War II. At
the war's beginning Miami still had many of the qualities of a
small town. As you walked down Miami Avenue or along Flagler Street
you met person after person you called by their first names. You even got
to know many of the "snowbirds" who spent their winters in Miami. The
war changed all that. Miamians returned home in late 1945 or early 1946
to discover that most of the old faces had disappeared. Or, if they had
not, the number of people you knew had become diluted by hundreds
you did not know. The war had brought countless young men and
women in uniform to Dade County. These young people did not forget,
and thousands of them, particularly those not yet tied down to one place
by the responsibilities of jobs or families, returned to try their fortunes.
Dade's population virtually doubled between 1940 and 1950, increasing
from 267,739 to 495,084.

The *Miami Herald's* daily circulation more than doubled during the
same period, increasing from 86,313 in 1941 to 175,985 in 1951. Circulation increased enormously during 1944 and 1945, when the military population was at its height. An expected postwar circulation loss did not occur. Instead, in 1946 the *Herald* gained 17,467 new daily readers, just under the record gain in 1944 of 17,585. The *Miami News,* meanwhile,
showed its first major signs of weakness, a portent of the disappointing
years ahead.

The slipping of the *News,* however, did not prevent it from beating the
Herald on an important story in June 1945, just before the war with
Japan was to come to an end. During the war censorship prevented both
newspapers from divulging more than a smattering of information about
the activities of Nazi submarines along the Florida coast. As soon as the

war with Germany was over, Hoke Welch, managing editor of the *News*, asked Commander Langley Hawthorne, in charge of public relations for the Seventh Naval District, to put together a story covering such activities during the war years. Because Welch and Hawthorne were drinking buddies, Hawthorne agreed to release the story exclusively to the *News*. Ironically, he gave the assignment to Chuck Watters, a former *Herald* editor and reporter who intended to return to the paper upon his discharge from the Navy. After Watters spent two weeks researching and writing the story, it appeared in the *News* on June 3, 1945. Ned Aitchison, the *Herald's* city editor, hit the ceiling when he saw the story, which covered two pages. Watters, whose byline had been deleted, had covered the Nazi submarine warfare from beginning to end. For the first time Floridians were informed that 111 ships had been torpedoed in the Gulf of Mexico, the Caribbean, and off Florida's east coast by Nazi submarines. Merchant seamen had suffered 882 casualties. The Navy had organized an elaborate system of hunting submarines with the help of destroyers, planes, and blimps. Despite these efforts, however, the Navy was able to claim only one positive and one probable kill. The Navy had been reluctant to give credit for a probable kill even when a large oil slick appeared after a submarine was repeatedly subjected to depth charges. Submarine commanders could release oil, fooling aircraft or surface ship commanders into believing a kill had been made, meanwhile lying quiet until it was safe to move again.

Watters revealed that Nazi submarine commanders had been able to obtain information that to the Navy seemed uncanny. As submarine attacks on merchant ships became increasingly hazardous, the main targets turned out to be important vessels. In a convoy bound for Key West, the only two ships torpedoed carried vital equipment, including electronic apparatus, for the defenses of the Key West Naval Station. How did the submarine commanders gain such intelligence? The Navy never learned. In only a few instances did planes or blimps catch surfaced submarines, making them fair game for guns and depth charges. One such encounter happened just east of Miami on the night of July 17, 1943, when Lieutenant Nelson Grills, commander of a Navy blimp, saw a surfaced submarine gleaming in the moonlight. As he approached, the Nazis started shooting, setting fire to his starboard engine. By this time he was virtually astride the submarine. At this precise moment Grills suffered a lifetime's greatest frustration and disappointment: the depth charge release stuck and refused to operate. Grills watched the submarine submerge while his blimp settled to the surface of the Atlantic, with one dead crew member.

The *Herald* was free to use this history of submarine warfare, in which the Miami area played so important a role, the day after it appeared in the *News* but did not. It was at a time of very strong competitive journalism, when the philosophy of "if you don't get it first you don't use it" prevailed. Thus thousands of *Herald* subscribers who did not get the *News* probably never saw the story.

Meanwhile, Lee Hills was in Europe as a war correspondent for Knight Newspapers, reporting on the wind-up of the war in that theater. While in London in July, on his way home, he got an astounding tip. A friend told him that the war in the Pacific might be brought to an end with a single bomb blast. He cautioned Hills not to talk about it or speculate about it, but related certain events from which Hills deduced the United States had developed an atomic bomb and might soon use it. The significance would be far greater than the event itself, greater even than the end of the war, said the friend. Thus Hills was mentally prepared when an Air Corps plane dropped the first atomic bomb on Hiroshima on August 6, 1945. The *Herald* gave the story tremendous play, and Hills, through every source available, sought to underscore the great impact this event would likely have on the future of the world.

A few days after Japan's war leaders signed the terms of surrender, on September 2, 1945, the *Herald* began keeping its readers informed about a major hurricane that was heading toward Florida from the eastern Atlantic. The war had come and had ended without Florida experiencing a hurricane. And it was a good thing, because the hurricane which hit Dade County on September 15, 1945, would have dealt the Navy a severe setback in its anti-submarine warfare had it hit during the war. Hills had watched the storm as it approached the Florida Keys, and late Friday he sent Arthur Peavy, Sr., and a photographer, Harry Steiger, to Key West to be in a prime location if the storm should hit the Florida Keys. Saturday afternoon as the storm approached Key Largo, Hills could only wait, chain-smoking, as the reports of the storm's ferocity reached his desk. Carysfort Lighthouse, a few miles north of the storm's center, reported winds of 143 miles an hour as the storm passed in late afternoon. The center of the storm continued a northwesterly direction, moving through the uninhabited Everglades south of Homestead, some sixty miles from Miami. Shortly after six, Hills' telephone rang. George Beebe, state editor, who had joined the staff early in 1944, was standing by. As he watched Hills jotting down notes in shorthand and listened to his clicking "yes . . . yes . . . yes" replies into the receiver, Beebe suspected something very important had happened. Upon hanging up the telephone, Hills jackknifed to his feet.

"We've got something bigger than a hurricane," he said. "The Navy blimp hangars at Richmond Field are on fire!"

The announcement electrified the newsroom. At that moment the

LITTLE WAS LEFT except wreckage and ashes after fire swept through the Navy's huge hangars at Richmond Field during the 1945 Hurricane.

center of the hurricane was passing fifty miles southwest of Miami, and the velocity of the wind in Miami was ninety-nine miles an hour. At Richmond Field, midway between Miami and the storm's center, the wind's velocity was nearly 150 miles an hour. But Hills began plans immediately to get reporters and photographers to the scene.

Meanwhile, fire was raging in three huge hangars, each covering an area as large or larger than a football field and the equivalent of a sixteen-story building in height—the largest wooden structures in the world. Inside the hangars had been stored twenty-five blimps, eleven inflated and fourteen deflated. Stored with the blimps were 213 Navy planes and 153 civilian planes, together with the firefighting equipment at the airbase and more than 150 automobiles, official and private. The hangars had been built to withstand winds up to 250 miles an hour. Because of the heavy rains accompanying the storm, nobody had figured the firefighting equipment would be needed, so the trucks were driven into the hangars and Navy personnel had parked cars about them. As the hurricane's intensity increased to seventy-five and then to 100 miles an hour, the roofs of the three hangars began to give way. A short time later the hangars started coming apart, and timbers began to fall among the blimps, planes, and automobiles. At 5:45 p.m., according to the Navy's report, a fire was spotted in Hangar Number One. How the fire was started could not be determined, but there was speculation that falling debris rent gasoline tanks in the planes, spilling flammable fuel on the hangar floor. A spark, or a match struck by a sailor, could have started the fire. In moments fire had spread throughout the hangar. Shortly thereafter the other two hangars were blazing furiously.

At the *Herald,* meanwhile, George Mangus, newsroom artist, volunteered to drive his car through the hurricane to Richmond Field. Hills asked Beebe if he wanted to go. He did. A photographer, Sam Beneckson, was called from the photographic department to accompany them. To prevent the wind from overturning the car, a thousand pounds of linotype lead was placed on the floor. The twenty-mile drive from the *Herald* to the entrance gate at Richmond Field would never be forgotten by any of the three. Beneckson later developed ulcers, but Beebe came pretty near having a hemorrhage right then when the lieutenant at the entrance gate refused to let them enter. They could see the bright glare of the fires through the hurricane-driven rain, but there they sat in the office with the Marine guards for company.

Meanwhile, Hills worried about whether Mangus had gotten through. Telephone lines were down and all communications had been cut between the *Herald* and outside. Hills decided to send a back-up crew. Volunteering were reporter John T. Bills, a blustery Texan who liked to think he was equal to any kind of adventure, and photographer Bill Kuenzel, who, although quieter than Bills, could be equally audacious. They, too, tied Bills' car to the road with a thousand pounds of linotype "pigs," and Kuenzel further fortified the expedition with a fifth of bourbon. By the time they hit the road toward Richmond the wind had begun to let up some, although it was still blowing at hurricane force. When they reached Richmond Field they found the members of the first expedition, cold and shivering in their wet clothes, still in the guard office at the entrance gate. Kuenzel broke out his bourbon and passed the bottle. Meanwhile, the gate officer had got in touch with the commanding officer, and shortly thereafter the newsmen were taken to him for a press conference, while the photographers were permitted to approach what was left of the burning hangars. The shots, made in the driving rain, showed very little when the pictures appeared in the *Herald* next morning. The hangars and their contents were a total loss, estimated to exceed $30 million. But although several persons were injured, only one life was lost. The body of Harry Schultz, chief of the civilian-manned fire department at the base, was found among the shells of his burned fire trucks.

About the time that Beebe, Mangus, and Beneckson were shivering in the front gate office at Richmond Field, a taxicab pulled up in front of the *Herald* building. In the taxi was Peavy, asleep in the rear seat. The driver shook him and got him out. Peavy, who had sobered some during the long drive from Key West, was accompanied to the newsroom by the driver who insisted upon being paid full taxicab fare for the 160-mile trip from Key West. The business office being closed, Hills told the driver to come back next morning. Hills was brimming with enthusiasm over the thought that a *Herald* reporter had come through a hurricane in a taxicab. This could be a story of immense human interest.

"Art," said Hills, "what about sitting down and writing us a first-person account of your experiences coming through the hurricane."

"What hurricane?" asked Peavy.

It was Peavy's last assignment. He had slept through the hurricane, unaware of the buffeting his taxi was getting. Later that evening Steiger arrived, having driven from Key West behind the storm. He had a story to tell but it didn't make the paper. Peavy had tried to follow the progress of the storm from a Key West bar, but lost it somewhere between drinks. Learning that the hurricane would cross the upper Florida Keys, Steiger abandoned the tipsy reporter and headed toward the mainland.

The coverage of the Homestead hurricane was the first attempt by the *Miami Herald* to do all-out reporting of a tropical storm, together with the damage it left behind. South Florida had not been hit by a hurricane since John S. Knight had become publisher, and Shutts had discouraged such coverage on the grounds that it caused "undue alarm" and gave the area a bad image. Hills did get some flak from Miami businessmen who wondered if the *Herald* hadn't gone out of its way to "play up" a storm in which so few lives were lost. Hills disagreed with that viewpoint, and so did Knight. From then on the *Herald* would cover hurricanes with due concern for their danger, and when the big one hit the coverage would be "all-out." Warning readers of the approach of a big storm, together with Red Cross suggestions of how to avoid loss of life and widespread property damage, was a necessary public service, and readers appreciated it.

Although the velocity of the wind from the Homestead hurricane hit ninety-nine miles an hour in Miami, little damage was done that was discernible by the beginning of November. Owners of Miami and Miami Beach hotels, which had been used by the military services during the war, rushed to refurbish. Thousands of visitors came to southern Florida that winter, the first tourist season since the beginning of the war. A record crowd of 200,000 saw the Orange Bowl parade that welcomed in 1946, and 38,000 fans crammed the inadequate Orange Bowl stadium to see the University of Miami win a freak victory of 13 to 6 over Holy Cross in the last nine seconds of play. A player on the Miami team intercepted a Holy Cross pass to run eighty-nine yards for a touchdown, reaching the goal line after official time for the game was over. Until those last seconds it had been a dull game, and as the end of the fourth period approached a third of the people in the stadium got up and left—including the *Herald's* photographer. Next morning the *Herald* devoted virtually its first page to the story about Al Hudson, who, in those last seconds, had become an instant hero. Sports editor Jimmy Burns, who wrote the lead story under an eight-column streamer, and two feature writers sought to enthrall readers with accounts of the electrifying happening, just as the feat had enthralled the surprised fans. Wilfrid Smith of the Chicago Tribune Press Service, whose story the *Herald* used, predicted that "Hudson's run will live forever."

But the glamor of Orange Bowl days were soon forgotten—Al Hudson as well as the pink elephants that waltzed in the Orange Bowl parade—and south Floridians turned their energy toward readjustment in the lively and challenging postwar period. The *Miami Herald,* no less than others, sought to take advantage of the opportunities in that sprightly era when new people with new ideas were pouring daily into Dade County. Early in January 1946, Lee Hills launched the Clipper Edition, a special, somewhat stripped-down version of the *Herald,* which was distributed to Latin American countries by air.

Although the beginning was slow, with only fifty copies shipped south, the Clipper Edition was to grow and to have a far-reaching influence in the Caribbean and Central and South America. But in the beginning Hills did no bragging. A Latin American edition of the *Herald,* or the *News,* had been the dream of managing editors for several years. Miami was in an enviable position as an aerial gateway to the nations in the south. But previous attempts to sell Miami newspapers in Latin American and Caribbean countries had been unsuccessful. One reason for the failures, Hills concluded, was the way the sales had been subsidized and managed from Miami. Why not sell the Clipper Edition FOB Miami, at the same wholesale price that a *Herald* cost a vender on Flagler Street? Then let the dealers in Bogota, Rio de Janeiro, Lima, or Buenos Aires set their own retail prices, based on the cost of airmail delivery. The airmail charge to Rio was one dollar, so the buyer would order only the number of Clipper Editions he had sales for.

Hills' idea worked. Among subscribers were U.S. embassies and U.S. business concerns in Latin America. Because a single copy cost so much, it might be passed among twenty or thirty persons. The papers were in great demand because they contained current stock market quotations, important national and international news, and full sports coverage as well as display advertising, which helped to keep United States citizens in foreign countries informed on prices back home. Classified and special advertising sections were removed to reduce mailing costs. Clipper Edition was the name selected because it was flown almost exclusively by Pan American Airways "Clipper Ships" which served Latin America. Several years later, after the name of "Clipper" no longer had any special significance, the edition would become known as the Air Edition. Twenty-five years after it was launched, the *Herald's* two Air Editions, one exclusive to Canal Zone residents, would reach 16,500 on Sunday and 11,000 daily. But while the circulation of the Clipper Edition may not have set any exciting records in 1946, its prestige grew enormously. By June 21, just six months after he had launched it, Hills could feel safe to carry a feature story about the success of the "Newspaper of the Americas."

"Throughout the Latin American countries," said Hills, "This new edition is forging a new link of cultural and economic understanding among all English-speaking peoples."

For the achievement Hills was awarded the Maria Moors Cabot Gold Medal, while the *Herald* received a Cabot Plaque, voted by the trustees of Columbia University for outstanding contributions to international friendship among the people and nations of the American continents.

The prestige of the *Herald* was increasing rapidly, and so was that of Lee Hills. In June 1946, the *Herald* had reporters scattered over a large part of the globe—Jack Bell in Germany, Jack Thale in Italy, Ernie Hill in Brazil, Jack Kofoed at Bikini to cover atomic bomb tests, and near the end of the month Hills himself was back in Western Europe writing about developments in Germany, Austria, and Italy for Knight Newspapers. At home, Steve Trumbull, a Midwesterner turned "Cracker," was covering Florida's "grits and catfish belt," as he described it, writing about such places as Yankeetown, Two-Egg, Sopchoppy, and Panacea. The *Herald* was no longer a small town "sheet" but was rapidly taking on the appearance, in makeup, story material, and readability, of a modern metropolitan newspaper.

As might be expected, Hills began to receive enticing offers from publishers in other parts of the country. Some offers included salaries that were difficult to turn down. But he did turn them down. None of the job offers came from newspapers he thought had the potentials of the *Herald*. Moreover, Miami was a great newspaper town where interesting things happened, where colorful personalities lived or passed through. Hills also liked the Miami climate. But what he liked most was working with the Knight brothers, and, what was equally important, they liked him.

20

Siding With the Alligators

W ORLD WAR II may have caused immense changes in Miami, but a 1947 tropical storm was to have a much greater effect upon the physical development of southern Florida than any war. Yet, the storm did not reach hurricane intensity, nor did it even get a name. Nobody would remember it like the 1926 Hurricane, the 1928 Hurricane, or the Homestead Hurricane of 1945.

On the morning of Saturday, October 11, 1947, the *Miami Herald* streamered on page one an announcement that a tropical storm had been discovered in the Caribbean south of the western tip of Cuba. "New Storm Heading Toward Florida," said the headline. It was the second tropical storm to threaten Florida within a month. Moreover, it was a "wet" storm. The storm that had hit the state on September 17 likewise had been wet. Although its winds barely reached hurricane force, it left the Everglades flooded, and water stood in the streets and about homes in outlying residential areas where drainage was inadequate. The Everglades was still brimming over in October. South Florida was ripe for disaster.

The storm reported on October 11 moved rapidly toward Florida during the day and that evening entered the peninsula south of Miami. It passed over Homestead, passed through the western edge of Miami shortly before midnight, then through Miami Springs, Hialeah, and Opa-Locka, moving on northward through West Hollywood, Davie, and Plantation, a new community west of Fort Lauderdale. Highest wind recorded was seventy-one miles an hour. It was an eerie, unforgettable storm, in which lightning winked so constantly and illuminated the night so brilliantly you had no need of a flashlight, even though the downpour was greater than anyone could remember seeing before in Florida. By midnight eighty percent of Dade and Broward counties was under water.

Water rose three to four feet in some areas of Hialeah and Miami Springs. Water covered the runways of Miami International Airport. Water covered the streets of Fort Lauderdale. The highways between Dade and Broward counties were closed. In low-lying areas of Broward water rose over windowsills. Thousands of hapless occupants of flooded homes were terrified as the downpour continued, as lightning flashed, as the water rose. In the midst of the storm a reporter reached the Miami Springs police station by telephone.

"Have you had much rain in Miami Springs?" asked the reporter.

"I'm up to my knees in it," replied the policeman.

The *Herald* summed up the storm's passage in an eight-column, three-line streamer: "71-mile Gales Lash Miami as Storm/Roars to Sea; Tor-

THIS SCENE was repeated throughout southeast Florida after a wet tropical storm passed over the area during the night of October 11-12, 1947, leaving 80 per cent of Dade, Broward, and Palm Beach counties flooded. A historic event of major importance, it resulted in a flood control project which was to open more than a million acres of former swamp land to development.

nadoes Rip Area;/Torrential Rains Flood Two Counties." Because the storm hit at such a late hour and reporters were unable to inspect the areas hit, the *Herald's* coverage failed to reflect the possible damage, the widespread suffering, or the distress of thousands of homeowners trapped in their flooded homes. Not until next day could reporters and photographers see for themselves what had happened or talk with police and Red Cross workers who had to operate boats through swimming water moccasins and rattlesnakes to rescue flood victims. The *Herald* on Monday ran eight-column photographs that showed the extent of the flood more dramatically than any reporter could do with words. Among the pictures were downtown Miami Springs with the Curtiss Parkway and Circle Park under water, as well as downtown Fort Lauderdale where all the streets looked like the city's New River. Water stood two to three feet deep about the Orange Bowl Stadium. Photographs showed highways, streets, and residential areas under water. The flood was not confined to Dade and Broward, but also hit Palm Beach County and the Kissimmee Valley north of Lake Okeechobee. Farms, groves, and cattle pastures were flooded. Thousands of cattle drowned.

South Florida appealed to the federal government for help, and in 1948 Congress authorized an engineering study of an eighteen-county area by the Corps of Engineers. The Corps held hearings, made surveys, and came up with a $208 million flood-protection plan, which with federal and state funds, was to be carried out over a period of twenty years. Florida would pay fifteen to twenty percent of the cost, the federal government eighty to eighty-five percent. Work on what would be one of the most controversial projects the Corps of Engineers ever designed, was begun in 1949. Although the project saved millions of dollars from flood losses, opened thousands of new acres for agriculture, and made it possible to expand the cities along the southeast coast miles westward into what once had been wet saw grass country, the engineers failed to calculate the effects on the area's environment—damage to the vast wilderness with its unique wildlife. Moreover, the *Miami Herald* supported this project without reservation when it was proposed, just as the paper had supported the creation of the Everglades National Park. To understand and appreciate how the engineers failed and how the *Herald* could support these two incompatible projects, you have to know the background of the Everglades—the Indians' River of Grass—and particularly the history of the Everglades National Park.

The Everglades National Park was dedicated less than two months after the wet 1947 storm, on December 6, by President Harry Truman. Through the efforts of John Pennekamp, the *Herald* played a major role in its establishment. The paper had adopted the project as the end of

World War II was approaching, as the result of a decision by John S. Knight. A short time earlier the publisher and Florida's Governor Spessard L. Holland had sat together during a flight between Washington and Miami. Holland, a booster of a proposed Everglades National Park, brought up the subject and suggested the *Herald's* support.

"If the *Miami Herald* would put its resources behind the park after the war," said Holland, "I believe we could soon get congressional approval."

"I gather that you consider the establishment of this park very important," said Knight.

"I think it is one of the most important projects under consideration in the state at the present time," replied the governor. "I believe we are in a position of seeing the park become a reality if we go after it. Furthermore, with the rapid growth of southern Florida, this might well be our last chance."

Knight asked Pennekamp about the park.

"All I know," said Pennekamp, "is that this man Ernest Coe has been fretting around for years, trying to establish a park in the Everglades. I'll be glad to get some information for you."

Next day Pennekamp reported to Knight what he had learned. The area of wilderness proposed for a federal park covered two million acres and included one of the most primitive parts of Florida. It consisted of saw grass prairies, sloughs, cypress strands, hammocks of tropical trees including mahogany, hundreds of miles of winding watercourses through mangrove swamps, as well as countless islands, lakes, bays, lagoons, and ponds. It also contained one of the finest saltwater fishing areas in the world—Florida Bay, Shark River, and the Ten Thousand Islands.

"Do you think this park would be a good thing for Florida?" asked Knight.

"The people whose opinions I respect tell me that it would be a wonderful thing for Florida," replied Pennekamp who had anticipated the question.

Conferring with Pennekamp and Hills, Knight informed them he wanted to put the *Herald's* editorial and news departments behind the project. He then directed Pennekamp to take whatever steps were necessary to get the ball rolling.

It was still wartime, however, with the United States engaged in major battles with Germany and Japan—not a propitious time to talk seriously about establishing a national park. So Pennekamp used this period to research the background and to get acquainted with this unique Florida wilderness. The first thing he learned was that the Everglades National

Park concept revolved about Ernest Coe, a slender, white-haired man in his upper seventies who had fought for its establishment since 1928. The public had come to identify Coe as the father of the park idea. Coe had headed the Everglades National Park Commission, a state agency created in 1929. But although Coe had worked tirelessly, interest lagged during the depression of the 1930s, and the commission was allowed to die. Still Coe hung on, using an office given him by the city of Miami, and spending his own meager funds to buy stationery and stamps. Pennekamp discovered that the park concept went back to the early 1920s before Coe, a landscape architect, came to Coconut Grove in 1925 to retire. Establishment of an Everglades park was one of the first subjects discussed by members of the Florida Society of Natural History after its organization in 1922. The group was composed mainly of naturalists who either had winter homes in Florida or were frequent visitors. Among them was Dr. David Fairchild, botanist and plant explorer; Harold H. Bailey, ornithologist and writer of a major book, *Birds of Florida;* Dr. Thomas Barbour, head of the Museum of Comparative Zoology at Harvard, and Dr. John K. Small, of the New York Botanical Garden and a writer of books and articles on the florida wilderness. These men had witnessed the progressive destruction of the wilderness—the slaughter of the plume birds, alligators, and otters, together with the drainage of the Everglades, the destrucion of hammocks by wild fires, and the removal of mahogany for timber, of orchids, and of colorful tree snails by collectors. The group discussed the essential areas which they thought should be saved, and Bailey, who knew the Everglades well, was asked to prepare a map delineating the boundaries. These men proved to be far ahead of their time, for while the park idea got some support from other naturalists, it received hardly any backing among politicians, the newspapers, or other sources which would have been needed to put it across.

After Coe arrived from New Haven, Connecticut, in the middle 1920s, he made friends with members of the society and became a member himself. Bailey took him on a tour of the southern Florida wilderness, including Flamingo, Cape Sable, Shark River, and the Ten Thousand Islands. The sensitive Coe was astounded by the primitive beauty, and his zeal for preserving this wilderness immediately matched that of his new friends. Retired and with time on his hands, Coe went to work. In 1928 he organized the Everglades National Park Association, and in 1929 induced the Florida Legislature to establish an Everglades National Park Commission, whose purpose was to acquire the land within the designated area and fulfill the requirements for the creation of a national park. Coe began the years of dogged promotion that brought the name of the proposed Everglades National Park to the attention of millions of people.

people. And in 1934, as the result of his work, Congress passed an act which, in essence, approved the park, if and when the property within the proposed boundaries was turned over to the Interior Department.

The park, as delineated by Bailey, covered a little more than one million acres, a sizeable part of which was state-owned overflow land or shallow bays and lagoons. But Coe kept finding reasons to expand the size until the area covered two million acres. Much of this property was in private hands and to acquire it would have cost the state several million dollars. While Coe had many supporters who agreed this much should be preserved, he was getting nowhere with the Legislature, which would have to appropriate the money to buy the private holdings. Meanwhile, Coe was growing older, and then the United States got involved in World War II. With the exception of a few faithful backers, Coe's park proposal seemed to have been forgotten. But among those who had not given up hope was Governor Holland, a longtime park booster. And this was the state of affairs when Holland suggested to Jack Knight that he put the *Miami Herald's* support behind the park. Holland, however, was a practical politician as well as a conservationist, and he knew that working for a two-million-acre park would be futile. So before he left office in 1945, Holland sat down with Governor-elect Millard F. Caldwell and Interior Department officials and reduced the park to practical and feasible dimensions. This eliminated 4,000 owners, a number of whom were strongly opposed to the park. Under an arrangement with Interior Department officials the state deeded to the federal government 847,175 acres—385,693 of land and 461,482 of shallow bays and estuaries—to be put under control of federal wildlife conservation until the park could become a reality. This left 400,000 acres to be acquired, which the state would have to buy.

Coe, who had come to look upon the proposed park as his private domain, objected strongly. He announced that if he could not get a two-million-acre park there would be no park at all. But Coe fell in 1946 and fractured a hip. Although tragic for him, it was a happy event for the future of the park. For when Pennekamp went to Governor Caldwell to ask him to reestablish the Everglades National Park Commission, Coe was in the hospital. Even then the governor was skeptical, because of the dissension Coe had created.

"I wouldn't mind recreating the park commission," said Caldwell, "if I were sure I wasn't trying to breathe life into a dead mule."

Pennekamp, who had been working for more than a year on his own plans, assured the governor that dissension over the size of the park would not be allowed to get in the way, and promised the *Herald's* full support to make it become a reality. The governor not only signed an order recreating the commission but named the members whom

Pennekamp recommended. August Burghard, Fort Lauderdale advertising executive and well known conservationist, was named chairman. Pennekamp reserved for himself the chairmanship of the legislative committee, a tough assignment since getting money from the Florida Legislature would be the commission's important reason for existence. Although Coe was not named to the commission no objections were heard, because there was no assurance that he would be active again.

With Coe out of commission, Pennekamp had one less critic to fight, but the remaining foes were difficult enough. They included powerful politicians, oil speculators, land speculators, fisherman, hunters, and scores of others who fought the park for a variety of reasons. Florida's attorney general, Tom Watson, friend of oil men and land speculators, went to court in an effort to kill the park. Dr. E. C. Lunsford, a Miami dentist whom Pennekamp recommended as a member of the park commission, bought a sizeable block of Cape Sable and fought to have the important area excluded. Meanwhile, senators and congressmen in Washington were surprised and confused to receive letters and telegrams from a dozen conservation clubs protesting the establishment of the park. These clubs, as Pennekamp had difficulty explaining convincingly, were hunting organizations rather than true conservation clubs, and were against the park because their hunting would be banned. Even more difficult to overcome was the opposition by politicians in Monroe County, in which much of the park would be located. Their chief complaint was that the park would remove "valuable" property from tax rolls, and they encouraged opposition among Monroe County residents by telling them fishing in the park would be prohibited. Pennekamp pointed out that virtually all of the Monroe County property within the park was either bay bottom or was low enough to be under water part of each year. And he challenged as untrue the claim that fishing would be prohibited.

The greatest obstacle was yet to be overcome—inducing the Florida Legislature to appropriate $2 million to buy the 400,000 acres needed to round out the park. Members of the park commission did not believe this big sum could be obtained all at one time, and it was decided to concentrate on getting an appropriation of $400,000 to buy 200,000 acres from the Model Land Company, whose owners, the heirs of the Henry Flagler fortune, had promised to sell for a token price of two dollars an acre. With a foot in the legislative door, it was reasoned, the commission would have less trouble getting the $1.6 million needed to buy the remaining 200,000 acres in the possession of many ownerships. Meanwhile, the Federation of Women's Clubs, which owned 4,000 acres within the proposed park boundaries, including Royal Palm Hammock, deeded this property to the state.

In 1947 the Florida Legislature was controlled by a group of north

Florida politicians which south Floridians had dubbed collectively the "Pork Chop Gang." They controlled the Legislature by virtue of the state's apportionment, which automatically permitted the smaller counties to dominate the more populous ones. The Pork Choppers, clever and hard-nosed politicians, had not gained their power and influence by being generous to South Florida, and particularly to Miami, which, to the Bible belt of north Florida, was a modern Sodom and Gomorrah. Furthermore, Pennekamp barely knew these leaders. But Pennekamp's friend, McGregor Smith, Sr., president of the Florida Power & Light Company, did know them. Smith, a native of Tennessee, had become acquainted with the north Florida leaders while lobbying in the state capital for his company. A bourbon drinker and an ardent but tough poker player, Smith could sit up all night with the boys and still have stamina left to pursue his business next day. Smith always carried a harmonica and whenever a little tension or boredom began to creep into a party, or a meeting, he would take out the harmonica and play a couple of tunes. He had the kind of earthy but outgoing personality that north Florida Crackers liked. Smith's relations with important legislators could hardly have been better when Pennekamp asked him to make it possible to meet them.

Some weeks before the opening of the Florida Legislature in the spring of 1947, Smith set up a meeting at a camp owned by the power company near Ocala. Present were State Senators William Shands of Gainesville, Dill Clarke of Monticello, B. C. "Bill" Pearce of Palatka, Wallace Sturgis of Ocala, and Sandy McArthur of Fernandina, as well as Judge Causey Green of Palatka. It was to be one of the memorable evenings in Pennekamp's life. Before sitting down for a dinner of north Florida style chicken and rice, the Everglades National Park was discussed over drinks, and particularly the $400,000 Pennekamp hoped to get to buy the Model Land Company property. What surprised Pennekamp was how personable and agreeable the senators were. Before dinner he had a firm promise of the $400,000, and the backing of a bill by these powerful leaders assured its passage.

After dinner the party settled down to a ten-cent limit poker game. Pennekamp, in high spirits, over having accomplished his mission so easily, enjoyed a winning streak. Normally a hard loser when the cards were going against him, but tending to be gregarious and elated when winning, Pennekamp now began kidding the senators good naturedly. And they were giving it back to him, especially after he drew to an inside straight and made it. Eventually he won a big pot after drawing a fourth king. One of the senators spoke of giving him what money he had left in his pocket and going home, since Pennekamp was sure to win it anyway.

Another senator accused McGregor Smith of setting up the game with marked cards. But Senator Pearce had another idea.

"Penny," said Pearce, "how much did you say you needed all together for that park?"

"Two million, senator," replied Pennekamp.

"Well," said Pearce stonily, "why in the hell don't you try to get it from the Legislature, instead of out of our pockets?"

"I guess you know I'm lobbying you all for that money," said Pennekamp, counting his winnings. He had thirty-three dollars before him, most of it won from the five state senators present.

"Why don't we just give him that money when the Legislature meets," said Shands. "Maybe he'll lay off us."

"I'll go along with that," said Clarke, president of the Florida Senate and at that time the most influential politician in the Legislature.

These Cracker politicians, who had surprised Pennekamp by their knowledge of the Everglades National Park and their appreciation of its possible benefits to Florida, were not kidding. One of the first acts of the 1947 Legislature was the appropriation of $2 million, assuring the creation of a national park. With Congress already having approved the park, all that was left was the purchase of the remaining property within the proposed boundaries which the Interior Department had agreed to do as soon as the state provided the money. And the money was soon in the hands of Interior Secretary Julius A. Krug, in the form of a check signed by Governor Caldwell. Krug signed the papers in June 1947 that created the Everglades National Park, and plans were soon being made for its dedication at the town of Everglades on December 6.

Among the VIPs invited to sit on the speaker's platform with President Truman, who was to make the dedicatory address, was Ernest Coe. He replied immediately that he would not be there. But as the date approached Coe changed his mind, and Pennekamp, chairman of dedication ceremonies, was surprised to see the slender, white-haired "father of the Everglades National Park" mounting the platform. When introduced, Coe received resounding applause from the 10,000 attending the ceremonies. But in later years there would be those who failed to remember that Coe had attended the dedication. Two of them purported to be historians. One writing of that day said Coe already was dead. The other said merely that Coe had not attended. Coe lived five years after the park's dedication, dying in 1952 at eighty-three.

Two years after the dedication of the Everglades National Park, Pennekamp was appointed by Governor Fuller Warren to the chairmanship of the newly created Florida Board of Parks and Historic Memorials, and he would be a member of the five-member board almost

PRESIDENT TRUMAN dedicates the Everglades National Park, December 6, 1947, at the town of Everglades. At his right is Governor Millard F. Caldwell of Florida, while U.S. Senator Spessard L. Holland stands facing the speaker's stand at left, clapping his hands. Behind him is John Baker, president of the National Audubon Society. John Pennekamp stands to left of unidentified admiral, clapping his hands. U.S. Senator Claude Pepper is in black suit, second to left of Pennekamp. Below, President Truman and Pennekamp chat.

continuously until its absorption by the Department of Conservation in 1969. He would see the state parks and memorials grow from thirty-four with 75,000 visitors a year to sixty-five with eight million visitors a year. In the meantime, Pennekamp would watch the Everglades National Park go through crisis after crisis as progress in the construction of the vast flood control works affected the normal flow of water southward through the Everglades to the park. A major misunderstanding and battle was to rage for years between the Interior Department on one side and the Corps of Engineers and the Flood Control District, state agency set up to operate and maintain the flood control program, on the other side. Conservationists joined with the Interior Department, while farmers, developers, and others with little interest in conservation joined the other side. It would not be until the arrival of the environmental revolution, in the 1960s, when so many persons began to get upset about the destruction of the wilderness, pollution of the air, streams, lakes, and bays, that the tide would be turned against those who thought the Everglades should be "taken away from the birds and alligators and turned over to the people."

Still, without the Corps of Engineers' flood control project it would have been impossible for southeast Florida to develop, as it was to, in the years ahead. By 1970, twenty years after construction was begun, more than a million people would live in areas that once had been the home of alligators, snakes, fishes, frogs, and aquatic birds. Although the price paid for Florida's progress had been tragically high, there could be no turning back of the clock. In fact, by the 1970s the growing concern would be that much which had been preserved might go the way of despoliation.

21

Christmas Strike

O N WEDNESDAY, December 22, 1948, the *Miami Herald* distributed to its employes a Christmas bonus of two weeks' pay, as was the practice at that time. Composing room employees picked up their bonuses and went to work as usual. At five o'clock the next morning, however, they met and voted 235 to four to strike. They did not notify the management; they just did not report for work that day. The only printers who did show up were pickets carrying strike signs and three or four others who entered the building to collect the bonuses they had failed to pick up the day before. And thus was begun a historic strike against the *Miami Herald* by Local 430 of the International Typographical Union, American Federation of Labor. The strike was important because the union lost and the *Herald* was able to replace outmoded production methods, which the ITU had insisted on retaining, with modern methods.

To appreciate the significance of the strike, and particularly the importance of the *Herald's* victory, one must be familiar with the relations which existed at that time between the ITU and newspapers throughout the country. The International's president, Woodruff Randolf, had set out to defy the Taft-Hartley Law, passed by Congress in 1947 after a wave of wildcat strikes, including slowdowns and sit-downs, swept the nation following World War II. The *Herald* and the *Miami News* had had experience with the postwar attitude of some of the unions when the pressmen of both newspapers decided on Saturday, January 5, 1947, to "go to lunch." It proved to be one of the longest lunches in history, lasting from Saturday until Tuesday. Walter Winchell, on his Sunday night broadcast from Miami, described it thus:

"The Miami newspapers are ready to go to press—but the pressmen are still out to lunch. They went to lunch at 5:00 p.m. Saturday—a new form of strike."

The pressmen were negotiating a new contract with the Miami newspapers at the time, but there was no hint that a strike was in the offing. The "lunch," a form of sit-down strike, was a local union decision. After the passage of the Taft-Hartley Act such strikes would be illegal, but at that time there was no law against such wildcat acts by labor. Only the International's president, George L. Berry, had enough influence over the pressmen to induce them to return to work. But he was unavailable. Berry, upon leaving his office for a weekend, could not be reached by telephone. In this instance he did not return to his office until Tuesday. He ordered the pressmen to return to work. The presses had not turned for three days. On Sunday, *Herald* subscribers received only the inserts, including the Sunday magazine, real estate section, women's section, and comics, which had been printed before the strike. On Monday and Tuesday mornings the paper consisted of two pages, the front page, containing a condensation of the news, and a pre-set page of comics and crossword puzzle, but published outside the *Herald's* plant.

This was an example of the kind of union activities which led to the passage of the Taft-Hartley Act. The law made unions subject to damage suits for strikes in violation of contracts and for other unlawful practices, including secondary boycotts and jurisdictional strikes. The traditional closed shop, in which only union members were permitted to work, was prohibited. Union leaders also were required to sign anti-communist affidavits and to file financial reports. Tagging the act as a "slave labor law," union leaders set out to use their political power to kill it. But none fought it more stubbornly than Randolf, who openly defied the law in speeches, in testimony before a Senate committee, and in directives to local unions. His prime target was the part of the act which outlawed the closed shop, through which the ITU was able to wield control over production methods in newspapers across the country. The result was that newspapers had been unable to introduce any important improvement in production since the perfection of the mechanical typesetting machine, the linotype, in the nineteenth century. Randolf was determined to maintain ITU control.

An opportunity for Randolf to test his will occurred soon after the Taft-Hartley Act became law—when the union's contract with Chicago's six daily newspapers expired on October 21, 1947. Among those papers was the *Chicago Daily News*, whose publisher at that time, John S. Knight, also was publisher of the *Miami Herald*. Nothing came of the meetings between the union and the publishers of the Chicago papers, because Randolf essentially demanded an illegal closed shop contract. In consequence the ITU struck the six newspapers on November 24, 1947. Foreseeing that a strike was unavoidable, the publishers had prepared to operate without the ITU, and managed to do so. The strike lasted twenty-two months and ended in a defeat for the union, which settled for a ten-dollar a week raise, exactly what the publishers had offered originally.

While the Chicago strike was in progress the ITU sought to bring pressure on newspapers published in other cities by the Chicago newspaper owners. At its national convention in August, 1948, the ITU discussed the possibility of calling a strike against these newspapers, among them the *Miami Herald*. With a new contract coming up for negotiation within a few weeks, the forewarned *Herald* management set up a school for the training of composing room workers, particularly teletypesetters, as the Chicago papers had done. Although the teletypesetter had been invented in the 1920s, few newspapers used it because of union opposition. The teletypesetter had a typewriterlike keyboard, which, when operated, punched out a perforated tape. The tape then was fed through a special unit to operate a conventional linotype machine. A teletypesetter operator could turn out 3,000 to 4,000 lines of type during an eight-hour shift, compared with 1,400 lines which an experienced union operator could turn out on an awkward linotype machine keyboard. One teletypesetter operator could keep two linotype machines going. The *Herald* made no secret about having a school in progress, but few of the union printers took it seriously.

The *Herald* and the *Miami News* began negotiations with the ITU at the same time. By December 23, thirty-two meetings had been held between management of the newspapers and union leaders. Negotiations were secret, in the traditional manner of meetings between management and unions. After the strike, ITU leaders claimed that disagreement over wages had been the cause of the breakdown in discussions. The *Herald*, in a statement signed by James L. Knight, insisted that the union's demands for a continuation of a closed shop arrangement was the main point of contention. The *Herald* published the printers' wage scale and what had been offered the union under a new contract. The figures put the printers in a bracket higher than any other craft union members in the Miami area.

On an hourly basis the printers were among the highest paid composing room employees in the nation. They worked thirty-five hours a week. Reduction in the work week had been made during the depression by the former publisher, Colonel Shutts, in order to keep all composing room employes working. This arrangement, which essentially amounted to a pay cut, received approval of the printers at the time. After the Knight brotl.ers acquired the *Herald* in 1937 and sought to return the work week to a normal forty hours, the printers insisted on maintaining the seven-hour-a-day work schedule, but demanded the same pay they would have received for an eight-hour shift. During World War II and for a time thereafter a shortage of printers forced the management to bow to the union demands.

Initially, the strike was limited to the *Herald,* the union's chief objective. If the ITU could bring the Knight brothers to their knees, they not only could whip the *News* into line, but, probably, would be able to break the resistance of the *Chicago Daily News.* The union leaders chose December 23 to strike because they concluded that the management would be least prepared and that nonstriking employees would be least willing to work over the holidays. Moreover, toward the end of negotiations, the union printers had been so inflamed against the *Herald* by their leaders that prospects of failure would not have kept many on the job.

Over the years the printers had managed to gain the upper hand in the composing room. The ITU not only required that the management use union foremen, it had set up strict rules to limit the authority and activities in the composing room of editors and other non-ITU members. It was necessary for editors and advertising personnel to work, at times, in the composing room, assisting in making up of pages, checking stories, or preparing ad layouts. But once a story or an ad was set, no one but a union employe could handle the type. For an editor to be seen carrying type from one place to another was to risk immediate stoppage of work by all ITU members on duty. An advertising salesman, Sam Bell, entered the composing room one morning to ask for a proof of a layout which a client had requested. Finding no one available to make a proof, Bell picked up the type, carried it to a proof-making machine, and ran his own proof. The union insisted that Bell henceforth be barred from the composing room.

The majority of the printers were friendly and easy to get along with. Some were fishing or hunting companions of editorial and advertising department employes, or social friends who visited each others' homes. But the foremen had gained considerable authority and looked upon themselves as privileged employees in the *Herald* building. If a foreman chose to exercise his privileges in excess, he could make things intolerable for editors. Most difficult union member was a makeup foreman, Bob Turner, an able and fast worker, but highly disagreeable when he chose to be. He had a special dislike for editorial employees and was frequently peeved at one editor or another. You could always tell when Turner had it in for you. If you asked him a question he would cut his eyes at you, look hard, even disgusted, and say nothing. For the next several days you had to look out, particularly if he was to make up pages for you. Turner disliked having editors looking over his shoulder as he worked. If there was time he would wait you out until you returned to the newsroom, after which he immediately began making up the pages you had hoped to watch. For there were often stories too long for the space allotted in the makeup dummy, and if you were on hand you could cut out one or more of the least important sentences or paragraphs to shorten the item. But if you were not on hand, Turner would cut a story at the line where the type spilled over. The "over" type was tossed into the "hell box." The cut might be made in the middle of a sentence; or some very important part of a story might be thrown away. You got criticized by your superiors for sloppy editing and makeup, but you got nowhere by blaming Turner.

As the bargaining between the union and management reached a climax your friends in the composing room were barely speaking. Kidding was dangerous. The groundwork for building an anti-*Herald* disposition had been started months before by ITU leaders. A few of the more perceptive and experienced printers, who figured the tactics being used could lead only to a strike, had given up their jobs and left Miami, or had made arrangements to leave in the event of a strike. The management, meanwhile, began to sense that a strike was inevitable. The leaders had succeeded in convincing the majority of the printers that the Knights were villains. But no one not privy to the union's conscience thought a strike might be called two days before Christmas.

CHRISTMASTIME strike by printers failed to stop publication of the *Miami Herald.* This is the front page of the paper published on December 24, 1948. Much of the copy was typed on electric typewriter and engraved—referred to as the "cold type" method of production to distinguish it from the "hot metal" set in separate lines by typesetting machines. In time the "cold type" method would be the preferred way of production.

Timing of the strike so incensed other employees, particularly in the newsroom, advertising, and business offices, that they were determined to see that the paper got published. While loyalty to the *Herald* and protection of jobs must have been major considerations on the part of employees who pitched in to help produce a paper under trying circumstances, generally this positive motive was overshadowed by negative feelings against the union. The union's chances of winning were further weakened when members of other unions, including the pressmen and mail room employees, crossed picket lines to go to their jobs.

When the early shift of editors, copyreaders, and reporters arrived in the newsroom on that Thursday morning everything appeared to be perfectly normal. There was a rumor, however, that the printers had gone on strike. A copyreader had heard it from his wife who worked in the composing room of the *News,* which was not immediately struck. It was not until pickets showed up, though, that the management could be sure. Immediately thereafter the newsroom became like bedlam as desks were shifted, packed together, and new production equipment was crowded in. Jim Knight was on the scene, directing activities with the aid of blueprints which had been prepared in the preceding weeks. Everyone available was commandeered to help. City Editor Ned Aitchison pitched in to help shift desks. Technicians began arriving to install teletypesetters, while young women who had been trained to operate the machines stood by ready to begin work. Meanwhile, employees who were on late shifts or were off duty that day were called in. So were the wives of many employees, volunteering their services in whatever capacity they could be used. Some became proofreaders, others learned to operate the typesetters, or, if they possessed no special skill, they cut copy and delivered it to the operators, or they fed the teletypesetter tape into the linotype machines. Several newsroom employees who had worked in newspaper production were transferred temporarily to the composing room. Jim Knight, who had gained some experience in page makeup on the *Akron Beacon Journal,* took charge of making up the classified ad pages. A few who transferred from the newsroom to the composing room that day would never return to their old jobs. One was Chuck Watters, state editor, who rose to an executive position in the production department.

To an outsider, the activities in the newsroom and composing room on that Thursday would have presented a picture of major confusion. A few late arriving employees had reason to wonder if they were on the wrong floor, or even in the wrong building. For there were twice the number of production people normally used to get out the *Herald,* many of them packed into the rearranged newsroom. But in spite of the apparent confusion the paper went to press as usual, coming out on Friday morning without the help of union printers for the first time since the *Herald* was founded in 1910. Indirectly, however, union members did help. Some of the type, particularly the classified ads, was set in the composing room of the *Miami News*.

When subscribers opened the *Herald* on that Christmas Eve morning they must have been surprised at the uneven appearance of the front page. Some of the type had been set on electric typewriters and processed by engraving rather than set on machines. But the newspaper was all there. The engraved type method, which came to be known as "cold type," eventually would become the preferred way of producing a newspaper, but in 1948 those cold type columns appeared crude and incongruous beside the conventional columns. During the succeeding days, however, the crudeness began to disappear. Everyone was learning rapidly, and this was a good thing, because within a week after the *Herald* was struck the printers on the *Miami News* walked out. Nothing could have been more objectionable to the union printers at the *News* than having to set type for the *Miami Herald*. They were able to withstand this indignity for only a week. Several began refusing to set the *Herald* type. General Manager Dan Mahoney ordered the recalcitrant printers fired, whereupon the entire composing room shift walked out.

It was now the *Herald's* turn to help the *News*. And it could do so because an amazing amount of know-how had been accumulated within the first week of the strike. It was becoming obvious that the *Herald* could continue to publish without the union printers. The appearance of the paper was improving daily. The young women operating the teletypesetters were becoming proficient, and most of the linotype machines in the composing room were being rapidly converted to tape operation. Still, Jim Knight left the door open for the union to return to work, or for any of the members to return. The pay scale would be that offered by the management originally for forty hours a week instead of the thirty-five-hour week the union had insisted in preserving. That pay, amounting to more than $100 a week, would still have made the printers among the best paid journeymen in Miami during that pre-Korean War era. Seeing that both newspapers could publish without them, the printers must have suspected that the strike was lost. Except for a few individuals, however, they refused to return to work. But in addition to shouting "dirty scab" and foul names at those crossing the picket lines, the striking printers began making threats. Then employees began experiencing various kinds of harassment, such as having their tires slashed or their automobiles dashed with quick-drying paint. Several homes were damaged with a dye which could not be painted over successfully. The one who got the most threats was Bill Sandlin, composing room superintendent. Although a long-time union member, Sandlin had remained loyal to the *Herald*. Sandlin lived in an apartment two blocks from the paper, and when he was ready to leave his office, after the city edition was run in the early hours of morning, he would call his wife and she would meet him. Mrs. Sandlin, a charming, calm and courageous woman, insisted on his calling her, not because she could do very much if her husband were attacked, but because she liked to believe her presence would have the effect of restraining those angry men. Sandlin, who passed out the word that he carried a revolver and a pair of brass knuckles in his coat pockets, was never touched. But Chuck Watters had his house splashed with dye.

On Saturday night, October 1, 1949, the *Herald* experienced one of the most destructive fires in Miami's history. A fire whose origin never was determined raged through the *Herald's* newsprint warehouse, adjoining the main plant. More than 2,000 tons of newsprint was destroyed and damages were estimated at $600,000. Discovered shortly after 9:00 p.m., the fire quickly spread out of control before firemen could set up firefighting equipment. Employees turned to assisting firemen or shoring up doors between the hot warehouse and the main plant to keep out a cascade of water as well as fire. But only a couple of pressmen lent a hand. The others lounged about between press runs and glared at those who sought to dam off water flowing into the press room, with the aid of sand and wet paper. The rapid spread of the fire, which went through the tight rolls of newsprint with virtually the speed of a flash fire, had all the marks of incendiary origin. If it was set, the evidence was destroyed.

In 1951 some 125 composing room employees went to Circuit Court to seek an injunction against the strikers, citing twenty-four incidents where damage had been done to automobiles or to homes. In a hearing before Circuit Judge Vincent C. Giblin, testimony revealed that the strike, then two and one-half years old, had cost the union $1,156,834 in strike pay. Giblin found the union guilty of intimidation and ordered the posting of a $15,000 bond against further harassment. The union sought without success to have the Florida Supreme Court reverse Giblin's decision. In late 1953 the union voted to end the strike, after three years and eleven months. Two weeks later this action was rescinded and the pickets returned to pace up and down for another year or two, until virtually all the printers had gone to work elsewhere or had moved from Miami.

The strike against the two Miami newspapers cost the ITU in excess of $1.5 million. Woodruff Randolf had battled in vain. Testifying before a United States Senate Committee investigating strike activities, Randolf conceded the ITU had been "compelled" to spend over $11 million in support of strikes and other defense activities to "preserve our union against the Taft-Hartley Act." Before Randolf's wave of strikes was over, the ITU had been found guilty of unfair labor practice charges and cited for contempt of court for refusing to comply with a court order.

The victory over the International Typographical Union proved to be of major importance to the *Miami Herald.* The newspaper won freedom to research, test, and install production improvements that in the years ahead would make it one of the world's most efficient newspaper plants, with many of its production facilities, including typesetting, operated by computers. Scores of newspapers on which the ITU has refused to allow any improvement in production facilities no longer exist, having gone broke as a result of being forced to operate at a loss with obsolete and costly methods.

22

Biggest Hoodlum Bust

D ADE COUNTY BECAME, for a time after World War II, the wintertime rendezvous for the top figures in the nation's underworld, including the Mafia and the Capone gang. They scattered widely in the luxury hotels at Miami Beach, or they quietly infiltrated into respectable neighborhoods to buy homes and act like decent citizens. None made a big to-do about being in the area, as did Al Capone who had sought unsuccessfully to get himself accepted in Miami society. The publishers and editors of Miami's newspapers were aware of this invasion. But for a time they could only guess how extensive it was. These underworld figures found it impossible to stay away from the horse tracks, however, and there they were easily spotted. Track owners, particularly Hialeah's President John Clark, who had an unpleasant experience with the Capone gang, became nervous about the presence of so many hoodlums. A former FBI agent who was able to recognize most of them on sight, Daniel P. Sullivan, was employed by Hialeah Park to investigate. Track owners also were interested in the possible connection between the mobsters and illegal horse bookmaking which had grown rapidly in Dade and Broward counties since the end of the war. Illegal bookmaking was taking considerable revenue from the horse tracks, and with this revenue went a sizeable amount of lost state taxes. By using Sullivan's investigation as a lever, track owners hoped to induce the governor to do something about bookmaking.

Florida appeared to be a neutral zone for the underworld. Here the mobsters felt free to cavort in the warm winter sunshine, fishing from their expensive boats, driving to the tracks in their limousines, and in the evenings slipping into tuxedos for a drive with their women to the Colonial Inn or Club Boheme in Broward for dinner and to gamble afterwards in the clubs' swank gaming rooms. Then they might drop in later at Club Green Acres, a sawdust place. These clubs, owned by members of the Mafia, had the protection of a corrupt sheriff. In wintertime they became hangouts for the top gangsters in the United States. If you wanted to see the who's who of the underworld, these were the places to see them. A news coverage policy adopted by Hills made it difficult for casinos to operate in Dade with the same freedom they enjoyed in Broward. But Sheriff Walter C. Clark ran Broward as his "own principality," and casinos could operate even in the glare of publicity.

While Hills' "routine coverage" of casino operations was keeping Dade casinos closed, he had not been able to use the same method to close the bookmaking establishments. After the end of the war a group which had established itself in 1944 as the S & G Syndicate to coordinate Dade's bookmaking, spread into an operation that proved impossible to combat by Hills' dogged harassment. The syndicate operated mainly at Miami Beach but furnished racing information for bookmakers throughout the county. Virtually every hotel newsstand or cigar stand was leased to the syndicate. Leases, called "key concessions," ranged from a few thousand dollars a year to $40,000 a year for a stand at the

CORRUPT OFFICIALS, maintained in office by a lackadaisical or cynical electorate, virtually turned Dade and Broward counties over to the Mafia and the old Capone gang after World War II. The *Herald's* continuing fight against the mobsters was to win it a Pulitzer Prize in 1950.

29 Killed in New Tornadoes; 250 Injured; 4 States Hit

Cold, Like Steam

Ah, Love

The Miami Herald

Sunday, May 22, 1949   No. 170   •   Florida's Most Complete Newspaper   39th Year 156 Pages 15 Cents

For Services Rendered

Next Year's Taxes To Be 63 Billion, And Here's Reason

By JEANNE BELLAMY

Chicago Gambler Muscles In On Rich S·& G Syndicate

White Slave 'Boss' Bared In Broadcast

Crime Commission Also Blasts Beach Police Case Anew

By JACK THALE

Injured Crowd Hospital

New Tornadoes Kill 29, Hurt 250; 200 Homes Destroyed; 4 States Hit

'Big Five' Yield To Pressure

'Deal' Gives Hold On Dade Operations To Outside Group

By WILSON McGEE

TORNADO CLOUD IN ACTION is shown in this unusual picture taken near Chadron, Neb.

Soviet Police   CAB Investigates

Roney Plaza Hotel. The syndicate also leased the rights to solicit horse bets at the hotel cabanas. Runners picked up bets. Other bets were made by telephone, or, if you walked up to a newsstand counter, planked down some money, and gave the name of a horse running at Aqueduct or Hialeah, you had a bet. The *Herald* could report bookmaking at such and such a hotel, but proving it was another matter. Corrupt law-enforcement officials were in cahoots with the S & G. The only bookmakers who got arrested were the "bad guys" whom S & G wanted to get rid of for one reason or another, the principal reason being theft. Periodically S & G sent a "beard" around to place bets. If a nonwinning bet went unrecorded, which could be easily spotted when the S & G office went over the bet sheets, that meant the operator had pocketed the bet money. Next day sheriff's deputies dropped in and arrested the operator on a charge of bookmaking. The gentleman got "the works" in court and his bookmaking days in Dade County were over.

The S & G Syndicate operated from plush offices behind a mirror-paneled door in the Mercantile Building Annex at Miami Beach. Headed by Jules Levitt, a suave, big-belted man, the S & G board of directors, the *Herald* learned, consisted also of Samuel P. Cohen, Harold Salvey, Charles Friedman, and Eddie Rosenbaum. Once getting through the door, you found yourself in a large office where bookkeepers, clerks, typists, and managers were occupied with their duties as in any other well-run business office. To run such a setup smoothly, operating in most Miami Beach hotels as well as supplying racing information to more than one hundred independent bookmakers, the S & G required protection. The only way this could be obtained was through the corruption of law-enforcement officials, the most important being the sheriff, Jimmy Sullivan.

Sullivan, a Florida Cracker with little education, earlier in life had won a reputation as a prize fighter. He had worked as a carpenter and a mason before becoming a member of the Miami police department in 1934. Stationed at the intersection of Southeast Second Avenue and Second Street in downtown Miami, Sullivan remained there for ten years, directing traffic and helping old ladies cross the street. Sullivan became known as the "smiling cop," and when the city editor could think of nothing better on a dull day, he would send a photographer to shoot Jimmy Sullivan smiling at a little old lady or giving directions to a bewildered stranger. The intersection became known as Jimmy's Corner. Everybody in the county knew the friendly, strapping policeman. Early in 1944, with a perfect record of having never made an arrest, Sullivan dropped into the *Miami Herald* to see John Pennekamp.

"Mr. Pennekamp, I'm going to run for sheriff," said Sullivan, grinning. "Will you announce that for me?"

The *Herald* ran Sullivan's announcement but no more. It supported neither Sullivan nor his opponent, an old-time constable. From his own pocket Sullivan paid the $225 county filing fee and the $150 Democratic Committee assessment to get his name in the Democratic primaries. Sullivan later estimated that his campaign cost him one thousand dollars. Yet he won the primaries with a 20,000 vote majority, which in 1944 was tantamount to winning the election because he had no Republican opponent. And Sullivan won without making a single campaign speech. He merely walked up to people and said: "I'm Jimmy Sullivan and I'm running for sheriff. Please vote for me." But he met most of his constituents on busses. In 1944 the United States was at war and gasoline was rationed, so everybody who could do so rode a bus rather than drive an automobile. Sullivan would board a crowded bus downtown just as the driver was about to depart. The driver would greet him with a loud "Hello, Jimmy Sullivan, our next sheriff!"

"Howdy, folks," Sullivan would say, smiling, "I hope you will vote for me—but vote anyway."

On the day of Sullivan's election, a reporter picked up a quote from a well-wisher:

"Jimmy Sullivan was the best traffic cop Miami ever had and he's going to be the best sheriff Dade County ever had."

Four years later, when Sullivan ran for reelection, he was described in the *Herald* as "the worst sheriff Dade County ever had." In the meantime, Sullivan had won a reputation as the county's most corrupt sheriff. By 1948 the S & G Syndicate was doing a racetrack bookmaking business estimated at $40 million a year, with earnings of $1.8 million a year, after payment for protection. And Sheriff Sullivan was doing well, too. His second campaign was greatly different from his first. By now he had the backing of powerful forces that stood to benefit by his remaining in office, and he was able to buy space on billboards, pay for ads in the newspapers, and for announcements on the radio stations. The *Herald* supported his opponent, Perrine Palmer, recently mayor of Miami, but Sullivan, conducting a campaign against the newspapers, won by a 15,000-vote majority.

In the meantime, the *Herald* had continued a relentless campaign against vice and its companion, corruption. Still, Dade and Broward counties were developing a reputation as safe places for the criminal. The area, particularly Dade, was growing rapidly. Postwar prosperity brought scads of money to Florida. New luxury hotels began to rise along the beach front. John S. Knight felt the pressure of fellow establishment members to relax the *Herald's* hard-nosed attitude toward casino gambling. They knew Knight liked to gamble himself, and that before the war he frequently was seen in the gambling places, rolling dice or betting on roulette. Knight, however had a change of viewpoint. While he saw no great harm in gambling, as such, he had become convinced that it was bad for the community. Gambling and bookmaking resulted in the corruption of law-enforcement officials and political leaders. Moreover, the widespread publicity Miami was receiving as a city of vice and corruption probably had the effect of discouraging desirable citizens who might otherwise settle in Dade. So Knight turned a deaf ear to his friends and gave Hills and Pennekamp freedom to swing the power of the *Miami Herald* against vice.

At first the *Herald's* stories appeared to make no important impression. There was too much public apathy. Moreover, both Jimmy Sullivan of Dade and Walter Clark of Broward were popular sheriffs whose numerous supporters did not want to believe anything said against the characters of their elected officials.

Clark was a friendly, gregarious man who had a warm affection for people, and people, including newspaper reporters, liked him. Clark seemed like a guileless, naive man, and he was a soft touch for the down-and-out. He gave away thousands of dollars. He was frequently compared with Robin Hood. Clark made most of his money through the Broward Novelty Company, which he organized in 1945 with the assistance of a brother, Robert, former deputy sheriff, and Gordon F. Williams. It was a most unusual firm for a sheriff to have a partnership in, because it dealt in slot machines and in the bolita business. It was Bob Clark who became rich, but Walter did all right. The higher things in life did not interest Walter Clark, a butcher before his election in 1932. It was all right with him if the hotel owners and business people of Broward County thought that gambling was good for the tourist business. In 1950 when Clark was questioned by the Kefauver Senate Crime Investigating Committee, he said of gambling in his county:

"I let them have what they want for the tourists down here."

Nor did Clark see anything wrong in dealing with Frank Costello, Joe Adonis, Meyer Lansky, Frank Erickson, and Joe Massei, allowing them to operate the Colonial Inn, Club Boheme, and Club Green Acres. When newspaper reporters called Clark and asked him about gambling in these places, he replied naively:

"What gambling?"

If pressed he would say:

"Well, nobody's said anything to me about gambling in them places. Ain't no taxpayer complained. I just don't know nothing about it."

The taxpayers weren't complaining. In Broward about the only complaint came from the *Fort Lauderdale Daily News.* Publisher Robert

SHERIFF Jimmy Sullivan grew rich and confident while in office. Above right, he sits behind his desk in the Dade County Courthouse in 1949, smoking a cigar and laughing at the world, but principally at his major critic, the *Miami Herald.* On the facing page, Sullivan sings a different tune while testifying before the Kefauver Senate Crime Investigating Committee in 1950 that he banked $70,000 during his first four years in office. Above left, Sullivan became famous in the 1930s and early 1940s as the "smiling cop" at Southeast First Avenue and First Street.

Gore, Sr., blamed the stagnation and lack of growth in Broward on the infiltration of the underworld. Clark brushed off Gore as "trying to sell newspapers." The *Herald* also tried to tell its readers about the increasing numbers of hoodlums who were spending the winters in the area. Perhaps the public thought the *Herald* was "trying to sell newspapers," too. But Hills came up with an idea that suddenly changed a lot of minds in both Dade and Broward. Hills organized a group of fourteen northern newspapers to investigate hoodlum activities in the nation and to interchange information. He built a large file on hoodlums who had infiltrated the Miami area from Detroit, Chicago, Cleveland, Minneapolis, New Jersey, and New York. Whenever Hills learned that a certain hoodlum had purchased a home in Dade County he would send a photographer to make a photograph and then proceed to build a dossier complete with a photograph of the hoodlum. After collecting a considerable file, Hills began running a daily feature, "Know Your Neighbor," including photographs of the hoodlum and his home. Residents, discovering that their "nice" next-door neighbor was Vincent Alo, alias "Jimmy Blue Eyes," or Joseph A. Doto, alias Joe Adonis, reacted immediately. But nothing could be done. The hoodlums couldn't be forced to give up their homes and leave the area. Al Capone had successfully defied efforts to oust him from Dade County. Concern grew among the majority of Dade citizens, however, and the relaxed attitude toward law enforcement that had prevailed since the founding of Miami began to change. Hills was winning the initial engagement of a battle he was determined to press to the end.

The Miami Herald

Senatorrid

Un-Darwined

Saturday, July 15, 1950   No. 224   Florida's Most Complete Newspaper   48th Year 40 Pages 5 Cents

Sultan Of Sweat Sullivan: He Had A Hot Time In The Old Town Last Night

JIMMY, FINDING IT NOT IN MANY WAYS, MOPS WITH RIGHT HAND   ... AND HE MOPS THE MOUTH THAT SPOUTED THOUSANDS OF WORDS   ... AND FINALLY HE SWITCHES TO HIS LEFT HAND TO FIND RELIEF

Fortune Grew, Sheriff Testifies

Jets And Mustangs Blast Bridgehead As Yanks Retreat

Griffin Denies Rapping Johnson

TOKYO (North Korean troops Saturday) crossed across the Kum river, drove the United States defenders back and ominously launched an encirclement push on the east flank.

Front dispatches said the main-sell attack was opened against South Korean troops who held the far east end of the American sector. It was in such force that the South Koreans called for Caesar Hodge artillery support.

The retirement left U.S. troops in Korea astride the stream.

They were pushing the pressure on the American lines at a point about 30 miles northwest of Taejon. There they planted a bridgehead after pushing the Americans backward.

At the same time, they were pounding the South Korean line to the east at a point where a breakthrough might send out to behind the American front position.

A field dispatch did not make clear whether the Reds had crossed the Kum in the direct Korean front or whether the fighting was on the north bank.

The Aggies told the pressure on the invasion front was slowly Saturday morning. The Americans were fighting a delaying action against the Reds pushing through the high forward in Taejon.

Iran Awaits New U.S. Arms

TEHRAN, Iran (AP)—Finance Day, as Secretary said today the United States offered and in cash China from citizens and in cash that, within six months the new month's aid had brought to Iran. Some are sufficient to carry it.

Crime Probe Cools Anger Of Crusader

It's Griffin the entire greater who carries engaging one of Maine in the Hills of Key event, he never stood to run Florida Warren are crime, was an crusading crowd when appeared before the Kefauver crime committee Friday night.

He absolutely was no longer at ease with Warren the long-time friend he helped elect, nor he couldn't remember even saying that it to his Johnson was friend for the Capone gang.

Griffin, admission, my tracks-up under and Los Wallace, before both citizens and crime, was led 55,000 in Warren from that under cross and Warren are had before the committee Friday and Johnson is one of the low-ing committee went had not to him.

The committee showed a note direct in the financial sources of Warren's campaign, but in Hipping brought up little parties that hasn't already been widely published.

MYER ACHNE

Erickson Had Roney Book, Schine Says

Lease Was Worth $40,000, He Asserts

Most telling, nationwide note mah Dagan-share operator, which had Friday night before the Kefauver Crime Committee that his Roney area with the incentives Frank Erickson in paying the highland figures and paid for the privilege of the Roan Hotel in Miami Beach.

Gang Death Feared By Witness

Russel Hides Away During Senate Probe

Harry Russell, Miami Beach and Chicago gambler, fled U.S. subpoena as the Kefauver Senate Crime committee investigation to feared peripheral death.

That was made plain in a note to the members from Russell's attorney, Lewis Kabuza, III at Chicago.

fixed at the night session at the hearing, testifying on the claims that Russell had heightened Kum, regarding he would not, to be not prominent, sensor nolo penta merits. Warner's later on passed.

He stated the Brought's case "Alphers" illustrated this point of

Charles Binaggio, gangland leader and politician of Kansas City, was shot to death in a typical gangland murder several months ago. The murder scene has been retired for a scene from gambling.

The Kum issue explained the Kefauver as the end of the front of M in Bing' Crosby, apples investigated its Gar Par of Korean.

Had $2,500 When He Took Office In 1945, Within Less Than Four Years, $70,000

By WILSON McGEE, BERT COLLIER and ROBERT H. HANSEN

Sheriff James Sullivan, not the Kefauver Senate committee investigating interstate crime and corruption Friday told the personal finances kept pace with his political fortunes after he took office in 1945.

His wealth, since a hearing $2,500 on Jan 1, 1941, had reached a "low estimate" of $70,000 by then he swears under oath.

He said he also kept as much as $12,000 cash in a "fishing box" at home.

He also said innumerable the questions of whether he had acquired property under the fictitious name of James Alexander Poulos and Poulos.

Sullivan said he "couldn't remember" Poulos, but admitted that his first two names were James Alexander.

It was that "can't remember" theme which at one point led Chief Counsel Rudolph Halley to warn him of contempt and perjury by meeting with a reply "no things you know are true."

The hearings will continue today but Sullivan probably will not be back. He was dismissed at the 4 p.m. recess. The committee, after two days, has heard only one-third of its witnesses.

Within the wide grin which earned him the name of Smiling Jimmy' where he was a Miami traffic cop from 1931 to 1941 when he resigned to run for sheriff. Sullivan testified he was having trouble with the government on income taxes.

He said that in 1930 he had first extended tax returns for the years running back to 1945.

But the sheriff told the committee that his then tax accountant, Martha McQueen, had kept some of the money due the government and that the auditing had since returned $1,000.

Testimony was that McQueen is in a hospital for removal of a cataracts.

McQueen declare that she had but discovered the error until the morning Revenue Bureau had started checking his returns. He said that Bureau recently did not glue with the records and revision, McQueen had given him.

Sullivan added that he paid McQueen $1 for each return that wrote in way a traffic cop. He showed up in court with a new tax report.

The sheriff asked that all he did was simply sign the income tax form.

Later he said, after McQueen's files were searched, he could not find one where bookkeeper upon which his tax had been completed and the "area of which he had turned over and records to McQueen.

Persisting and asking his face with a handkerchief in the event of a crumpled courtroom in the federal building, Sullivan said that he face, at the end of 1949 said in four banks, a total of just the $ various at $7,500 borrowed about $1,200

Again Full Coverage

Today's Herald continues with complete text and picture coverage of the Miami Crime Probe hearings. Turn to these areas special crime probe pages — 17, 18, 21, 22, 23 and 24-A as well as 1-B. All Photos are taken by Herald Staff Photographers Tony Garner and William Kuenzel.

summer June and various note and mortgages owed to him.

After several earlier files with Channel Valley, Sullivan placed a "low estimate" of $70,000 to $75,000 on his holdings.

Reporters who struggled with apply to keep up with the sheriff's pace notes, arrived at a variation of roughly $10,000 this that was not official.

Earlier he had testified that he had brought 11 houses during the recent period at but the on the additional section of Miami, he retains only his present home, he said.

It was Halley's prodding at the failure to list on his income tax the net gain from sale of one of the homes in 1949, that opened up the whole financial look.

All through the morning Jams Estes, Kefauver of Tennessee and Charles

Turn to Page 18, Col 1

Turn to Page 2-A, Col 4

Turn to Page 15-A, Col 4

Turn to Page 2-A, Col 8

Partial Mobilization Imminent, Senator Says

Guard, Reservist Calls Expected

Hearing Stalled By Dade Sheriff

Probers Get A Lesson In Filibustering

By STEPHEN TRUMBULL

Turn to Page 15-A, Col 4

Today's Chuckle

Where To Find It

Early in 1948 six Miami leaders met in the office of Frank Katzentine, attorney and radio station owner, to discuss hoodlum infiltration. They were James L. Knight and Dan Mahoney, general managers of the *Herald* and the *News*; McGregor Smith, president of Florida Power & Light Company; George Whitten, president of Burdine's; and John Clark, principal owner of Hialeah, and Katzentine. The meeting received no publicity. No attempt was made to form any kind of organization. But determined to find out how extensive were vice and corruption in Dade County, and how outside hoodlums fitted into the picture, the "Secret Six" hired Daniel P. Sullivan, former FBI agent, to investigate. Having just completed an investigation for Hialeah Park, Sullivan was familiar with the extensive bookmaking activities in the county, and he knew the hoodlums.

The Dade County Bar Association, likewise concerned about the reported corruption among public officials, had appointed a group to investigate. But progress was slow. On March 31, 1948, however, leaders of the bar association met with 250 delegates representing ninety Dade organizations, and founded the Crime Commission of Greater Miami. Under the leadership of Katzentine, himself an influential bar member, the Crime Commission merged with the Secret Six and Sullivan was employed as operating director.

Hills assigned a reporter, Wilson McGee, to spend full time covering the crime beat. "Red" McGee, as his associates knew him, was just past his middle thirties. He had been for a time managing editor of the *Orlando Morning Sentinel.* Coming to Miami in 1945 as city editor of the *News,* he decided in 1946 to shift to the *Herald* as a reporter. He was assigned to the Miami Beach beat. Combining an aggressive spirit, curiosity, and skepticism with an ability to win the confidence of people in high and low places, McGee was soon well acquainted with the widespread bookmaking activities along luxurious hotel row, and he was learning how that efficient organization, the S & G Syndicate, conducted this complicated operation. When assigned to cover the underworld in Dade County, coordinating his efforts with the Crime Commission, McGee was well prepared. In the succeeding months McGee wrote numerous crime stories but came up with little that was not known. His most exciting experience was accompanying photographer William Stapleton into the headquarters of the S & G Syndicate at Miami Beach. It was a busy day at S & G. Bookmakers were coming and going. McGee and Stapleton managed to enter the office without anyone noticing them, even though Stapleton carried a bulky Speed Graphic camera. But immediately after Stapleton raised the camera and fired off a flash the normally quiet office suddenly became the scene of an uproar. Stapleton turned and fled.

McGee merely walked out and took an elevator to the ground floor. Next morning the picture Stapleton had shot appeared on the front page of the *Herald* along with a McGee story on the mechanical setup and ramifications of the powerful S & G. The display must have caused some nervousness among S & G officials, but it could hardly affect an outfit that was in so solidly with law-enforcement officials.

McGee's contacts grew, though, and in time he was able to develop sources that brought him tips which appeared to come from near the top of S & G's echelons. And it was through these tips that in early 1949 McGee heard that Al Capone's old mob was trying to muscle in on S & G's exclusive control of Miami Beach bookmaking. At first he was skeptical because the reports seemed fantastic—a strong hint of connections between the Capone gang and the office of Florida's new governor, Fuller Warren. A Florida dog track operator, William H. "Bill" Johnson, who formerly had been a partner of the Capone gang in the operation of a Chicago horse track, was reported to have made a contribution in excess of $150,000 to the Warren campaign fund. Although skeptical of politicians, McGee could not bring himself to believe that Warren was involved with the Capone mob. Nevertheless, McGee kept hearing that Harry "The Muscle" Russell of the Capone mob, accompanied by "two dog track men." had served an ultimatum on the S & G Syndicate. They demanded to be cut in, but S & G, still confident of its power, turned them down.

Then a whole new set of facts began to develop. Governor Warren, under pressure to stop the widespread bookmaking because Florida's tax receipts from the horse tracks were declining at a time when the state was in dire need of revenue, sent a special investigator to Miami with orders to close bookmaking establishments. The state agent began raiding S & G's prime locations at Miami Beach's leading hotels and hauling the bookmakers to jail. Next day a new bookmaker showed up to take over a raided concession. But he was not an S & G man; he had been sent by Harry Russell. S & G's hierarchy was thrown into turmoil. This once powerful organization could no longer guarantee a bookmaker protection from arrest. S & G might have been in good with Sheriff Sullivan and Miami Beach police, but something had gone awry at Tallahassee. On May 22, 1949, the *Herald* broke the story under a page one, six-column, two-line head: "Chicago Gambler Muscles In/On Rich S&G Syndicate." McGee had the full account. Russell had demonstrated his power when the Continental Wire Service of Chicago cut off the S & G Syndicate's bookmaking information. Efforts by S & G agents to get racing information through New Orleans or other sources proved futile. The Capone mob had everything sewed up. Harry Russell was taken into the syndicate as a full partner. Wire services were restored and the raids by the Tallahassee agent ceased. The story had the effect of a major explosion. Dade County had paid an enormous price for a liberal policy which was supposed to help the tourist economy. Not only had local government been corrupted, the corruption had reached the state government level, while the money that gambling was supposed to funnel into the local economy was now going to hoodlum overlords in Chicago. Governor Warren's press agent issued a release describing the McGee story as a fabrication.

Thus was the stage set for the hearings of the Senate Crime Investigating Committee, headed by Senator Estes Kefauver of Tennessee. The committee had been established to investigate the influence of organized crime in the corruption of public officials. Miami hearings were not on the agenda, however, until McGregor Smith went to Washington to see Kefauver. Smith, a native of Kefauver's state, had met the senator, who donned a coonskin cap while campaigning in the Tennessee hills. Showing Kefauver documentary evidence of organized crime and its corrupting influences in southeast Florida, Smith convinced the senator that Miami should be put on his agenda.

The Miami hearings were held during a hot mid-July week in 1950 in the old federal building on Northeast First Avenue. Kefauver's investigating staff, working with Dan Sullivan, had done its homework well. While avoiding the subpoenaing of those who could be expected to invoke the Fifth Amendment, the investigators concentrated on persons who could not very well refuse to testify or who had volunteered. Among them were the sheriffs of Dade and Broward counties, deputies, police officials, state investigators, former employees of the S & G Syndicate, hotel owners, and politicians. The investigation had extended to the governor's office, resulting in Governor Warren being subpoenaed. Warren refused to comply, later being upheld in his right by the United States Supreme Court. But testimony confirmed what Wilson McGee had heard and reported—that dog track owner Bill Johnson indeed had contributed $154,000 to the governor's campaign fund. Contributing equal amounts were C. V. Griffin, central Florida citrus grower, and Louis Wolfson, Jacksonville financier and junk dealer. The hearings revealed widespread connections between hoodlums and law enforcement officials, and the *Herald* ran the recorded testimony verbatim. Stories, testimony, and pictures filled six to eight pages daily, which was far more coverage than the *Herald* had ever given a local story, or perhaps even a national story. Of eight stories starting on page one on July 15, 1950, five involved the Crime Committee hearings.

Lee Hills assigned his top reporters to cover the hearings from every angle, and employed a team of public stenographers to record the testimony and transcribe it for delivery to the *Herald's* composing room. It had been a year and a half since the printer's strike, and in the meantime the *Herald* had set up one of the most efficient composing rooms possible at that time. Thus local citizens, who could follow the verbatim testimony of witnesses, were fully informed of hoodlum activities in southeast Florida, together with the corruption that reached all the way from the lowest policeman to the highest office at Tallahassee. (In deference to Governor Warren, no proof was offered to show that he was involved directly with corruption, but testimony provided abundant evidence that top people in his administration were involved.)

The hearings were opened with a background of hoodlum activities given by Dan Sullivan. But it was the testimony of Sheriff Sullivan that proved to be the most dramatically revealing. Sullivan, like other witnesses, was afraid to lie and face a possible prison term for perjury. While there was much Sullivan could not remember, when Kefauver and his assistants primed the sheriff's memory with facts he candidly admitted that during his first four years in office, 1945 to 1949, he had banked $70,000, although for much of this period his salary was $10,000 a a year. In 1944 Sullivan had listed his personal assets at $2,991.50. Failure of the air conditioning on that hot July day was devastating to members of the committee and to witnesses alike, but Sullivan, in the hottest seat, sweated most. A *Herald* photographer sat there making shot after shot of the uncomfortable "Sultan of Sweat," as he mopped his wet face. Was this fair? Sullivan's friends thought not. But no one could deny that the strips of pictures which appeared in the *Herald* next morning were among the most magnificent shots ever made of an uncomfortable witness under fire. Sullivan never forgave the *Herald*, but he also became disenchanted with the Internal Revenue Service, which already was investigating his income.

Deputy Tom "Sailor" Burke followed his boss to the stand. He admitted that between 1945 and 1949 he had been able to buy, on his $350 a month salary, an $11,000 home, a $26,000 farm, and a $4,000 automobile—a lot of automobile at that time. Burke, like Sullivan, was a former boxer. On the witness stand this dapper witness felt obliged to tell all.

Although a more difficult witness than Sullivan, Sheriff Clark of Broward admitted with a little prodding that he had permitted casino gambling and bookmaking to flourish. As soon as a transcript of the testimony of the two sheriffs reached Governor Warren's desk he suspended them from office. Clark was to die the following year, of leukemia, while Sullivan, bitter and protesting his innocence, sought to make a political comeback but was soundly defeated. A federal jury freed Sullivan of tax evasion charges, but the IRS collected thousands of dollars in back taxes and penalties from him. Sullivan was to live until 1969, dying a bitter and tragic figure, insisting upon his innocence to the end.

Hills' six-year drive against organized crime in Miami came to a climax with the Kefauver hearings, which marked the end of an era. The free-wheeling days of the hoodlum in southeast Florida had come to an end, for a time at least. Broward's Mafia-owned casinos were closed for good, and the expensive roulette wheels, dice tables, and other apparatus were sent to Havana. A new federal law silenced the racetrack wire services. A number of hoodlums, their backgrounds revealed in the Kefauver hearings, went to jail for income tax violations. The Mafia, finding the spotlight too bright in Florida, transferred its activities to Havana or to Reno. A refreshing new atmosphere prevailed in Dade and Broward counties, the cleanest atmosphere Miami had experienced since its founding.

For its part in achieving this, the *Miami Herald* was awarded the Pulitzer Prize.

A RECESSION, or depression, expected to follow World War II, like that which had followed World War I, did not occur. Southeast Florida felt the effects of growing national affluence in the 1950s, with rapid development and great wintertime crowds, like the sunseekers on Miami Beach.

23

Writing it Readably

A REVOLUTION IN NEWSPAPER writing occurred after World War II and the *Miami Herald* played a role in bringing it about. The cataclysmic events of the war itself, together with the dropping of the first atom bomb, which signaled an end to the conflict, inspired much outstanding and enduring writing. Such events are in themselves of such compelling interest that a sensitive observer with the gift of communication is able to capture a moment in history and make it memorable. But as every editor knows, it is much more difficult to chronicle the day-to-day happenings in a community, a city or nation, or even the world, in language that commands the attention of the average reader. Yet that is what a newspaper like the *Miami Herald* tries to do every day.

While rebuilding his decimated staff after the war, Lee Hills began some serious self-examination of how well the *Herald* was doing the daily job of reporting. While he had bright and talented reporters, he still felt the *Herald* wasn't doing a good job of presenting the news. Discussing his concerns with editors in other parts of the country, Hills discovered they felt much the same way he did.

Surveys had demonstrated that a lively, clean appearance in the display of stories and pictures helped to attract readers. Many newspapers, including the *Herald,* were engaged in typographical face-lifting. But readership surveys revealed that content and readability were even more important than visual attractiveness. Hills was acquainted with these surveys—those of Dr. George Gallup, made before the war, followed by similar studies made by Carl Nelson. And he also was familiar with the readability analyses done by Robert Gunning and by Dr. Rudolf Flesch.

Hills' concern for clarity in writing did not stop with *Herald* writers. The wire services writers were capable of turning out stories as obscure as any of his reporters. Unless he could begin a campaign on a national scale for clarity in writing Hills realized that his efforts on the *Herald* could never be more than partially successful. This opportunity occurred when Hills was named chairman of a committee in the Associated Press Managing Editors Association (APME).

The APME had been organized by managing editors in an effort to improve news coverage by the Associated Press, a cooperative wire service to which virtually every daily newspaper subscribed. Once a year the managing editors met to discuss the faults they had found with AP reports during the past twelve months, and to make recommendations for improvements. After Hills was elected to the APME board of directors, he and Bill Stevens of Minneapolis suggested that in addition to meeting once a year, a continuing study committee be appointed to handle problems as they came up. Appointed chairman of this committee, Hills soon added another goal for the managing editors: better writing of AP stories.

Meanwhile, a Vienna-born student of communications, Dr. Rudolf Flesch, had written two important books on clarity in writing. The first, *The Art of Plain Talk,* was published in 1946, followed by *The Art of Readable Writing* in 1948. The young Jew had fled Austria in the 1930s ahead of German troops after Hitler's takeover of that country. While working for a degree in communication at Columbia, Flesch read a variety of newspapers and magazines. He found the *New York Times* difficult to read despite its reputation as a great newspaper, while the *Readers Digest* he found easy to read. The articles in the *Times* were complicated and tended to be long, while the articles in the *Digest* were short and the writing simple. The writing in the *Times* was generally forbidding and dull, while that in the *Digest* was bright and interesting. The writers in the *Times* made no effort to write simply and clearly, but clouded their long articles with Macauley-like prose, phrased to sound erudite and authoritative. It was obvious that the writers and editors of *Readers Digest* had gone to a lot of trouble to achieve simplicity, clarity, and brightness. Flesch's observations led to a Ph.D. thesis analyzing writing. Published under the title of *Marks of Readable Style,* the thesis was a sellout. His other books followed.

Flesch told writers to forget the pedantry of English composition they had learned in high school and college, which put the writer in a straitjacket. He preached a doctrine of almost primitive simplicity—short words, short sentences, short paragraphs, shorter stories. If you wanted others to understand you, you avoided long words of many syllables and difficult sentences punctuated by a multitude of commas, semicolons, and dashes. Newsmen were advised to "talk straight" to readers, as one would in everyday conversation. The most readable stories, Flesch discovered, were the simple, narrative type, while "genuine dialogue is the most readable thing there is."

Hills was quick to use Flesch's books to help achieve his goal. Reporters were advised to forget the heavy literature and to write for Mr. and Mrs. Everyman. Write for college graduates, said Hills, and not even college graduates would read you. But if you wrote for the ninth grade level reader you were writing for everyone. The older writers and editors found the new ideas difficult to accept. They were being asked to abandon a long respected rule of journalism—getting who, what, where, when, and how into the first paragraph of a story, followed by an elaboration of details in the order of importance. This was the "inverted pyramid" method. Generations of reporters had worked hard to develop an individual style on the bones of this journalistic skeleton. A few bright, imaginative, or colorful reporters did well indeed. But ordinarily a story written by formula had to be about a subject of compelling interest to be readable. To encourage brighter, easy to read stories, reporters were advised to stray from the inverted pyramid straitjacket. Many of the early efforts, however, were far from laudable. One day Ned Aitchison called a reporter to the city desk and threw back at him a story he had just turned in.

"Take this and rewrite it," grouched Ned. "You tell what happened in the fourth paragraph and you wait to the sixth paragraph to tell who it happened to. Maybe Dr. Flesch will read that far to find out what a story is all about, but nobody else will."

Although Aitchison gave lip service to Hills' efforts to improve the writing of his reporters, he privately took a dim view of Flesch. Ned had a number of excellent writers and he feared the new theories would spoil their styles. But Hills was not trying to change anyone's writing style. He only recommended Flesch and Gunning as guides to clear and concise writing. He never suggested adopting "I see a cat; you see a cat" simplicity. Flesch was a psychologist specializing in the analysis of writing to determine its readability. The art of writing was another matter. Hills never lost sight of his goal. Young, bright, and impressionable editors who were in sympathy with Lee Hills' goal were eventually installed on the city desk.

By the early 1950s the seeds of clear writing had been planted, not just on the *Herald,* but among newspapers throughout the country. Journalism schools began to feel the influence, and in the years ahead journalism graduates would arrive at newspaper offices already indoctrinated in the new theories of achieving clarity. And the time would come, in the affluent 1960s, when journalism graduates, better trained and ever more confident, would be unaware of the long, quiet revolution in newspaper writing. Many would believe their own generation had brought about the changes.

While still engaged in his campaign, Hills in 1951 was given the job of managing the editorial departments of two newspapers 1,300 miles apart—the *Detroit Free Press* and the *Miami Herald.* The *Free Press* had thrived after Jack Knight became its publisher in 1940, but in 1944 Knight Newspapers acquired the *Chicago Daily News,* which had more problems than all the other newspapers in the Knight group. With Knight having to keep his shadow in Chicago, where he had bought a lot of debt with a newspaper, the *Free Press* made little progress. But a newspaper can mark time just so long before it begins to slip, and this was the position of the *Free Press* in 1951.

Hills had been managing editor of the *Herald* for nine years. Knight had watched his progress with increasing admiration. He liked Hills' quickness of mind and ability to communicate. Hills was an altogether different type from the cigar smoking, cajoling, and prodding "Stuffy" Walters, executive editor of the *Chicago Daily News,* or another of Knight's favorites, the blunt, impatient, and driving Ben Maidenburg, at that time managing editor of the *Akron Beacon Journal.* But, like them, Hills' mind was quick, incisive, clear, and in conversation he came immediately to the point, tackling a subject head-on. Several years later when reviewing his impressions of Hills as a younger editor, Knight would remember how quickly he and Hills could "get on the same frequency." Knight possessed great communicative ability himself, but he was a publisher of underlying irritation and impatience, with many things to do and seldom with enough brilliant minds to call on. Hills had been a great discovery. But he was reluctant to sever his connections with the *Herald.*

"All right," said Knight, "you can have the *Herald,* too. Keep your home in Miami and rent yourself an apartment in Detroit."

So Hills was made executive editor of both newspapers and given the choice of selecting his own managing editor on each paper.

During the next twenty years Hills was to set some kind of record for air travel between Michigan and Florida. He would recall, after the jet liner was introduced, that during the era of the propeller planes he seemed to spend almost as many of his working hours in the air as he did on the ground. But the *Free Press,* a poor third in circulation and advertising behind the *Detroit News* and the Hearst *Detroit Times*, required much more of his time than did the *Herald,* whose circulation had doubled and advertising had tripled during the past decade. Meanwhile, a managing editor was needed for the *Herald,* and Hills sought to lure J. Montgomery

Curtis away from the American Press Institute at Columbia University. When Curtis turned him down, Hills selected George Beebe, passing over Aitchison, who was fifty-eight. Hills would have no regrets about his selection of Beebe, who not only was experienced, capable, and loyal but in addition had a certain style. Moreover, Beebe was a person of unquestionable integrity; he was mature yet still a young forty-one, and willing to work the long hours the managing editor's job demanded.

A native of Pittsfield, Massachusetts, and a graduate of the Boston University School of Journalism, Beebe came from a family of five straight generations of physicians. Beebe had worked for the *Herald* since 1944, demonstrating his ability on whatever job Hills gave him. He formerly had worked for the Billings, Montana, *Gazette* and for the *Florida Times-Union* in Jacksonville. Getting out of school in the depth of the depression, Beebe had gone West after being unable to land a job in the East that paid him more than twelve-fifty a week. The editor of the *New York Daily News* had offered him a job as copy boy, while Harold Anderson, editor of the *Sun,* was contemptuous of his college education.

"Look, young man, I can get reporters who can cover fires, police, and City Hall for a dime a dozen," said Anderson. "Go out in the world and get some experience and then come back to see me."

After writing to several editors in the West, Beebe got a job on the *Billings Gazette.* He was to remain in Billings ten years, while there marrying a charming school teacher, Helen Plato Lewis. In 1943 Beebe came to Miami to visit a sister, and also to look for a chance to change jobs. Neither the *News* nor the *Herald* had an opening, but he landed a job as telegraph editor on the *Times-Union.* Although happy to make the change, Beebe found himself working for another company newspaper. The *Gazette* was owned by copper interests while the *Times-Union* was owned by railroads. In Billings you could carry no story critical of the copper industry, and on the *Times-Union* you could run no story adverse to the interests of railroads. One night Beebe learned that the Sun Queen, a crack passenger train, had derailed just north of the city. Excited, he hastened to the city editor.

"I know you'll want to get a reporter out on this story," said Beebe.

"Beebe, you haven't been around very long," said the editor. "The *Times-Union* does not cover train wrecks."

"But this is just outside of Jacksonville. There may be local people killed or hurt."

"The AP will cover it. We'll use the AP story, if the story's worth using."

"What about pictures?"

"The AP will get them, too, but I doubt we'll use any."

The train accident was reported deep inside the paper. But a couple of weeks later when a bus accident occurred in New Mexico, in which three or four persons were injured, Beebe was ordered to place that story on page one. Some months later while in the composing room making up pages, Beebe glanced up to see Sam Butts, managing editor, conducting a tour of several persons, among them Lee Hills. Catching Beebe's eye, Hills edged over and spoke.

"You still interested in working for us?" asked Hills.

"I sure am," replied Beebe.

"Well, I've got an opening, if you want it."

So pleased was he that Beebe accepted the offer without knowing what kind of job Hills had in mind or what the salary would be. He arrived at the *Herald* early in 1944 and Hills put him on the copy desk. Hills later moved him to the state desk, then to the Sunday desk before making him a special assistant. After the end of World War II, Beebe was to play a role in the making of typographical changes on the paper, gaining experience that would be valuable to him in the years ahead. Hills sent him and Aitchison to the American Press Institute Seminars at Columbia.

The *Herald,* meanwhile, continued its growth at an average exceeding 12,000 new subscribers a year. In 1952 daily circulation passed 200,000, Sunday, 234,000. The expected slowdown in growth after World War II had never happened. Now the United States was engaged in the Korean War. And while Miami's future was uncertain, one thing was sure: if the city's growth continued the *Herald* would be forced to expand. In the late 1940s James Knight had sought to buy property on Miami Avenue, separated from the *Herald* building only by a spur railroad track. But Knight thought that the asking price was out of reason, and while he and his brother, Jack, were trying to make up their minds whether to go ahead and pay the price, the property was sold. The buyer was Jose Manuel Aleman, exiled Cuban and former minister of education.

The loss of an opportunity to buy that property only emphasized to Jim Knight the problem the *Miami Herald* was facing. Jim discussed the problem with his brother and Blake McDowell, Knight Newspapers' general counsel and an important stockholder. But when Jim began talking about building a new plant, the two older men balked. Better minds figured the nation was certain to suffer a depression in the 1950s, as had happened after the prosperous 1920s. Jack Knight and McDowell felt the predictions were realistic. Moreover, the *Herald's* operation in the conglomeration of old and new buildings on Miami Avenue was highly profitable. Acquiring new property and building a new plant would be a costly venture, to say nothing of the added weight of taxes resulting from a much higher property tax assessment. Still, they were reluctant to say no to Jim's argument that they buy a site. For Miami continued to grow and property prices were rising every year.

After World War II a number of newspapers, faced with the problem of plant expansion, had decided to move their production plants into industrial areas outside the city, keeping their editorial, advertising, and business offices downtown. The Knights watched this trend without enthusiasm, but felt that in Miami they might be forced to follow the trend. For obtaining sufficient property in a downtown location to build a major newspaper plant not only would be difficult but tremendously expensive. However, Knight Newspapers owned Miami Radio Station WQAM, purchased in 1945. Its broadcasting tower was in Biscayne Bay, a short distance offshore from waterfront property the station owned between MacArthur and Venetian causeways, almost exactly one mile from the *Herald* building. The area was an unusual mixture of zoning, with apartment houses, night clubs, restaurants, single family residences, doctors' offices, a sports arena, a huge dance hall, an automobile dealer, and various kinds of small businesses. On the waterfront were some of the largest display signs in Florida, several of them having cost more than $50,000. It was a key location because the signs could be seen from the two causeways, particularly at night when the enormous neon displays looked like Times Square reflected in Biscayne Bay. Jack Knight thought the site was too far from downtown, but at that time no more suitable location appeared to be available closer in. If the Knights could buy the run-down property between the causeways without the owners knowing who the purchasers were until it was all acquired, they probably could obtain it cheaply. Because he was based in Miami, Jim Knight was given the responsibility of seeing if this was feasible.

Secrecy was essential, but a limited number of key people would have to know. Among the first Jim discussed his plans with was Orra Townsend, business manager of WQAM.

"I'm interested in finding a real estate broker who can buy this property, but he must be able to keep a secret," said Knight.

Townsend suggested H. W. MacDonald, a broker who had an office on Biscayne Boulevard a few blocks from the property.

"'Big Mac,' everybody calls him," said Townsend. "He knows the real estate game as well as anybody I know—and he's reliable."

"All right," said Knight, "would you call MacDonald and make an appointment? We'll meet in my office. And I'd like to repeat, this must be highly confidential. We want that property—all the property on the waterfront between the two causeways."

A few days later Townsend took MacDonald into Knight's office and introduced the two men. Looking up at the six-foot-three broker, Knight

realized why he was called "Big Mac." Although reasonably slender, Big
Mac exceeded 200 pounds. Handsome, confident, and possessing a man-
of-the-world personality, Mac might have passed as a strapping movie
hero. Knight figured he was forty-five, but underestimated the broker's
age by eight years; Big Mac was fifty-three. After a few minutes of conversation, Knight decided he had the right man.

"Mr. MacDonald," said Knight, "do you think it's possible to buy all
that property without anybody learning about it until we have made the
final purchase?"

"I don't see why not," replied MacDonald. "I've handled lots of
property this way—in St. Louis and in California before I came to Miami
in 1943."

"And what about your fee?"

"Five percent of the purchase price—plus the enjoyment of the
challenge," replied the broker.

And so was begun early in 1953 one of the most unique real estate
purchasing operations in Miami's history. It was to take MacDonald five
years to acquire the property. Yet during those five years, although some
forty parcels were acquired, the identity of the buyer—Knight
Newspapers—was never revealed.

PLANNING TO BUILD a major new plant, the *Miami Herald* in 1953 began buying this
conglomeration of waterfront property on Biscayne Bay, between MacArthur and Venetian
causeways.

24

Some Were Oddballs

W HILE LEE HILLS had brought a new era of professionalism to the *Miami Herald* with the hiring of able editors and re- porters, his hiring of Ned Aitchison as city editor provided a unique human touch to the newsroom. It was a touch that was warm and occasionally tender, but sometimes strident and even traumatic for the erring or blundering reporter. Ned was forty-nine when Hills hired him from the city desk of the *St. Petersburg Times* in 1942. In the years ahead a reporter would look upon a forty-nine-year-old city editor as an ancient graybeard. But in 1942 a war was in progress and able young city editors were scarce.

Edward Aitchison, a native of Council Bluffs, Iowa, was a tall and im- posing person, beneath whose courtliness were fused paradoxical qualities of tenderness and toughness. Except for a hitch in World War I, in which he served as captain of a machinegun company, Ned had been in the newspaper business all his working life. He had done his early repor- ting on a motorcycle, roaring off to fires, accidents, and murders. Ned maintained a childlike interest in aviation and in automobiles, particular- ly sports cars. He had a fondness for air travel and was partial to news stories about aviation. Automobile shows he usually covered himself. His principal weakness, however, was animals. Almost any story about an animal that came across his desk got into the paper. He encouraged reporters and photographers to be on the lookout for animal stories and pictures. Although never able to shoot it, a photographer came up with a suggestion for Aitchison's ideal picture—a dog driving a sports car at an airport.

Ned was married to the newspaper game, his wife being a newspaperwoman. If Hills had any complaint about Ned as a city editor, it was about his insistence on doing virtually all the work on the city desk himself. He was never able to make efficient use of assistants, which bode badly for him and the *Herald* in the years ahead. Nor did he like to cut the copy of his better reporters. Ned's greatest qualities as a city editor came out after World War II, when he had at his command a group of bright, energetic reporters and photographers who were always ready to jump whenever he called. The staff was small and the *Herald* still had some of the qualities of a small town newspaper. A capable city editor could still run everything himself. Ned loved his staff and would defend his reporters even when they were wrong. It was all right for him to give a reporter hell but nobody else could. Hills recognized this broody hen attitude. If he had reason to criticize a reporter's work he was careful to do it through the city editor rather than going directly to the reporter. Ned's ablest reporters were young and full of fun. They liked to horse around in the city room when there was little to do, while Ned rocked in his swivel chair in a tolerant mood. Although Ned would visit his washroom locker two or three times during a shift, returning to the desk with his face flushed, he restricted his reporters from the Music Box, a favorite bar a block from the *Herald*. When things were not going right, or when Ned was cross for whatever reason, the reporters were likely to feel his temper. He seemed to be hardest on his better reporters, and whenever he was in one of his bad moods they trod water quietly to avoid making a discordant sound. If a reporter came in late Ned would glance up at the clock and look sternly at him to express his displeasure. One morning when Jack Thale arrived thirty minutes after the hour, sauntering nonchalantly across the newsroom, Ned jumped to his feet and dashed with long strides toward the reporter.

"Look at that clock," shouted the city editor, his face beet-red as he shook a nervous finger in Thale's face. "You're thirty minutes late. I'm not going to put up with it."

"But-but, Ned," said Thale, placatingly. "I'm not working today. I just came in to pick up my pay."

"I don't care," replied Ned, so built up he was unable to settle down immediately, "from now on you get in here on time."

Thale was one of Ned's star reporters, who had mastered a colorful but simple style that Hills admired. Two other of Ned's top reporter's, Charlie Fernandez and Lawrence Thompson, often were victims of his ire, particularly when he imagined they stayed out too long for dinner. One evening he left his desk and strode across the street to the Herald Grille, where Fernandez and Thompson were eating, and ordered them back to the office.

"But, Ned, we've still got twenty minutes on our lunch hour," complained Fernandez.

"I don't give a damn," shouted the angry city editor. "You're always taking a long dinner hour. Now get back to your desks."

The embarrassed reporters got up from their half-finished meals and followed Ned back to the city room. Ned didn't speak to them the rest of the evening, but next day he couldn't have been kinder.

Reporters who misspelled names or used wrong addresses were reminded of their errors in caustic terms, and for the next several days they knew they were on the city editor's "list." When a reporter missed an important story, however, Ned would question him to find out how it happened, then commiserate with him, knowing from experience the disgrace the reporter felt. But while Ned was fond of his staff, it would be incorrect to say that he had equal regard for all the individuals who worked for him. Hills, in hiring a staff with widely varied talents, wound up with many reporters and editors of uneven ability, some of whom had strange personalities. The older members of the city desk staff, like Henry Reno, Cy Berning, and John T. Bills, were good legmen and competent reporters but hardly colorful writers. Ned liked to keep his best writers, like Thale, Miss Bellamy, Fernandez, and Thompson, close at hand so they would be available in emergencies. But Fernandez spent much of his time on the road, covering Latin America as Steve Trumbull, the *Herald's* "Mr. Florida," covered the state. Aitchison lost one of his ablest reporters in 1950 when Henning Heldt, the paper's political writer, died after a long bout with a heart ailment. But he gained an equally able reporter when John McDermott, World War II European correspondent for the United Press, joined the staff as political writer. A New Englander and a graduate of the University of Georgia, McDermott had a cosmopolitan outlook but passed himself off as a plain guy. He was to become one of Florida's best known newspaper writers among the state's politicians. Although a teetotaler, his skill at playing gin rummy won respect for him among the Cracker leaders of north Florida.

Among Ned's more promising young reporters was David Kraslow, destined to become one of the University of Miami School of Journalism's outstanding products. Kraslow was a serious newsman who made hmself thoroughly disliked on the city hall and county beats because of his insistent probings and his suspicion that everybody was hiding something from him. Where older legmen had made a career of winning the friendship and confidence of politicians and bureaucrats, Kraslow treated them as enemies of the press and the public. The example he set, of severely monitoring the activities of the people in government, was to have a positive influence on the *Herald's* future coverage of public offices. Although Aitchison failed to see in Kraslow a potential star, he had the heart of a great reporter and would go to the top in the profession, winning a Nieman fellowship at Harvard.

The reporter with the best credentials was John F. Bonner, a Harvard graduate who was twenty-nine when he joined the staff. A World War II veteran with seven battle stars, Bonner was tall, handsome, and had one of the most imposing personalities in the newsroom. While he may have lacked color, he made up for it in confidence and communicative ability. Beebe, however, felt that Bonner lacked enthusiasm for newspaper work. After a stint as assistant city editor, Bonner succeeded Bills as financial editor. Meeting the Mackle brothers, builders of Key Biscayne and other major Florida developments, he impressed them so much they hired him to head their public relations department.

Jack Bills, who joined the *Herald* before World War II, became the paper's first financial editor. Prior to the war the state editor had handled the financial page, on which appeared the daily quotations of the leading stocks, bonds, and commodities, together with a lead story on market activities transmitted by the Associated Press. Bills took over the job with a stout bluster expected of a Texan who had gone through flight training with Jimmie Doolittle in the old Army Air Corps. Although crippled as a result of a training plane accident, the big, confident Texan was quick to take a position—always on the conservative side—on whatever subject might come up. His opinions were positive, hard-driven, and spoken with small consideration for how the flak might fly. Bills usually succeeded in intimidating the weak and insecure, and sought to throw off balance even the more robust and resolute. As a reporter he had succeeded in intimidating Ned Aitchison, whom he impressed by his bombastic and confident manner. As financial editor Bills wrote glowingly of Florida's business opportunities, as the late W. F. Therkildson had written of the state's agricultural opportunities. Bills later moved to the job of real estate editor with the same bombast. Florida was making amazing growth and his positive viewpoint would prove justified. Bills had married the *Herald's* star woman reporter, Jeanne Bellamy, and appeared to enjoy a special rapport with Hills and the Knights. Nevertheless, Hills passed over him to select George Beebe as managing editor. Bills left the *Herald* to go into banking, and, at the time of his death in 1967, had risen to be a director and senior vice president of Midtown Bank.

Miss Bellamy left the news department in 1951 after Hills departed for Detroit, joining John Pennekamp and Arthur Griffith in the quieter atmosphere of the editorial page office. She had lost her enthusiasm for the city desk, with which she had been associated since joining the *Herald* in 1937. The staff was growing and there was an increasing turnover of reporters and editors. The *Herald* was no longer the family affair it had been before World War II when the staff was small. Although Miss Bellamy thought Hills was the greatest newspaperman she had ever worked for, she feared the confusions and frustrations she imagined would plague the newsroom after his departure, and asked for a transfer.

Her fears of confusions and frustrations would prove justified, but they were the result of the *Herald's* continued growth and the improvements Hills was forever pressing as well as the failure of Aitchison to adjust to the onward and upward trend.

While the city desk lost one of its better reporters when Miss Bellamy departed, in 1953 it gained one destined to rise to the highest levels in the newspaper business, Al Neuharth. Bright, ambitious, and an eager opportunist, Neuharth worked only two years as a reporter before beginning his meteoric rise in Knight Newspapers. Neuharth's most important story as a reporter was his exposure of a mail order racket that grossed three Jewish brothers $1.5 million from the sale of cheap religious trinkets to naive Catholics. Benjamin, Henry, and Max Kram, operating through Catholic Products of America, mailed more than three million pieces of unsolicited plastic crucifixes, figures of saints, and other religious trinkets to Catholics throughout the country. For a trinket costing the Kram brothers a nickel or a dime to make they charged a dollar. They worded their sales pitch to suggest that the buyer was helping a religious cause.

Neuharth's stories brought demands by Catholic officials for an investigation. Congressman Dante Fascell asked and got a Congressional investigation. The Post Office Department ordered its own investigation. Meanwhile, the Krams were hailed into court on charges of using false and misleading advertising and found guilty. The pressure forced brothers Ben and Henry out, but roly-poly Max Kram defied the police, the courts, the *Herald,* Congress, and postal officials. Shouting at them all, and particularly at reporter Neuharth, Kram claimed his rights were being taken from him. His cries made no impression on the unimpassioned Neuharth, who continued until he put Max out of business. Neuharth's stories resulted in a rewriting of postal regulations, giving authorities more control over the sending of unsolicited merchandise through the mails.

The city desk's fastest rewrite man—one of the fastest who ever worked for the *Herald*—was Lawrence Thompson, whose father, Dr. Carl Thompson, was a swine specialist at Oklahoma State University. Hills hired Thompson from the *New York Herald-Tribune* in 1945. For several years he was given the big stories which involved coverage by several reporters—hurricanes, sensational murders, big fires, the annual Orange Bowl festival. He knew the right questions to ask and was able to cover a story so thoroughly from the rewrite desk that few details were left for the opposition to develop as "new" angles. His big stories, written from reporters' notes and from the observation of eyewitnesses, read as true as if he had been on the scene. He had a habit of talking louder and louder over the telephone as his enthusiasm grew until he seemed to be shouting. At such times it was difficult for others in the newsroom to work. Hills, and later Beebe, would give Thompson a concerned look across the newsroom, but the engrossed reporter was unaware of the disturbance he was making. The prolific Thompson began writing a weekly column in addition to his regular assignments. He wrote mostly about his family, nearly always on the ridiculous side. Thompson wrote of a world in which everybody else was "stupid," but always gave himself away in the end as the village idiot. The management had reservations about the column. Readers, however, found Thompson immensely funny. They evidently found in the column release from their own frustrations and miscalculations, and Thompson's popularity grew until he was writing his column daily and receiving volumes of mail from folksy fans. Most of his fans were "middle-aged squares"—at least this was the view held by the younger reporters who thought his column was "for the birds."

Another talented writer was Jack E. Anderson, who came up from copyboy. His best production, however, was reserved for the newsroom bulletin board and for the Sigma Delta Chi's annual Ribs and Roast scripts. When given an assignment by the city desk, Anderson turned in competent but usually routine copy. Lacking in the boldness that one needs to be a top-notch reporter, Anderson got stuck covering school board meetings and the *Herald's* annual spelling bee. The best he got out of this was a trip to Washington every year. When the management decided it could save money by having Knight Newspapers' Washington bureau cover the spelling bee finals, Anderson had good reson to think he'd "had it." But Anderson was to take charge of the television section and to write one of the liveliest TV columns in the country.

Steve Trumbull was one of the more colorful personalities who ever worked on the *Herald*—and his writing was just as colorful as Trumbull was in person. A native of Indiana, Trumbull had worked on a dozen newspapers before he and his wife, Jane, wound up in south Dade County in the early 1930s to plant an avocado grove. While waiting on the trees to grow, he decided to return to newspapering, where he was to remain until retirement in 1963. Trumbull's sense of humor and ability to tell salty stories in the primmest of company won friends everywhere, and, like any other fervent newspaperman, he sought friends among all levels of society. Although Trumbull had attended college, he had never learned how to spell; in fact, he was so bad other reporters hesitated to let him use their typewriters lest the machines pick up his bad spelling habit. When he returned from World War II, Hills sent him throughout Florida in search of colorful feature stories. Trumbull made the back country familiar to *Herald* readers, and, traveling on his boat, the Po Ho, he took readers down the Saint Johns, the Oklawaha, and the Suwannee rivers. He discovered many unusual and delightful stories, like one about a sandhill crane, which, having been raised as a household pet after breaking a wing, thought it was a dog. Trumbull was more than a writer about colorful people, animals, and places. He also was a sharp-eyed reporter always on the lookout for hard news stories. He liked to think of himself as the Nemesis of real estate developers who subdivided Florida swamps and promoted the sale of lots as "high and dry" and a "short distance from Miami."

"Hold onto your pocketbook," he started one story, "another land pirate has subdivided a swamp wetter than the Okefenokee and is offering lots to suckers."

Hills would not have tolerated such a lead written by any other reporter, but Trumbull was given great freedom. All Hills asked was proof to back up such statements. And Trumbull had the proof, including photographs of submerged street signs. One subdivider sued but the suit was thrown out. Trumbull wrote as pungently about the lobbyists whose activities he observed while covering the Florida Legislature, but none sued. About the lobbyists of one legislative session he wrote:

"The lobbyists have prowled the halls throughout this session, most of them with smug and self-satisfied smiles, because they got what they came for."

Trumbull prided himself as an outdoorsman and camp cook, particularly of fish and game. He introduced a cooking story with this lead:

"Grab the smelling salts and start fanning yourselves, you gourmets, the old swamp rat is about to do a piece on game and fresh water fish cooking."

In succeeding paragraphs you could hear the speckled perch sizzling in deep fat and smell the wild, country-chicken aroma of young rabbit frying in a black skillet resting on live campfire coals.

Charlie Fernandez, a native Floridian and a decorated Navy pilot, came to the *Herald* after World War II. Of Spanish extraction, Fernandez was a handsome, suave, able reporter and a fast and able writer who could handle any kind of assignment—a Lee Hills' ideal newspaperman. Fernandez spoke Spanish fluently and Hills assigned him to the Latin American beat. For several years he was in Latin America about as much as he was in Miami. Every other reporter was envious of Fernandez, but only one thought he could do a better job. That was Stuart Morrison, Sr., telegraph editor, who thought of himself as a Latin American expert. In deference to Morrison, a rough hewn, gregarious man in his fifties, he was bright, widely experienced, and clever. Morrison spent much of his off-duty hours interviewing Latin American travelers flying in and out of Miami between Washington and Central or South America. His contacts were as mysterious as the stories he came up with. Morrison was always dashing out to the airport to to meet someone, returning with a notebook filled with information on Communist intrigue, palace uprisings, developing revolutions, threatening invasions. Working over a typewriter with enormous enthusiasm, Morrison turned out stories of compelling readership. Widely read in the *Herald's* Clipper Edition, some of them created sensations—and denials. Hills read Morrison's stories as he cleared his throat nervously. He wondered about the credibility of the reporter's sources, yet Communists were active throughout Latin America and there was always the same old palace intrigue taking place. The stories Fernandez sent back reflected the unrest and impending troubles that Morrison sensationalized. Hills, however, entertained enough doubt that he gave Morrison no encouragement. But Morrison so impressed John Montgomery, a Miamian who owned the *Brazilian Herald,* an English language newspaper in Rio de Janeiro, that he hired him as editor. Morrison departed, taking with him his wife, Margaret Miles, one of Hills' better writers and editors.

You saw more women in newspaper offices after World War II than you did before. Except for a few like Jeanne Bellamy and her predecessor, Doris Stone, women writers before the war often found themselves assigned to "sob-sister" stories. The tear-jerking story was a common part of newspaper writing after the war, too, and editors were always looking for a gal who could be turned into a sob-sister. But it was becoming increasingly difficult to find women who would endure the role. Like Miss Bellamy or Miss Miles, they insisted on doing much the same kind of reporting and feature writing as men, which they frequently did with keener insight. Gals got some derring-do assignments heretofore reserved for males. In 1951 reporter Jeanne Voltz, mother of two children, learned to fly a plane in one day and soloed after seven and one-half hours of continuous instruction. Mrs. Voltz, who worked in the woman's department, could have done an outstanding job for the city desk, but, being a gourmet cook, preferred to write about food. An excellent writer, Mrs. Voltz had a knack for making food stories interesting. She made trips through the state, collecting recipes from Key West, Tampa, Ocala, Cedar Key, and writing about them against the background in which they originated. She collaborated with Trumbull to do features on the preparation of fish and game at campsites. It was no surprise when Mrs. Voltz became a nationally known food editor in charge of the food section of the *Los Angeles Times*.

Mrs. Doris Reno, part-time music and art critic when the Knights purchased the *Herald,* was a niece of Publisher Frank B. Shutts. As Doris

Smith, daughter of his sister, Mrs. George Smith of Aurora, Indiana, "Uncle Frank" had given her a minor position in the newsroom in the early 1930s and had assisted her through college. He objected to her plans to work for a master's degree, giving as a reason that she already "had enough education for a woman." But Uncle Frank objected even more upon hearing of her plans to marry Paul Reno, son of the *Herald's* photographer, Bob Reno, and brother of Henry Reno, the police reporter. Neither objection stopped her, however, but upon returning to Miami after receiving her master's degree, the best Uncle Frank would do for her was to give her part-time work as music and art critic, with piddling pay. Having heard a rumor that the Knights planned to fire all members of the Shutts family working for the *Herald,* Doris pleaded with Pennekamp "not to tell on her." And, although she was to become respected and influential as the *Herald's* music and art critic in the years ahead, Doris reached retirement age in the late 1960s without overcoming the fear that she would be fired if the Knights learned the former publisher was her uncle.

Aitchison had a few among his staff who were so unsuited for newspaper work that he was often at his wit's end to make good use of them. One was James Lyons, a Harvard student and graduate of Boston University School of Journalism. Although in his twenties, Lyons had the figure of a forty-year-old clerk. He had an excellent mind, and, having attended the New England Conservatory of Music, had an enviable knowledge of music. He thought of himself as an expert in all the arts and jumped at any opportunity to review an art show. But Lyons was happiest on those rare occasions when Mrs. Reno was unavailable to cover a concert. Lyons was given to extravagant phraseology and long, complicated sentences, making himself the bane of Hills' efforts to achieve clarity in writing. Routine reporting bored him and his writing showed it. Hoping Lyons might prove to be a successor to Oxford-educated Arthur Griffith, Pennekamp gave him a trial at editorial writing. Although erudite, Lyons' writing was as obscure as it was verbose. Pennekamp eventually let him go.

Another reporter Aitchison found difficult was Robert Armstrong Andrews, of South Carolina. Andrews worked with great energy but produced little. To Ned he was a Santa Claus type minus the beard. He gushed with good will, promoting himself and his ideas, dashing off memos to Hills and to Aitchison and signing them in black ink with a broad-pointed pen—"Robert Armstrong Andrews." Or he would send reporters notes on personalized cards, half-written, half-printed, lauding them for especially good stories. The reporters were at first flabbergasted but soon learned that such notes from Andrews were routine. Aitchison tried Andrews on rewrite, reporting, feature writing. But he exasperated Ned so much that finally the city editor refused to give him anything to do. Andrews returned to South Carolina, from where he wrote stacks of cards to puzzled editors and reporters. After a time the cards stopped coming.

Cliff Thurmon, a copyreader, one night came back from lunch and disappeared. Fifteen minutes later News Editor Charlie Ward noted Thurmon's absence and asked if anyone knew what had happened to him.

"He went to the john," said a copyreader.

Noting Thurmon's glasses and cigarets on the desk, Ward thought no more about him. But Thurmon did not appear that night, the next day, or the next week. A year later Ward received a letter from him in Spokane.

"If my glasses are still around," wrote Thurmon, "would you send them to me?"

Ward mailed the glasses without comment.

The drinking breed of reporters and copyreaders, common on every city newspaper before World War II, was fading out, but a few were still around. Some were so good that the management was reluctant to let them go. One was Jack Thale, whom Aitchison considered his most colorful writer. Some days were dull, though, and when Thale went to dinner in the evening he might not return. Nor would he return for a couple of days. Sometimes he stayed away as long as a week. But the management kept him, deducting his pay for the days he took off. Thale was to work for several years under this arrangement before going into public relations.

Al Hallman, a former Associated Press writer who worked on the copydesk, was a different type of drinker. His breakfast consisted of milk toast and three bottles of Ballantine ale. And he continued to drink all day and through working hours, going periodically to his washroom locker where he kept a bottle of gin. Having a brilliant mind and years of writing and editing experience, Hallman was an excellent copyreader. Hills knew of Hallman's drinking but tolerated it. Eventually Hallman's health began to fail and his doctor insisted that he go on the wagon.

"I won't drink," Hallman told Charlie Ward, "but it'll put me in the hospital."

Sure enough, Aitchison called Ward next day to tell him to get someone in Hallman's place; that he was in the hospital. On the following day Aitchison called Ward again.

"You know something, Charlie," said Aitchison in a trembling voice, "Hallman's dead."

25

New Stars Arise

L EE HILLS could report to John S. Knight in 1954, three years
after his moving to Detroit, that both the *Free Press* and the
Miami Herald were doing well. Although he had little time to
spend in Miami, capable people headed the various editorial departments
of the *Herald*. Before leaving Miami he had hired Dorothy Jurney,
Northwestern University School of Journalism graduate, as women's
editor to succeed Mary Shuck who died in 1950. Within four years Mrs.
Jurney had built one of the nation's outstanding women's sections. Jimmy Burns, veteran sports writer whom he had hired in 1943, had continued to raise the stature of the *Herald's* sports section. Jack Bell was at
his peak as the Town Crier columnist. George Beebe had proved to be a
capable managing editor, and he had a capable staff of reporters, department editors, and copyreaders. But by 1954 Beebe was having troubles
with the city desk.

Ned Aitchison may have been a competent and beloved city editor, but
the newsroom staff had expanded enormously—and Ned had aged. The
Herald no longer bore much resemblance to the newspaper Ned had
started to work on twelve years before. Yet, he was still insisting on doing
virtually everything on the city desk himself. Aitchison never had been
able to make efficient use of assistants, except for Arthur Himbert, whose
main job was answering the telephone, processing the staff's expense accounts, and sitting at the desk late at night. Himbert, a graduate of Notre
Dame, had joined the *Herald* in the early 1940s. Being dependable and
congenial, he soon got stuck on the city desk doing menial jobs, including
the rewrite of handouts, the writing of late obituaries, and taking dicta-
tion from beat reporters. Aitchison had come to look upon Himbert as a
minor edition of the city editor's alter ego. If Ned suddenly wanted a
quotation from the mayor, a judge, or some other official to insert in a

story, Himbert could get it. And if Ned wanted to send a photographer on an assignment, Himbert could arrange it. But Himbert had no title. Assistant city editors came and went, as much to their frustration as to Ned's; but the ever faithful Himbert remained. As the 1950s progressed, however, the city desk became progressively more difficult to manage. While insisting on handling all the important copy that passed over the city desk, Ned merely put commas and periods in the correct places. Because he loved his scribes it pained him to cut out their bright metaphors and descriptive phrases or to remove their colorful although superfluous paragraphs. Moreover, Ned had a penchant for running picture strips across the top of the local page when a single good photograph would have illustrated a story just as well. He was especially a sucker for airlines' picnics and Captain Eddie Rickenbacker in various poses. And nothing melted his heart more than a stack of photographs made at the crippled children's hospital. You could see a picture strip forming in his mind as he shuffled the photographs and began laying them side by side. With the growing staff, particularly of specialists, together with the new activities that had to be covered in booming Dade County, there was less space now for long-winded stories and extravagant use of art. Moreover, Hills was pressing George Beebe and Charlie Ward to get a greater number of stories in the paper. Exasperated, Ward would run to Beebe and throw down on his desk a pile of long-winded stories Ned had just handed the copy desk.

"Look, George," lamented Ward, "where am I going to find the space to run all this stuff? And if I cut anything Ned will get mad as hell. What can I do?"

What Ward wanted was for Beebe to have a showdown with the city editor. That would keep Ned off the news editor's neck. But Beebe knew that wouldn't be easy. So, instead of going directly to Ned, Beebe said to Ward:

"Go ahead, Charlie, and cut anything you have to. I'll back you up."

Ward returned to the copydesk with a long face. He could cut some but feared to do as much as he wanted to . Two or three of those long stories would show up next day in the leftovers. A showdown was avoided, but Beebe knew it had to come. Hills was monitoring the *Herald* daily and Beebe was under constant pressure.

"Fun in Florida," a new tabloid magazine with Betty Garnet as editor, was started in 1954, with the paper's installation of a three-color process. Beebe improved Latin American coverage by adding Puerto Rican and Panamanian editions. Hills in the meantime succeeded in having all advertising matter removed from page two of the first section, making it possible to continue, or "jump," all the long, important page-one stories to a single open page inside. On top of it all there was constant prodding from Detroit for "tighter writing and tighter editing."

Beebe insisted that the only way to achieve Hills' goal was to replace Aitchison, sixty-one, with a younger, more pliable city editor. But in the entire newsroom was not one person they could agree on who was qualified for the job. Wilson McGee and Charlie Fernandez, either of whom might have been qualified, had departed—McGee into law practice, Fernandez into the operation of a radio station with a brother in Sarasota.

"Well, I need help," complained Beebe. "We've got all this writing talent—almost too much—but there's not one strong man on the staff that I can use to help me."

With the hope that he might contribute to the solving of the city desk problem, Hills sent William A. Townes from Detroit as Beebe's assistant. Townes had the reputation of being one of the more brilliant newspaper editors in the business. He was a Nieman Fellow and had moved from one high-paying job to another. Hills was impressed by the inexhaustible flow of ideas from Townes' facile mind and his uncanny ability at improving newspaper typography. With the title of "night managing editor," Townes arrived at the *Herald* like one who had been sent to put out a fire. Brimming with ideas, he went about the newsroom talking with reporters and special writers. After a conversation with Townes you were likely to receive a memorandum suggesting a story, together with the night managing editor's ideas about how the story should be approached and written. But Townes' approach was often overly simple; life was too complicated to be reduced to the brittle white and black format that Townes demanded, without considering the nuances that a reporter finds whenever he goes out on the scene where stories happen. Moreover, Townes neglected to consult the city editor when making assignments, frequently disrupting Aitchison's plans for the use of his staff. Townes, meanwhile, was of small assistance to Beebe. Despite his title, Townes worked the same hours as Beebe, the day managing editor. But Townes made one contribution that made Beebe happy: he fuzzed Ned Aitchison into a mood sufficiently discouraging to ask for a transfer from the city desk. Pleased to accommodate, Beebe assigned Ned to write travel and aviation stories, and put on the city desk the only person on the staff he thought to be both qualified and able to get along with the staff—Merlin Test.

Test, forty-eight, was a native of Dayton, Ohio, and a hardworking, veteran newspaperman. Although Test lacked the aggressiveness of Bills or the personality of Bonner, Beebe reasoned that he would have better rapport with the staff. But soon after becoming city editor, Test began to undergo a personality change. Feeling the pressure from two bosses, and particularly from Townes with his incessant flow of ideas, the problems became too great for him. Test no longer smiled. He worked tensely. Wincing under pressure, he tended to lose his cool when dealing with his staff. Reporters lost their respect for him, then began to take him as a joke. Al Neuharth delighted in tantalizing Test. Neuharth was one of those rare reporters of such ability and orderly mind that he could research a story until minutes before a deadline, then, hanging up the telephone, turn to his typewriter and bang out perfectly typed "takes" of copy as a copyboy ran the pages one by one to the nervous city editor. The confident reporter seemed to delight in putting new worry lines in Test's already heavily creased brow. There were times when he came very near to driving Test into a muttering idiot by his waiting until fifteen minutes before deadline, then turning to his typewriter to beat out his story, completing it within a minute of deadline. Such experiences sent Test to his washroom locker. Defeated and dejected, he gave up in 1956 after less than two years on the job. Test went to less demanding jobs, but never recovered his lost confidence. Three years later he suffered a fatal heart attack.

Beebe, in the meantime, had discovered that he did have a "strong man" on his staff—Neuharth. The reporter was thirty-two when elevated to executive city editor, a new position. Under him was put Luther Voltz, in his forties and handicapped from a fall he had suffered when a child. Bright and aggressive, Voltz had started working for the *Herald* as a school reporter in 1925 when he was in junior high school. Jack Bell joined the *Herald* as sports editor about that time, and Voltz idolized him as a teacher and friend. When his father died two years later, Voltz lived with Bell in his bachelor apartment. Voltz went to school and held down a regular job alongside the one-armed Bell. One day Bell was writing a story with Voltz watching intently over his shoulder. When Bell reached the end of a page, Voltz rolled in fresh paper. Jack took the paper from the machine, put it back on the desk, picked it up again and rolled it in himself with one hand. When he had finished the story, Bell said tartly:

"Let me give you a piece of advice, Luther: never help a one-armed man unless he asks you."

Voltz would never forget. Himself a cripple, he took the advice and was determined to make his own way. Following in the shadow of the colorful Bell, Voltz worked aggressively at every job he was given and endured criticism from the sports writer, who showed him less sympathy than he would have had he not been handicapped. Moreover, Bell made Voltz pay the rent. But when Voltz left for college Bell returned the money to him. Voltz returned to the *Herald* in 1945 after working for

Mobile and New York papers. Along the way he married an attractive newspaperwoman, Jeanne Appleton, and sired two children. In 1950 Hills sent Voltz to the American Press Institute seminars at Columbia. Although not a colorful writer, he made a highly competent reporter on city hall and county building beats, being blessed with an insight that a lot of more sure-footed reporters lack. Voltz did a competent job as city editor, too, but the job required more energy than he could spare, and after six months he transferred to the editorial page office.

Voltz was succeeded on the city desk by John McMullan, who moved over from the same job on the *Miami News.* McMullan was a strong-man type like Neuharth, highly competent, and with an uncanny nose for news. He had a law degree from the University of Miami Law School but had not practiced. His leaving the *Miami News* was a serious loss to the evening paper.

The *Miami Herald* meanwhile made fantastic growth as Miami was in the midst of a boom much greater than that of 1925, although less spectacular. The daily *Herald* was running sixty, eighty-two, and ninety-six pages, and the Sunday *Herald* was running up to 252 pages. Pressure on the city desk had grown so much that Ned Aitchison could be happy he no longer was city editor. McMullan was given four assistants, Derick Daniels, Arthur Himbert, Jim Miller, and George Southworth. By now Townes had departed and Neuharth moved into his job, with the title of assistant managing editor, in charge of the city desk. The title of executive city editor was abolished. The *Herald's* circulation made a record increase in 1957, gaining an average of 17,800 daily and 24,900 on Sunday. Beebe now had more capable assistants than any previous managing editor could claim. Of the six who shared the duties of the city desk in 1957, let's look ahead and see what would happen to them. Only Himbert, a retiring man with a lame hand and a mild personality, would remain on the desk, staying there until his death from cancer in 1970. Miller, bright and competent but lacking the ambition to go places as an editor, would leave to enter law school. Southworth, a facile writer and dependable editor, but lacking in administrative drive, would go to the University of Miami as a journalism instructor. Neuharth would leave Knight Newspapers to become president and chief executive officer of Gannett Newspapers. McMullan would become executive editor of the *Philadelphia Inquirer* and *News,* then a vice president of Knight Newspapers. Daniels, a member of the Daniels newspaper family of Raleigh, North Carolina, would go to the *Detroit Free Press* where he became executive editor when Hills was elevated to publisher of the *Free Press* and the *Miami Herald.*

While the *Herald* may have had some outstanding editors, in 1956 it acquired three exceptionally capable reporters and writers, two of them women. Denne Petitclerc, a young Californian, gave readers a glimpse of newspaper writing that would not be seen again until the late 1960s. Joy Reese Shaw, a striking blonde from Jacksonville, Florida, wrote with a warmth and in a style that reflected her glamorous personality. Juanita Greene, a Louisiana Cajun who came to the *Herald* from Daytona Beach, would develop into one of the outstanding reporters in the newspaper's history.

As a result of Hills' efforts the *Herald* had become widely known as a newspaper which encouraged individual style and original writing. Good straight reporting was encouraged, too, of course. Hills won a Pulitzer prize in 1956 for his behind-the-scene reporting of negotiations between the United Automobile Workers and Ford and General Motors for a guaranteed annual wage arrangement. But Hills and Beebe also encouraged writing that was different. Steve Trumbull's writing was an example. His salty leads and colorful phraseology were likely to take unusual turns, but his readers were accustomed to them. Jim Russell, who had just come to the *Herald* from the United Press, was quick to learn that Trumbull's style was "sacred." Sitting on the city desk one evening, Russell read copy on a Trumbull yarn and concluded it needed clarifying. He took it upon himself to rewrite Trumbull's lead. Next day he caught hell from the management.

"I didn't know there was any writer in the world who couldn't be rewritten," complained Russell who as a U.P. editor had rewritten countless stories without repercussions.

Petitclerc was an altogether different type of writer from Trumbull. After a couple of years on the *Herald* he would leave to rewrite what he hoped would be the great American novel. His novel was eventually published, but, like so many similar efforts, it was born in obscurity and died in obscurity. Petitclerc's talent was displayed in the *Herald* in his ability to combine the technique of fiction writing with newspaper writing. He was one of the first to make a successful attempt at this, long before magazine writer Tom Wolfe and *New York Times* writer Gay Talese came along to get the credit for influencing news writing with the application of fiction technique. Although older reporters and copyreaders tended to look upon him as an odious upstart, Petitclerc's writing pleased both readers and the management. He might have been considered the *Herald's* star writer—next to Trumbull, who was in a class by himself—if it had not been for Mrs. Shaw. While Denne may have had the most individual writing technique, Mrs. Shaw wrote with a warmth that was lacking in his stories. Petitclerc was a serious student of Hemingway, and Papa's style came through in his writing. When Denne arrived, Neuharth was trying to make a star out of an attractive gal from Kansas and Oklahoma, Dixie Gilliland. She was sent out to write about the things that struck Neuharth's fancy. What he wanted was the reaction of a Midwest gal to glittering Miami Beach and magic Miami. He wanted her to write with wide-eyed fascination. On one occasion he assigned her to write about her reaction to the royal poinciana, among the tropic's most colorful trees. Neuharth also assigned Petitclerc to write his reaction. The observations of both writers were run one after the other and we have them for comparison. Miss Gilliland began:

"The blazing beauty of the royal poinciana now in bloom in Miami have taken a great weight off the mind of this Midwestener.

"There is a way to tell the change of season in South Florida."

It was a straightforward statement of a writer's reaction to one of Miami's most beautiful trees, which blooms in late spring and early summer. Petitclerc was concerned more with reducing his reaction to an artistic achievement than in revealing his feelings. He started like this:

"And there were the trees with the branches altar-like over South Miami Avenue, and the brilliant bursts of flowers that are, in brightness, like the twinkling of shellfire on a pitch black hill.

"'What are they?' my wife asked.

"'Royal poinciana,' our guide said. 'Named for M. de Poinci who was once a governor of the French West Indies.'"

Petitclerc could have been starting a novel or a short story. His approach had the flavor of Hemingway. But it had been Hemingway who had seen shells explode on a "pitch black hill." Old-timers in the newsroom gagged.

After meeting Hemingway, Petitclerc tried even harder to imitate him. Assigned to interview Hemingway at the Miami International Airport, the reporter was invited by the noted author to accompany him and "Miss Mary" to nearby Miami Springs Villas. By no means immune to praise, Hemingway was taken in by the glib young reporter. A warm friendship developed between them. A few weeks later George Bourke, the *Herald's* amusement editor, was on board a Cuban ferry pulling out of Key West on its way to Havana when he spotted the black hull of Hemingway's cruiser, Pilar, off the port. Bourke recognized the familiar stocky figure of Hemingway. But who was the slender fellow with him? Raising his binoculars, he recognized Hemingway's companion—Denne Petitclerc. Meanwhile, Hemingway had read some of Petitclerc's writing, and because it sounded so similar to his own, praised it.

"You're the best qualified," said Papa, "to take the master's place after he's gone."

Hemingway, of course, never thought anybody would be able to take his place. Nevertheless, the naive reporter repeated Hemingway's praise in the newsroom. More gags. The praise did nothing to improve Petitclerc's writing, and may have done it harm. It was shortly afterward that he began talking about writing a novel. By the time Denne departed in 1958, to become a highly paid writer in television, he was of much less value to the *Herald* than upon his arrival, when he was fresh, enthusiastic, hard-working, and eager to please his editors.

By the time Petitclerc announced he was leaving a new star had risen—Joy Reese Shaw. Even if she had not sparkled as a writer she would have as a blonde beauty, for she was the most glamorous reporter who had walked across the newsroom threshold. Beebe hired her from the *Jacksonville Journal,* where she had starred as an investigative reporter. A series of stories she did on the activities of crooked school officials caused a major scandal in Jacksonville and resulted in the superintendent of public schools going to prison. Neuharth, having failed to make "stars" out of two other women writers, was determined to make one out of the talented Mrs. Shaw. Miss Gilliland, lacking the flair for a Brenda Starr role, departed for Houston, to die six years later of infectious hepatitis at thirty-seven. The other "disappointment" was Juanita Greene. Miss Greene, her own woman, insisted on being a straight, hard-hitting reporter. Thinking that Neuharth was trying to make a sob-sister of her, she wanted none of the "warm and human" assignments he urged on her. Working variously on the federal, county, and city hall beats, Juanita found satisfaction in being compared with Dave Kraslow as the "impossible" reporter. And although she may have been a disappointment to Neuharth, she was a star to the new, hard-nosed city editor, John McMullan. Taking an equally hard-nosed view of her beat, she considered it her duty to check on what the "politicians and bureaucrats" were doing for the public; that it was not her job "to propagandize their positions." At Neuharth's encouragement, Juanita stole a copy of the City of Miami's budget before it was released. While this pleased Neuharth, his reporter was Mrs. Shaw. Juanita was McMullan's reporter.

Neuharth, having read Mrs. Shaw's stories in the *Journal,* knew what she could do well. While she may have been a knockout as an investigative reporter, she also could do those heart-warming stories that Neuharth liked. And whatever she wrote a certain sparkle and glamor came through, too. Mrs. Shaw reported for work in late December, 1956, and her first assignment was the Orange Bowl parade. This was one story the *Miami Herald* gave blockbuster coverage every year. Reporters were given various assignment in connection with the parade and attendant events. Most of the reporters called in details to Larry Thompson, who did the lead story which started on page one and jumped inside to run on and on ad infinitum, together with spectacular picture coverage. Mrs. Shaw was assigned to ride the *Miami Herald's* float in the parade and write her reactions. Neuharth couldn't have been more pleased with her story, which started like this:

"Suggestion for viewing your next parade:

"Float by.

"I did. Right on the back of the *Herald* float in Monday night's King Orange Jamboree.

"I watched the human parade, while the human parade watched me."

Next day the beautiful Mrs. Shaw was assigned to sit on the bench between the players in the Orange Bowl game. During the first half she sat with the beefy Clemson players, then spent the second half with the Colorado bulls. So hung over was Mrs. Shaw from the New Year's party the previous night at Steve Trumbull's that she felt rotten. But a three-column photograph which accompanied her story showed "little Joy" as

GLAMOROUS REPORTER Joy Reese Shaw sits between Colorado's husky gridironers at the 1957 Orange Bowl game in one of her first assignments on the *Herald*. She discovered that football players spit a lot and played every minute of the game, whether in the field or warming the bench.

bright and as pretty as ever. "A Blonde Beauty Rides Bench/Between Mountains of Muscle," said the three-column headline over her story, which she started like this:

"Ball players play every minute of the game whether they're warming the bench or not.

"They coach, too. And spit.

"They are excellent spitters."

Mrs. Shaw proceeded to report what she saw and heard in a candid and spirited way. Despite her monstrous hangover, she was able to add up the weights of the Clemson squad to discover she was sitting between 6,852 pounds of beef. Even a small crush on the 120-pound reporter could have been fatal.

Neuharth failed, however, to make Mrs. Shaw into a full-fledged sob-sister. Independent and hard-headed, she resisted Neuharth's efforts to make her "cry" over heart-rending stories. She insisted on thinking of herself as an investigative reporter, and, indeed, her beauty, together with a deceptive naivete, made it possible for her to "con" people into talking freely to her. A series she did on the sorry conditions of Miami nursing homes resulted in major reforms. One of her most unusual stories was written after interviews with sex offenders serving life terms at Raiford prison. But probably her greatest beat was inducing Candace Mossler to grant an interview before her arrest on a charge of complicity in the murder of her husband, banker Jacques Mossler. Mrs. Shaw left the *Herald* in the middle 1960s to head the Dade County School Board's public relations department. By the time she was preparing to leave, another promising woman writer was rising on the *Herald*. She was Jeanne Wardlow, who had studied under Fred Shaw, one of the University of Miami's outstanding teachers of creative writing. But, for the most part, the era of the "woman" writer, in contrast to the strictly "male" writer, was disappearing. "Women's Liberation," together with the desexing of hair styles and dress, would take care of that. An era would come when the males, not the women, would "cry" over stories.

26

Metro, Libel, and Dynamite

DADE COUNTY in the 1950s undertook an experiment in government that ignited a political controversy that was to continue for the next several years. The experiment, in which the *Miami Herald* played a major role, was metropolitan government, or Metro. It was designed to consolidate Dade County's scattered municipalities under one government. Consolidation, as originally visualized, was only partially achieved. The failure was viewed by Metro supporters as tragic, while to Metro's enemies the failure was a godsend. Never was an experiment in government, outside of communism or fascism, more bitterly condemned or more stubbornly fought by its enemies.

Between 1896 and 1949 Dade County's incorporated communities had grown to twenty-six. Miami was first to be incorporated, followed by Homestead in 1913, Florida City in 1914, and Miami Beach in 1915. During the boom years of 1925-26 seven were created—Hialeah, Coral Gables, North Miami, South Miami, Opa-Locka, Miami Springs, and North Miami Beach. Six more were created between 1928 and 1939—Golden Beach, Miami Shores, Biscayne Park, Surfside, El Portal, and Indian Creek. Nine additional municipalities were created between 1941 and 1949—Sweetwater, North Bay Village, Bal Harbour, West Miami, Bay Harbor Islands, Virginia Gardens, Hialeah Gardens, Pennsuco, and Medley. Each community had its own city hall, police department, and fire department, tax assessor, tax collector, building and zoning department, garbage and trash collection service, with almost as many separate water and sewage systems. If all these functions could be taken over by the county government, the supporters of Metro argued, costly local governments would be eliminated. This would bring an end to spiraling local taxes.

John Pennekamp has been given credit for introducing the Metro concept in his column, "Behind The Front Page." Pennekamp earlier had succeeded in a campaign to consolidate the Dade County school system, then divided into ten inefficiently managed districts. Later, he brought about the consolidation of the city, county, and state health departments. Although Pennekamp's column was never flashy or a work of brilliant prose, the writing had an editorial quality greater than these—believability. Where other columnists depended on clever use of language, compelling human interest, fresh angles, and even contrived controversy, Pennekamp began his column in 1941 as a simple statement of the facts he had at hand. Whenever he took a stand he was direct and firm. This format never changed, and in time "Behind The Front Page" became the most influential newspaper column in Miami, a position it would enjoy for several years.

After his experience with the consolidation of the schools and the health departments, it seems only natural that Pennekamp should have been the first to suggest the consolidation of Dade County's numerous municipalities under one government. The idea, however, grew out of the meetings of a group of citizens, a group that had nothing to do directly with the founding of Metro. These citizens were members of the establishment—businessmen, lawyers, bankers, the head of the electric power company, together with representatives of the newspapers. The meetings, in the form of Thursday evening dinners in a downtown hotel, were called to discuss the problems of rehabilitating the Miami area after the pullout of the military following World War II. An economic recession was feared. It would take some time to renovate the hotels and office buildings which the military had used during the war. There was the problem of rebuilding the image of Miami and Miami Beach as a winter resort and re-establishing business and banking on a normal civilian-oriented basis. Taking a recession for granted, these leaders discussed means of cutting the cost of operating the government of Dade County and those of the numerous municipalities. Pennekamp had been given a springboard from which to jump—a springboard set up by the establishment.

Achieving consolidation and true metropolitan government might have been simpler had a recession occurred. Instead, Dade County experienced the greatest boom in its history. Although the boom may not have been so wild as that of the 1920s, many more people were involved, and a great deal more money. Where the boom of the 1920s had built Miami from a small resort town into a city, the boom of the 1950s would expand Miami into a major metropolitan area, bringing half a million new people to Dade County. When the germ of consolidated government was planted at those Thursday dinner meetings Dade County's population was under 400,000, and most of the people lived in Miami and Miami Beach. Coral Gables and Hialeah, the two largest satellite communities, each had populations of under 15,000. Many areas northwest and west of Miami were in cattle and dairy pasture, much of which was under water after the hurricane rains in the fall of 1947. But a major drainage and flood control program, begun in 1949 with federal and state funds, would encourage the spread of residential areas in parts of the county which heretofore had been part of the Everglades. Land which once could have been bought for ten to twenty dollars an acre jumped to a thousand and eventually would soar to ten thousand or more an acre. Where there had been two dozen dairies in Dade County at the end of World War II, by the end of the 1950s the number would be reduced to two or three. And many of the little communities that could boast few more residents than the employees of city hall and the police department in 1950, would begin calling themselves cities by 1960.

In the meantime, political changes were taking place that would have immense significance when the proponents of metropolitan government sought to make consolidation a reality. Prior to 1949, Charles H. Crandon, a member of the county commission, had been the most important political figure in Dade County. Crandon, owner of a wholesale drug company, came to Miami in 1917. In 1928 he was elected to the county commission. He wanted to establish a countywide park system such as he had seen in California while serving with the military during World War I. He found that to achieve his aims he would have to get himself elected to the county commission. Then he had to campaign to get other commissioners elected who would support him.

Despite a Massachusetts accent, Crandon was able to hide his Yankeeism behind a folksy way of greeting and talking to voters, a large percentage of whom were from Florida or Georgia. Crandon remained on the county commission for five successive terms before retiring at the end of 1948. During that time he had built one of the finest county park systems in America, and at little cost to taxpayers because he got most of the land donated. The land for Haulover Park, which included a mile and a half of ocean beach, he obtained by having the county attorney forclose on property which owners had abandoned during depression years, and buying, in secret, lots on which owners had paid taxes. Use of public funds to buy property secretly would be impossible after the passage of a "government in the sunshine" law by the Florida Legislature. Crandon's greatest achievement was the building of Crandon Park on Key Biscayne. In the late 1930s he made a deal with the Matheson family, which owned 4,000 acres of the 4,400-acre key. If the family would give Dade County the northern two miles of Key Biscayne, which was half of the Matheson holdings, the county would build a causeway to the island. The family accepted the offer and the county sold revenue bonds to build Rickenbacker Causeway.

Crandon ran the county commission like the board of a private corporation. He was content to let the mayor of Miami be the greeter of visiting dignitaries, which, traditionally, had been the mayor's role. A prelude to weekly county commission meetings was held in Crandon's office in the Dade County Courthouse. Reporters were welcome to witness how the chairman of the board whipped other board members into line prior to appearing in formal session before the public to transact the county's business. Crandon's departure from public office ended the "Big Daddy" kind of government. No one on the commission was capable of stepping into Big Daddy's shoes. I. D. MacVicar, a building supply dealer, tried but ran afoul of Pennekamp and the *Herald*.

After MacVicar became commission chairman in 1953 he sought to operate the county's affairs with the tactics he had learned under Crandon. Much of the commission's business was conducted in secrecy. Pennekamp, who had reservations about Crandon's methods, wasn't about to let MacVicar develop as Big Daddy's successor. He went after MacVicar and the other commissioners with sledge-hammer editorial attacks. Editorials, written by Arthur Griffith, were some of the best examples of Oxford invective. But MacVicar, a decorated combat major in the Army during World War II, defended his position firmly. Meanwhile, a scandal erupted at the Miami International Airport. A. B. Curry, a director of the the the Dade County Port Authority, which administered the affairs of the airport, was indicted on grand larceny charges and accused of accepting $1,000 a month from an engineering company doing business with the Port Authority. He was accused of moving a building from the airport to his own private property, and of using Port Authority employees to work on his own premises. The *Herald* was given more ammunition for its attack on the county government after charges against Curry were dropped and he was permitted to save his skin by resigning. Shortly thereafter other irrregularities were discovered at the airport by *Herald* government reporter Dave Kraslow. The major airlines not only were receiving a special low rental preference over the smaller airlines, Kraslow found, but paid less in Miami for the lease of airport facilities than they paid in any other large eastern city. Then the *Herald* found that MacVicar's building supply firm was selling to a company which was doing a major construction job at the airport. MacVicar denied any conflict of interest.

Neither the *Herald* nor anyone else suggested that MacVicar was lacking in integrity. He was patriotic, was active in civic affairs, and a com-

MR. DADE COUNTY, Charles H. Crandon, left, watches fellow county commissioners and other officials get their feet wet during an inspection of Crandon Park a short time before Crandon's retirement in 1949. With Crandon, left to right, are Congressman Richard Oelkers, Jr., Commissioner Hugh Peters, Congressman William C. Lantaff, and Commissioner I. D. MacVicar. Although MacVicar inherited Crandon's position as county commission chairman, Crandon failed to pass on his influence and power in the county. That mantle fell to John D. Pennekamp of the *Miami Herald.*

pulsive achiever. His fault was a lack of sound political judgment. The airport scandals helped him none. But his most unwise decision was to engage Pennekamp in a head-on battle. MacVicar was to discover that the mantle of Charlie Crandon's power and influence had not come down to him. John Pennekamp was at this time the most powerful individual in Dade County.

Between 1954 and 1956, while all the unfavorable news involving the county commission was erupting in the news and editorial columns of the *Miami Herald*, the newspaper was at the same time putting its full editorial support behind efforts to establish a metropolitan form of county government. A proposal to abolish the city of Miami and turn over the responsibilities of government to the county commission had been narrowly defeated at the polls in 1953. Shortly thereafter the Miami City Commission created a Metropolitan Miami Municipal Board and directed it to make a study of government in Dade County and to determine how best to consolidate, simplify, and curtail the growing costs of government in the several communities and the county. This study, completed in 1954 by the University of Miami and the Public Administration

Service, was the basis of a bill in the 1955 Florida Legislature proposing an amendment to the State Consitution, granting home rule to Dade County. The amendment, which essentially gave the Dade County Commission authority to set up a metropolitan type of government and to consolidate the twenty-six municipalities with that of the county, was approved in the general election of November, 1956. But two things happened which helped to weaken Metro.

The *Herald*, while supporting consolidation without reservation, succeeded in getting the entire county commission voted out of office—except for one member who had announced his intention to retire anyway. The old commissioners—MacVicar, Hugh Peters, Preston Bird, who retired, Jesse Yarborough, and Grant Stockdale—were replaced by Charles "Chuck" Hall, Johnny McLeod, Faris Cowart, Ralph Fossey, and Edwin Lee Mason. None had held an important public office before, none was qualified for the big job ahead, and, in addition, the new board was far from being unanimous in its support of consolidated government.

The second blow to Metro was a no-holds-barred fight by the mayors of the various municipalities who feared the loss of both jobs and prestige. The battle was fought through the Dade League of Municipalities, and the leaders who emerged at the top proved to be far superior to the new county commission leaders who gave lip service to Metro. By the time a Metro charter was ready to be offered to Dade voters in the spring of 1957, the public's enthusiasm for metropolitan government had all but diminished. The charter was approved by a very narrow margin.

Under the charter, the Metro board would grow from five to eleven members in 1958 and to thirteen in 1961. But it was those first five commissioners who had the job of implementing the new charter and beginning the job of consolidation. Juanita Greene, first *Herald* government reporter to cover Metro, has since described those commissioners as the most irresponsible elected officials she had ever seen in action. She blamed them, through their incompetence and lack of interest, for the failure of consolidation being achieved.

"The commission wasn't interested in Metro," said Miss Greene. "Metro had more critics than supporters on the commission."

It is ironic that Johnny McLeod, whom the *Herlad* had recommended over MacVicar, was the commission's most outspoken and cynical opponent of Metropolitan government. Pennekamp had known the salty teller of ribald stories since the time when he was a theater usher. McLeod preoccupied himself at the commission meetings by uttering satirical "asides" to focus attention on himself, when he was not baiting the county manager, O. W. "Hump" Campbell, or the county attorney,

Darrey Davis. Leo Adde, who followed Miss Greene as Metro government reporter, remembered McLeod as a person who didn't care what
was said about him in the *Herald* as long as he appeared to be clever,
which he wanted to be more than anything else in the world.

It was the men like McLeod who helped to pull the teeth of Metro and
cause disillusionment with consolidation among the residents of Dade
County. Although Metro did take over a few functions of the
municipalities, like tax assessment and tax collecting, none of the twenty-
six communities "faded away." Thanks to the newspapers, however, efforts by its enemies to have the Metro concept abolished failed. The
home rule authority of the county government remained to give the commissioners power in the years ahead to establish countywide laws governing pollution, to improve water and sewer services, to coordinate traffic
control, and to set up the machinery for the construction of a rapid tran-
sit system.

In kicking out an entire county commission and getting men like Johnny McLeod elected, Pennekamp had displayed the awesome power of a
newspaper. And while the personable "Penny" was loved by his friends,
he was hated and feared by his enemies, who identified him and the
Herald as synonymous. Many members of the establishment viewed
Pennekamp with concern, and he in turn viewed them with mistrust. He
was likely to look upon their civic and charitable activities as possible
cover-ups for their own nefarious schemes. Meanwhile, Pennekamp
remained aloof from civic or charitable enterprises. His column and the
Herald's editorials reflected his strong likes or dislikes.

Both Knight brothers observed these developments with reservation.
The publisher had great respect for Pennekamp, however, and he sincere-
ly liked the personable, dominant editor. Despite a difference in the concept of newspapering, Jack Knight and Pennekamp had managed to get
along well since the publisher took possession of the *Herald* in 1937. Yet
they had their disagreements. Pennekamp felt that when a newspaper
took an editorial position on anything, the full weight of the newsroom
should be thrown behind him. Jack Knight disagreed, but otherwise he
nearly always backed Pennekamp in his editorial policies. "Well, if you
think you're right, then go ahead," was Knight's usual answer. But
Pennekamp's suspicions of what Knight called the "Miami Club crowd"
bothered him. The club was the gathering place at noon for the Miami establishment. Jack Knight once called the Miami Club "Dodge City in
business suits." Still, he and his brother were members; they were part of
the establishment. What bothered Knight was that as a result of
Pennekamp's suspicions, the *Herald* editorial attitude to many
worthwhile civic enterprises was negative. Knight felt that the paper was

failing to get behind the things needed most for a vital downtown, which, in the 1950s, was going to pieces. He felt that Pennekamp had failed to recognize that Miami was making a transition from a resort town to a burgeoning metropolis. Moreoever, Knight agreed with his brother, the general manager, that the *Herald* should take a stronger interest in civic affairs and in charities. In the middle 1950s Dade County was growing at a record rate, but Jim Knight felt that the newspaper was not keeping up despite a soaring circulation. He put some of the blame on editorial policy.

In 1956 Pennekamp got the *Herald* involved in a libel suit that did nothing to make the Knight brothers happy. In late April of that year a grand jury drew up a report that criticized the conduct of two Circuit Court judges. State Attorney George A. Brautigam sought to suppress the report on the grounds that it censured public officials without returning indictments. Brautigam drew rebukes from several sources including the Grand Jury Association and the *Herald*. On April 28 the *Herald* came out with a stinging editorial written by Griffith. Under a heading "Why Does State Attorney Muzzle the Grand Jury?" the editorial said Brautigam's actions raised two questions:

"Is he afraid of something, or of someone?"

"Is he trying to protect someone?"

A cartoon, done by Quin Hall, accompanied the editorial. It showed Brautigam putting a gag—"Action to Halt Report"—over the mouth of a citizen identified as "Grand Jury." Two days later the *Herald* came out with a second editorial, under the heading "State Attorney Brautigam/ Runs Out on the People." The editorial hinted that something sinister was behind the state attorney's action and recommended Brautigam's removal by the governor.

Meanwhile, Circuit Judge Robert L. Floyd refused Brautigam's petition to suppress the grand jury report. Released, the report hit like a bomb. It condemned Circuit Judges George E. Holt and John W. Prunty and recommended that they resign. It strongly criticized the judges for their handling of receiverships, masterships, guardianships, appointment of curators, and the awarding of fees, particularly to lawyers. Given as an example was the handling of the estates of Jewell Alvin Dowling and Ina I. Dowling, aged couple of Brookline, Massachusetts, and Miami Beach. During a two-year period $208,841.04 was distributed to guardians, receivers, physicians, lawyers, and other court-appointed agents. The Florida Bar Association conducted an investigation and Holt was tried by the Florida Legislature. The House of Representatives voted to impeach him but the move failed by a slim margin in the Senate.

Meanwhile, Brautigam brought suit against the *Miami Herald* for $2 million. This suit was filed in March 1957, after the Florida Supreme Court agreed with Brautigam that a grand jury had no right to criticize a judge without returning an indictment on specific charges. This made Brautigam appear to have been right in his efforts to suppress the grand jury report, and, under the circumstances, improved his chances of winning a libel suit. But what gave him an even better chance to win was his employment of Melvin Belli, nationally known trial lawyer.

Brautigam, elected to the office of state attorney in 1952, was a very serious person. Like Pennekamp he was Catholic, and he was a graduate of Notre Dame. During the heyday of the Joe McCarthy Communist hunt in Washington, Brautigam had conducted a hunt in Miami. He unearthed little but won considerable publicity. He began to dream of becoming governor of Florida. But not only did the *Herald's* editorials stem that ambition, he was defeated for re-election by Richard Gerstein. Brautigam told a *Herald* reporter that Pennekamp had ruined his career and that he could never forgive him.

Jack Knight had backed Pennekamp, although he thought the editorials had been too strong.

"I thought Brautigam was derelict in trying to suppress the report of the grand jury," said Knight. "The grand jury is the people's protector, you know. I think that maybe our editorials were pretty strenuous. A skilled copyreader with an eye for libel could have struck two or three adjectives, or substituted less strong adjectives, and I don't think the suit would ever have arisen."

Knight looked upon it as Pennekamp's fight, not his. But during the trial, when Belli was making the *Herald's* defense lawyers look like Ivy League soda jerks, Steve Trumbull dashed over from the courthouse to Knight's office.

"Boss, they're murdering our guys over there," said Trumbull, who knew it soon would be Knight's turn to testify. "This guy Belli's got the jury completely awed. When you go over to testify, don't you let this guy murder you."

The courtroom was jammed when Knight entered to take the witness stand. Knight looked over the faces staring at him, then turned to the flamboyant Belli, dressed in an Italian silk suit and Texas boots. The lawyer cut an impressive figure. He sucked in his breath, heaved out his chest, and fixed his eyes upon Knight.

"Now, Mr. Knight," said Belli, "tell us about the tricks in the newspaper business."

"We don't have any tricks, Mr. Belli."

"Well, tell us about the artifices and the strategems you employ."

"We don't employ artifices or strategems, but if you want to return to your first term—tricks—my impression is that I have found many more of these in your profession than in mine."

"Do you have reference to anyone in particular?"

"Yes."

"Who is it?"

"You!" replied Knight, pointing a finger at Belli.

The courtroom let out a roar. Judge William Herin admonished Knight. Belli turned to the jury and said:

"There sits the emperor who instructs the colonial governors on what to do. We are suing for two million dollars. Mr. Knight can well afford this. When you go out bring back the full verdict, the full two million dollars."

The jury returned a verdict awarding Brautigam $100,000. Jack Knight, later reflecting on his experiences in the witness chair, acknowledged that he may have done nothing to help win a victory. But the way the boss met Belli head-on made a deep and lasting impression in the newsroom. It was almost worth $100,000 as a morale builder. Brautigam, however, would never enjoy his winnings. The *Herald's* lawyers appealed the verdict. A few months later Brautigam died of a heart attack. His widow was the beneficiary—after settling with Belli.

Meanwhile, Don Shoemaker, a graduate of the University of North Carolina and former editor of the *Asheville Citizen*, had succeeded Pennekamp as editorial page editor. Pennekamp retained his title as associate editor, but his authority as editorial director had been taken away, and now he only wrote his column. There could hardly have been greater difference between two individuals. Shoemaker was a reflective, reserved, intellectual type. He wore form fitting suits that emphasized his athletic slenderness, while the way he tightened his tie gave you the impression of someone bent on strangling himself. Shoemaker was forty-five in comparison to Pennekamp's sixty-two. Although a person of strong convictions, Shoemaker was by no means dogmatic. His editorials took both sides of an argument, and there were times you felt he bent too far in his efforts to be fair. The result was that for a long period after Shoemaker arrived the *Herald's* editorial page seemed to go down the middle of the road on every issue in the gutless manner of a newspaper which wanted to offend no one. It was easy to come to this conclusion, however, because of the sharp contrast between the Shoemaker editorial page and the Pennekamp editorial page. To Pennekamp an issue was either black or white, while to Shoemaker the two sides of an issue often appeared to merge into a cloudy gray. Shoemaker, in time, would take a firmer stand, but in the beginning he chose to feel his way and to tread softly. This would pay off. Shoemaker would be an important member of a new "breed" of editors and managerial executives like Alvah Chapman and George Beebe who were to put the *Herald* in the middle of civic, charitable, educational, better government and nonsectarian religious activities aimed at identifying the newspaper with the aspirations of the community.

Jack Knight had been looking for some time, before the Brautigam libel suit, for someone to succeed Pennekamp. He was in no hurry for he found nothing greatly wrong with Pennekamp. But Miami was growing and the scene was changing. Knight thought the *Miami Herald* needed a reorientation. Moreoever, in 1958 plans were being made for a new *Herald* plant. He told Lee Hills that it was time to begin looking in earnest for a new editor.

Hills knew of Shoemaker, who at that time was head of the Southern Education Reporting Services (SERS) in Nashville, Tennessee. The service had been set up by Southern newspaper editors and educators after the 1954 U.S. Supreme Court decision which ordered an end to segregation. Hardly anyting was known about the problems of integration. With a Ford Foundation grant, SERS began to make a study and to fill in the void. The details were published in a newspaper, *Southern School News*, which could be obtained by request. Shoemaker had been editor of the *Asheville Citizen* seven years when he departed in 1955 to head SERS. With his wife, Lyal, he had been a leader in civic and charitable activities in Asheville. Mrs. Shoemaker had served as president of the Junior League and was a director of the National Conference of Christians and Jews. Shoemaker's record appealed to Jack Knight. Moreoever, Shoemaker had done an outstanding job at Nashville. The integration story needed to be told. There were fears of social upheaval following the Supreme Court decision. The press was not covering the field. Because of a mixture of ignorance and fear the press seemed unable to realize that it was sitting on one of the most significant stories in the history of the United States. It was at a time, however, when newspapermen were much less knowledgeable of sociology and community affairs reporting than later generation newsmen would be. Shoemaker, in a sense, had been pioneering a new field for a newspaperman. But when he received a call from Hills, inviting him to Detroit to talk about the possibility of going to work for Knight Newspapers, Shoemaker jumped at the opportunity.

Shoemaker's communicative ability impressed Hills. Moreover, Shoemaker had a relaxed, easy manner, the reflection of social confidence. Hills had reason to believe that he could take care of himself if thrown to the Miami Club lions. So Hills and Shoemaker took a train for Chicago to see Jack Knight.

Knight questioned Shoemaker sternly about his views on integration.

Although the publisher was in accord with the Supreme Court's decision, he wanted to see integration accomplished in a patient and systematic manner, and he hoped it could be done without turmoil. He wanted his newspapers to support integration, but he cautioned his editors against becoming impatient, or letting themselves be taken in by those on opposing sides. Shoemaker would long remember the hard time Knight gave him on the integration issue, and how surprised the publisher was when he realized that their views were pretty much the same. Shoemaker, who knew as much about the problems of integration as anybody else in the country, realized it couldn't be accomplished overnight. On other issues they did disagree, but each found grounds for sympathy with the other's views. Knight, impressed by Shoemaker's facile mind and his independence, decided he was the man for the Miami job. And Shoemaker felt that "here is the guy I want to work for."

On August 1, 1958, Shoemaker started to work on the *Herald* with the newly created title, "editor of the editorial page." Shoemaker's arrival coincided with the retirement of Arthur Griffith, crusty mold of erudition who was thought too old and set in his ways to work under a new boss. The transition was painful enough without Griffith. It was not until the *Herald* management built Shoemaker a new office, laid wall-to-wall carpeting and installed new, expensive furniture that no doubt was left among the staff about who the top man was. Shoemaker at first had only Jeanne Bellamy and Luther Voltz to assist him, but soon added Bert Collier from the newsroom. Each morning the staff would walk around Pennekamp's office for the daily editorial conference with Shoemaker. It would be several years, however, before all *Herald* readers could believe that Pennekamp was no longer the power behind the editorial page—"Mr. Miami Herald." Pennekamp continued to write his column and to serve on the Florida Board of Parks and Historic Memorials. Then, in December, 1960, Governor LeRoy Collins dedicated the John Pennekamp Coral Reef State Park, covering seventy-five square miles, in his honor. The first underwater park in the continental United States, it is one of the most beautiful coral reefs in the world, with myriad forms and unusual and colorful marine inhabitants. Governor Collins called Pennekamp "Florida's best known conservationist" and referred to his achievement in making the Everglades National Park a reality.

Naturally it was difficult for many readers to believe that Pennekamp was no longer a power on the *Herald*. To have a major park named for you in your lifetime is rare recognition. Moreover, Pennekamp's name remained on the masthead of the editorial page as associate editor. Even more confusing, Pennekamp and Shoemaker shared the same views about metropolitan government. Shoemaker was an ardent supporter of consolidation, and he threw the full weight of the *Herald's* editorial page behind Metro, fighting stubbornly when its numerous enemies sought its destruction. A dramatic incident was needed to emphasize Shoemaker's position on the *Herald*—the bombing of his home on the night of February 18, 1962.

Donald W. Branch, twenty-six, a meter reader for a utility company and a Navy veteran, knew who was in charge of the *Miami Herald's* editorial page. Moreover, his house was easy to find in exclusive Bay Point, because the address was in the telephone directory. Branch's mistake was to place the bomb, charged with dynamite, beneath the window of the Shoemakers' young daughter, Elizabeth. Branch thought he was placing the bomb beneath the window of "Mr. Shoemaker's bedroom." A member of the State's Rights Party and the Minutemen group, Branch had fed himself freely on propaganda that made him believe the country was going to hell and that the liberals and the United State Supreme Court were responsible. He had gorged himself on such works as *Witness* by Whittaker Chambers and imagined that the Communists were on the verge of taking over. Branch identified Shoemaker as a liberal who was preparing the way for the Communists.

"I only wanted to scare him," said Branch in a confession.

Although no one was hurt, he did succeed in scaring the Shoemaker family. But change the editorial policy of the *Miami Herald* he did not. For his extreme and violent effort, Branch was sentenced to twenty years in the Florida State Prison at Raiford. Branch did succeed in doing something he had not planned. The story of the bombing, followed by Branch's arrest and confession, got so much attention in the news columns that no reader would doubt again who called the shots on the *Herald's* editorial page.

JOHN PENNEKAMP   DON SHOEMAKER

27

Big Mac

O NE OF THE *Miami Herald's* lucky breaks came when Jose Manuel Aleman, exiled Cuban politician, in 1948 purchased the property next door, making expansion of the Miami Avenue plant impossible. The Knights had sought to buy this property but thought the
asking price was too high. Had the old plant been expanded it would
have been a costly mistake, and the *Herald* might have lost its chance to
occupy a beautiful site on Biscayne Bay between MacArthur and Venetian causeways. But in 1954, a year after Jim Knight had been given the
go-ahead to buy the valuable bayfront property, the Knight Newspapers'
board of directors was far from a meeting of minds, not only about the
size of a plant that should be built, but whether a plant should be built at
all. Jack Knight kept saying that the site, a mile from downtown, was too
far from the center of activity. C. Blake McDowell, Knight Newspapers
counsel and third member of the board, reminded the brothers that the
greatest profits were made in an old plant where the overhead costs were
small. But in Jim Knight's view, remaining at the old site would be impossible. New presses had been added in 1946, 1948, and in 1952, while in
1954 the last remaining space had been occupied by the addition of color
presses. Still there were no signs of a slowdown in population growth or
in the *Herald's* circulation growth. Seeing there was small likelihood of a
meeting of minds, Jim suggested the employment of a consulting
engineering firm to seek the answers. This was agreed on, and Methods
Engineering Company of Pittsburgh began a study aimed at answering
two questions:

First, was the bayfront site a suitable location for a newspaper plant,
and, if not, where was the ideal location? Second, what plant should be
built, based on the projected population growth and circulation of the
Miami Herald in 1980?

The report of Methods Engineering, delivered some months later, affirmed what Jim Knight had believed all the time—that the bayfront site between the causeways was an ideal one for a newspaper. The site was described as being "like the hub of a wheel," the spokes representing streets, causeways, and highways radiating in all directions. And this report was prepared before the Interstate-95 expressway sytem had been planned through Miami, with its huge midtown interchange located a few blocks west of the "hub," connecting with the East-West Expressway to be completed in the 1960s. Indicating the size of the plant the *Herald* would need in 1980, based on population growth and the paper's probable continued ratio of circulation, Methods Engineering recommended facilities for a circulation of one million. It would be a plant designed for expansion in all departments, and should satisfy the *Miami Herald's* production needs beyond 1980.

Still, Jack Knight was in no hurry to make up his mind. Knight Newspapers only recently purchased the *Charlotte Observer*, while also sinking millions into improvements at the *Detroit Free Press* and the *Chicago Daily News.* Moreoever, Jack was by no means as optimistic as his brother that all the bayfront property could be acquired. One holdout in the middle of the site would make it impractical to put up any kind of building. In 1955, H. W. MacDonald, real estate broker who had been given the job of acquiring the property, all together more than ten acres, was having difficulties making deals with several owners. One was Arthur B. "Mickey" McBride, Sr., of Cleveland, operator of a horse racing information service. McBride, who owned a fifty-foot lot almost in the middle of the bayfront strip, had turned down all offers by MacDonald. Furthermore, McBride had a violent dislike for Jack Knight, who had written critically of the wire service lord's suspected friendship with underworld personalities. Should he learn that the Knights wanted this property he might refuse to sell at any price.

In 1953 when MacDonald began buying the conglomeration of ownerships, he was able to obtain the first parcel, an inside lot, for $6,-000. For vacant bayfront lots he offered $25,000, but got only one for this price. By 1955 he had boosted offers to McBride for his lot to $75,000 but was still being ignored. He had no trouble buying two lots from the *Miami News* at a reasonable enough price, but an adjoining lot was owned by Leo Edwards, a local sportsman and a tough trader. Big Mac got Dan Mahoney, general manager of the *News*, to introduce him to Edwards. Edwards told him he wanted $150,000 for the lot, an unrealistic price. After that Mac had lunch several times with Edwards, at the LaGorce County Club, at Hialeah, and at Gulfstream racetracks. By this time Edwards and MacDonald had become warm friends. One day Edwards invited him for lunch at LaGorce.

"Mac," said Edwards, "I need $100,000 cash to make an investment."
"Leo," replied Mac, "I'll give you $100,000 for that lot."
"It's a deal," said Edwards.

MacDonald was making no headway, however, in purchasing an important piece of property on the north end of the tract. This property ran 140 feet along the bayfront and 270 feet along Northeast Fifteenth Street at the entrance to the Venetian Causeway. It was owned by a family named Ginsberg who used it as a parking lot for an automobile agency on the north side of the street. MacDonald had offered the Ginsbergs $90,000 for this property, but Daniel Ginsberg, a lawyer who had an office in a small building on the property, advised the family to turn it down.

To avoid the risk of revealing the actual buyers, MacDonald purchased all parcels of property in the name of one of four persons who worked in the offices of attorney Blake McDowell in Akron—William C. McMasters, F. I. Snyder, Robert Rene May, and Mary Smith, who was McDowell's secretary. MacDonald recorded the warranty deeds in the Dade County Courthouse and sent them to Akron where the "buyers" in turn deeded the property to Knight Newspapers. These deeds McDowell locked in his safe, where they were to remain until the Knights were ready to announce plans for the building of a new *Herald* plant on the site. This did not occur until August 17, 1958, five years after MacDonald purchased the first lot in the name of William C. McMasters. McDowell then removed the deeds to forty-two parcels of property from his safe, took them to Miami, and recorded them under the name of Knight Newspapers.

The purchase of such a diverse collection of properties had proved to be an adventure for MacDonald. For funds he had to obtain cash from the *Herald*, delivered by Charles F. Eberly, the comptroller, or by Arthur Gucker, the treasurer. To avoid the possibility of anyone becoming suspicious, MacDonald seldom went to the *Herald* but met Eberly or Gucker in some prearranged place, such as a parking lot. As much as $100,000 at a time was delivered to him. The money was deposited in banks under the names of the four dummy buyers, and later transferred to northern banks from which he would draw funds as needed. He operated with the aid of a power of attorney which gave him authority to act in behalf of the buyers.

Big Mac had a background that gave him unique credentials for a tough and complicated assignment. A native of Dayton, Ohio, MacDonald went to St. Louis in the 1920s where he developed the H. W. MacDonald Mortgage Company. After going broke in the 1929 stock market crash, he moved to Los Angeles where he handled real estate for such concerns as the Bank of America and Atlas Corporation. He played polo in Beverly Hills and moved easily in the Hollywood scene. Coming to Miami in 1943 to visit his mother, he liked the city so well he decided to move to Florida. Establishing himself on Biscayne Boulevard, on the edge of downtown, Big Mac—handsome, dominating, experienced—soon became identified with the more successful real estate brokers. Moreoever, he was accepted as a member of the exclusive Bath Club at Miami Beach, where, gregarious and a free spender, he entertained himself and his friends in the style to which he had become accustomed in Beverly Hills.

Jim Knight could hardly have chosen a broker better equiped mentally and physically for the job. And no more diverse area, with its unusual mixture of zoning, existed anywhere else in Dade County. The area, formerly shallow bay bottom, had been filled after the Army Corps of Engineers established a harbor line in 1916. The dominant building was the Frolics Club, eighty feet wide and 187 feet long, built in the 1920s. Extending through a block from Bayshore Place to Bayshore Court, the building occupied one-third of an acre. For a time the Frolics Club was Miami's jazziest place, but in the late 1930s it lost favor. It was opened for a short period in 1941 by former boxer Max Rosenbloom under the name of Slapsie Maxie's. His backers, knowing the people in the right places, thought they could operate casino gambling without being molested. But Captain Otis Huttoe of the Miami Police Department raided the place, making a hundred arrests, seizing $40,000 in cash, and carting away all the expensive gambling equipment. Another 700 patrons were permitted to go free. The courts ordered the money and the equipment returned, but Huttoe's raid, the most spectacular ever conducted in Dade County, closed the place for good.

For a time during and shortly after World War II one of the swankiest night clubs in Miami's history, the Little Palm Club, was operated in a less-than-spectacular building next door to the Frolics Club. The owner, Art Childers, had operated the Royal Palm Club on Biscayne Boulevard south of Miami's Bayfront Park before the Coast Guard took it over at the beginning of World War II. The Royal Palm had a successful combination of night club and high class casino gambling, and Childers sought to offer the same at the Little Palm. Walter Winchell described it in his column as the "Stork Club of the South." The *Herald's* Town Crier, Jack Bell, in a nostalgic piece written after the Little Palm was demolished, described it as "one of the best eating places in the world." If you wanted to dine, all you needed in order to get into the Little Palm was plenty of money. The dining room walls were lined with rose-tinted mirrors. Even the columns in the dining room were covered with the tinted glass. There was another long, rose-tinted mirror behind the highly polished mahogany bar. The bar stools were of leather, with backs. On the shelves beneath the mirror was glassware for every imaginable kind of drink. And the bartenders at the Little Palm had a reputation of being able to mix any concoction in the drinker's dictionary. In the fall of 1958, when a steel ball was swung on what was left of the Little Palm after its interior had been stripped, Bell, who watched, turned and walked away. He was certain Miami would never have another Little Palm Club, with its great food and delightful people who patronized it.

If you went to the Little Palm to gamble, you turned to the left after entering the foyer. If you got through the first barred door you still had another barred door in front of you. The peep holes were visible and you knew you were being studied for identity. And you had to be a known gambler to get in. Kibitzers were as unwelcome as were the police. But the *Miami Herald* knew, through its police reporter, Henry Reno, when the Little Palm's gaming rooms were in operation, and a short item with this information would appear next morning in the paper. As a result of harassment by police and by the *Herald*, Childers was eventually forced to close the casino. And without gambling to support his expensive food operation, which in itself never came close to paying its way, he was forced to close the restaurant.

Except for some difficulties in clearing up the titles, MacDonald had no trouble buying the buildings which had housed the two former clubs. In the meantime, however, he found himself in a double role. In addition to being the purchasing agent, he was now the buyers' agent in collecting rents and leases on apartments, offices, buildings, and space for huge signs that lined the waterfront. By the end of 1956 MacDonald was collecting $96,948.02 a year on rentals. And he was collecting more than $2,000 a month from Webster and Outdoor advertising companies for the space occupied by their huge waterfront signs. During the five years MacDonald was engaged in purchasing these properties nothing was disturbed, lest someone become suspicious that a big project was in the making. But Jim Knight wanted to keep all the income property intact for another reason. Knight Newspapers would continue to enjoy the income from it until ready to begin construction. Moreover, there was a chance that one or more key property owners might refuse to sell, making it impossible for the Knights to go ahead with their plans. And McBride, whose fifty-foot lot was so vital that construction could not have been started without it, held out to the last. For nearly five years Big Mac periodically had raised his offer to McBride, until he reached $175,000. But McBride showed no interest in selling until, with Jim Knight's nod, Big Mac offered him $200,000, the highest price to be paid for a parcel.

In 1958, as the time approached when Jim Knight hoped to announce plans for a new *Herald* building, only one holdout remained, the Ginsberg family. When MacDonald's offer reached $200,000 the family showed some interest, but insisted that Big Mac's client also buy property on the north side of Fifteenth Street for which the Ginsbergs asked $300,-000. After a meeting with Knight, MacDonald could inform Daniel Ginsberg, with whom he was dealing, that his client had agreed to the family's demand. In the meantime, however, the shrewd Daniel thought he had figured out who the actual buyer was—the *Miami Herald*. Checking the records at the courthouse, Daniel determined that the four buyers MacDonald used as dummies had purchased all the property in the block except two pieces, the Ginsberg property and the lot owned by Radio Station WQAM. Since the radio station was owned by the *Herald*, Daniel figured that the newspaper had to be behind the purchase of the surrounding property. Seeing an oportunity to get an even greater price than half a million dollars for the Ginsberg holdings, Daniel advised the family to hold out. But while the property was important in the building plans, it was not that vital, and Jim refused to pay more. Some years later Knight Newspapers would be able to buy the Ginsberg property on the south side of Fifteenth Street, amounting to more than three-fourths of an acre, for $100,000, half the original offer.

The holdout by the Ginsbergs resulted in an unexpected break for the *Herald*. Had the property been acquired, the new building would have been pushed north against Fifteenth Street at the entrance to the Venetian Causeway. Instead, the building had to be pushed south against Thirteenth Street, at the entrance to the MacArthur Causeway. And this is where the break came. At that time traffic moved freely between Thirteenth Street and Bayshore Place, a two-block-long street which would become Herald Plaza after completion of the new *Miami Herald* plant. But in the construction of the East-West Expressway, Interstate-395, the elevation of Thirteenth Street was raised four feet above the south end of Herald Plaza, and the drop was too great to allow a flow of traffic at this interseciton. A chain-link fence would be erected along the expressway after it was opened in 1969, permanently closing the south end of Herald Plaza. But Jim Knight could not have foreseen this in 1958 when plans to construct a "$20 million *Herald* plant" were announced. It was essential for the newspaper's operation, however, that the flow of traffic at this intersection be cut off, and Knight took steps to purchase from the city of Miami the two-block-long street facing the building, in order that it could be closed at Thirteenth Street. But the city commissioners, particularly B. E. Hearn, took a hard-nosed view, and, after several months of negotiations, wound up asking the *Herald* to pay $350,000. With street improvements in the area already planned by the

Herald, this would bring total costs above half a million dollars. Disappointed, Knight wanted time to study the city's demands. The morning after Knight's frustrating experience with the commissioners, Big Mac popped into his office.

"Forget that deal with the city," said MacDonald.

"What do you mean by that?" asked Knight.

"Look, I've been checking on the East-West Expressway they're planning to build within the next few years," said MacDonald. "The drawings I saw show the pavement running at least four feet higher than the *Herald* property. Furthermore, the building's going to be too close to Thirteenth Street for them to build a ramp. So you're going to have a closed street in front of the *Herald* after all."

"Humph," said Knight, studying Big Mac with a sparkle in his eyes. "I'll be doggoned."

"He'll, let the city keep its street," added MacDonald. "Furthermore you won't have to pay taxes on it and the city will have to maintain it."

Knight ordered Gucker to check and he confirmed what MacDonald had found. So Knight cut off negotiations with the commissioners and the city lost an opportunity to receive a sizeable windfall, in addition to the chance of saddling the *Herald* with taxes on a high-priced piece of property.

At the insistence of Jack Knight, the job of designing the new *Herald* plant had been given to a Danish-born architect, Sigurd Naess, who designed the *Chicago Daily News* and *Sun-Times* buildings, which the publisher admired. Naess, sixty-eight, was planning to retire, but on the promise that Knight Newspapers would build the plant he designed, Naess agreed to postpone his retirement. The decision on determining the size of the plant, however, was given to Jim Knight.

Jim was uniquely qualified to make this big decision. He had been for years a member of the American Newspaper Publishers Association (ANPA) and the Southern Newspaper Publishers Association (SNPA). This had given him a chance to meet the publishers of all the large newspapers, and he had spent a great deal of time visiting newspaper plants, talking with production experts about what was right or wrong with these plants. Jim served on the associations' committees and was a member of ANPA's Research Institute. In 1949-50 he had served as president of the Associated Press Dailies of Florida. In 1951 he was engaged in helping SNPA establish what would be a half-billion-dollar newsprint industry in the South, with mills in Alabama, Tennessee, and Texas. In 1955 he became the publisher of the *Charlotte Observer*. With his growing prestige he was elected president of SNPA in 1956, after which he served as chairman of the board. Meanwhile, he was elected

PRINCIPAL person behind the planning of the new Miami Herald building was James L. Knight, who foresaw the need for a large and spacious structure.

president of ANPA's Research Institute, which he had helped to build. All the while he was gaining these experiences Jim was active in the expansion and improvement of Knight Newspapers. Living in Miami, he was well aware of the area's vitality. The slowdown in economic and population growth which had been forecast by experts from the postwar period had not occurred. Sunday circulation rose to a peak of 414,000. Moreoever, the number of *Herald* employes had increased from 383 in 1937, when the Knights purchased the paper, to 1,113 in August of 1958 when an announcement was made that a new building was being planned.

Jim Knight had been working for months on space figures for the various departments which would occupy the new *Herald*—space for presses, for production, editorial, advertising, business; space for newsprint storage, newspaper loading facilities, for employee parking. Moreoever, since the plant was to be built on the waterfront where the ground level was only a few feet above the bay, all the important facilities, including the presses, would have to be built above the first floor as a protection against possible hurricane-driven tides.

Every department was given a hand in the planning. Department heads were sent to inspect other recently built newspaper plants. Les Griner, vice-president in charge of Knight Newspapers production, toured plants to study the latest product improvements, particularly methods of automatically counting, stacking, tying, and delivering bundles of newspapers to waiting trucks. Some thought was given to putting the cafeteria on the roof, but after a study of the rooftop cafeteria at the new Louisville *Courier-Journal* plant this idea was abandoned. That rooftop view was so great employees stayed overtime at lunch and at coffee breaks. With the fantastic view employees would have had from the

Herald's rooftop, the management feared nobody would want to return to work after lunch. Jim, remembering the problem the management had at the old *Herald* with employees keeping liquor in their lockers, scratched plans to have lockers installed in the washrooms of the editorial department. The planners overrode Jack Knight, who objected to a private elevator for the executives, but he overrode the planners when they suggested penthouse apartments for visiting executives from other Knight newspapers.

"Hell, no," he said, "we're not going to have any apartments."

That ended any further discussion about the subject.

With the rough drawings and square footage handed him, architect Naess began translating the details into architectural reality. It must have been a major challenge to an architect who had been given one of the dominant settings in Miami and virtually complete freedom to design the structure that was to be built there. When Naess got through he had a beautiful building, but it would be a huge one, the largest in Florida up to that time. The building would stretch 631 feet along Biscayne Bay, with a width of 220 feet, its six stories rising 117 feet. A football field could be fitted into the space planned on the fifth floor for the editorial department, while the building itself would be as massive as the Orange Bowl Stadium. The structure would house the most modern production equipment available. When completed no other newspaper plant in the world would compare with it.

In 1960 when the floor plans and elevation drawings were unveiled before the Knight Newspapers board of directors Jack Knight studied them with disbelief.

"Jim," he said gruffly to his brother, "you have lost your sense of values! This is a monster that could destroy us!"

Jim Knight smiled as a sparkle flashed in his eyes.

"You're wrong, Jack," he said. "You've lost touch with our needs. That's the *Miami Herald* plant we're going to need in 1980—perhaps before. Let's build it."

There was force and conviction in the younger brother's voice. Looking at him, Jack realized there was no sense in arguing; that Jim was determined to build this fantastic new plant.

"Well, all right," said Jack, "we'll build it. I hope it doesn't break us."

Ground was broken on August 19, 1960. Instead of the $10 million cost that board members had discussed with apprehension in the early 1950s, when a new plant was first proposed, the new building and equipment would cost in excess of $30 million. The boldest decision was the order for presses—seven presses of sixty-three units capable of printing seven 144-page newspapers at one time. It was the largest press order in

DESIGNED originally to face Biscayne Bay, with the press building on the MacArthur Causeway side, the structure had to be reversed when Knight Newspapers was unable to buy an important piece of property on the Venetian Causeway side.

history, while the press drive was the largest to be installed anywhere in the world up to that time.

Bold, yes, but in the years ahead, after the dedication of the new plant in 1963, these immense presses would be inadequate to print the gigantic issues of the *Miami Herald* that were to follow the fantastic economic surge South Florida was to experience during the affluent 1960s. Two press expansions were to be needed in the building's first decade, but, thanks to Jim Knight's foresight and hard-headedness, the *Herald* still had ample space to accommodate additional press units in the years ahead.

The Miami Herald

Tuesday, April 18, 1961   No. 138   Florida's Most Complete Newspaper   51st Year   56 Pages   5 Cents

Eight Great Services

Associated Press   AP Wirephoto
United Press Int'l   UPI Photo
U.P.I Business Wire   Science Service
New York Times News Service
Chicago Daily News Foreign Service

Counter Revolu-sun

3 Beachheads Secured,
Cuba Invaders Push On

Arrows Show Where Invaders Stabbed Into Castro-Dominated Cuba

Castro Takes Troops Helm; Losses Heavy

By DOM BONAFEDE

Stage Set to Ask Eichmann's Death; Atrocities Cited

The Issue: Fidel Vs. Cubans

Army Photographs Show a U.N. by Raul Roa

Giant Pincer Drives To Cut Cuba in Two

By JAMES BUCHANAN

Cuba Tells U.N. U.S. Backs Rebels

Joy, Worry Fill Exile Colony

By F. V. W. JONES

Full Cuba Story Inside

Role of the 114	7-A
Russia Opposed	7-A
Public Alert	2-A
Latin Reaction	16-A
Rush of Recruits	16-A
On the Radio	21-A
Havana in the La...	11-A
Her Son at War	7...

Turn to Page 7A Col. 7

SPECIAL
Life Behind Bars

Dr. Bernard Finch, Carole Tregoff lose their federal sentences; Life imprisonment 8-A

● CONGO PRESIDENT Kasavubu is ready to be friends with the U.N. ... 3B

● BREAST CANCER a startling new treatment ... 1B

● BEN-GURION AIDE'S contention he was fired spy chief light on anti-American ... 1B

KASAVUBU

Today's Chuckle

It's smart to pick your friends, but not to pieces.
— Dailey Paper

INSIDE YOUR LEGISLATURE

Full Coverage, 14A

Turn to Page 5A Col. 7

Volunteers for Revolutionary Army Get Medical Examinations
... at 127 SW Fourth Ave., one of the recruiting stations in Miami

---

BEAUTIFUL HEADLINES for Miami's Cuban population on the morning of April 18, 1961, but what a prelude they were to the tragic truth which appeared next day! Larry Jinks, serving as city editor, was so perplexed over conflicting reports on the night of April 17 that he inserted a box listing the claims of the invaders and the invaded under a headline of "Which Side Do You Believe?"

28

The Cuban Story

T HE CUBAN STORY, which began in 1959 after Fidel Castro arrived in Havana at the head of a bearded, fatigue-clad guerrilla army, would nose out the Florida land boom of the 1920s as the biggest local story ever covered by the *Miami Herald*. Looking back, the Boom had everything—continuous action, continuous drama—and it had a total effect upon Miami, transforming it from a resort town of 30,-000 into a city of more than 150,000 within five years. Moreoever, the 1926 hurricane, which sounded the death knell of the Boom, could hardly have been more dramatic and tragic. But the Cuban story would pack more action and drama, more romance, suspense, and tragedy—together with Don Quijote interludes—than a dozen wild real estate booms. It would involve the transformation of Fidel Castro from hero to villain, as well as the breaking of diplomatic relations between the United States and Cuba, the Bay of Pigs tragedy, the ransoming of the surviving invaders, the Cuban missile crisis, together with the coming of the Cuban refugees to Florida, and the transformation of Miami into a Latinized, bilingual community within a decade.

Castro and his followers get the blame for the destruction of Cuba's political, economic, and social structures. But the pages of the *Miami Herald* recount a history of violence and corruption long before Castro. Upon becoming a republic after gaining its freedom from Spain, the corrupt and brutal leadership of the Spanish governors fell to equally corrupt and brutal presidents. Gomez, Menocal, and Zayas, who preceded Machado, won reputations as "thieves, bribers, and murderers." The United States, which assumed a "big brother" attitude toward Cuba after the Spanish-American War, felt obliged to send warships to Cuban ports on several occasions when anarchy threatened. Machado's regime became so intolerable corrupt and brutal that in the early 1930s he was ordered by Washington to make reforms or resign. Finding it impossible to make the reforms Washington demanded, Machado fled. But conditions got little better. Between the time of Machado's exile in 1933 and 1959 when Castro came to power, Cuba had a dozen chief executives, including the personable and quick-witted Fulgencio Batista, who rose from sergeant to general and chief executive. An admirer of Abraham Lincoln, Batista dreamed of emulating him in Cuba. The trail of his failure was to be marked by violence and bloodshed, corruption and gangsterism, disillusionment and cynicism, and, in the end, by political, economic, and social disorganization before Cuba gave its soul to Castro.

The 1930s was a period of utmost confusion and violence throughout the island. Cuba had three presidents in 1933, two in 1934, three in 1936. Exiles shifted back and forth between Havana and Miami depending on whose party was in or out of favor. Batista was elected president in 1940, and, as a result of soaring prices for sugar and tobacco during World War II, prosperity followed. The sugar barons made millions. So did the politicians and bureaucrats. But because of the scheming and the plotting, tumult continued. Those who were out of the government sought to get in and those who were in sought to stay in. After Batista was succeeded in 1944 by President Grau, a new kind of exile began arriving in Florida. Many of them were rich. Among them was Batista himself. He moved into an oceanfront home at Miami Beach, later moving to Daytona Beach.

Many of the new exiles invested money in Florida. Biggest investor of all was Jose Manuel Aleman, Cuban minister of education until dismissed by Grau. Aleman fled to Miami Beach in 1947, buying a mansion on Pinetree Drive. Within two years he had invested millions of dollars in real estate, but information about his activities was difficult to obtain. Aleman refused to see reporters, while his henchmen were tight-lipped.

Lee Hills assigned reporter Bert Collier to do an investigative story on Aleman. At first he got nowhere. Then came help from an unexpected source, Batista. At the instigation of George Beebe, who had done some stories on Batista, the exiled president ordered his henchmen to help Collier. After six months of investigation, Collier was able to trace $20 million worth of Aleman's investments in Dade County, including 526 acres on Key Biscayne. Aleman had built the Miami Baseball Stadium, costing $1 million, and had bought the Miami Sun Sox baseball team. Among his purchases were Miami Beach hotels and apartment houses. He also had built a 400-car parking garage on property he had purchased next to the Miami Herald building on Miami Avenue.

The *Herald* ran Collier's story on September 18, 1949. A story by reporter Charles Fernandez, datelined Havana, revealed that two years before his arrival in Miami Aleman had been a clerk in the Ministry of Education in Havana, earning less than $200 a month. A few days after the story came out Aleman suffered a heart attack, dying six months later at forty-five. But Aleman wasn't the only Cuban politician sending vast sums to Miami. Collier quoted a "prominent Miami businessman" who estimated the flow of money from Havana to Miami as much as $100 million during the four years since the end of World War II.

"This reciprocal flow of investment capital is bound to be good," said the businessman. "When people develop mutual interests, they're more apt to be good friends."

This cynical attitude toward the wholesale investment of stolen Cuban money in Florida changed after Batista seized the government from President Prio in 1952 in a bloodless coup. "Lucky" Luciano, Meyer Lansky, and other top Mafia leaders who had gained a foothold in Cuba during the Prio administration became more dominant under the Batista dictatorship. According to Hank Messick, a *Herald* crime reporter of a later era, it was Lansky who made arrangements with Prio for Batista's return to Cuba. Lansky, with Batista's blessing, built a major gambling empire in Cuba. But Havana already was a wide-open city where gambling and prostitution flourished against a background of what the *Herald's* travel writer, Silvan Cox, described as "riotous gaiety and un-bridled merrymaking." Havana had everything—horse racing, jai-alai, cockfighting, casino gambling, lotteries, the most beautiful purchasable women in the hemisphere, gourmet restaurants, and continental architecture in an atmosphere of tropic luxury. You "ptissed" for a waiter, tax-icab driver, or bell-boy, who jumped to serve you with the expection of a fat American tip.

Bastista could not have dreamed when he seized power in 1952 that a shadow would fall over his regime—that of Fidel Castro, twenty-four, a graduate of the University of Havana with a doctorate in law. He unwittingly gave Castro a popular cause. While Prio's government may have been corrupt, Cuba was still a democracy and the government could be voted out of office. Bastista's action, however bloodless, took away Cubans' constitution rights. Batista had set up the atmosphere for the rise of a leader who possessed as much charisma and political ability as he himself had in 1933 when he headed an enlisted men's revolt and was himself rocketed into notoriety.

An attack by Castro and his follwers on the Moncado Army Barracks at Santiago on July 26, 1953, appeared to be the perfect bungle of a wild-eyed plan to seize arms and spur an uprising aimed at toppling Batista. But in the trial that followed, Castro emerged a revolutionary hero. George Southworth, *Herald* reporter covering the trial, reported that

Castro, instead of being penitent and apologetic for the uprising, which resulted in a number of deaths, defended his action. The timid court gave him fifteen years in the Isle of Pines prison. Two years later Batista ordered his release, along with eighteen followers, in an effort to stem growing unrest. Castro was in Miami shortly thereafter, raising funds among exiles and calling upon Southworth at the *Herald*.

"Soutwort, I'm here to raise money to overthrow Batista," said Castro, wearing a thin mustache that was hardly more than a pencil smear on his upper lip. "I'm going to Mexico to raise and train an army to invade Cuba."

The *Herald* put the story inside because in 1955 Castro was hardly to be taken seriously. But as he promised "Soutwort," Castro did fly to Mexico City, where he met Che Guevara, a restless medical doctor from Argentina who recently had participated in Communist guerilla warfare in Guatemala. Castro was soon joined by his brother Raul and other loyal followers. A year later he and his followers landed in eastern Cuba.

Meanwhile, Miami's exiles chose sides and began battling. In May 1957, fifty Cubans were arrested after a downtown fracas between Batista and Castro supporters. Several heads were skinned, including those of policemen. In 1958 Prio was charged in Miami Federal Court with buying arms for Castro; he was ordered jailed. The handcuffed former president of Cuba was marched several blocks through downtown Miami to jail in the Dade County courthouse, followed by a parade of Cubans chanting the anthem of Castro's 26th of July movement and eager to bloody any Batista supporter.

In July 1958, the *Herald* sent reporter Jim Buchanan to Guantanamo Bay to do an on-the-scene story about twenty-one servicemen and some thirty other United States citizens who had been kidnapped by Raul Castro's forces and were being held in the Sierra Cristal mountains north of the Navy base. Taking no chances of having another citizen kidnapped, the Navy restricted Buchanan to the base. But he soon found a Castro sympathizer among the Cuban workmen on the base, who helped him to slip past Marine gate guards and then arranged for his visit to Raul's headquarters. Buchanan could report that the servicemen and civilians held by Castro "were having a ball."

"Raul was only trying to show the United States that Batista's army wasn't able to provide any protection," reported Buchanan.

The reporter noted that Castro's followers were well armed, well supplied with food, and that their morale could hardly have been better. Moreoever, Raul claimed to have an army of 6,000. Brother Fidel wasn't admitting how many followers he had, but rebellion was spreading throughout the island. By the middle of 1958 Batista was assured of the support of only his bureaucrats, the police, and army officers. Assassinations and bombings, blamed on the rebels, were common. Batista's henchmen retaliated with terror campaigns, torture, and executions. Such stories frightened tourists. Travel writers and columnists were invited to Cuba to see for themselves that the reports of violence in Havana "were exaggerated." Horace Sutton, syndicated writer whose articles appeared in the *Herald's* travel section, reported Havana "a happy land of manana." Jack Kofoed, *Herald* columnist, dined at Centro Vasquez and found almost every table filled. And he reported that the Monseigneur, the "Stork Club of Havana," was jammed. Revolt spread nevertheless. On December 7 the *Herald* reported that federal agents had confiscated $100,000 worth of arms in a Miami warehouse and seized $50,000 worth of ammunition stored at abandoned Opa-Locka Air Base. Both caches were slated for Castro. On December 14 Southwroth wrote that Castro's rebels were active in five of Cuba's six provinces, and that the rebel leader claimed to have 12,000 armed guerrillas under his command. Although Batista had some 35,000 trained men, with the "best equipment money could buy," there was "some doubt as to their desire to fight," Southworth added. The *Herald* noted on December 19 that Batista had suspended constitutional guarantees "for another forty-five days." On December 22 Castro began an all-out offensive. On January 2, 1959, the *Herald* reported in a six-column, two-line head: "Mobs Pillage Havana;/Castro to Take Over." Batista's army had collapsed. Other stories appeared inside, including an interview with Batista, who had fled the island. He blamed a lack of arms for his defeat. And the *Herald* carried an editorial which would seem rather curious when reread some years later.

"Cuba, in its hour of decision," said the editorial, "needs strong, dedicated leadership and there is none immediately in sight."

It was obvious that the editorial writer failed to take Fidel Castro seriously as leadership material; that the success of the rebels was viewed as one more bloody chapter in Cuba's turbulent history. And this probably is why the *Herald* had failed to send anyone to Cuba to cover the bloody events of December which preceded the overthrow of Batista on January 1. Three reporters, George Southworth, Steve Trumbull, and E. V. W. Jones, were sent to Havana on January 2. But, except for Southworth, these reporters had little background to understand the rapidly changing events, and the stories they filed gave *Herald* readers little more information than desk men had been able to glean from tourists holed up in Havana hotels during the crisis. Beebe hoped Southworth would be the first reporter to interview victorious Fidel Castro. But Castro waited a week before entering Havana, until his advance army, headed by Che Guevara and other revolutionaries, could restore order and prepare for *Numero Uno's* gala entry. Southworth remained in the capital and other reporters beat him to Castro, who dallied to received a hero's welcome from towns and cities along the road. It was not until January 8 that he entered the city at the head of an armored caravan, to be greeted by more than a million cheering citizens.

The hero worship of the bearded rebels, who now had full control of Cuba, even reached some newspaper correspondents, as was reflected in their stories. But the attitude was to change. The rebels quickly rounded up Batista supporters and began executing them. By January 10 more than 150 had been shot. On January 12 seventy-five were lined up in front of a bulldozer-dug trench at Santiago, shot with automatic weapons, and covered like so many lengths of cordwood. Editorial criticism began to appear in U.S. newspapers arriving in Havana, and Castro didn't like it. "Don't meddle" in Cuban affairs, he cautioned critics of the executions, "or 200,000 will die." Later claiming he had been misquoted, Castro told reporters that what he really said was that 200,000 Marines would die if the United States should invade Cuba.

Everyone who had been associated with the Batista regime had reason to fear, and countless numbers who were unable to book air passage or flee by water went underground. By April and May 1959, Miami was beginning to get a new influx of exiles. By June 22, the Immigration Service reported, 497 political refugees had been processed in Miami since January 1. During a three-week period from June 22 until July 13 another 103 streamed into Miami. Two Cuban colonies with opposing views were developing, and it was becoming dangerous to be openly pro-Castro. In the middle was a neutral group of several thousand former Cubans who looked upon Miami as home. Propagandized, and even threatened by both factions, the neutrals wanted to be left alone. Miami was rapidly becoming the "Casablanca of the Caribbean," the *Herald* reported. Police were kept busy dispersing Cuban bands bent on making trouble for their enemies. Angry Cubans gathered at the Miami International Airport to meet planes in an effort to spot and rough up their political opposite members. Consul Alonso Hidalgo, representing the Castro government, was knocked unconscious during a melee on Biscayne Boulevard. The previous consul, Eduardo Hernandez, representing the Batista government, had been attacked several times in public by Castro supporters. Miami businessmen employing Cubans began receiving handbills threatening them with physical harm if they kept persons of "undesirable" political faith. Miami Mayor Robert King High ordered a crackdown on Cuban dissidents, and promised jail for rioters and other troublemakers. The hot summer, with its head-skinnings, passed. By fall of 1959 Miami had so many anti-Castro exiles that no Cuban dared open his mouth in defense of the bearded leader. While Castro was denying the new Cuban government was Communist, industries in increasing numbers were being seized and nationalized, while a political and economic policy which would force the entire middle class of Cuba into exile was being implemented. Castro was now turning on many of his veteran followers, who were jailed, tried, and either executed or sentenced to prison. The rebel leader was making four-hour speeches castigating the United States. Visitors from the United States no longer felt welcomed in Havana, and *Herald* reporter Jim Buchanan discovered that it was easy for a newspaperman to get into serious trouble in Cuba.

Early in December 1959, a Miami free-lance pilot, Frank Austin Young, was found guilty by a Cuban court of charges he transported Batista supporters out of Cuba and was sentenced to thirty years in prison. But the day after his trial Young escaped from jail in Pinar del Rio and made his way by the underground to Havana where he checked in at the St. Johns Hotel. From there he called a girl friend in Miami, Evelyn Hill. Would she come to Havana right away?

Lacking funds to make the trip, Miss Hill called on the *Herald*. If the paper would pay her way, she told Rose Allegato, assistant city editor, she would arrange for a reporter to interview Young. Miss Allegato took up the proposition with City Editor Derick Daniels and they went to the managing editor. Beebe agreed to give Miss Hill $100 on her promise to set up the interview, and Buchanan was called from his courthouse beat. Buchanan flew to Havana ahead of Miss Hill, waited for her at the airport, and they took a limousine together to Young's hotel. Promising to meet Buchanan in the hotel bar after talking with Young, Miss Hill went her way and the reporter went into the streets to find a pay telephone to call Beebe in Miami.

"I'm hoping to see the 'manufacturer' this evening," said Buchanan, referring to Young.

Beebe in the meantime had experienced a change of heart. The accounts of summary trials and executions which Beebe had been reading about had all come back to him after Buchanan departed. He thought of Castro as a madman, and considered the reporter to be in a very dangerous situation.

"Forget the manufacturer," said Beebe bluntly. "We don't want to do any business with him. Come on back to Miami."

The unhappy Buchanan returned to the St. Johns. As the hour approached for his appointment with Miss Hill, he went into the bar and ordered a drink. Soon Miss Hill came in and sat at his table and he ordered a drink for her.

"He's in Room 408," she said. "He'll talk with you. Knock three times—two quick knocks, pause, and then another knock."

Buchanan took an elevator to the fourth floor and knocked on Young's door. By the time the interview was over, Buchanan was on the track of an even more fascinating story—how to escape from Cuba by way of the underground. He would follow Young along the underground route, and upon his return to Miami would have a terrific story. As Buchanan was about to leave the room, Young asked him to bring back some bandages to wrap a badly swollen sprained ankle he had received in jumping over a wall while making his escape from jail. Buchanan went to a drugstore and bought the bandages. Returning to Young's room some time later, he knocked on the door. When the door opened the room was full of policemen.

"Come in," a voice commanded.

"What a lousy Grade B movie," thought Buchanan as he entered.

Buchanan and Young were hauled off to jail. John S. Knight spent much of the next two weeks trying to get the reporter's release through diplomatic channels. But Buchanan had been accused of shielding Young and assisting him to hide in Havana, a serious offense. On December 22 Buchanan was whisked to Pinar del Rio for trial before a military tribunal. Next day he was sentenced to fourteen years in prison, then heard the sentence suspended. Returning to Miami and an airport welcome on Christmas Eve, Buchanan was driven to the *Herald.* As he stepped off the elevator and entered the newsroom, reporter Phil Meyer stood upon the city desk and blew a rather bad fanfare on a bugle. And when Buchanan looked up he was greeted by a large banner stretched across the room:

"Welcome Home Jailbird!"

By the middle of 1960 the Castro government had seized more than half a billion dollars worth of property owned in Cuba by U.S. interests, and relations between the two countries approached a breaking point. By this time President Eisenhower had listened to one of his advisers on Cuban affairs, William D. Pawley of Miami, former ambassador to Peru and Brazil, and had given CIA Director Allen Dulles authority to begin training Cuban exiles for an invasion of Cuba. The president had become convinced that Castro was a Communist, as Dulles and Pawley insisted all along. By now Miami had become the number one center for Cuban exiles. Hundreds were fleeing the island weekly. By March of 1960 the exiles in Miami exceeded 40,000. Pawley told Eisenhower that recruiting an invasion force would be no problem, because overthrowing the Castro regime was the exiles' only hope of returning to Cuba.

Because Cubans proved talkative, the *Miami Herald* heard plans for an invasion in the summer of 1960. Members of the Cuban colony were signing up with invasion forces. A *Herald* copy boy, Mario Abril, a young Cuban, signed up. Planes began using the Opa-Locka Air Base, which had been abandoned by the military. Observers saw planes arriving and departing at night, and without lights. But guards stopped reporters at the gate. Beebe sent Southworth to Guatemala where the exiles were reported to be training. He wound up in Retalhuleu, northwest of Guatemala City, where a major airstrip had been constructed in recent months, but was denied entry. Meanwhile, the *Herald* sought unsuccessfully to find out something from Washington sources. As the end of 1960 approached, with Eisenhower soon to leave office, *Herald* editors figured an invasion of Cuba could happen any time. John McMullan, assistant managing editor, wanted to break the story and publish what reporters had gathered, which was considerable. But Beebe insisted on talking first to Lee Hills. Hills conferred with Jack Knight, who ordered the story held. Knight wanted to avoid putting the *Herald* in the position of revealing information that might affect national security. The *Herald* held up the story until January 11, 1961, after the *New York Times* broke the news of invasion preparations in a story from Central America.

As it turned out, the *Herald* could have run its story without giving any secrets to the enemy. Castro was well aware of invasion preparations. Invasion fever was running high among exiles, whose number now exceeded 50,000. On January 2 Castro had made a long speech in which he described the United States Embassy in Havana as a center of espionage and subversion. He demanded that the staff be reduced to the same level as the staff of the Cuban Embassy in Washington, eleven. Since the employees of the U.S. Embassy numbered eighty-seven, to meet Castro's demand would have meant calling home seventy-six employees. Eisenhower on January 4 ordered the embassy closed and severed diplomatic relations with Cuba. It was the break Dulles and Pawley had been waiting for. A tentative Cuban government in exile could be set up, which Washington would be in position to recognize and support with arms after the invaders established a beachhead.

The rapidly changing events in Cuba made it timely to send a reporter to Havana. But when Beebe and Daniels began looking around they could find no reporter they thought qualified for the delicate assignment. The reporter not only would have to be an astute newsman, he would have to speak Spanish and know his way about Havana. It was approaching three in the afternoon and a decision would have to be made soon. At about this time Beebe spotted Al Burt, night city editor, entering the newsroom.

"Let's send Burt," said Beebe. "He knows Havana and speaks enough Spanish to get by."

Burt was given no time to sit down before finding himself assigned.

Hastening to the airport, he discovered that 100 persons had booked flight on a plane with only eighty-four seats. But he waited, and only seventy-eight showed up.

"You're on," said an attendant to Burt. "I hope you get back."

Burt arrived in Havana to find it a madhouse. The militia was setting up artillery and antiaircraft guns along the Malecon and the Prado, and digging trenches in preparation for an expected invasion. The U.S. Embassy was in a state of confusion, and hundreds of Cubans seeking visas were milling about the building. The embassy had been issuing 1,000 visas a week to Cubans seeking to flee the island, a practice that suddenly had stopped. Burt was told that more than 50,000 Cubans had applied for visas.

Burt remained in Havana five days, making himself inconspicuous as possible as he sought to see and hear what was going on. Meanwhile, two correspondents and a photographer, Frank Beatty of the United Press Bureau in Miami, were arrested. Beatty was accused of photographing military preparations. Correspondents Bob Berrellez of the Associated Press and Henry Raymond of the United Press were accused of espionage.

Burt's stories reflected the pathos and the tragedy of people involved in revolution and in the confusion and frustration of not knowing what traumatic events were to happen next. Reading the stories, you could almost feel the pain he saw in the faces of people, who seriously believed an invasion was coming. The reporter was convinced they would fight if an invasion should occur. While Burt's stories contained none of the sophisticated observations of an expert, he was the first *Herald* reporter to capture the realities of the revolution which was then beginning to take a new and hard course that would steer the island beyond the influence of the United States and into the lap of Russian Communism. The series won Burt the Ernie Pyle Award.

It was two days after Burt's return that the *New York Times* broke the story about the CIA's training of a brigade of Cuban exiles in Guatemala. But January passed without anything happening, and now the nation had a new president, John F. Kennedy. While he had been briefed on the invasion plans, Kennedy postponed making a decision. His advisers were against it. For one thing, no Cuban leader of stature acceptable to the Cuban people was available to succeed Castro. But by April everything had been readied for an invasion. The brigade of exiles was reaching the peak of training. If the invasion was to take place at all it would have to be soon. Moreoever, Castro's forces were becoming stronger with every week of delay, although the MIG fighters promised to Castro by his new ally, Khruschev, had not arrived. Other Russian armament, however, was arriving in quantity. Pressed to act and assured of victory, Kennedy gave his assent, with the understanding that U.S. armed forces were to take no part.

B-26 bombers of the CIA's air force hit Cuba on Saturday, April 15. One bomber landed at the Miami International Airport. The two fliers reported they had deserted Castro, taking off from a Cuban airport and dropping bombs on their way to Miami. Shortly therafter the *Herald* got word of a second bomber landing at the Boca Chica Naval Air Station near Key West, while a third had landed in Jamaica. Confusion shook the city desk. The bombings appeared to be a prelude to invasion. But from where would the invasion be launched, and when?

At that moment the brigade of invaders, which had been flown from Guatemala to Nicaragua to board vessels, was steaming toward Cuba. Meanwhile, the bombing and strafing of Cuba had created such a furore abroad that Kennedy ordered the use of planes limited to the support of invading forces. Failure of the invasion attempt would later be blamed on Kennedy's order. Pre-invasion bombings had been expected to destroy Castro's air force. But unknown to the CIA and to Cuban exile leaders, the Cuban air force had moved its planes to new sites and had placed obsolete planes as decoys about military fields.

Beebe, upon receiving a tip that the invaders had departed from Puerto Cabezas, Nicaragua, sent Southworth to Central America. Burt was dispatched to Jamaica, to be ready to follow the invaders into Cuba from a neutral country. On Monday, reports of the invaders' landing began coming in from three sources—Castro, the Cuban Revolutionary Council in Miami, and from a public relations firm, revealed later to have been employed by the CIA. On Tuesday, the *Herald* announced the invasion with a black headline across the top of page one: "3 Beachheads Secured,/Cuban Invaders Push On." Dom Bonafede had written the story from reports obtained from the wire services and from the sources mentioned above. Invasion leaders in Miami reported their forces were moving ahead to victory, while Castro reported they had been repulsed.

It was a frustrating night for Larry Jinks, who had been drafted into Burt's place on the night city desk. Jinks had been on the *Herald* only a few months, having come from Charlotte where he had been city editor of the *Observer*. Although a well trained newspaperman—he had a master's degree in journalism from Columbia—none of his training had taught him how to stay relaxed in a situation where reliable information was impossible to obtain. Moreover, Jinks had never been to Cuba. To balance the reporting and to prepare readers to the possibility of "anything happening," he ran a box under the heading of "Which Side Do You Believe?" He quoted the announcement of the exile leaders that the invasion had been successful, that heavy casualties were being inflicted on Castro's defenders, together with reports that "much of Castro's force of 300,000 militia had defected." Below, Jinks ran the reports from Castro's government which claimed that the invaders had been repulsed. Not until Wednesday did local leaders admit that invading forces had been defeated at the Bay of Pigs. More than 15,000 distressed Cuban exiles congregated in Bayfront Park in downtown Miami to pray for a miracle. On Thursday a streamer across page one told the agonizing truth: "Cubans Admit 'Tragic Losses.' "

Months would pass, even years, before the whole truth about the invasion was to be known—the unwise decisions, the foul-ups, the quixotic actions, and the miscalculations of Castro's power and influence over the people of Cuba. Moreoever, the invaders had been assured by their CIA advisers that a United States aircraft carrier, standing by, would provide air assistance for the invasion. It did not. President Kennedy had ordered the admiral in charge to give no assistance. The invaders had only obsolete bombers of the CIA's task force. Exiles in Miami claimed the invaders had been betrayed.

Of the 1,297 who landed, 1,180 were taken prisoner. Eighty died in fighting. Another thirty-seven drowned after their ship was sunk by Castro's planes. Ironically, they had refused to leave their ship after learning the brigade was to receive no air cover for the landing. Only those who could swim made it to shore. Nine or ten more died of their wounds or from suffocation while being transported to Havana in crowded vans. Meanwhile, presidential pretender Cardona, his cabinet, bureaucrats, and secretaries remained at the Opa-Locka Air Base for two days while awaiting word to fly to Cuba and set up a provisional government. That word never came and gloom fell upon Miami's refugee colony. There were recriminations, too. The Cubans blamed Washington for the failure. Pawley blamed Kennedy's "liberal" advisers who he said were "playing into the hands of the Communists." But Kennedy took the blame himself. After months of negotiations. James Donovan, a New York attorney, succeeded in making arrangements to ransom the prisoners in exchange for $53 million worth of food and medical supplies.

Failure of the invasion caused the United States to suffer a great loss of face. Moreover, Castro's influence over the Cuban peple was greatly increased. At the same time, he was thrust into closer ties with Russia and the Communist cause. In December 1961, Castro turned his back on the Western democracies and his liberal friends for good. He claimed to have been a Marxist-Leninist—a Communist—all the while. Strong anti-Communists, like Bill Pawley, cried in unison: "I told you so." Castro turned Cuba into a Russian island, and Khruschev, taking advantage of what he believed was a lack of will on the part of the United States to do anything about it, began preparations to build a nuclear Gibraltar in the Western Hemisphere, ninety miles from Florida.

Scores of Russian ships began unloading military supplies in Havana, while Russian advisers and technicians were arriving by the thousands. Kennedy warned Khruschev that "offensive weapons" would not be tolerated in Cuba. By the fall of 1962 it became obvious that a showdown was developing. On October 20 the *Herald* noted that South Florida was experiencing a military buildup. Caravans of Army trucks were moving through Miami, heading southward to Key West. Tent cities were going up on the outskirts of Miami, where radar and other electronic sensing devices were set up, together with antiaircraft missiles. It was all a prelude to Kennedy's announcement of an arms blockade of Cuba. Only then did the president tell the nation that the United States was virtually on a wartime alert. Naval vessels had been ordered to the Atlantic to stop any further landing of Russian war materials in Cuba. The Russian government had been warned. Khruschev replied that Russia would assist Cuba if the United States should invade the island. Next morning *Herald* headlines—an eight column two-line streamer—screamed out the developments: "Cuban Blockade Ordered:/JFK Warns of War Peril." An aerial photograph showed the Key West Naval Station berths empty of warships and nuclear submarines. Another photograph, made by a U-2 spy plane, showed Russian missile pads in Cuba which had caused the crisis. Governor Farris Bryant of Florida put the National Guard on alert. The Cuban colony, expecting an invasion of Cuba, rejoiced. The headlines continued. Twenty-five Russian ships, most of them loaded with armaments, including missiles, still headed toward Cuba. Aerial photographs of the flotilla appeared in the *Herald*. What would happen if the Russian ships kept coming and the United States Navy had to stop them? Would Russia order its Navy to resist? The *Herald* sought to cover all angles. Reporter Gene Miller was sent in a private plane to the Key West area to see if he could find any Navy ships patrolling the Florida Straits. He did. Returning, he started his story like this:

"Fly south from Key West and a destroyer will point guns at you.

"I know. I got pointed at."

Miami was tense. Renewed interest was shown in the building of bomb shelters. On October 24 Kennedy ordered Russia to remove its missiles from Cuba. "JFK Tells Nikita Missiles Must Go," said an eight-column *Herald* streamer the next morning. Nervous residents began to pack up and flee Miami. Among them was Judge W. R. Culbreath of Juvenile Court, who closed down his court and fled with his family. Miller found him in Caruthersville, Missouri.

"I guess I'm getting my brains kicked out down there," said the judge, a man with one leg. He added that he had worried about "the irresponsibility of that guy Castro."

Khruschev, meanwhile, backed down, ordering the ships carrying armaments to turn around before they reached the American Navy's blockade line. The Russian leader squirmed from his embarrassing position under a flurry of rhetoric inspired by his shrewd peasant's mind. He would remove the missiles from Cuba provided Kennedy gave a pledge that the United States would not invade or let anyone else invade Cuba. Miami quickly returned to normal. Most of the armed forces departed. But the radar installations remained, together with antiaircraft missiles. Those who fled Miami returned, including Judge Culbreath. But those who stayed and sweated out the crisis did not forget. When the judge came up for re-election the voters booted him out of office.

Despite the mounting significance of the Cuban developments, the *Herald* had waited until just before the beginning of the missile crisis to create a full-time Latin American department. Al Burt and Dom Bonafede were assigned as permanent staff members. But the *Miami News* had assigned Hal Hendrix to the full-time job of Cuba-watching several months before. As a result of his contacts with the CIA, Hendrix was able to beat the *Herald* on the coverage of the missile crisis, winning a Pulitzer Prize.

Miami's Cuban exiles were disappointed over the outcome of the crisis, particularly with what seemed to be Kennedy's pledge to permit no invation of Cuba. But it had a quieting effect on them. The exiles knew they would not be returning to Cuba any time soon, and many felt they might never return. They began settling down in Miami, to make a new life in trades, businesses, and professions. By the beginning of 1963 at least 100,000 Cuban exiles lived in the Miami area. Most of them had moved into cheap apartment houses and old residences close to downtown. To alleviate the crowding and to make it possible for the Cubans to obtain jobs, the federal government sought to resettle thousands of them in other parts of the nation. But, being gregarious and preferring to stick together, most of them returned to Miami, even at the risk of added hardship, to be with their relatives and friends. By the 1970s the number of refugees fleeing Castro's Cuba would exceed 400,000, three-fourths of whom lived in Dade County.

29

Moving Day

TWO MAJOR EVENTS in the life of the *Miami Herald* occurred on August 19, 1960: ground was broken for a new $30 million plant, and a new employee, Alvah H. Chapman, Jr., began work as James L. Knight's assistant. A decade later, after Chapman had risen to president of the *Herald* and executive vice-president of Knight Newspapers, it would be difficult, in retrospect, to tell which of the events had been the most significant to the newspaper. Chapman proved to be an achiever in a league with Lee Hills. He was to introduce the *Herald* to the computer age, to modernize, streamline, and improve the production, circulation, advertising, and business departments much as Hills had done with the editorial department in the earlier period.

Upon hiring Chapman, Jim Knight had no special plans for him. He had no thought at that time of training a successor. Knight had just passed fifty, and, although he was executive vice-president of Knight Newspapers and publisher of the *Charlotte Observer and News*, as well as general manager of the *Herald*, he did not look upon his extensive responsibilities as unduly burdening. However, with the double job of running the *Herald's* business side, together with overseeing the building of a new plant, he figured he would need an assistant. Moreover, Knight was on the lookout for promising executive talent for Knight Newspapers, and upon discovering that Chapman was at "loose ends," offered him a job. If Chapman should fit into the Knight organization he might, upon completion of the new *Herald* plant, go to some other Knight paper in an executive position.

Chapman, like the Knight brothers, had been born into the newspaper business. His grandfather, R. W. Page, purchased the Columbus, Georgia, *Ledger* in 1888 and published it until his death in 1920. Alvah's father, A. H. Chapman, Sr., was for twenty-four years the president of

ALVAH H. CHAPMAN, JR.

the Ledger-Enquirer Company in Columbus as well as the Bradenton (Florida) *Herald*. Young Alvah had worked as a newsboy, printer's devil, mailroom worker, truck driver, reporter, and copyreader during his school years. He was a devoted, bright, and tireless achiever who quickly rose to the top in whatever he attempted. Graduating from The Citadel as top-ranking cadet in 1942, he entered the Army Air Corps and flew thirty-seven missions over Europe as commander of a bomber squadron. After the war he went to work on the family's Columbus paper, going through two years of training in all departments before becoming business manager in 1948. So thoroughly did he master the newspaper business that after attending a seminar in newspaper management in 1950 at the American Press Institute, Columbia University, Chapman was invited back for the next seven years to conduct sessions. In 1953 he left the family operation to become executive vice president and general manager of the *St. Petersburg Times*. In 1957 he became a partner of Mills B. Lane, Atlanta banker, in the ownership of the *Savannah Morning News* and *Press*. But the opposing concepts of banking and publishing came into conflict, and, after three years, Chapman and Lane sold their interests in the Savannah papers. Jim Knight, who had known Chapman for several years, asked him if he would like to give Knight Newspapers a try. Chapman, wanting to buy a newspaper rather than become an employee of one, didn't jump at the opportunity. But he was only thirty-nine, so why not work for the Knights a couple of years? He admired the Knight brothers and was fully aware of the reputation of their newspapers. To work for such an outfit, particularly in the position of assistant to the general manager of the *Herald*, could be a worthwhile experience. So Chapman took the job, and, one month later, when the Executive Committee of Knight Newspapers was organized, he was selected as one of the five original members, along with John S. and James L. Knight, Lee Hills, and Blake McDowell.

Both Jim Knight and Chapman were uncertain about what the younger man's duties would be, but this problem soon resolved itself.

Not only did Knight have a multitude of decisions to make in connection with the construction of the new building, in the meantime he was facing a showdown with the pressmen's union. Confident in his ability and eager to take responsibilities to show what he could do, Chapman soon found himself handling an increasing number of the general manager's duties. Watching the younger man in admiration—astonishment, really—Knight sat back, chuckled a bit, and gave him more rein.

"I soon learned," said Knight in retrospect, "that here was someone who knew more about the newspaper business than I did. I had said before that if I should find such a person I would turn over my job to him."

But Knight wanted first to settle the difficulties with the pressmen's union. The trouble with the pressmen had developed with the rapid circulation growth of the paper in the 1950s. During the peak periods it was necessary to keep pressmen on the job overtime, paying them time and a half time for extra hours. As the paper continued to grow, the *Herald* found itself paying overtime all year to some ninety pressmen—because the union refused to permit the hiring of additional men. A pressman's salary in 1960 was in excess of $7,000 a year, high pay during that pre-inflation period. With overtime, however, most pressmen were making in excess of $9,000 a year, while at least fifteen received in excess of $10,000 a year. In addition, the *Herald* was having to hire pressmen from the *Miami News* at the overtime rate, although they might work for the *Herald* only one day a week. As the time approached for negotiating a new contract in 1961, Knight was looking ahead to the day when the *Herald* would be moving into a new and modern plant. With greatly expanded facilities, the number of pressmen would have to be substantially increased. Moreoever, Knight was determined to end what he considered a ridiculous situation wherein overtime pay had become a normal thing with the pressmen. The union's action, which Knight looked upon as an undisguised "holdup," was costing the *Herald* more than a quarter-million dollars a year. But Knight foresaw that the pressmen were unlikely to agree to the management's demands. To give him leverage in dealing with them, Knight ordered Les Griner to set up a pressmen's school. Should the union insist on continuing what Knight considered an "unreasonable and intolerable situation," he would be prepared for a showdown.

Griner set up his school in an auxiliary press building several blocks from the *Herald's* Miami Avenue plant, making no effort to maintain secrecy. He already knew from experience that the training of pressmen was no "big deal;" that it was possible to teach a reasonably intelligent person how to operate a press after a week of intensified training. He had helped to conduct an experimental course at the *Los Angeles Times*, set up under the auspices of the Southern Printing Production Institute. Using the same course in Miami, Griner began training volunteers from several departments in the *Herald*. Within a few weeks Griner "Tech" had seventy-five graduates. Still the union remained adamant. The pressmen had a good thing and refused to give it up. They laughed when Griner told them the *Herald* intended to run the presses without them.

"They really thought they were indispensable," said Griner later.

Meanwhile, both the white union pressmen and the *Herald* management were courting the black newsprint handlers, who came closer to being indispensable than the white union pressmen. While the pressmen sought to turn the blacks against the *Herald*, sticking with them in the event of a strike, Griner sought to convince the blacks that it would be in their interest to stay on the job. The relationship between the black paper handlers and the white pressmen was a typically segregated arrangement of that era. The blacks, who were nonunion, rolled the heavy rolls of newsprint on dollies to the presses while the whites loaded them onto the machines and set up the automatic pasters. The blacks cleaned up after the pressmen, carrying away the scrap paper and the empty reels. Although their work did not appear to be highly skilled, it was vital in the pressroom, and was the kind of work that required experience.

The groundwork for winning the loyalty of the blacks was prepared by Nick and Yorick Kemp, Bahamian brothers who were the *Herald's* oldest employees. Nick, a large, rawboned, intelligent, and communicative black, had begun work on the *Herald* in 1918. Nick worked in the stereotyping department, keeping the lead pots going. With a relaxed confidence and easy manner, Nick was liked and respected by both blacks and whites. Moreover, there was a closeness between him and Jim Knight that made most of the black employees on the paper look to him for leadership. Nick's brother Yorick, a thickly set, muscular man who was more likely to brandish his fists rather than use conversation to get his ideas across, was a paper handler. He had worked for the *Herald* since 1921. Griner found it convenient to go through these brothers in his efforts to keep paper handlers loyal. When it became obvious that negotiations with the union were making no progress and that a showdown was approaching, Griner called the paper handlers into a meeting in Jim Knight's office and explained what the *Herald* was prepared to do for them if they remained loyal.

"You have worked as paper handlers long enough that you can load those rolls of paper on the presses as well as the white union pressmen," said Griner. "If they strike, you will step right in take their places."

"But what will happen to us if the strike is settled and the whites come back to work?" asked a doubting paper handler who could foresee trouble ahead.

"I have Mr. Jim Knight's word that your jobs will be guaranteed no matter what happens," said Griner. Seeing that some doubt still existed, Griner added that he would ask Knight to meet with them so they could get the word directly from him.

"That won't be necessary," said Yorick Kemp. "We all know that if you say Mr. Knight's going to do something he's going to do it."

The showdown with the union came on August 1, 1961. The union refused to budge on its stand against hiring additional journeymen pressmen, while the management refused to continue the overtime pay policy. The union struck and set up picket lines. Unexpectedly, the mailroom employees refused to cross the picket line and the paper had a double strike on its hands. Although few papers were mailed any more from the mailroom, that's where the papers from the presses were counted, bundled, and distributed to route carriers, and a strike there was a serious thing. But first the paper had to be printed. Griner called in his "seven-day wonders" to take over the operation of the presses and ordered paper handlers to take over the jobs vacated by the union pressman on the paper-loading floor. Although the blacks may have lacked technical knowledge of the press operation, they stepped in and took over the whites' work with scant difficulty. Because of the loyalty of the paper handlers, the *Herald* was able to continue publication without missing a single edition.

The Kemp brothers, who played major roles in gaining and retaining the confidence of the paper handlers, would remain with the *Herald* until 1970, retiring after together working a total of 101 years for the newspaper. Nick, seventy-two, had been with the *Herald* fifty-two years, while Yorick, sixty-eight, had been employed forty-nine years.

To overcome the difficulties created by the striking mailroom employees, Jim Knight called for volunteers from all departments. With the help of circulation managers, paper route men, truck drivers, *Herald* executives, and everybody else he could snag, the papers were counted, bundled and delivered to waiting delivery trucks. Meanwhile, the *Herald* ran an ad offering employment in the mailroom. More than 300 showed up, mostly Cuban exiles. Neither the striking pressmen nor the mailroom employees had a chance of winning. Only two months before Knight had signed a new agreement with the mailroom union. He viewed the walkout as a breach of contract.

Having finished with his washing of the *Herald's* "dirty linen," as he put it, Knight was ready to turn over to Chapman the position of general manager. Although Knight moved into the position of *Herald* president, he backed away completely from the responsbilities of the newspaper's day-to-day operations. He was now able to devote more time to the fun of being a "super-sidewalk superintendent" at the new plant. And even with his other duties, he was finding more time to fish in the Bahamas during the tuna and marlin runs. It was a new experience for him and his family, and, unlike his more tensely put-together brother, Jack, he was quite capable of enjoying the opportunities for relaxation.

"I had turned the management of the *Herald* over to Alvah, and I was satisfied that he could get along without me," said Jim some years later. "I did make myself available for consultation in case I was needed, but that was seldom, I can assure you."

The operating styles of Knight and Chapman were miles apart. Where Knight's style had been highly personal, that of Chapman was businesslike and streamlined efficiency, to the oberver sometimes less humane than that of Knight. Over the years Knight had depended on department heads who were several years older than himself. It was his nature to develop a strong attachment to older employees who had demonstrated their loyalty to the *Herald*. But nobody knew better than he that the newspaper had outgrown its management as well as its plant. Several of the department heads were no longer in touch with the realities of the newspaper business. Knight had permitted the aged production manager, Harry Reese, to occupy an office in the crowded *Herald* building even after it was necessary for a nurse to accompany him.

Although the *Herald* was a highly successful operation, Chapman's trained and searching eyes began to spot countless deficiencies. Even before becoming general manager, Chapman initiated a number of changes, including the method of handling money received from paper route managers. Heretofore circulation route men had mailed checks or cash to Box 302, Miami Herald. Chapman looked upon this system as needless duplication, and with Knight's assent arranged to have route men mail funds directly to the bank with which the *Herald* did business.

Chapman's long-range plan was to develop a staff of key department heads who, with capable, bright, and loyal young assistants, could operate with a minimum of supervision. He demanded efficiency and communicative ability in department heads and required demonstrations of achievement in all responsible employees. His system of delegating total responsibility to department heads made it possible for him to devote much of his time to other important things, such as adopting data processing for the business and advertising departments and preparing the *Herald* for the computer age. And there was still time for the general manager's involvement in a wide number of civic and charitable enterprises. So successful was Chapman in the streamlining of the various

HARRY TRUMAN, a frequent critic of the press while President, was invited by John S. Knight to edit the *Miami Herald* for a day. He appeared in the old building at 200 South Miami Avenue, a short time before the paper moved into its present building on Biscayne Bay, and went through the motions of editing copy, to the delight of photographers, editors, and reporters. Then rising, he turned to the news editor and said: "Hell, I've got enough of this; you take over."

departments that by the time of the *Herald's* move into its new plant he would be awarded the added title of vice president and elected to the Knight Newspapers board of directors.

The move from the old building on Miami Avenue to the new plant on Biscayne Bay took place on the weekend of March 23-24, 1963, after three months of planning. The new presses already were in full operation and were being used to print Sunday supplements. But not all the equipment in the new plant would itself be new. Typesetting and stereotyping machines, and a lot of other equipment which the computer would make obsolete, were to be transferred from the old building. This equipment, with files from the business and advertising departments, together with typewriters and files from the newsroom and library, amounted to more than 2,000 tons. Moreover the moving had to be done so that no edition would be missed. All day on Saturday, then all night and until noon on Sunday, the moving continued, with swarms of men operating forklifts, cranes, and a fleet of big vans. Two moving companies were involved. To simplify the removal of heavy equipment from the third floor composing room, a section of the concrete wall of the production building was knocked out. Equipment was moved to the opening by forklifts, where it was picked up by cranes and loaded onto trucks. Electricians, plumbers, machinists, and pipefitters worked at both buildings, disconnecting machines in the old building and installing them in the new one.

A weekend was selected for moving because most of the Sunday paper, including all the sections except the classified, the current news, and sports sections, are normally printed earlier in the week. The preparation of most of these sections is done before the first edition is printed. Thus much of the equipment in the composing room could be moved before the running of the final edition. Movers began transferring files from the business and advertising departments on Saturday morning, along with the tagged typewriters and labeled files of editors and reporters not working on Saturday. The rest was moved early Sunday.

Several days prior to moving, editors and reporters had begun sorting their files and cleaning out their desks. They would get new desks and new files in the new building, but would keep their old typewriters. Columnist Jack Bell spent parts of three days going through an old wooden filing cabinet, wound up tossing out everything.

"Didn't find a thing worth saving," said Bell sourly. Can't understand why I saved the stuff in the first place."

Columnist Jack Kofoed tagged his typewriter but put into his briefcase everything from his desk that he wanted to save. Kofoed had the kind of mind that needed no extensive man-made filing system. His filing system was in his head.

George Bourke, the amusement editor, never did get around to cleaning off his desk, leaving everything behind when he moved into a new desk at the new building. If he missed anything from the clutter on top of his old desk he never mentioned it.

Those reporting to work Sunday afternoon to get out the Monday paper showed up at the new address, 1 Herald Plaza. Monday's paper, produced in a new building and rolled on new presses, came out with a page one letter to readers signed by Jim Knight.

"Well," he began, "we made it!"

Those in a position to appreciate the meaning of the move to Knight felt it unnecessary to read further. In those four words, as far as Knight was concerned, he had said it all.

"Yes, we moved," said George Beebe, who as managing editor had been getting out a paper under almost impossibly crowded conditions for several years, "but if by some unhappy fate we had to return to that old building, we wouldn't be able to stuff everything back even if our lives depended on it."

RISING ABOVE the shoreline of Biscayne Bay, the new Miami Herald plant was the largest building in Florida when completed in 1963.

JOHN S. KNIGHT greets visitors who trek through the new Miami Herald building during open house on April 7, 1963.

More than 10,000 persons trekked through the new *Herald* building upon its dedication on April 7, 1963, to gape in wonder at the expensive equipment and the immense space occupied by the various departments in a splendid modern setting. But the most inspiring view of the building was from the causeways, where it stood out as the most striking structure on the bayfront. The yellow color trimmed in blue, a combination selected by architect Sigurd Naess, seemed just right on a building that rose from the edge of a tropical bay and against a blue sky. But inside Jack Knight quickly discovered a deficiency. It was the absence of a telephone in the executives' private elevator. Knight visualized leaving his spacious office on the fifth floor late in the day after the other executives had departed, entering the elevator, stalling between floors, and remaining there until discovered the next morning. With that dismaying thought, Knight refused to ride the elevator until a telephone could be installed.

LEE HILLS, president of the American Society of Newspaper Editors, welcomes John Kennedy to the April, 1963, meeting before which the President spoke. The year before, Kennedy had invited Hills to the White House to report on a visit to Russia and of his impressions of Khrushchev. A warm friendship developed between the President and Hills. At Hills' invitation, Kennedy addressed the Inter-American Press Association in Miami on November 18, 1963, four days before his death in Dallas on November 22. Because of Miami's history of violence, elaborate precautions were taken to protect the President here, while only routine precautions were taken in Dallas.

30

Print It, But be Fair

G EORGE BEEBE would remember the feeling of "emptiness" in the auditorium-sized newsroom. This emptiness bothered others besides the managing editor. And they complained, despite the beautiful view of the bay, framed within tinted glass windows. The new building was "too new." It lacked atmosphere, and you felt lonely sitting out there with row after row of empty desks all round. For a time even the telephones seemed too quiet. Moreover, the city desk seemed so far away. You could see the people working up there, and see their lips as they talked, but unless they raised their voices you heard nothing. It was uncanny. Many reporters liked the old building better, despite the awful crowding. They had been close to the city desk and to the managing editor. Now the city desk was so far and the managing editor seemed unapproachable in his wood-paneled, glass-enclosed office, with its sanitized atmosphere.

But changes were coming. The staff grew rapidly with the addition of reporters, special writers, and editors. The newsroom staff was to grow from 185 in 1963 to just under 300 by 1973. Those empty desks not only became occupied but additional desks had to be brought in as the staff expanded. Immense changes were occurring in southeast Florida during the 1960s, and the editors were kept busy trying to stay abreast of the demands on the paper by a rapidly growing population. It was a decade of major events—the assassination of President Kennedy in November of 1963, followed by the assassinations of Robert Kennedy and Martin Luther King in 1966; the coming of the Cuban refugees and their resettlement in the Miami area; the beginning of the greatest building boom in Florida's history, with record numbers of new people moving into the state; the environmental revolution, with the awakening of the public to the destruction of natural resources and the senseless despoliation

WHILE RISING in position on the *Miami Herald,* George Beebe became widely known as a result of his activities in various press associations. Here he is with Governor Nelson Rockefeller of New York in 1965 at a meeting of the Associated Press Managing Editors Association in Buffalo, the year Beebe served as president. Rockefeller and Beebe later traveled together in Latin America. Meanwhile, Beebe rose to associate publisher of the *Herald.*

through pollution; the confusion and frustration among black people and youths of all colors; the reaction against the Vietnam War; the rioting and head-skinnings accompanying three national political conventions at Miami Beach, and the mounting problems associated with the widespread use of drugs by young people.

Vast sums of money were pumped into Florida's economic machinery in the 1960s, producing the most affluent period in the area's history. The *Miami Herald's* circulation and advertising grew rapidly, which meant that more space had to be provided for editorial copy—news, features, photographs, sports, and special departments. The *Herald* found itself ranked among the top newspapers in the United States, in space given to news coverage, in advertising, and in the use of color. By the 1970s the *Herald* had passed the *New York Times* in space given to news coverage. In 1972 the *Herald* devoted 34.8 million lines to news coverage, compared with 31.9 million lines devoted to news coverage by the *Los Angeles Times,* which ranked second.

In 1974 *Time* magazine selected the *Miami Herald* as one of the "Ten Best" dailies in America. Sharing this designation with the *Herald* were the *Boston Globe,* the *Chicago Tribune,* the *Los Angeles Times,* the *Louisville Courier-Journal,* the *Milwaukee Journal, Newsday,* the *New York Times,* the *Wall Street Journal,* and the *Washington Post.*

"These ten papers stand out," said *Time,* "for several reasons. They make a conscientious effort to cover national and international news as well as to monitor their own communities. They can be brash and entertaining as well as informative. They are willing to risk money, time, and manpower on extended investigations. Through 'Op-Ed' pages and dissenting columns they offer a range of disparate opinion."

The selections were made on the "basis of editorial excellence rather than commercial success," said *Time*, "but economically these papers range from the sound to the very prosperous."

Illustrating how the *Herald* staff works together in the coverage of a big news break, *Time* related the story of the tragic crash of a cargo plane into a Miami residential area just before Christmas, 1973, killing nine persons, including the three crewmen. Editor Larry Jinks was at a party attended by several fellow newsmen when, just before midnight, he was reached by telephone from the city desk.

"Jinks took a carload of reporters from the party to the crash," said *Time*, and "had thirty men on the story by 3:00 a.m.

"Such hell-for-leather legwork has become almost routine at the *Herald*, the strongest link in the Knight newspaper chain."

The growth of the *Herald* during the past ten years, in circulation and advertising, attests *Time's* estimation of it as a newspaper. Daily circulation grew from 322,500 in 1963 to 404,846 in 1973, with Sunday circulation reaching 507,777. But the *Herald's* most spectacular growth was in advertising—from 59.7 million lines in 1963 to 84.5 million lines in 1970. Then, in 1973, advertising exceeded 92 million lines—a figure projected for the early 1980s. The Sunday *Herald* often ran more than 400 pages, and occasionally reached 500 pages, exceeding five pounds in weight. Production costs, however, increased enormously. As a result of sharply rising costs of newsprint and ink, tied in directly or indirectly with the energy crisis, the *Herald*—and other newpspapers—faced the necessity in 1974 of making some hard-nosed readjustments. One thing was certain, newspapers could not expect to continue getting bigger and bigger.

The greatest change occurring on the *Herald* during the first decade in the new building, however, was all behind the scenes—the introduction

LARRY JINKS

THE MIAMI NEWS in 1966, feeling the pinch of declining circulation and advertising, closed down its own costly production facilities and moved its editorial department into the Miami Herald Building. Under contract, the *Herald* took over production, selling of advertising, and circulation. Ownership of the *News* as well as editorial independence were retained by the Cox family.

of the computer to newspaper production. Work on the new building was just beginning when Alvah H. Chapman, Jr., was given the go-ahead to set up a computer experiment in cooperation with International Business Machines (IBM). So successful was the implementation of the computer that by 1963 it was ready to begin taking over the setting of type. In succeeding years the computer was to take over more and more of the slow manual operations in production, until by 1972 all classified advertising copy was being set electronically. An electronic device called OCR (Optical Character Reader) read copy prepared by typists and fed the information into a computer, which set it into type, thus eliminating the slower teletypewriter and the traditional typesetting machines. A year later OCR was extended to editorial copy. Reporters saw their old manual typewriters picked up and replaced by IBM electric machines whose typefaces OCR had been programmed to read. OCR not only read the reporters' copy, but also inserted corrections and changes made by editors.

Except for a change of typewriters and the necessity of producing cleaner copy, the invasion of the newsroom by the computer had no effect on jobs. In the production department, however, enormous job changes had to be made. Many doing jobs which had been routine in newspaper production for nearly a century had to be retrained for other work. Some sought employment on newspapers elsewhere, while a smaller number of older employees chose early retirement. While the computer had revolutionized newspaper production, as well as providing a vast source of instant information for the various departments, particularly circulation and advertising accounts, it had not succeeded in reducing the number of employees. The 383 *Herald* employees when the Knights acquired the paper in 1937 never stopped growing, and by 1973 employees exceeded 1,700.

While the *Miami Herald* had grown, so had Knight Newspapers, Inc., the parent company, which had its beginning at Akron, Ohio, in the early part of the century. C. L. Knight, the father of John S. and James L. Knight, and founder of Knight Newspapers, had begun his career as a lawyer, but his principal interest was in newspapering and politics. In 1897 "C. L." gave up law to found the *Winston-Salem Journal.* Early in the century he became business manager of the *Akron Beacon Journal,* and, in 1907, after having acquired stock in the paper, became its publisher. The majority stock, however, was owned by Cleveland capitalists. But in 1915 an Akron banker, E. R. Held, who also owned a sizeable amount of *Beacon Journal* stock, took the advice of his son-in-law, C. Blake McDowell, and helped C. L. to acquire control. Upon the death of C. L. in 1933, son John S. Knight succeeded him as publisher of the *Beacon Journal* and the *Massillon Independent,* which the family also owned, while son Jim set about mastering the business side of newspapering. What the brothers learned about newspaper management during those depression years they would utilize in the building of Knight Newspapers into a major corporation.

Knight Newspapers purchased its first out-of-state newspaper, the *Miami Herald* in 1937. In 1938 Knight Newspapers purchased the failing *Times-Press* in Akron, closed it down, and moved into the new *Times-Press* building. The *Detroit Free Press* was purchased in 1940, and in 1944 controlling interest in the *Chicago Daily News* was acquired. (The *News* was sold in 1959 to Marshall Field, Jr., who paid the Knights $17 million for their stock.)

Acquiring the Charlotte (North Carolina) *Observer* in 1955, Knight Newspapers followed up with the purchase of the *Charlotte News* in 1959. Six years later, in 1965, the *Tallahassee Democrat* was acquired, then, in 1969, Knight Newspapers took a giant step and purchased five dailies—the *Philadelphia Inquirer*, the *Philadelphia Daily News*, the

Macon Telegraph, the *Macon News*, and the *Boca Raton News*. The purchase of the Philadelphia papers, from Walter Annenberg, was a $55 million deal. Five additional dailies were acquired in 1973—the Lexington (Kentucky) *Herald* and *Leader*, the Columbus (Georgia) *Ledger* and *Enquirer*, and the Bradenton (Florida) *Herald*.

Knight Newspapers also owns the following community newspapers: Coral Gables *Times* and the *Guide*, the Florida Keys *Keynoter*, the *North Dade Journal*, and the *Union-Recorder* of Milledgeville, Georgia.

Realizing from years of experience that financial soundness is essential for the independence of a newspaper, the Knights never apologized for a heavy emphasis on the business side. A newspaper that doesn't make money is soon up for sale or is out of business. Worse, a financially weak paper may find itself at the mercy of the kind of advertisers or money-lenders who are not averse to using their power in an attempt to bend editorial policy under their influence. Knight Newspapers long has had a public image of a successful organization. This the Knights never discouraged. The validity of this image was confirmed when Knight Newspapers became a public corporation in 1969. The first public stock offering was immediately sold out at $30 a share.

But while Knight Newspapers has a record of good earnings, the *Miami Herald* has been the biggest money maker. The *Herald* in 1973 was among the most valuable business properties in Miami. During the intervening years the *Herald* had increased more in value each year, on an average, than the $2.25 million the Knights paid for it in 1937.

A good investment, surely, but the Knights never forgot that they were publishing a community newspaper—in a community where they had interests as deep and as broad as anybody else. The brothers were more than businessmen-publishers, interested in earnings reports. Through the Knights' leadership the *Herald* has played a major role in community affairs. But, while many civic enterprises have had the weight of editorial support behind them, the editor, at the insistence of the Knights, maintained his independence. He could comment and criticize according to his best judgment. Moreover, the Letters to the Editor department of the editorial page was open to comments by readers who could feel free to disagree with anything they read in the newspapers—a policy which made this one of the most widely read departments in the *Herald*.

The separation of the editorial department—both the editorial page and the news side—from the business side and administrative side of newspaper operation was something the brothers had agreed upon since their earliest association in publishing. While Jim Knight never showed any interest in becoming involved in the editorial side himself, he never lost sight of the fact that it was the editorial content that sells newspapers.

JOHN SHIVELY KNIGHT, editorial chairman of Knight Newspapers, stands before his reading bench in his *Miami Herald* office. Early in his career Knight made a habit of reading a wide variety of newspapers every day. He developed an eagle eye for what is good in other newspapers and what is bad in his own—in editorial content as well as appearance.

Jack Knight, on the other hand, had spent his whole career in the editorial side, even through the years when preoccupied with the problems of publishing the growing Knight Newspapers. His journalistic abilities were recognized in 1968 when he received journalism's highest award, the Pulitzer Prize, for "distinguished editorial writing." It was the second Pulitzer Prize in successive years for *Herald* writers. Gene Miller received the award in 1967 for investigative reporting. He was able to free Joseph Shea and Mary Hampton, who had been sentenced to prison for murders he proved they did not commit.

For Knight the winning of the Pulitzer Prize was the golden topping on a career of award winning, beginning with the Poor Richard Club's citation in 1946. During the twenty-three year interval Knight was to win virtually every important award that a top newspaperman can receive in recognition of his standing in the profession.

Knight's editorial "Notebook" was begun in 1936 and first appeared in the *Akron Beacon Journal*. In the succeeding years he seldom missed writing this feature, which millions of readers developed the habit of turning to on Sunday mornings. The Notebook stood out sharply and clearly in both opinions expressed and in the manner of expression. Never a flamboyant or eloquent writer like his father, Jack Knight nevertheless turned out material of compelling readership quality. He always gave the impression of knowing what he wanted to say, and he said it directly in a way that held the reader. Knight was never reluctant to criticize state or national leaders, although he may have supported their election. His attacks on Johnson's Vietnam War policies were an almost every-Sunday affair over a long period.

Knight had spoken out against involvement in Southeast Asia since 1952, because he failed to see how it would benefit either the United States or the rest of the world. He remained consistent in this viewpoint as he observed progressive escalation, which began with the sending of technical advisers to Saigon during the Eisenhower administration. He contended that the white man's influence in Asia was over and that it would be extremely costly for the United States if the nation's leaders failed to realize this. Although Knight had served in World War I and had lost a son in World War II, his experiences had not embittered him; they had made him a realist in the estimation of what can be accomplished through warfare. The harm done to this country's morale by what he considered the pointless expenditure of lives and resources in Vietnam was even greater than he had foreseen, and you agonized with him as you read his Notebook. It disturbed him, too, that while keeping us involved in Southeast Asia, President Nixon, mainly through Vice President Agnew, sought to brand critics as anti-American or as being on the side of the enemy.

But whatever his own opinion might have been, he steadfastly insisted on unbiased reporting of the news and studied news columns and headlines for any evidence of prejudice or slanting by reporters and copyreaders. While he encouraged reporters to get the news, he insisted on being fair. An example was the handling in 1972 of reports heard by reporters of Knight Newspapers that Senator Thomas F. Eagleton, Democratic vice-presidential nominee, had received psychiatric treatments. Instead of forthwith breaking the story, Knight Newspapers held it until Eagleton, confronted, could answer. But the answer went to all newspapers simultaneously and Knight Newspapers missed the chance to break the big campaign story of a decade. While this may have disappointed Jack Knight, it did not worry him. His reporters and editors had been fair.

Thirty-one years before, at a breakfast gathering of reporters and editors, shortly after the *Miami Herald* had moved into a new office building on Miami Avenue, Knight made a frank talk about what he as a publisher expected of his staff. One crisp statement would remain in the memory of those present:

"Get the news and print it, but be fair."

And what could be a better guiding maxim for all news media?

Index